HIR DAMODAR

HIR DAMODAR

Context, Translation and Analysis

SURINDER SINGH

MANOHAR
2025

Cover illustration: Epitaph on the grave of Hir-Ranjha. Situated in Jhang, near River Chenab, West Punjab.

First published 2025
First eBook edition 2025

ISBN 978-93-6080-375-9 (hardbound)
ISBN 978-93-6080-581-4 (eBook)

Published by
Ajay Kumar Jain *for*
Manohar Publishers & Distributors
4753/23 Ansari Road, Daryaganj
New Delhi 110002

Cover design by Manoj Kumar

Typeset by Ravi Shanker, Delhi 110095

Printed and bound in India

To

the transformative power of love

na koi akhoh hire mainun, na koi kahe saleti
zaat sanaat pachhano nahi, main chake naal chaketi
kadon chuchak maa peyo mainda, main kiddan unhan di beti
dawan aaye laggi main tainde, je pavaan qabool jateti

Let no one call me Hir.
Nor refer to me as a Siyal girl.
Do not identify my caste or lineage.
I am now the maid of the herdsman.
When was Chuchak my father and mother?
When was I their daughter?
I am tied to your lappet, if you accept this Jat girl.

tora trutt geya hire da, jo boli itt bhatti
hoi khak zimin di loka, rahi uss mani naa ratti
gall vich pallu dast pairan te, ishq machayi matti
jiyon piraan ranjhe nu ratta, teyon hir ranjhete ratti

The pride of Hir crumbled.
As she spoke in this manner.
Folks! She became dust of the earth.
Without even a bit of conceit.
A scarf around neck and hands on feet.
But love has aroused her intelligence.
As the saints dyed Ranjha in red.
So did Ranjha dye Hir in red.

(*Hir Damodar*, Stanza nos. 228 and 229)

Contents

Preface

At the outset, it is essential to recapitulate the experiences of Hir-Ranjha, the famous lovers of medieval Panjab. Ranjha, the son of Mojam, was born in Takht Hazara. Hurt at the enmity of his brothers, he left his home and walked towards the Chenab. At a ferry on the river, Panjpir bestowed Hir on him. Hir saw him sleeping in her boat and fell in love with him. She persuaded her father Chuchak to employ Ranjha as a herdsman. Every day, the lovers met in the moors. The gossip spread all around. The Siyals feared disgrace as Hir had been betrothed to a Khera youth. Hir declared her love for Ranjha and opposed the parental choice. Following a forced marriage, she left for Rangpur Khera. Ranjha returned to Takht Hazara. Hir refused to consummate the marriage and formed a compact with her sister-in-law Sehti. Ranjha received a message from Hir and, travelling to Tilla Balnath, converted to Jog. He arrived in Rangpur Khera as a Jogi. In a visit to a sesame field, Hir acted as if a snake had bitten her. The Jogi met Hir in Sehti's house on the pretext of providing medical treatment. After staying together for five weeks, the lovers eloped. The Kheras chased the lovers, who took shelter with the Nahars. During a trial at the Qazi's court in Kot Qabula, Hir was restored to the Kheras and Ranjha was whipped. A big fire spread in the town. The people forced the administration to reverse the verdict. The Jogi extinguished the fire through a miracle and attained Hir. The lovers left for the south, while the Kheras were beaten and expelled.

The present study comprises six chapters. Chapter 1 recalls

some prominent love tales that were rooted in different parts of Asia. Circulating for long in the oral tradition, they carved a niche for themselves in medieval literatures. The ruling elites and Sufi lineages took a keen interest in these stories. The former sponsored the versification of these narratives to enliven their leisure and patronize their poets. The latter explained complexities of the spiritual path with metaphors from the love tales. The fluidity of the storylines did not erode their appeal across the ages. The story of Vis-Ramin, located in pre-Islamic Persia, uncovered the life of a ruling class, which was wedded to wealth, luxury and intrigue. Mobad, the powerful Parthian monarch, failed to win the love of Vis as his desire was irrational. His younger brother Ramin, in spite of his foibles and waywardness, attained Vis as well as the empire. Laila and Majnun were born in prosperous Arab tribes. Unable to unite in marriage, they chose a life of suffering and remained true to each other. Laila refused to consummate her marriage with Ibn Salam, while Majnun composed poetry in the wilderness. In Egypt, Zulaikha could not impose her will on her handsome slave Yusuf. Unable to seduce Yusuf, she subjected him to cruel persecution. Only when she lost her wealth and beauty, she undertook a sincere repentance and succeeded in softening Yusuf's mind.

Amir Khusrau, the distinguished Persian poet of the Delhi Sultanate, implanted famous love tales in the cultural landscape of South Asia. In addition to the adventures of Alexander and Bahram Gur, he versified the love tales of Laila-Majnun and Shireen-Khusrau. He could not be blamed for the choice of themes that were vastly distant from the Indian mind. Waves of Muslim immigrants, uprooted from their homelands during Mongol invasions, settled in the urban centres of northern India and interacted with diverse indigenous groups. The mixed urbanites, learned in Persian and groomed in Islamic ambience, turned to the accounts of legendary warriors, lovers and saints. Amir Khusrau, evolving in this cultural environment, met the needs of his contemporaries. Out of humility, he admitted his inability to match the excellence of Nizami Ganjawi in the craft of narrative poetry (*masnavi*). Owing to a favourable turn of events, he was assigned the task of versifying the story of Dewal Rani-Khizr Khan, which was intertwined with contemporary political developments. During the late Sultanate and early Mughal period, Sufi networks were established in all parts of the Indian subcontinent. Away from the hegemonic influence of the royal capitals at Delhi and Agra, the Sufi masters delivered spiritual discourses to lower social orders. In this onerous task, they forged a new vehicle of communication. They discovered numerous love tales from the vast reservoir of oral tradition and narrated them in the language of the people. This gave rise to what has been designated as the Indian Islamic literary tradition. During the mid-twentieth century, the texts of these works were published along with scholarly introductions. Aditya Behl examined this distinct body of literature and established its role in the making of medieval Indian culture. Precisely when the medieval Sufi poets were narrating these romances in Awadhi, Shah Husain and Damodar reconstructed the story of Hir-Ranjha in different poetic forms.

Chapter 2 seeks to build the context in which Hir-Ranjha lived and Damodar narrated their story. Here, we are engaged with a period of two centuries, extending from Timur's invasion to Akbar's death. During the reign of Firoz Shah Tughluq, the state formed alliances with rural elites and prominent Sufis, resulting in agrarian expansion in south-east Panjab and Multan. The arrangement was dismantled during the dislocation of Timur's invasion. The ruling class, undergoing intense internal conflict, enthroned the Syed dynasty. Powerful landholders (*zamindars*), particularly based in cis-Satluj area, sided with rival nobles to maximize their political gains. Jasrath Khokhar, with his mountainous base north of Sialkot and beyond the Chenab, became a formidable force. Carrying out predatory raids in the plains of Panjab, he overpowered petty warlords and even captured fief holders (*muqtis*) of the Delhi Sultanate. The steady convergence of Afghan immigrants in Sirhind enabled Bahlol Lodi to acquire sovereign power in Delhi. Two Sufis, enjoying the support of rural magnates, began to rule in Malerkotla and Multan. The Afghan State under Sher Shah and Islam Shah, in spite of sustained military operations, could not impose its authority on tribes such as Gakkhars, Niazis, Balochis and Langahs. The Mughal control, in spite of Akbar's military pressure, faced stiff resistance from Bhatti landholders of central Panjab and Rajput chiefs of hill principalities. The Jogis, both as inmates of monasteries and wandering ascetics, exercised a strong influence on the people. The Chishtis and Suhrawardis, gaining a strong presence in western Panjab, slipped into the political orbit of the Delhi Sultanate. The new Sufi orders, Sabiris and Qadiris, assimilated the Jogi practice of breath control in their meditational techniques. The Sikh Gurus, rejecting asceticism, sought to achieve social equality with the uplift of depressed castes. If Guru Nanak raised his voice against the suppression of women, Shah Husain built his mystical thought on physical love and examples from the story of Hir-Ranjha. In the foregoing context, Damodar composed his long poem (*qissa*) on the love life of Hir-Ranjha.

Chapter 3 comprises the English translation of Damodar's text. The poet has narrated the story in 963 stanzas of four lines each. While undertaking the task, he employed the western dialect of Panjabi as spoken between Chiniot and Multan. In accordance with the contemporary linguistic practice, he has assimilated a large number of Persian words. Irrespective of their philological roots, the words have existed alongside each other in organically whole sentences and did not betray any unnatural imposition. This translator has performed his chosen job with a difference. Instead of offering the stanzas in a uniform pattern of four hemistiches, he has presented them in the form of prose. In this manner, the translation has become more readable and easier to grasp. However, the original sequence of lines has been retained as in the stanzas. Every paragraph of the translation has put together a few stanzas, keeping in mind the thematic unity of the events described. The translator has placed Panjabi and Persian words within brackets so that the readers are free to make personal judgements. Every effort has been made to preserve the literal sanctity of the words, while giving equal primacy to the practical meaning. Wherever two characters were engaged in a dialogue, their respective exchanges have been cast in the manner of a play. For example, Hir had conversations with Kundi, Jogi and Qazi. On two occasions, she conversed with her sister-in-law Sehti. Similarly, Ranjha had verbal interactions with Hir's confidant Hassi as well his former fiancée. The translator has provided copious footnotes to explain the terms pertaining to the social order, political structure, agrarian economy, historical geography, social values, belief systems and local customs.

Chapter 4 seeks to analyze Damodar's narrative. At the outset, it examines the circumstances in which the poet settled in Chuchkana (Jhang Siyal) and developed a keen interest in the story of Hir-Ranjha. It assesses his claim of being personally present on several occasions in the story. More importantly, it delves into some crucial aspects of the tale, ranging from the landed clans to the legal apparatus. Damodar has paid maximum attention to the socio-political role of the landed clans, with reference to their internal organization, functions of the chiefs and procedure of making decisions. Apart from growing crops and raising cattle, the landed clans formed matrimonial alliances among themselves. In their endeavours to attain local dominance, they made frequent use of their armed retinues. Damodar was certain that the lives of the protagonists were inseparable from the rule of the landed clans. His narrative enables us to understand Ranjha's refusal to settle as a farmer and, instead, choose the humble option of herdsmanship. In spite of his honesty and simplicity, Ranjha suffered throughout his life. Hir also faced acute opposition from patriarchal forces. In contrast to Ranjha, she grappled with obstacles with her tenacity, courage and articulation. This chapter investigates the reasons that helped the lovers to unite in spite of sustained hostility. Damodar's narrative indicated that the case of the lovers was not entirely hopeless. On the one hand, they were truly committed to each other and, on the other hand, they made an ingenious use of deception and received invisible support from Panjpir and black warriors. It was wise on their part to take shelter with the Nahars. Equally crucial was the support from the people of Kot Qabula who, through an angry demonstration, brought the administration to its knees. This chapter places three characters under a scanner. It finds that Kaido was devious, Sahiba was an idiot and Sehti was wise. It interprets the numerous references to Akbar, who loomed large in the life of the landed clans. The Khera-Nahar conflict was significant owing to a number of legal issues. In conjunction with it, our discussion takes a close look at the judicial system prevailing in the late Sultanate period.

Chapter 5 navigates through the versions of the story of Hir-Ranjha that were produced after Damodar. These reproductions appeared during 300 years, extending from the late seventeenth to the late nineteenth century. Panjab witnessed tectonic changes during this phase. The Mughal State, after reaching the pinnacle of its power, underwent a slow decline. Subsequent to the defeat of Banda Bahadur, the Sikh warrior bands attained power in different pockets of Panjab and, in the process, empowered the depressed castes. The invasions of Ahmad Shah Abdali contributed to the ongoing political turmoil. Ranjit Singh created a large kingdom north of the Satluj. Following the Anglo-Sikh wars, the British annexed Panjab to its expanding empire. The colonial state, in order to control its territories, began to document the provincial topography, demography, economy and customs. All through these changes, the interest in the story of Hir-Ranjha remained intact. In cross-cultural movements, the story entered the Persian historiography as well as the Sikh tradition. Three Panjabi balladeers (*qissakars*) – Ahmad Gujjar, Shahjahan Muqbal and Waris Shah – produced major narratives on the romance. Bulle Shah, following in the footsteps of Shah Husain, formulated his spiritual discourse with the help of soulful yearnings of Hir. The genre of narrative poetry (*qissa*) reached a high watermark during the reign of Ranjit Singh. The trend was manifest in the prolific compositions of Ahmadyar and Hashim Shah. The consolidation of the colonial state enabled Ganesh Das Vadhera and Maulavi Nur Muhammad to chronicle the history of the province and locality, resulting in fresh retellings of Hir-Ranjha love. Richard Carnac Temple, the distinguished historian and folklorist, compiled the legends of Panjab and, thus, underscored a continuity in the narration of our story.

In view of our discussions in the preceding chapters, we are in a position to formulate an assessment of Damodar's narrative. It is possible to identify its outstanding features that were not visible in the works of Damodar's successors. Our poet did not begin his story with the circumstances in which the protagonists fell in love. Instead, he has described their childhood when they displayed exceptional traits. During this period, they were betrothed through the contemporary inter-clan relations. Damodar's story revolved around ordinary people, not the members of the elite classes. In a parallel approach, he has located most events in the open countryside of western Panjab, not in the exclusive residential spaces with high boundary walls. Damodar has shown that the entire experience of the lovers was enacted in accordance with a divine plan, not due to human volition. The lovers were destined to love, suffer and unite. In their relation with each other, the lovers were not equal. Since they were tied in a master-disciple bond, Ranjha was ahead of Hir in spiritual progress. Damodar understood love as a convergence of work, sex, struggle and spirituality. In his portrayal of characters, Damodar has drawn a distinction between the supporters of lovers and their opponents. The poet has been kind towards the former and harsh towards the latter. Damodar's narrative has attained considerable complexity owing to inevitable interaction between the lovers and the dominant landed clans. In describing the internal organization and public functions of these clans, Damodar has remained unsurpassed.

While working on this book, I incurred a number of debts. This is an opportune moment to acknowledge them. I am grateful to the staff of a number of libraries that opened their doors to me. These are A.C. Joshi Library and the library of the Department of History, Panjab University, Chandigarh; Shri Natnagar Shodh Samsthan, Sitamau, Madhya Pradesh; Institute of Advanced Study, Shimla, Himachal Pradesh; Rampur Raza Library, Rampur, Uttar Pradesh; Institute of Islamic Studies, Jamia Hamdard, New Delhi; Punjabi Reference Library, Punjabi University, Patiala and Bhai Gurdas Library, Guru Nanak Dev University, Amritsar. Priyatosh Sharma offered valuable suggestions on medieval Indian culture, besides enabling me to avail the facilities at our departmental library. Jasbir Singh provided me with his insights on the nuances of Panjabi literature. Ashish Kumar lent me his books and procured articles for me from online sources. At different points of time, I received assistance from Manohar Singh Ranawat, Azizuddin Husain, Raj Kumar Hans, Zaheer Husain Jafri and Virinder Kalra. Many former students have taken a keen interest in my research. In particular, they are Yogesh Snehi, Harjeshwar Pal Singh, Rajni Sahota, Kamalpreet Singh Grewal and Sona Singh. At Manohar, Ajay Jain has been meeting my perpetual need for books. In the end, I pay warm tributes to the late Ramesh Jain for supporting my ongoing academic efforts. Needless to add, I alone am responsible for the views expressed in this book.

CHAPTER 1

Love Tales in the Medieval Times

In all parts of the world, human societies have nurtured their love stories with care. It is nearly impossible to fix them in definite chronological frames. Without exception, they underscore the commitment of protagonists to pure love and describe their immense suffering culminating in premature death. To begin with, these stories were communicated across generations through oral traditions and, during their varying journeys, retained their somewhat fluid character. Cultural changes, particularly development of Persian literature and increasing availability of paper, gave impetus to the craft of poetic composition. Prominent Persian poets – Fakhruddin Gorgani, Nizami Ganjawi and Abdul Rahman Jami – composed iconic versions of some stories that attained great popularity. In the Indian subcontinent, Amir Khusrau, who was associated with both the ruling class of the Delhi Sultanate and leadership of the Chishti order, pioneered the production of narrative poems (*masnavis*), both romantic and historical. The Awadhi Sufi romances (*premakhyans*), developing in the hands of Sufi masters, retold classic love tales as allegories of the spiritual quest. The interest of the Mughal State in the indigenous stories was reflected in a major work from the pen of Abul Faiz Faizi. As Damodar's narrative constituted a link in this chain, it would be appropriate to trace the storylines.

Erotic Passion in Persia

Sometime in the mid-eleventh century, Fakhruddin Gorgani versified the story of Vis-Ramin. This first Persian romance derived from the period of the Parthians (247 BC - 224 CE), described the customs of ancient Iran.[1] The ruler Mobad had two brothers, Zard and Ramin. The former served the king as advisor and minister. The latter, handsome in looks, was devoted to music, poetry and wine. During a royal festival, Mobad was attracted to Shahru, the beautiful queen of Mahabad. Already married to King Qaren, she signed an agreement with Mobad. If she gave birth to a daughter, she would be married to Mobad. After some time, Shahru was blessed with a daughter, who was named Vis. The child was sent to Khuzan, where a nurse brought her up along with little Ramin. At the age of ten, Vis was brought back to Mahabad. Shahru tied her in matrimony to her brother Viru, as custom permitted incestuous marriages. Mobad reminded Shahru of the agreement and demanded the hand of her daughter. Vis blamed her mother of promising an unborn child to Mobad. She ridiculed Mobad for desiring a marriage in old age and expressed disgust at the filthy customs of Merv. Mobad invaded Mahabad where Qaren was killed. Mobad, fleeing towards Isfahan, learnt that Vis was residing in the fort of Gurab.[2]

Ramin, experiencing a revival of his childhood love for Vis, asked Mobad to abandon his desires. Mobad, invoking the agreement, bribed Shahru and abducted Vis to Merv. On the way, Ramin saw Vis and lost his heart to her. The nurse, an expert in occult arts, prepared a talisman that rendered Mobad impotent for a year. Since the talisman was swept away in floods, Mobad lost his virility forever. The nurse became an intermediary between Vis and Ramin. Vis saw the physical beauty of Ramin and succumbed to her desire. Ramin entered the palace from rooftop. The lovers exchanged vows of love and surrendered themselves to erotic passion.[3] Mobad asked Ramin to join him in Mahabad along with Vis. During a hunting trip, Mobad slept with Vis but could not have sex with her. The nurse asked Vis to see Ramin from the rooftop, as he was bound to leave soon. Mobad, overhearing the conversation, fell into a rage. He accused Vis of committing infidelity and bringing disgrace. He ordered his vassal Viru to civilize Vis and punish the nurse. He banished Ramin from Merv. Vis, speaking to Mobad, declared her undying love for Ramin and dared the king to punish her. Viru advised Vis to reconcile with her husband Mobad. She must abandon Ramin who was a slave to many vices. She admitted being deceived by Ramin's looks, wealth and eloquence. Since love was blind, she chose Ramin over heaven. Mobad returned to Merv, while Vis left for Mahabad. Ramin went to Gorgan and lived with Vis for seven months.

Surprisingly, Mobad still regarded Vis as his wife and vowed to kill Ramin. His mother dissuaded him from the act, as Ramin was his advisor and heir. She urged Mobad to marry a new bride and produce a successor. Mobad threatened to attack Viru and shame Vis in public. Mobad, as Viru's guest, stayed in Hamadan for a month and returned to Merv with Vis. He ordered Vis to appear before a ceremonial fire and take an oath of purity. A massive blaze was raised in the presence of the aristocracy. Vis and Ramin, fearing their annihilation in the inferno, escaped from the palace along with the wealth they could carry. They travelled for ten days across a desert and reached Rey, where they stayed with Ramin's friend Bahroz. Mobad undertook a massive search for Vis in Iran, Turan and Byzantium. After six months, he returned to Merv and discarded his hostility towards the lovers, who were urged to come back.[4]

Mobad, Ramin and Vis celebrated their amity in a drinking party. Ramin sang songs and played on his harp, besides exchanging fresh vows of love with Vis. While Ramin lay drunk, Mobad led Vis to his bed. He berated her for shamelessness and pleaded for her love in lieu of provinces, throne and the seal of authority. Vis went upstairs to make love to Ramin, leaving the nurse on the king's bed. Ramin asked Vis to kill Mobad, but she advised patience. When the Romans invaded Persia, Mobad mobilized his vassals including Ramin. He imprisoned Vis in the Devil's Fort and ordered Zard to guard her. Ramin climbed to the place with a rope and lived with Vis for nine months. Mobad vowed to punish the lovers. Ramin escaped from the Devil's Fort. Mobad, accusing Vis and the nurse of betrayal, beat them up. Bowing to the demand of Shahru, he allowed Vis and the nurse to return to Merv. He forgave Ramin and allowed him to join Vis. Everyone was happy. Mobad built a wall around his palace and left for Zoval on a month long visit. Ramin climbed over the wall and reached the palace. Vis jumped into the garden and injured her feet, though she succeeded in joining Ramin.

Mobad rushed back to the palace, forcing Ramin to escape.

Mobad grabbed Vis by the hair and raised his sword to kill her. Zard dissuaded him from committing a murder, as there was no evidence of Vis's infidelity. Vis explained that an angel, appearing in a dream, brought her to meet Ramin in the garden. Mobad was reconciled to the lovers, but the goodwill was short lived. During a royal festival, Mobad attacked Ramin with a dagger, but fell down. A famous astrologer predicted that Ramin would become the king. He was advised to forget Vis for a year and leave for a distant place, where he could find more beautiful women. Ramin accepted the advice. Mobad secured an oath of fidelity from Vis and permitted Ramin to leave for Mahabad. Ramin and Vis bade farewell to each other. Ramin established an efficient rule in Isfahan, Rey, Ahwaz, Baghdad and Gorgan. During his stay in Gurab, he fell in love with a charming woman Gul and married her. Ramin gave offence to Gul when he expressed her resemblance to Vis. To placate Gul, he wrote to Vis that Gul had given him three times more happiness. Vis must forget him and instead devote herself to Mobad.[5]

Vis, on reading the letter, drowned in grief and pined for Ramin. She had both a husband and lover, but the former hated her and the latter deserted her. Vis sent the nurse to Ramin with a letter. She accused Ramin of betrayal but urged him to keep his wife as well as lover. Ramin condemned the nurse for tricking him into the love of Vis, who was a shameful sinner. Vis fell sick and dictated a long letter for Ramin. Accusing Ramin of treachery, she related her suffering. She reiterated her attachment to him and hoped for a reunion. Ramin, tired of Gul, felt like a stranger in Gurab. He found no joy in pleasures and stood exposed for his fickle nature. He rode out of Khurasan to meet Vis. On the way, he broke down on receiving a letter from Vis along with a tunic dyed in her blood.

Ramin reached the palace in Merv, while Vis appeared on the balcony. A long conversation ensued between them. Vis revealed that she was loyal to Mobad and, if he became suspicious, he would kill her. Ramin had been inconstant and untrustworthy. A compulsive adventurer, he was as dangerous as a snake and scorpion. During the last ten years, she had been faithful to him. He was the only man with whom she had sex. Since she was still beautiful, he coveted her. Ramin, standing in freezing cold, tried to answer all her questions.

He attributed his mistakes to human nature. The world was not static and everything was in constant motion. In Merv, he had lost his reputation and, therefore, left for greener pastures. He fell in love with Gul, while his love for Vis smouldered like fire. He deserved mercy and forgiveness. Vis remained unmoved. She refused to give him facilities of a guest and asked him to leave forthwith. She placed guards around the palace to prevent his entry. Feeling humiliated and frustrated, he rode away.[6] Vis repented of slamming the door on good fortune. She sent the nurse to stop Ramin and herself followed the suit. On meeting him, she revived her teasing arrogance. His repeated acts of betrayal had hurt her. She was not only beautiful, but also came from a noble ancestry. Ramin, while expressing remorse for his offensive acts, hardened his stance. Vis was self-righteous and only found faults in him. She failed to show compassion when he apologized. He would remain committed to Gul, who was her opposite in temperament. Vis broke down and confessed her rashness. She held that reproaches were integral to love and, therefore, she would never desert him. Ramin, having woken to reality and wisdom, remained firm and forced Vis to leave. His anger was momentary. He caught up with her and regretted his cruelty. Reconciled to each other, they stayed in a hunting lodge and, for one month, immersed themselves in amorous play.[7]

Ramin returned to Merv and appeared in the royal court. Mobad was overjoyed. His writ extended to Syria, Mosul and Armenia, while Ramin ruled over Gorgan. Ramin continued his secret intimacy with Vis, though Mobad did not get a wind of it. At the onset of spring, Mobad went to Gorgan on an hunting expedition and took Ramin along with him. Vis and the nurse hatched a conspiracy. They would displace Mobad, enthrone Ramin and grab the treasure. Vis dispatched a letter to Ramin, asking him to return. He rode back with 40 men through secret paths. Vis hosted parties for women. Zard, who was handling the administration, did not suspect anything. Ramin entered the palace with 40 men, who wore the veils of women. Ramin killed Zard and the guards. Ramin was proclaimed the king. Vis sat besides the throne, while Viru was made the Wazir. Ramin marched to Dailaman, carrying the treasure on 10,000 camels and mules. Mobad died at the hands of a wild boar. The people, relieved at their deliverance from Mobad's long misrule, hailed Ramin's accession to the throne. The benevolence of the new rule was reflected in settlement of villages, construction of inns, patronage of scholars and punishment of marauders. There was never a king like Ramin, though Vis exercised the real power. Their two sons, Khurshid and Jamshed, governed the eastern and western lands of the empire. Following the demise of Vis, Ramin erected her tomb in the temple of Borzin. He abdicated in favour of Khurshid and, for three years, lived as a recluse besides Vis's tomb. At his death, his body was placed besides that of Vis. As their souls were united, they lived as man and wife in heaven.[8]

Madness in the Arabian Desert

According to tradition, Laila and Majnun lived in the western part of the Arabian Peninsula during the second half of the seventh century. After a gap of five centuries, Nizami Ganjawi recapitulated (1188) their love story at the instance of a trans-Caucasian chief Shervanshah.[9] He acquired the basic facts from early Arabic sources that contained notes on Majnun's life, his verses and their textual commentaries. Nizami, while developing the rudimentary material to fullness, made important additions such as Naufal's attack on Laila's tribe, Majnun's rule over the animals, the visits of his mother and uncle, and the arrival of a youth from Baghdad. Nizami understood three elements of the traditional Majnun – his love, his insanity and his poetical genius – as a single indivisible unity. He converted an ancient Arabian tale into a work of art, which elevated love to a high spiritual plane.[10] For the lovers, love did not mean aspiring for a physical union. Instead, it meant a lifetime of intense physical suffering. Laila, refusing to consummate her marriage, erased her libido. Majnun, withdrawing from the human society, isolated himself in a cave and survived as a physical wreck among the wild animals. In their inner lives, the two felt inseparably attached to each other.

A great lord named Syed lived among the Bedouins of Arabia. He ruled over the tribe of Amir. His country surpassed all others in prosperity. Generous to the poor and successful in all enterprises, he commanded great respect. He was blessed with a son, who was named Qais. By the age of ten, the boy's beauty grew to perfection. At school, he mastered the arts of reading, writing and oratory. One of his classmates was a beautiful girl named Laila. Immersed in each other, they began to sip the wine of love. The other boys reproached them out of jealousy. Qais praised Laila's beauty in their presence. The parents and tribe of Laila, concerned about their honour, kept her at home and shifted their tents to the hills of Najd. They employed guards to block the paths. Qais paid frequent visits to the place. At night, he secretly reached Laila's tent and, kissing the threshold, returned at dawn. Since he had become a poet of melancholic songs, he came to be known as Majnun or the mad man.[11]

Syed summoned all the elders and discussed the case of Majnun. If he were married to Laila, he would recover his sanity. Forming a delegation, they met Laila's tribe. Syed proposed a marriage between the youngsters, as it would strengthen the ties between the two tribes. Syed was the most prominent man in his tribe. He had numerous followers and ample wealth. He could be a valuable friend or a formidable enemy. He would fulfil any demand for dowry. Laila's father rejected the alliance because of Majnun's madness. The boy must be cured of his malady before a proposal was put forth. The delegation returned in sadness. Majnun was advised to look at the girls of his own tribe, who were more beautiful than Laila. In despair, he ran away from home and, moving among the tents, cried the name of Laila. Lost to himself and the crowd, he appeared to be conversing with Laila on the depth of his love. When he fell down unconscious, the crowd brought him to his father's tent.

Syed, following the suggestion of his counsellors, took Majnun for Haj. He joined a caravan and carried Majnun in a litter. On reaching Mecca, he asked Majnun to pray at the Kaaba and seek freedom from his affliction of love. Majnun did the opposite. He prayed that his love for Laila might be strengthened. The caravan returned in frustration. The madness of Majnun grieved Laila and offended her tribe. The latter sent two emissaries to the caliph's prefect with a complaint. Allegedly, Majnun roamed the countryside like a madman, reciting his sonnets (*ghazals*). People memorized the lyrics that violated custom and decency. The prefect passed a death sentence on Majnun, who could not be traced. A Bedouin informed

Syed of a strange creature, who crawled like a snake in a mountain gorge. Syed met Majnun in the gorge and tried to dissuade him from the pursuit of love. Majnun, attributing his love to fate, expressed his willingness to die for love. He continued to stay in the hills of Najd. The travellers carried his poems in all directions. Laila collected these poems. Having herself become a poet, she composed answers to the lyrics and threw these scraps of paper to the wind. In this manner, melodies were exchanged between the two nightingales.[12]

Naufal, a Bedouin chief, brought Majnun to stay with him and vowed to unite the lovers. He offered to pay a huge sum in lieu of Laila. Assembling a large tribal army, he fought two battles against Laila's tribe but failed to secure the consent of Laila's father. Majnun, upset at the violence, broke his friendship with Naufal and sought forgiveness from Laila's tribe. Meanwhile, the reports of Laila's beauty spread in all directions and attracted a number of suitors. In order to marry Laila, they approached with various forms of wealth. None of them succeeded in his aim. Ibn Salam, a famous warrior with a large retinue, tried his luck. He fitted out a caravan of camels and scattered gold coins on the way. Laila's father wilted under the pressure of an eloquent emissary and glitter of wealth. The marriage ceremony, amidst sumptuous festivities, was held in accordance with the Arab custom. Ibn Salam, leaving behind tonnes of goods, returned with his bride in a rich palanquin. Laila, inseparable from the thoughts of Majnun, refused to share her husband's bed. First he waited with patience. Then, he used force. Laila hit him so hard that he went nearly deaf and blind. Asking for forgiveness, he remained satisfied with merely glancing at her. Majnun learnt from a stranger that Laila, refusing to consummate her marriage, was faithful to him. Syed, bent with age, searched out Majnun and urged him to take his position in the tribe. Majnun could not agree with his father, as wisdom was the antithesis of love. Syed, after returning home, breathed his last. Majnun grieved at the tomb of his father, who had sacrificed so much for his sake. Expressing his loss, he returned to the wilderness.[13]

Majnun lived in the company of wild animals such as lions, stags, wolves, foxes and vultures. To them, he was different from other men. He did not hunt them for their meat. He ate roots, grass and fruit. He did not fear the beasts. When he found them in a trap, he released them to freedom. If he received food from strangers, he shared it with them. Quick to catch his scent, they collected around him. Besides protecting Majnun from unwelcome visitors, they provided him with all manner of comfort. He lived among them as an exiled ruler in a foreign country. Alienated from the world, he began to interact with the stars in the sky. He spoke to Venus and Jupiter, asking for their help. Praying to God, he sought the transformation of the darkness of his life into light of the eternal day. An old man, who had conversed with Laila, brought her letter for Majnun. As soon as he held the letter, he fell into ecstasy and collapsed on the ground. Laila had acknowledged his love and suffering. Her husband had never shared her bed, so that Majnun's treasure of love remained sealed. They would build their nest in this world, but he must act with hope and patience. Majnun, in his reply, wrote that Laila was his Kaaba with a beautiful face. Trampled like dust at her feet, he was a slave who carried her saddlecloth on his shoulders. Though her pearl was intact in its hiding place, he could attain it only if Ibn Salam was driven out of her life.

Salim Amiri, the maternal uncle of Majnun, searched out Majnun among a host of animals. He was shocked to see that Majnun was sick and naked. He brought out clothes and eatables. Majnun did not touch the clothes and gave food to the animals. Salim brought his hapless sister to meet Majnun. She said that his father had died and she was nearing death. Majnun must return with her. Majnun replied that he had not chosen his life, but fate had allotted it to him. He would not leave his cage of love to enter the worldly prison. He fell at his mother's feet and asked for forgiveness. Learning of her demise, he went to her grave and mourned her departure. The people, taking pity on Majnun, urged him to stay with them. However, he vanished like a cloud in the wind. Laila decided to meet Majnun for once in a garden and hear his verses. She requested an old man to arrange a meeting with Majnun and, as expenditure, gave him a few pearls of her earrings. The old man placed a garment over Majnun and brought him to the garden, while his animals formed a caravan behind them. Majnun reclined against a palm tree, while Laila stood still ten paces away from him. In his poem, Majnun identified the uniqueness of his love. Though their bodies were separate and mortal, their souls merged to survive in the eternity. He became suddenly silent and fled from the garden like a shadow.[14]

Salam Baghdadi, who had heard of Majnun's verses, travelled from Baghdad to meet him. Majnun allowed Salam to stay with him for a short time. True to his understanding of love, Majnun remained wedded to the absolute suppression of senses and differed with Salam. The visitor, returning with a stock of Majnun's verses, shared them with amazed listeners. On the other hand, Laila kept her love for Majnun a closely guarded secret. Her husband Ibn Salam loved her without enjoying her body. Ultimately, Ibn Salam fell ill and died. Outwardly, she mourned for Ibn Salam and, inwardly, she grieved for Majnun. As a widow, she followed the Arab custom. For two years, she veiled her face and imprisoned herself in her tent. Sensing her end, she revealed her inner thoughts to her mother. On her death, she should be clad in a red garment, which was associated with martyrdom and festivity. Majnun would come to her grave for mourning. Her mother must be kind to him. She must tell him that Laila, while dying, was thinking of him and that she always treated his grief as her own. Below the earth, her eyes would look forward to him. Saying these words, she breathed her last. As she had foretold, Majnun rushed to her grave and, while crying, praised Laila for her beauty. He guarded her grave like a serpent. He paid frequent visits to the site along with his animals. After his death, his body remained in this state for many months. His bones crumbled to dust and blew away with the wind. The animals, who remained on guard around him, did not allow the onlookers to approach. When his body entirely vanished, they withdrew into the wilderness in deep sorrow.[15]

Princess-Slave Tussle in Egypt

Nuruddin Abdur Rahman Jami (1414-92), a distinguished Sufi and prolific writer, versified the tale of Yusuf-Zulaikha.[16] According to his narrative, Yaqub belonged to a lineage of prophets like Adam, Seth, Idris, Noah, Abraham and Isaac. His banner flew over Syria and

Kinaan. He possessed a vast multitude of sheep and rams. He was blessed with twelve sons. Of them, the youngest Yusuf was endowed with matchless beauty. When he was two, his mother passed away. His aunt, acting through deceit, acquired his custody. Following her death, Yusuf went back to his father. Yaqub, gaining complete control over Yusuf, made him the locus of his actions and thoughts. The story shifted to King Taimus, who ruled over a country in the west. Having conquered new lands, he fulfilled every aim. His daughter Zulaikha was incomparable in beauty. Every part of her body was made to perfection. Her apparel was fashioned out of raiment from Egypt, Syria, Greece and China. Her golden ornaments were studded with diamonds. Untouched by passion and love, she lived a life of ease, happiness and luxury.

In a dream, Zulaikha saw a handsome youth and surrendered her heart him. She kept her dream a secret, but lost her sleep and appetite. During the next twelve months, Zulaikha remained obsessed with the youth and declined in health. In a second dream, she saw the same youth and asked his identity. The youth, admitting the purity of her love, urged her to preserve it only for him. Taimus, upset at her mental condition, consulted the physicians. For a year, she was feterred in a golden chain but longed for her beloved. In her third dream, the youth revealed that he was the Grand Wazir of Egypt. Zulaikha, overjoyed at the revelation, was freed of her chain.[17] Taimus rejected marriage proposals from numerous kings and, instead, pledged Zulaikha to the Grand Wazir. Zulaikha, seated in a golden litter, left for Memphis with a large cavalcade. Stealing a glance through a hole in her tent, she was shocked to find that the Grand Wazir was not the youth of her dreams. She had been deceived. In a message from Jibrail, she was assured that her husband was the instrument through which she could attain her love. The aristocracy of Memphis welcomed her. Outwardly, she wore a cheerful demeanour and, inwardly, she pined for her love.[18]

Meanwhile, Yusuf had grown up into a personable lad. He received numerous favours from Yaqub and earned the envy of his brothers. From Jibrail, he received a magical staff, which would guide him throughout his life. One night, Yusuf dreamed of sun, moon and eleven stars bowing their heads before him. Yaqub warned Yusuf to keep the dream a secret from his jealous brothers. Somehow, the brothers learnt of the dream and unable to digest Yusuf's elevation above them, considered several plots to get rid of him. They planned a picnic to the countryside along with Yusuf and promised to protect him from the wolves. Yaqub gave his silent consent. On the way, the brothers subjected Yusuf to physical torture and, tying a rope around his waist, lowered him into a well. Providentially, he was stuck to a stone jutting out from the side. From Jibrail, he received a shirt, which had been transmitted from Abraham. According to a heavenly message to him, his brothers would bend before him in due course. Malik, a merchant who was thirsting for water, pulled out Yusuf. The brothers, claiming Yusuf as their slave, sold him to Malik for a pittance.[19] Malik reached Memphis and presented Yusuf in the royal court. The gathering was amazed at his beauty. Zulaikha swooned on finding that the youth was the man of her dreams. A public announcement was made regarding the auction of the slave. Thousands of inhabitants, selling their valuables, converged in the market. A penniless old woman came out with a bit of cotton yarn to purchase Yusuf. Zulaikha dug out her treasure to outbid the king. At her insistence, the Grand Wazir secured the king's permission to buy Yusuf. She was jubilant on acquiring Yusuf as a slave.

Zulaikha clothed Yusuf in glittering clothes, combed his curls and fed him rich food. Yusuf, uneasy at the attention, opted to serve as a shepherd for a flock of sheep. Zulaikha provided him a diamond studded sling and appointed guards for his protection. She employed a series of devices to win over Yusuf. She sent her nurse to him with a message of love. Yusuf, offering a refusal, was conscious of his lowly status. Zulaikha had purchased him as a slave with her gold. The Grand Wazir treated him like a son. His spiritual inheritance was traceable to Yaqub, Isaac and Abraham. His heart was imbued with the wisdom of Jibrail. Zulaikha sent a bevy of lovely damsels to a picturesque garden. One after the other, they tried to seduce Yusuf. In contrast, he gave them a sermon on divine love and turned their minds to the worship of God. Zulaikha, spending her treasure like water, built a magnificent palace with seven chambers. All its surfaces were covered with paintings of Yusuf and Zulaikha in amorous postures. Leading Yusuf through six chambers, she narrated the stages of her love, particularly her sacrifices of wealth, faith and prudence. Yusuf, demanding a release from his burdens, refused to be locked alone with her in the chambers.[20]

On entering the seventh chamber, Zulaikha felt that it was her last chance. She fastened the door with a golden chain and, making Yusuf sit on a seat, threw herself by his side. She asked him to satisfy her hunger. In response to her loving entreaties, he identified a dual fear. God would reveal his sin on the day of judgement and the Grand Wazir would kill him. Zulaikha declared that she would poison the Grand Wazir and spend her wealth to win God's forgiveness. She threatened to stab herself and shift the crime to Yusuf. He forced her to drop the dagger and, during a scuffle, she took his lips in a long kiss. He broke free from her grip and ran out. During a chase, she fell down and pulled the corner of his coat from behind. Yusuf rushed to the Grand Wazir and described the incident. Zulaikha, fearing exposure, alleged that Yusuf had tried to violate her while she slept. She caught hold of the fleeing culprit, whose garment was torn. The Grand Wazir was outraged. He had chosen Yusuf as the chief of all slaves and, along with the maidens, appointed him to guard his wife. He had betrayed his trust and proved untrue to his salt. In a spirited defence, Yusuf exposed Zulaikha's frantic passion for him and her numerous attempts to seduce him. True to his duty and morality, he escaped from her custody and lost a part of his coat. Zulaikha swore in the name of the throne, the state and her husband. The Grand Wazir imprisoned Yusuf until the case was investigated.[21]

In his confinement, Yusuf prayed to God for the vindication of his honour. A maid's child was the sole witness of the incident. He urged the Grand Wazir to examine Yusuf's coat. If it had been torn from the front, Zulaikha was right. If it had been torn from behind, Yusuf was innocent. The Grand Wazir went to the prison and found Yusuf's coat torn from the back. He condemned Zulaikha for her lies, but asked Yusuf to seal his lips. The women of Memphis reproached Zulaikha for surrendering her heart to a Hebrew slave and facing rejection at his hands. Zulaikha invited them to a feast. At the end of a banquet, they beheld Yusuf and lost their senses. One of them, instead of cutting an orange, sliced her own fingers. They realized that Yusuf's beauty was responsible for Zulaikha's misery. Yet they looked at him with desire. Yusuf sought divine protection from the wiles of women and saw his safety in prison. In utter humiliation, Yusuf was escorted through the streets as a slave who had dared to look at his master's wife.[22]

Still concerned about Yusuf, Zulaikha kept gazing at his prison from the heights of her palace. She paid secret visits to his cell and saw him bent in prayer. Yusuf helped prisoners with his ability to interpret dreams. The king of Egypt, in a dream, saw seven healthy heads of cows, who suffered subjugation at the hands of seven weak ones. He also saw seven healthy ears of corn meeting destruction at the hands of their weak counterparts. The king summoned Yusuf to explain the vision. Yusuf stated that the former reflected plenty of rain, grain and happiness. The latter pointed to drought, starvation and death. The women of Memphis, appearing in the court, declared that Yusuf was pure in his action and thought. Zulaikha confessed her guilt from beginning to the end. The king ordered the release of Yusuf and prepared to abdicate in his favour. Along the route from the prison to the court, large crowds congregated to welcome Yusuf.[23] The king seated him on the throne and handed over his authority. Yusuf gave advice on the ways to meet the impending crisis. During abundance and rains, the people must be ordered to plough the fields, raise crops and store grains. During drought and scarcity, the state was required to distribute grain to each individual. Meanwhile, the Grand Wazir died. Zulaikha began to wear white clothes according to the practice of Hindustan. Repenting her maltreatment of Yusuf, she sank into a sea of sorrow. Bent with age, her body became disfigured and face acquired wrinkles. When her money exhausted, she built for herself a hut on the highway. Having lost her eyesight, she hoped for the attention of Yusuf.[24]

One day, Yusuf heard the cry of an old woman and her tale of woes. Zulaikha, revealing her identity, recalled her sacrifices for his love and her loss of wealth. Yusuf, deeply touched, vowed to fulfil her desires through his supernatural powers. She asked for the restoration of her beauty and eyesight. While Yusuf moved his lips in prayer, she regained her youthful splendour. She also demanded his love so that the sugar of his ruby lips became a balm to her wounded heart. Yusuf heard the sound of Jibrail's wing. The angel conveyed a message from

God, 'I have seen Zulaikha's humility, prayers and suffering. My pity has risen to free her soul from despair. By my throne, I betroth her to you.' Jami has provided an abrupt end to this epical tale.[25]

Narrative Poems of Amir Khusrau

Amir Khusrau (1253-1325) has made an outstanding contribution to the development of Persian literature in the Indian subcontinent. Composing Persian poetry at a young age, he earned the patronage of Malik Chhajju and Bughra Khan. He spent five years (1280-5) at Multan where, along with Amir Hasan Sijzi, he lent luster to the court of the governor Sultan Muhammad, the son of Balban. His elegy (*marsiya*) at the tragic death of the Prince and his own misery in Mongol captivity was an important episode in his career. In 1289, he joined the court of Sultan Muizzuddin Kaiqubad and henceforth remained associated with the royalty until his death. He witnessed the political developments during the rule of five Sultans. Throughout his literary career, he enjoyed affectionate intimacy with Shaikh Nizamuddin Auliya. The Chishti saint advised the poet to compose poetry in the style of the Isfahanis and accordingly compose love poems revolving around tresses and moles. Whenever he completed a work, he presented it to the saint who, after reciting the *fatiha*, returned it.[26] Khusrau was a prolific writer. In prose, he wrote an account of Alauddin Khalji's military campaigns and Nizamuddin Auliya's spiritual discourses, besides a voluminous treatise on the nine styles of writing prose. He has produced a vast corpus of lyrical poetry, including panegyrics (*qasidahs*) and sonnets (*ghazals*), that were preserved in five collections (*diwans*). However, his fame rested on his narrative poems (*masnavis*) that were divided into two categories, romantic and historical. Generally speaking, the genre of *masnavi*, which comprised couplets with rhyming hemistiches, was ideal for narrating the varying moods of love stories.

Amir Khusrau, adopting the models of Nizami Ganjawi, produced a quintet (*khamsah*) of five romantic poems. *Matla ul-Anwar*, comprising twenty unequal parts, expressed Khusrau's views on diverse themes, ranging from the superiority of man over other creatures to the benefits of knowledge and speech. It brought home the value of the five pillars of Islam and the ingredients of Islamic spirituality. In the last section, the poet advised his daughter Maimunah on the fidelity of women, the need for seclusion (*pardah*), attainment of domestic harmony and dangers of immoral conduct. In the *Ainah-i Sikandari,* Khusrau has narrated the military expedition of Sikandar against the Chinese, Russians and Almanis. In addition to the king's discourses with Aristotle and Plato, it described a number of technological devices of the times.

The remaining three *masnavis* reconstructed the famous love legends of Persia and Arabia. In *Shirin-Khusrau*, the poet described the life of the Persian king Khusrau in the context of his political engagements. While struggling against his rebellious noble Bahram Chobin and the Qaisar of Rum, he fell in love with Shirin (niece of the Armenian queen). His love affair came under stress due to his marriages with Maryam and Shakar. Meanwhile, Shirin fell in love with Farhad, a sculptor who was hired to construct a canal. Khusrau's pressure induced Farhad to commit suicide, while Shirin contrived the death of Shakar. Khusrau and Shrin, following their reconciliation, married and lived in happiness. In his *Laila-Majnun*, the poet differed from Nizami's plot on two points. Naufal, the chief who failed to persuade Laila's father to give his daughter in marriage to Majnun, accepted the lover as his son-in-law. The marriage could not turn Majnun's heart away from Laila. Towards the end of the tale, Majnun led Laila's last journey. When her coffin was lowered, he clasped her to his chest and gave up his life. The people, astonished at the sight, buried the lovers in the same grave. In *Hasht Bihisht*, the poet has recreated the life of the Persian king Bahram Gur who was famous for his hunting expeditions. He was in love with a Chinese beauty Dilaram. Bahram, offended at a minor lapse, exiled her to a forest. She learnt music from an old master and, appearing as a great musician, won over Bahram. At the advice of Wazir Numan, seven palaces were built and a princess was installed in each. Every day, Bahram visited a princess who narrated a story. Bahram, weary of this life, left for his last hunt, never to return.[27]

A story, as the Tatari princess Gulnari narrated to Bahram, has been set in Multan and Kamrup. Typical of Amir Khusrau's technique and literary devices, it deserved a closer attention. A group of five young men – a Prince, merchant, tunnel digger, carpenter and gardener – lived in Multan. They went on a trip to Kamrup. In an imposing temple, they saw the beautiful statue of a woman. Its caption, Kamrani, was a combination of the two words of love (*kam*) and woman (*rani*). The statue was a replica of the city's beauty. She lived on the top of a tower. No one had ever seen her. If anyone uttered her name, his tongue was pulled out. The local king, climbing the tower on a ladder, enjoyed the beauty along with wine. The Prince fell in love with Kamrani, while his friends provided all help. An old woman, who carried flowers for Kamrani, conveyed their messages to her. A plan was formulated to unite the lovers. The merchant built a seven-storey house with rooms, chambers and terraces. The tunnel digger made an underground passage from the house to the tower. The carpenter fashioned a secret ladder leading to the top of the tower. As the king was absent for a few days, the Prince stayed with Kamrani. They became steadfast in their mutual attachment. In the second part of their deception, the visitors planned to bring Kamrani with them to Multan. For seven consecutive days, they invited the king to banquets in their bungalow. The king, excessively drunk, was baffled on seeing Kamrani as the cupbearer (*saqi*). He was astonished even more on finding her in the chamber at the tower. His suspicion was removed. Grateful to his hosts, he equipped them for their voyage. The conspirators sailed away with Kamrani. The king was horrified on the disappearance of Kamrani, besides the presence of the tunnel and ladder. The king died of shock, while the lovers rejoiced at their union.[28]

Amir Khusrau earned the censure of his contemporaries for repeating Nizami. According to Ubaid Shair (a close associate of Muhammad bin Tughluq), it was irreverent presumptuousness on Khusrau's part to boil his meat and rice in Nizami's cauldron. In an angry response, Khusrau stated that his *Majnun-Laila* might not equal Nizami's classic. Since the work of his critics was worthless, they sang Nizami's praise only to console themselves. Originally, he aimed at recreating Nizami's magic and cast a similar spell. However, he was convinced of his own shortcomings and eminence of Nizami. The latter had the advantage of collecting that was excellent without leaving anything for him. Khusrau was forced to construct his *masnavi* out of the stuff Nizami discarded. Further, Nizami confined himself to a single branch of poetry (*masnavi*) and did not fritter away his energy in all directions. A combination of secluded life and princely patronage enabled him to produce excellent poetry. In contrast, Khusrau was burdened with lack of peace and unbridled worldly ambition. Day after day, he stood with folded hands before a patron till he sweated from head to foot. The payment was made to him as a gift, not as a remuneration for his toil. He was torn between the material need to praise his kindly patron and express the poetic aspirations of his soul. If the arduous task of earning a livelihood had left him more leisure, he would have shown his real potential. According to Mohammad Habib, Khusrau neither equalled nor surpassed Nizami. Rather, he was Nizami's best imitator. His basic problem lay in the choice of the subject. Instead of the old Persian legends, he should have explored a new field in the wide reservoir of Indian stories.[29] This criticism, as we shall see in the next section, was addressed in the Awadhi Sufi romances.

Amir Khusrau, as the official chronicler of the Delhi Sultanate, penned five historical *masnavis*. In the *Qiran us-Sadain* (The Conjunction of the Two Auspicious Stars), he described the meeting between Sultan Muizuddin Kaiqubad (r. 1286-90) and his father Bughra Khan, who ruled over Bengal. The text throws light on the majesty of the Kilokhari palace, Jama Masjid and Hauz-i Shamsi that received water from the Yamuna. This was followed by the celebration of Nauroz and the expedition of Khan-i Jahan against the Mongols. The main subject comprised Kaiqubad's march to the east, his correspondence with Bughra Khan, lavish festivities and exchange of gifts. In the *Miftah ul-Futuh* (The Key to Success) Khusrau recorded the military campaigns of Jalaluddin Khalji (r. 1290-6) against Malik Chhajju, the local chiefs of Awadh and the stronghold of Jhain. The *Nuh Sipihr* (Nine Skies), instead of narrating contemporary events, was an anthology of diverse themes. Eulogizing Qutbuddin Mubarak Shah Khalji (r. 1316-20) and the architectural monuments of Delhi, it advanced ten arguments to prove the superiority of India as a country. The case revolved around the changing seasons, quality of products, forms of knowledge, diversity of languages, merits of Hinduism and supernatural abilities of the Brahmins and Jogis.

It offered advice to rulers on war, justice and consultation. In the *Tughluqnama*, the poet has described the circumstances in which the Khalji rule came to an end and Ghazi Malik attained sovereign power. In his view, Qutbuddin Mubarak Shah Khalji neglected state affairs and failed to exercise caution in making appointments. The poet provided a minute account of Ghazi Malik's march to Delhi, the composition of rival armies, the proceedings of battles and the fate of the vanquished. He drew attention to Ghazi Malik's distinguished military career, loyalty to the Khalji regime and the rationale of his anti-Khusrau Khan campaign.

Amir Khusrau, while composing his *Dewal Rani wa Khizr Khan*, intended to match the famous lovers such as Vis-Ramin, Azra-Vamiq and Laila-Majnun.[30] As one of his five historical *masnavis*, it was free from legend and fantasy. It was built on an actual historical event that unfolded before the poet.[31] Khizr Khan, the eldest son of Alauddin Khalji, was a patron of literature and a disciple of Shaikh Nizamuddin Auliya. Khusrau held him in esteem and affection. One day, the Prince summoned the poet and, giving him a draft (*dibacha*) of the story of his love for Dewal Rani, requested him to versify it.[32] He completed the task in four months of 1316. He employed the various artifices of Persian poetry to lend a touch of the picturesque, romantic and heroic.[33] As in other *masnavis*, the text opened with the praise of God, Prophet Muhammad and Shaikh Nizamuddin Auliya.[34] The next portion comprised the Turkish occupation of Hindustan and conquests of Alauddin Khalji. The real story began with the Khalji occupation of Gujarat under Ulugh Khan. With the defeat and flight of Rai Karan, his treasure and women were sent to Delhi. The Rai's beautiful wife Kamla Devi entered the harem of the Sultan. She was the mother of two daughters. One of them had died, while the six-month old Dewal Devi was left behind. Kamla Devi, finding the Sultan in a happy mood, persuaded the Sultan to bring her to Delhi. She suggested that the girl could be married to Khizr Khan. The Sultan, accepting the proposal, sent a command to the Rai. Happy at the development, the Rai made preparations to send his daughter to Delhi. The Sultan, intending to annex Gujarat, dispatched Alp Khan and Panjuman to accomplish the task. Rai Karan fled to Devgiri. He was induced to marry Dewal Devi to

Bhilam Dev, the brother of Rai Shankar Dev of Devgiri. Following the ceremony, the bride was escorted to Devgiri. On the way, she fell into the hands of the Delhi army. Ulugh Khan sent her to Delhi under escort.[35] As she joined her mother, the Sultan and Queen Malika-i Jahan prepared to marry her to the Prince. Khizr Khan aged ten and Dewal Devi aged eight fell in love. Communicating with each other through confidants, they held a secret meeting and kept their passion under control. Malika-i Jahan shifted Dewal Devi to the Red Palace (*qasr-i lal*). The distraught Khizr Khan shaved his head and, sending a curl to his beloved, received a ring in return.

Malika-i Jahan, with the concurrence of the Sultan, organized the marriage of Khizr Khan with her brother Alp Khan's daughter. The women of the harem conveyed their opposition to the move in view of Khizr Khan's betrothal with Dewal Devi. Malika-i Jahan had her way. The capital, including its streets and bazaars, were decorated. Entertainers displayed their artistic talents. The festivities continued for three years.[36] Khizr Khan did not show interest in his new bride. Thinking of his beloved, he read the story of Laila-Majnun and abandoned recreational activities. A rumour caused misunderstanding between the lovers. Dewal Devi, learning that Khizr Khan had accepted his bride, felt shattered. In a letter, she accused Khizr Khan of betrayal and cruelty. She appealed to the Sultan for help. Khizr Khan, in his reply, refuted the accusations and asserted the purity of his feelings. He prayed to heaven and invoked the memory of true lovers like Majnun and Farhad. A mysterious voice assured him of union with his beloved. He sent an emissary to Malika-i Jahan and pleaded his case. It was improper to sacrifice a son for a niece. A man could marry four wives, while the royal family needed a large number of women. If the matter did not receive urgent attention, it might be too late. In these circumstances, Khizr Khan was quietly married to Dewal Devi. This was a turning point in his life, as he became disciple of Shaikh Nizamuddin Auliya and abjured all bad habits.[37]

The original *masnavi* ended here. After a gap of nearly ten years, Amir Khusrau appended to it a section of 319 verses, tracing the miserable fate of Khizr Khan. During the illness of Alauddin Khalji, Khizr Khan went on a pilgrimage to Hastinapur. He failed to seek the blessings of Shaikh Nizamuddin Auliya and lapsed into alcoholism. Malik Kafur created a gulf between him and the Sultan. Deprived of the symbols of heir-apparent, he was ordered to stay at Amroha.[38] During a visit to Delhi, he was reconciled with the Sultan. He was imprisoned in the fort of Gwalior. Following the Sultan's death, Malik Kafur had him blinded.[39] Dewal Rani served her husband with devotion. The new ruler Qutbuddin Mubarak Shah Khalji proposed to release Khizr Khan and demanded Dewal Rani as his slave. Khizr Khan, having lost the throne, saw her as his only possession. As the women wailed, Khizr Khan and his brother Shadi Khan were murdered. Khizr Khan was buried in the Vijay Mandir, while his soul felt like Farhad, not Prince Khusrau. Dewal Rani sank into a sea of mourning.[40] The lovers were two flowers blooming in a garden. Since this tale was written with the blood of the lovers, every line was imbued with many secrets. The story offered a lesson to the reader, who was urged to learn the way of love.

Awadhi Sufi Romances

During the late Sultanate and early Mughal period, the eastern Gangetic plain witnessed the inauguration of a new literary and devotional culture. The poets, being disciples of Sufi masters and members of Persian-speaking courtly elite, made their spiritual agenda comprehensible and appealing in the Indian cultural landscape. For this purpose, they composed romances (*premakhyans*) in Hindavi and, in the process, used terms, symbols, concepts, techniques and gods from their local milieu. Recited in the evening story telling sessions at the royal courts, these were ritually performed in the Sufi shrines to awaken the novices to spiritual realities. In order to understand these love stories, Aditya Behl points to three interlinked historical processes – cultural assimilation and transformation, creation of a new literary media and canons, and articulation of spiritual practice, using local terms and concepts.[41] The plots of these romances indicate some formulaic elements – awakening of hero in a dream or description of heroine's beauty, the transformation of hero into a Jogi, the hero's abandonment of his first wife in order to consummate love with the divine heroine, the agony of the first wife during twelve months, the hero's death and self-immolation (*sati*) of the two wives – all alluded to earlier common stereotypes that were reshaped into a distinctive formula.[42] In this manner, the essential characteristics were embedded in the content of the narrative poems.

In 1379, Maulana Daud, a disciple of Shaikh Zainuddin who, in turn, was a nephew and spiritual successor of Shaikh Nasiruddin Mahmud Chiragh-i Delhi, composed the *Chandayan* at Dalmau. His narrative was set in the north Indian city of Govar. Its ruler Mahar Sahdev and his wife Phularani were blessed with a daughter of the Padmini category, Chanda. The tales of her beauty spread in a vast area from Gujarat to Tirhut and from Badaun to Malabar. Princely families sought the hand of Chanda. Sahdev accepted one of the proposals and married Chanda to Bavan, the son of Jait. Her husband not only lived in squalor, he was also short-statured, one-eyed and impotent. Since the marriage remained unconsummated, Chanda returned to her parents in Govar. A beggar named Bajur saw Chanda and, during a visit to Jaipur, described Chanda's beauty to the ruler Rupchand. The latter, deciding to acquire Chanda by force, led a military expedition against Govar. Sahdev sought the help of a great warrior Lorik. In the ensuing battle, Lorik forced Rupchand to flee. The victorious army seated Lorik on an elephant and carried him in a procession. Chanda saw him from her terrace and suffered a heart stroke. During a public celebration, Lorik saw Chanda and lost his senses. Brihaspati, the handmaiden of Chanda, met Lorik. She suggested a plan for the union of lovers. For one year, Lorik lived in the temple and, performing austerities as a Jogi, chanted Chanda's name. Chanda visited the temple with 60 companions and saw her lover. On a stormy night, Lorik climbed to Chanda's balcony with the help of a rope and hook. The lovers not only professed their love for each other, but also ended up making love. Though Chanda concealed the presence of Lorik in her chamber, the secret was revealed to the world.

Lorik's wife Maina cornered her husband for his absence. Lorik convinced her of his fidelity. In the festival of Somnath, a fight erupted between Maina and Chanda, while Lorik succeeded in pacifying them. Lorik eloped with Chanda and escaped towards Kalinga.

Bavan, the lawful husband of Chanda, made an unsuccessful attempt to overpower the fugitives. The lovers faced numerous ordeals. Twice, Chanda suffered from snakebite, but an occultist (*garudi*) revived her. The lovers took shelter with the king of Hardi Patan. In response to a message from Maina, Lorik returned to Govar. The inhabitants strengthened the fortifications to defend themselves against an attack. Lorik met Maina and became convinced of her chastity. Another fight erupted between Maina and Chanda. Lorik established peace between the two women and, accompanied by them, entered Govar. Chanda's father, in order to avenge himself, took away the herds of Lorik and killed his brother Kumvaru. Repentant at his actions, Lorik sought forgiveness from Maina. Mulla Daud concluded his story at this point.[43] It appears that Maina reconciled with Lorik's attachment to Chanda and, thus, agreed to share the affection of her husband with another woman.

What was amazing, the above romance gained acceptance in Muslim circles, both mystical and theological. Abdul Quddus Gangohi (1456-1537), a prominent Sufi of the Chishti-Sabiri lineage, nurtured a keen interest in *Chandayan*, which conformed to his preoccupation with Jog. In his letters to Jalaluddin Thanesari and Shah Muhammad, he explained mystical themes with the help of quotations from this text. He discussed its content with the same intensity as his lectures on the works of Ibn Arabi, Fakhruddin Iraqi and Saadi Shirazi. His references from *Chandayan* figured alongside his quotes from the Quran. More importantly, he undertook a Persian translation of *Chandayan*. Unfortunately, its manuscript was lost in the upheaval of Rudauli during the Lodi-Sharqi warfare.[44] Towards the close of the sixteenth century, Badauni observed that there was no need to praise *Chandayan* as it had acquired great fame (*az nihayat shohrat dar een diyar*). Shaikh Taqiuddin Waiz Rabbani used to recite its verses from the pulpit in Delhi. The recitation had a strange impact on the listeners. Some learned men asked the Shaikh to state the reason of selecting this *masnavi* in Hindavi. The Shaikh replied that it comprised divine truth and pleasing subject. For devout lovers, it was worthy of ecstatic contemplation. It conformed to the interpretation of some Quranic verses and presentation of melodious singers of Hindustan. Its recitation captured the human hearts.[45] Sufi romances, other than *Chandayan*, might have undergone the same cross-cultural experience.

In 1503, Shaikh Qutban Suhrawardi, who was disciple of Shaikh Buddhan and associated with the court-in-exile of Sultan Husain Shah Sharqi of Jaunpur, composed the *Mrigawati*. In the narrative,[46] a king was blessed with a son. The Pandits, looking into his future, predicted a happy life, except his suffering in the love of a woman. By the age of 10 years, the Prince began to read the Puranas and excelled in physical sports. One day, he left for hunt and, separating from his retinue, saw a seven-coloured doe. The doe plunged into a pool and disappeared. The Prince jumped into the water and, even after a diligent search, did not find it. He established himself at the spot, refusing to return. The king constructed a temple at the site. The building had a number of paintings, including that of the magical doe, Mrigavati. The Prince, while looking at the picture, kept on crying. After a year, a group of nymphs bathed in the pool and flew away. The Prince was captivated on seeing the most beautiful of them. She was the magical doe Mrigavati, who had appeared in the garb of a woman. Her disappearance made him sad. His nurse suggested the way to unite with Mrigavati. Next Nirjala Ekadashi, she would come to bathe in the pool. If he hid her clothes, he would fulfil his desire. Mrigavati, who was also attracted to the Prince, anxiously waited for the occasion. While she bathed along with her companions, the Prince took away her clothes and refused to give them. She was induced to wear a new set of clothes that the Prince gave her. She entered the temple along with the Prince. He wanted to have physical intimacy with her. Mrigavati agreed to do so only if her companions gave the green signal. He accepted the proposal.[47]

The Prince and his beloved lived in happiness for some time. One day, he received a summons from the king. He placed Mrigavati's clothes in the custody of the nurse and left for the capital. Mrigavati managed to retrieve her original apparel and flew to the top of the temple. She told the nurse that she hailed from Kanchan Nagar and that Rup Murari was her father. The Prince, on returning, was shocked to know Mrigavati's departure. Turning a Jogi, he went out in her quest. He reached the seacoast and, boarding a ship, reached a mound. He overpowered two huge serpents and a cruel demon. He rescued Rupmini, the princess of Subhodaya. Her father forced the Prince to marry his daughter. The Prince never had sex with his wife and, putting on the guise of a Jogi, escaped to Kanchan Nagar.[48] Mrigavati, after the demise of her father, ruled over the kingdom. She acquired information about the Prince from Jogis and, bringing him back, installed him on the throne. A demon abducted the Prince. Mrigavati secured the help of God Pavan and brought him back.[49] He went to Subhodaya with Mrigavati and, joining Rupmini, came to Chandragiri. When a quarrel erupted between the two wives, he intervened to bring peace. During a hunt, he died at the hands of a wild animal. His wives committed Sati on his funeral pyre.[50]

In 1540, Malik Muhmmad Jaisi composed the *Padmawat*. According to this epic,[51] Padmavati was the daughter of Gandharvasen, the king of Simhal (Lanka). At the age of twelve, she began to live in a separate palace along with numerous companions. She was deeply attached to her parrot Hiraman, with whom she often discussed esoteric matters. Gandharvasen, angry at the intimacy, ordered the parrot to be killed. Hiraman escaped to freedom, leaving Padmavati in depression. A hunter caught Hiraman and sold it to a Brahmin, who brought it to Chittor. Raja Ratansen purchased Hiraman owing to its intelligence. The queen Nagmati wanted to kill Hiraman, as it hinted at the beauty of Simhalese women. Ratansen heard from it the incomparable comeliness of Padmavati and decided to acquire her at all costs. He became a Jogi like Gopichand and Bharthari. Travelling under the guidance of Hiraman, he was accompanied by a retinue of 16,000 followers, who had converted to Jog. He borrowed a fleet of boats from the ruler of Odisha. Arriving at Simhal, he performed austerities at the Shiva Temple. Padmavati met Hiraman and learnt of the arrival of her lover. On Vasant Panchami, she came for prayers at the Shiva Temple and saw Ratansen absorbed in a Jogic trance. Since he was unaware of her presence, she inscribed a message on his chest with sandalwood paste. Ratansen, armed with Shiva's magical boon, besieged the royal fort with the help of 16,000 Jogis. Gandharvasen surrounded the besiegers and ordered Ratansen to be hanged. Hiraman carried letters between the lovers and revealed their love to Gandharvasen. The king organized the marriage of lovers, who spent one year in enjoyment. The 16,000 Jogis were united to an equal number of Padmini women.[52]

Back in Chittor, Nagmati bore the pangs of separation. A bird carried her message to Ratansen, who decided to return against the wishes of Padmavati. During their voyage to Puri, a storm separated the lovers and killed all the retainers. Samudra and Lakshmi united them. Reduced to penury, they travelled across the Gangetic plain to reach Chittor. A quarrel between the two wives resulted in a fight. Ratansen, while bringing peace between them, asserted that he was equally attached to both. He banished a Brahmin hypnotist Raghav Chetan for lack of academic integrity. Ratansen banished him from the kingdom. While departing, Chetan received a bangle from Padmavati and was stunned on seeing her beauty. He went to Delhi and, meeting Alauddin Khalji as a beggar, described Padmavati's loveliness and intelligence. The Sultan besieged the fort of Chittor and demanded Padmini. Ratansen rejected the demand and offered to pay a tribute. Disregarding the advice of his vassals Gora and Badal, he allowed the Sultan to survey the fort. The Sultan managed to behold Padmavati in a mirror and took Ratansen in captivity. Padmavati directed Gora and Badal to march to Delhi to rescue their master. The two warriors, disguised as Padmavati and her 1,600 companions, entered the fort of Delhi and rescued Ratansen. Gora died fighting during the retreat, while Badal returned to Chittor with Ratansen. Devpal, the ruler of Kumbhalmer, took advantage of Ratansen's absence and tried to entice Padmavati. Ratansen, learning of the attempt, attacked Devpal. Both were killed in a combat. Nagmati and Padmavati committed Sati. When the Delhi forces besieged Chittor, the women burnt themselves in the rite of Jauhar, while their menfolk died fighting. The Sultan found the fort empty.[53]

In 1545, Mir Syed Manjhan Rajgiri composed the *Madhumalati*. The poet was associated with the court of Islam Shah and the mystic circle of the Shattari saint Muhammad Ghaus Gwaliari. The narrative opened with Surajbhan, the ruler of the kingdom of Kanaigiri.[54] He served an ascetic for twelve years and, as a reward, was blessed with a son. The Pandits named the child as Manohar and predicted his future. At the age of 14 years and 11 months, he would fall in love and, in separation from his beloved, would wander as a Jogi for one year. When he attained the age of twelve, Surajbhan abdicated in his favour. After three years, he underwent a strange experience. A group of nymphs saw him sleeping and, impressed with his looks, searched for his suitable partner. They chose Madhumalati, the daughter of king Vikramajit of Maharas. Through their miraculous power, Manohar's bed was placed besides Madhu's. Seeing each other, they recalled their love from previous births. They exchanged vows of love, but stopped short of physical union.[55] As soon as they awakened from their dream, they began to suffer from the pangs of separation. A senior officer advised Manohar to abandon his involvement with a woman. Manohar rejected the advice and, assuming the garb of a Jogi, left Kanaigiri along with a large retinue in search of Madhu. At the sea coast, he boarded a ship. After a voyage of four months, a storm destroyed the vessel and swallowed the followers. Somehow, Manohar remained safe and found himself in a jungle.[56]

Manohar killed a demon and rescued Pema, the daughter of Raja Chitrasen of Chitbisraun. Manohar informed Pema of his search for Madhu. Pema stated that Madhu had been her childhood friend and paid a monthly visit to them with her mother. He restored Pema to her parents. He declined the offer of the kingdom and Pema's hand. Next day, Madhu and her mother arrived in the city. Pema enabled Manohar to meet Madhu. Madhu expressed her anger at Manohar's desertion but reconciled with him. The two slept together, but vowed to make love only after their marriage. When they woke up, they found themselves in their respective native places. For a second time, Manohar turned a Jogi and left in search of Madhu. At Maharas, the Queen Rupmanjari confronted her daughter Madhu and urged her to forget her love. Failing in her attempt, she converted Madhu into a bird. The bird flew out and, in a quest for Manohar, reached Pavaneri. Prince Tarachand caught the bird and brought it back to Maharas. Rupmanjari restored Madhu to her human form. Her parents offered her to Tarachand in wedlock. Tarachand declined the match, as Madhu was bound to unite with Manohar. The parents sent a letter to Pema informing her of the happenings. Madhu, in a separate letter, expressed her miserable state in separation from Manohar, particularly her suffering during the last twelve months (*baramasah*).[57]

The messengers, travelling from Maharas to Chitbisraun, delivered the letters to Pema. Precisely at this time, Manohar also reached the place. Since Pema was conversant with the miserable state of lovers, she became instrumental in arranging their marriage. Pema and Manohar sent their letters to Maharas. Vikramajit, along with his household, travelled to the venue. So did Pema and Chitrasen. Manohar and Madhu were tied in a marital bond. The newlyweds invited Tarachand to stay with them. Tarachand saw Pema and lost his senses. Manohar and Madhu revived Tarachand. Manohar secured the approval of Chitrasen for the marriage of Pema with Tarachand. The two couples, after staying together during the monsoon, left for their respective homes. Madhu expressed her gratitude to Tarachand, while Pema acknowledged her indebtedness to Manohar. The story, though crowded with descriptions of struggles and sorrow, ended on a happy note.[58]

In 1594, Abul Faiz Faizi retold the tale of Nal-Daman at the instance of his royal patron Akbar.[59] We learn that Nal, the king of Ujjain, possessed the noble qualities of good looks, wisdom, wealth, justice and generosity. Hearing stories of love from his courtiers, he became restless. The royal physician declared that Nal had become a victim of the fire of youth. As a remedy, the courtiers narrated stories of love to distract his troubled mind. One story dilated on the beauty of Daman, a daughter of the king of Bidar. Nal, without seeing Daman, fell in love with her. Daman, undergoing the same torment, discovered the identity of Nal through imagination. A strange bird, possessing miraculous powers, became a conduit between them. It conversed with Nal, who gave it a letter for Daman. The princess sent a reply, reciprocating her love for Nal. The affair became known in the palace. The king decided to tie Daman in a marriage. Royal suitors were invited to try their luck. A number of princely suitors, including Nal, reached Bidar. Some pagan gods assumed the physical form of Nal. Daman, in her predicament, prayed for divine assistance. A beam of light, accompanied by a voice, revealed the signs of gods.

With this knowledge, Daman recognized Nal and garlanded him. The lovers were married and came to Ujjain.[60]

Married life did not turn a bed of roses. Nal surrendered himself to pleasure (*nishat*), so that love (*ishq*) and frenzy (*junun*) formed an alliance against intellect (*aql*). In a bout of gambling with his brother, Nal lost his kingdom and possessions. Rendered destitute, he went into wilderness along with Daman. Nal, unable to live with Daman in this misery, deserted her. Thus separated, they faced numerous ordeals involving change of identity and encounters with supernatural elements. Daman reached a kingdom where she was employed as a companion to the princess. Nal repented of his mistakes and, vowing to unite with Daman, underwent a series of trials. His complexion turned black due to a snakebite. He strayed into a city and, assuming the name of Bahuk, began to serve King Rutbarn as a horse keeper. The real identity of Daman was discovered and she was sent to her parents in Bidar. She reconvened an assembly of suitors (*swyamwar*) in order to search out Nal. Rutbarn, accompanied by Bahuk, reached Bidar to try his luck. No assembly was held. Daman subjected Bahuk to a vigorous interrogation and test of skills. It was proved that the man was Nal. He attained his original complexion and united with Daman. The lovers returned to Ujjain. Nal forgave his brother and began to rule. After some time, he abdicated in favour of his son and, retiring to a forest, desired to end his worldly life. Daman reproached him for wishing to leave her when they had united in love. Nal breathed his last, while Daman burnt herself on his funeral pyre.[61]

During the medieval times, West Asia took the lead in versifying prominent love tales. In most cases, the protagonists were associated with the privileged ruling classes. The career of lovers witnessed three phases. In the first, they fell in love amidst mutual attraction. In the second, they endured prolonged agony and, in the third, they met an uncertain end. Vis and Ramin, owing to their unsteady natures, often became hostile to each other. Majnun, failing to marry Laila, withdrew from the society and became a reclusive poet. Yusuf faced acute persecution because of his moral principles clashed with the desires of a capricious mistress. Owing to the cultural intercourse between central Islamic lands and the Delhi Sultanate, Amir Khusrau retold West Asian tales in Persian narrative poetry (*masnavis*). His composition on the life of Dewal Rani-Khizr Khan, revolving around contemporary political developments, was embedded in the Indian cultural milieu. The Sufi poets, associated with the Islamic literary tradition, placed the adventures of Hindu ruling elites in the realm of fantasy and established the motif of Jogi in the quests for union between lovers. A study of these literary trends enables us to assess Damodar's narrative on Hir-Ranjha, the most famous lovers of medieval Panjab.

NOTES

1. The poet hailed from Gorgan, which lay to the east of the Caspian Sea. He assumed the task at the instance of Amid Abul Fateh Muzaffar, the governor of Isfahan on behalf of the Seljuqid ruler Abu Talib Tughril Beg. From eleventh century onwards, Persian poetry showed a strong nostalgia for pre-Islamic Persia. The story was confined to the Parthian royalty, which was occupied with power and pleasure. The opulence and splendour was reflected in military conquests, hunting, feasting and drinking. The narrative, essentially a celebration of eroticism, included episodes of intrigue and conflict. The plot, moving slowly, was interrupted by descriptive passages, rhetorical speeches and hyperbolic expressions of extreme emotion. Nizami Ganjawi, who lived a century after Gorgani, adopted his predecessor's scenes, themes and rhetoric. Fakhruddin Gorgani, *Vis and Ramin*, Eng. tr. with an Introduction, Dick Davis, New York: Penguin Books, 2008, pp. ix-xliv.
2. Ibid., pp. 1-44.
3. Ibid., pp. 45-128.
4. Ibid., pp. 129-80.
5. Ibid., pp. 181-307.
6. Ibid., pp. 308-430.
7. Ibid., pp. 431-52.
8. Ibid., pp. 453-99.
9. Nizamuddin Abu Muhammad Ilyas (1140-1203), born in the Trans-Caucasian city of Ganja, was one of the greatest poets of Persia. He studied in Sufi circles under Shaikh Farrukh Raihani. He claimed to have avoided the bustle of royal courts and had an ascetic conception of life. Yet, all his great poems were dedicated to the rulers of his times. His works marked the zenith of epic poetry in Persia. For the first time,

the antithesis between language of the lyric and the archaic style of the epic was overcome and the epic was brought into the milieu of the court style, which at this time was already fully developed in the lyric. At the same time, the epic lost its heroic character and increasingly devoted itself to psychological characterization at which Nizami was a master. M.T. Houtsma et al., ed., *The Encyclopaedia of Islam*, vol. III, Leiden: E.J. Brill and London: Luzac & Co., 1946, pp. 937-8.

10. Nizami Ganjawi, *Laila and Majnun*, Eng. tr. Rudolph Gelpke, E. Mattin and G. Hill, New Lebanon: Omega Publications, 2011, pp. vi-xvii.
11. Ibid., pp. 1-15.
12. Ibid., pp. 16-46.
13. Ibid., pp. 47-104.
14. Ibid., pp. 105-56.
15. Ibid., pp. 157-77.
16. Jami, formally attached to the Naqshbandi order, trained under Saiduddin Kashghari and Ubaidullah Ahrar. His chief contribution lay in presenting Ibn Arabi's thought in intelligible terms. In him, Sufi traditions of Ibn Arabi and Jalaluddin Rumi were united. In *Lawaih* (Gleaming Lights), he summarized the doctrines of Ibn Arabi, while his *Nafhat ul-Uns* (Breath of Familiarity) provided accounts of the Sufis of Central Asia and Persia. His long poetic work *Haft Aurang* (Seven Thrones) comprised seven odes (*masnavis*), including Yusuf-Zulaikha and Laila Majnun. His *Baharistan* was composed on the lines of Saadi's *Gulistan*. He translated 40 Prophetic traditions (*hadis*) into Persian quatrains. His verses gained fame from Turkey to Malaya and, thus, he earned the honorary title of the Seal of Poets (*khatam ul-shuara*). Seyyed Hossein Nasr, ed., *Islamic Spirituality: Manifestations*, vol. II, New York: The Crossword Publishing Company, 2012, pp. 174, 344.
17. Abdur Rahman Jami, *Yusuf and Zulaikha: A Poem by Jami*, Eng. tr. Ralph T.H. Griffith, New York: Routledge, rpt., 2013, pp. 33-70.
18. Ibid., pp. 71-103.
19. Ibid., pp. 71-126.
20. Ibid., pp. 127-202.
21. Ibid., pp. 203-18.
22. Ibid., pp. 219-41.
23. The twelfth chapter of the Quran narrates the story of Yusuf. Jami, while developing his plot, relied heavily on the first part of this chapter (12: 4-58). It focused on Yusuf's dream, his ill treatment at the hands of his brothers and his sale to a merchant as slave. The merchant's wife

tried to seduce Yusuf and, vindicating her action before the women of the city, locked him in prison. Yusuf interpreted the king's dream, secured his release and became manager of the royal storehouse. The second part of the Quranic chapter (12: 59-111), which Jami has overlooked, describes the relations between Yusuf and his brothers. During scarcity, they came to the city and received grain from Yusuf. At Yusuf's insistence, they brought his uterine brother Benjamin to the city. Yusuf, employing a stratagem, ensured Benjamin's stay with him. As he revealed his identity, his brothers felt repentant. Yusuf sent his shirt to Yaqub, who recovered his eyesight owing to a miracle. His parents arrived in the city and prostrated before him. The prophecy of Yusuf's original dream proved true. A.J. Droge, *The Quran: A New Annotated Translation*, New Delhi: Oxford University Press, 2013, pp. 142-9.

24. Abdur Rahman Jami, *Yusuf and Zulaikha: A Poem by Jami*, pp. 242-89.
25. Ibid., pp. 290-6.
26. Amir Khurd, *Siyar ul-Auliya*, Delhi: Matba-i Muhibb-i Hind, 1885, pp. 311-15.
27. Mohammad Wahid Mirza, *The Life and Works of Amir Khusrau*, Delhi: Idarah-i Adabiyat-i Delli, rpt., 1974, pp. 190-203.
28. Sunil Sharma, *Amir Khusraw: The Poet of Sultans and Sufis*, Oxford: Oneworld Publications, rpt., 2006, pp. 99, 126.
29. Mohammad Habib, 'Hazrat Amir Khusrau of Delhi', in *Politics and Society during the Early Medieval Period: Collected Works of Professor Mohammad Habib*, vol. I, ed. K.A. Nizami, New Delhi: People's Publishing House and Aligarh: Centre of Advanced Study, Department of History, 1974, pp. 333-5.
30. Sunil Sharma, op. cit., p. 62.
31. A reading of the *masnavi's* text based on content leads to the traditional division between history and literature. The first third of the text on Nizamuddin Auliya, Alauddin Khalji, the Delhi Sultans and their victories related to historical information, while the remainder of the text provides a story of the romance. On the other hand, reading the form inverted the historical and romantic sections. The first third of the text becomes a literary panegyric created by Khusrau in praise of his patrons and Delhi Sultanate. The remaining text, describing the romance between Khizr Khan and Dewal Rani, is a biography using Prince's draft as a historical source. Michael Boris Bednar, 'The Content and Form in Amir Khusraw's Duval Rani va Khizr Khan',

Journal of the Royal Asiatic Society, 3rd series, vol. 24, no. 1, January 2014, p. 33.

32. Amir Khusrau, *Duwal Rani Khizr Khan*, ed. Rashid Ahmad Salim Ansari and Khaliq Ahmad Nizami, Delhi: Idarah-i Adabiyat-i Delli and Aligarh: Centre of Advanced Study in History, Department of History, Aligarh Muslim University, 1988, p. 41.
33. Mohammad Wahid Mirza, op. cit., pp. 178-9.
34. Amir Khusrau, *Duwal Rani Khizr Khan*, pp. 5-21.
35. Ibid., pp. 80-7.
36. Ibid., pp. 152-73.
37. Ibid., pp. 216-29.
38. Ibid., pp. 233-40.
39. Ibid., pp. 241-64.
40. Ibid., pp. 273-88.
41. Aditya Behl, *Love's Subtle Magic: An Indian Islamic Literary Tradition, 1379-1545*, New York: Oxford University Press, 2012, pp. 1-2.
42. Ibid., p. 23.
43. Naseem A. Hines, *Maulana Daud's Candayan: A Critical Study*, New Delhi: Manohar, 2009, pp. 45-51.
44. Saiyid Athar Abbas Rizvi, *A History of Sufism in India*, vol. I, New Delhi: Munshiram Manoharlal, 1975, pp. 348, 365.
45. Abdul Qadir Badauni, *Muntakhab ut-Tawarikh*, vol. II, ed. Maulavi Ahmad Ali, Aligarh: Centre of Advanced Study in History, Department of History and Publication Division, Aligarh Muslim University, rpt., 2018, p. 250.
46. This text is a perfect example of the Sufis' use of the Sanskrit technology of the sublimation of desire into divine love in order to express their own ideology of Islamic monotheism. The inner journey is depicted as a Yogic quest, denoting the historical interaction with the Gorakhnath Panth. Its poetic logic of sublimation, using the language of emotion (*bhava*) and essence of aesthetic and devotional experience (*rasa*), evolves in dialogue with the practices of the sects devoted to the worship of Krishna, who may themselves owe something to the ladder of ordinate love that shapes the Sufi path of asceticism. Aditya Behl, *The Magic Doe: Qutban Suhrawardi's Mirigavati*, New York: Oxford University Press, 2012, p. 36; Aditya Behl, 'The Magic Doe: Desire and Narrative in a Hindavi Sufi Romance, circa 1503', in *India's Islamic Traditions 711-1750*, ed. Richard M. Eaton, New Delhi: Oxford University Press, 2003, pp. 180-208; Aditya Behl, 'Emotion

and Meaning in Mrigavati: Strategies of Spiritual Signification in Hindavi Sufi Romances', in *After Timur Left: Culture and Circulation in Fifteenth Century North India*, ed. Francesca Orsini and Samira Sheikh, New Delhi: Oxford University Press, 2014, pp. 273-98.

47. Qutban, *Mirigavati*, ed. Mataprasad Gupt, Agra: Pramanik Prakashan, 1968, Stanza nos. 13-89, pp. 9-70.
48. Ibid., Stanza nos. 90-183, pp. 70-152.
49. Ibid., Stanza nos. 188-300, pp. 156-259.
50. Ibid., Stanza nos. 301-425, pp. 260-368.
51. Contrary to popular perception, *Padmawat* is not a Sufi allegory. It does not aim at luring the reader in the name of a love story and than giving her a tutorial in Sufism. It was also not a call to arms in the name of community honour. In the text, love is primary and the battle secondary. More than two-thirds of the epic is about the epitome of the beauty of Padmavati and Ratansen's quest (*saadhna*) for her. Far from being a dry discussion on Sufism, its characters are seen coming to terms with the vagaries of love and life in general. Through creative imagination, it transforms an episode of history into an intricate tapestry of love, desire, struggle and sacrifice. Placing a local episode into a wider cultural perspective, Jaisi makes it the basis of a classic through his vast knowledge of mythology and folklore. This work is located in the Indian tradition that celebrated the pleasure and pain of erotic love. Purushottam Agrawal, *Padmavat: An Epic Love Story*, New Delhi: Rupa Publications, 2018, pp. 9-11.
52. Ibid., pp. 51-117.
53. Ibid., pp. 118-80.
54. This text, being both allegorical and symbolic, contained a variety of suggestive incidents. These were an allegorical centrepiece in the form of the seductive divine heroine, a genuine commitment to a range of poetic meanings and a sense of the poem suggesting and evoking poetic flavour (*rasa*). Manjhan employed three classes of mystical symbols – pilgrim on the way (*salik*), lover searching for his Beloved (*ashiq*) and seeker of inner transformation (*sadhak*) – allegorically and intertwined them into a beautifully constructed narrative. In Manjhan's scheme of events, it was possible to focus on the narrative stages of awakening, purification, illumination and consummation of desire. Manjhan, *Madhumalati*, Eng. tr. Aditya Behl, Simon Weightman and Shyam Manohar Pandey, New York: Oxford University Press, 2000, pp. xxxvii-xlii.

55. Mir Syed Manjhan Rajgiri, *Madhumalati*, ed. Mataprasad Gupt, Allahabad: Mittar Prakashan, 1961, Stanza nos. 44-135, pp. 37-113.
56. Ibid., Stanza nos. 139-80, pp. 116-52.
57. Ibid., Stanza nos. 182-417, pp. 153-365.
58. Ibid., Stanza nos. 430-534, pp. 376-478.
59. Abul Faiz Faizi (1547-95), was the eldest son of Shaikh Mubarak Nagauri and elder brother of Abul Fazl. In 1567, he gained access to the Mughal court and travelled with Akbar to Bengal, Ajmer, Kashmir, Kabul and Panjab. He taught the princes (Salim, Murad and Daniyal), supervised land grants in Agra, led a diplomatic mission to Deccani states and fought against the Yusufzais. In 1588, he was honoured with the title of Malik ush-Shuara. He was unsurpassed in poetry, composing enigmas, prosody, history, philology, medicine and prose. Apart from a *diwan* of 9,000 verses, his *Lataif-i Fayyazi* comprises letters to the emperors, nobles, relatives, physicians and saints. He wrote an undotted commentary on the Quran and an undotted Arabic treatise on moral maxims. On the lines of Nizami's quintet, he intended to compose five *masnavis*, viz. *Markaz-i Adwar*, *Sulaiman wa Bilqis*, *Haft Kishwar*, *Akbar Nama* and *Nal-Daman*. He began working on all, but completed only the last. Z.A. Desai, 'Life and Works of Faizi', *Indo-Iranica*, vol. XVI, no. 3, 1964, pp. 5-35.
60. Muzaffar Alam and Sanjay Subrahmanyam, 'Love, Passion and Reason in Faizi's Nal-Daman', in *Love in South Asia: A Cultural History*, ed. Francesca Orsini, New Delhi: Cambridge University Press, 2007, pp. 119-29.
61. Ibid., pp. 130-5.

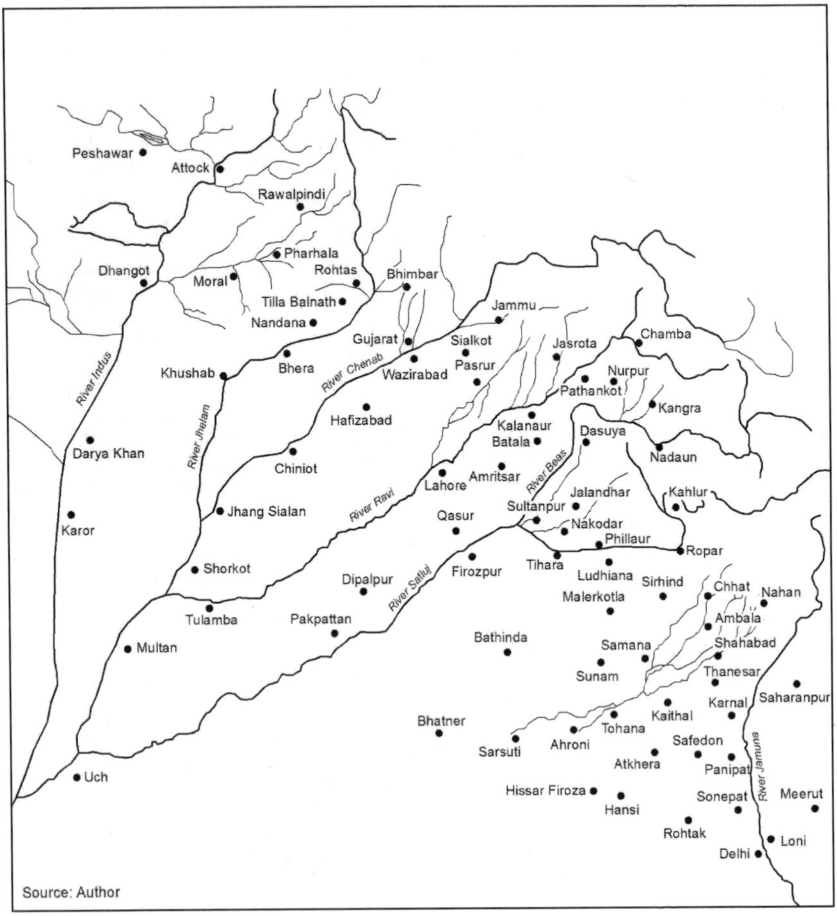

Source: Author

Map: Medieval Panjab

CHAPTER 2

Historical Context

Some time in the second half of the fifteenth century, Hir and Ranjha lived on the Chenab. By the early sixteenth century, their story had spread across Panjab. Shah Husain, the Sufi poet of Lahore, made frequent reference to it. Damodar Gulati documented the entire story in a Panjabi narrative poem (*qissa*) in 963 stanzas. These developments took place in a specific historical context. The protagonists lived in the rural society, which the landed clans dominated. Damodar was also located in the same social space. Hence, it is imperative to understand the process of state formation (Turkish, Afghan and Mughal) with special reference to the role of local elements including tribes, chiefdoms and *zamindars*. While the local elites, aspiring for autonomy, engaged in a perpetual struggle against the Delhi-based polity, diverse spiritual traditions rooted themselves in the sociocultural life. Jogis and Sufis, having come out in support of Hir-Ranjha, attained a strong presence in the region. Guru Nanak and Shah Husain, though distinct in their spiritual roots, lent strong support to female sexuality. The Sikh movement, raising its voice against caste-based inequality, uplifted the depressed castes in social estimation and political empowerment. Shah Husain deserved a separate treatment because he was the first to note Hir's suffering in her quest to unite with Ranjha and, in the process, spiritualized the story. Since he became notorious for singing and dancing in the streets of Lahore, he might have succeeded in giving a wide currency to the story. Possibly, he inspired Damodar to narrate the story in fullest detail and in its social context.

Political Transitions

At the opening of the fourteenth century, the intermediaries (*khuts* and *muqaddams*) stood out for their wealth, power and splendour. They did not pay any land tax. Nor did they accept the authority of the government officers. As soon as the Delhi Sultanate gained strength and stability, the intermediaries suffered an erosion in their status.[1] A uniform system of agrarian taxation, which was introduced in the Indo-Gangetic plain, deprived the intermediaries of their privileged position. An increase in the burden of taxes and natural calamities ignited a widespread agrarian uprising in the Ganga-Yamuna Doab. The unrest spread to south-east Panjab including Sunam, Samana, Kaithal and Karnal. The rebels comprised a number of tribes such as Bairahas, Mandahars, Jiwans, Bhattis and Minas. In addition to chiefs, intermediaries and peasants were involved in the insurrection.[2] The Delhi Sultanate, learning from this experience, adopted new strategies of state formation. During the second half of the fourteenth century, it roped in diverse local elements, particularly the intermediaries and Sufis, to develop canal-based irrigation and agrarian expansion in south-east Panjab.[3] A similar project was undertaken in the Multan region with the help of the local beneficiaries such as the peasants, intermediaries and chiefs (*ahali wa arbab*).[4] As the structure of polity became strong, positive results were noted in the settlement of new villages, sedentrization of pastoral groups, increase in agricultural output, introduction of winter crops, emergence of new urban spaces and creation of fresh administrative units.[5] The symbiotic relation between the state and local elements did not survive the dislocation resulting from Timur's invasion.

After the death (21 September 1388) of Firoz Shah Tughluq, the Delhi Sultanate underwent political fragmentation. The focus of polity gravitated to Panjab and remained so for several decades. The new ruler Sultan Muhammad, facing opposition of the Firozi slaves, shifted to Nagarkot. Ghiasuddin Tughluq, a contender for power, sent into the hills a punitive expedition, which included Sultan Khushdil, the *muqti* of Samana, and Rai Kamaluddin Muin, the *zamindar* of Ludhiana. At Delhi, the Firozi slaves enthroned Abu Bakr. Sultan

Muhammad descended on Samana and, with the support of *muqtis* and *zamindars* of the cis-Satluj tract, mustered a force of 50,000 men and made three attempts to occupy Delhi. On his orders, the Firozi slaves posted in the cities of Panjab (Lahore, Multan, Samana, Hansi and Hissar Firoza) were massacred. On 31 August 1390, he succeeded in occupying Delhi and ruled for four years.[6] At this time, Sarang Khan, the governor of Diplapur, was engaged in a tussle with Shaikha Khokhar. Securing the assistance of prominent chiefs like Rai Juljain Bhatti, Rai Kamaluddin Muin of Ludhiana and Shaikh Daud of Jalandhar, he recovered Lahore from Shaikha Khokhar, who withdrew to Jammu. As a fresh conflict broke out among governors, Sarang Khan snatched Multan from Khizr Khan, but failed to take Samana from Ghalib Khan. For six months, he defended Multan against Pir Muhammad (the grandson of Timur) and became a prisoner in the hands of the invaders. His brother Mallu Iqbal Khan, following several manipulations, converted Sultan Nasiruddin Mahmud Shah into a puppet and overpowered many rival nobles.[7] In these circumstances, Timur crossed the Indus and entered Panjab.

Timur, long before invading India, placed his grandson Pir Muhammad over Afghanistan and lands up to the Indus. The prince, aiming at the subjugation of south-western Panjab, captured Uch and Multan after protracted sieges. At both the forts, Sarang Khan's dogged resistance did not produce the desired results. Meanwhile, Timur crossed (20 September 1398) the Indus and received tributes from the chiefs of the Salt Range. Marching across a vast desert (Chaul-i Jalali), he reached the Jhelum and defeated Shihabuddin Mubarak Shah Tamimi, who ruled over a fortified tract on the river. Timur established his camp at Tulamba and extracted a ransom from prominent citizens. In the countryside, the local chiefs offered resistance and, in the combing operations, lost 2,000 men and unlimited wealth. Pir Muhammd, losing his horses in an epidemic of plague, faced opposition from the landed potentates. The inhabitants of Dipalpur and Ajodhan fled to Bhatner in panic. Timur refrained from attacking Ajodhan owing to its association with Baba Farid. Thousands of fugitives took shelter in the fort of Bhatner, while the invaders ravaged the countryside and surrounded the citadel. The defenders were killed, the buildings were burnt and women committed self-immolation. Timur, occupying the fort of Bhatner, entered south-east Panjab. He targeted Sarsuti, Fatehabad, Ahroni, Tohana, Samana, Kaithal and Panipat. At every place, the inhabitants were killed and grain was looted. Countless prisoners were put to death. Timur occupied the stronghold of Loni and, crossing the Yamuna, encamped at Firozabad. On the other side, Sultan Nasiruddin Mahmud Shah and Mallu Iqbal Khan mustered 10,000 cavalry, 40,000 infantry and 125 armoured elephants. The Sultan and his minister, losing 600 men in an ambush, retreated into the city only to escape from it. The invaders committed atrocities in Siri, Jahanpanah and old Delhi. Thousands of artisans were captured for relocation to Samarqand. Timur, marching from Meerut to Lahore via Haridwar and Jammu, ravaged the Siwaliks and extracted ransoms.[8] In the spring of 1399, he travelled through the Salt Range and crossed the Indus.

Growth of Sufism

Sufism was the most important ingredient of the Panjabi culture. Almost all medieval towns (Lahore, Multan, Uch, Gujarat, Batala, Jalandhar, Malerkotla, Sirhind, Bathinda, Hansi and Panipat) were identified with prominent Sufis. Popular tradition has linked the earliest Sufi, Baba Haji Rattan, with Prophet Muhammad. Ali bin Usman Hujweri (d. 1072), the author of *Kashf ul-Mahjub*, lived in Lahore during the Ghaznavid rule. The emergence of the Delhi Sultanate coincided with the establishment of two major Sufi lineages, Chishtis and Suhrawardis. Most Sufis endeavoured to bring an increasing area under their influence and, as a result, developed the competitive notion of spiritual domains (*vilayat*). They have left behind a variety of evidence in the form of biographies, conversations, letters and poetry. On the one hand, the Sufis trained disciples in the intricacies of Islamic spirituality and, on the other hand, guided lay aspirants on the path of piety and devotion. The Sufi lodges (*khanqahs*) served as residences and seminaries. When prominent Sufis were buried in their premises, they evolved as centres of pilgrimage (*dargahs*). A plethora of periodic rituals, coupled with the performances of Qawwals, lent a popular character to these sacred sites. The rulers and local magnates, appreciating the social influence of the Sufis, cultivated friendly relations with them. They sought to legitimize their political power through conferment of land grants and cash allowances on the Sufis. At the same time, the Sufis received large donations from the merchants and small offerings from devotees.

A Sufi establishment (*khanqah*), besides providing residence to the Sufi and his family, served as a school for grooming novices and an open house for visitors. The Chishti hospice comprised a large hall (*jamaatkhana*), which was little more than a roof standing on a number of pillars. At the foot of each pillar, a disciple resided with his bedding, books and rosary. The disciples slept, prayed and studied on the floor. If food was available, it was shared among all and, if not, they collectively endured hunger. The physical work was distributed among the disciples, who looked after the personal needs of the Shaikh, brought wood from the forest, plucked wild fruits from trees, fetched water, cooked food, cleaned utensils and managed the common kitchen.[9] They received a large amount of unasked charity (*futuh*), but distributed it among the visitors, so that nothing was kept for the next day. When wild fruits (*kareel* and *delah*) were not available, the disciples were sent to the neighbouring localities with begging bowls to collect food.[10] The hospice was open to all classes of people, ranging from mighty rulers to indigent peasants, who sought answers to their existential and spiritual needs. In contrast to the simplicity and openness of the Chishti hospice, the Suhrawardi establishment at Multan was large and exclusive. Built on a grand scale, it provided separate accommodation to inmates and visitors.[11] Its opulence could be traced to its close ties with the nascent Delhi Sultanate and ample financial resources. Its wealth and granaries flowed from the possession of land grants and liberal disposition of the long distance merchants. It helped the local authorities with grain and silver in times of exigency. The Suhrawardi accumulation of wealth invited a strong criticism from the Chishtis.

In the middle of the fourteenth century, the Suhrawardi hospice of Multan was a busy place. Its structure comprised courtyards, cells and terraces. All parts had doors that opened into a courtyard, so that everyone could follow the prayer leader. Built like a mosque, it was open to local inhabitants and travellers. There was always a stream of visitors from foreign lands. Apart from permanent residents and workers, the number of visitors often touched 1,000. In addition to prayers, one came across perpetual recitation of the Quran, continuous remembrance of God, distribution of food, grant of allowances to the Sufi and his dependents. Books were read in an academic setting, where a tutor instructed the students in the correct transmission of a text to the posterity. Alternatively, books were read in a devotional framework, where a Sufi elder profusely wept while listening to literary evocations of the love for God. Extra prayers corresponded to the occasion of liturgical calendar and followed prescriptions of the local leaders of the fellowship. On every Thursday night, there was a special recitation of the Quran, followed by public prayers and distribution of sweets (*halwa*). On these nights, some disciples kept a vigil and performed prayers of the rosary. Every year, a fast of six months was observed in seclusion. In order to prepare the aspirants for this arduous undertaking, special food was provided for twenty days to build their strength. As an incentive, these devotees were favoured with a separate cash allowance. During the recitation of poetry, the emotionally agitated listeners engaged in ecstatic movements, which the presiding master calmed down.[12]

In the hands of Baba Farid (1175-1265), Chishti mysticism was built on the foundations of Quranic recitations. It was followed by the study of Hadis from Abu Shakur Salimi's *Tamhid ul-Muhtadi* and principles of mysticism from Shihabuddin Suhrawardi's *Awarif ul-Maarif.* The fame of Baba Farid as an erudite scholar and diligent teacher spread far and wide. Though he did not keep any book in front of him and sat with a sheet around himself, his scholarship and eloquence appeared divinely inspired.[13] In Chishti circles, the prayers followed three ways of Prophet Muhammad. The first was determined by time, the second by a specific cause and third by neither of the two. The Chishtis also benefited from Ghazzali's prescriptions for supererogatory prayers that were drawn for the day, week, month and year. Baba Farid preferred such prayers in congregation, as on 14 Shaban. Besides the *Ayat ul-Kursi*, he recommended reciting four times a line on God's oneness and omnipotence. However, he suggested chanting *Surah-i Fatiha* thousands of times. Senior

Chishtis performed the inverted 40-day retreat (*chilla-i makus*) without attracting attention. An aspirant, suspended upside down into a well with feet tied with a rope, spent the whole night in prayer. During normal days, Baba Farid remained engrossed in remembrance of God and mystical contemplation, with his head prostrate on the ground. During small breaks for meals, he took flavoured sherbet and two loaves of bread that were often shared with others.[14]

Shaikh Bahauddin Zakariya (1182-1262), who established a Suhrawardi hospice in Multan, laid emphasis on the outward form of religious observances. He disapproved any deviation from the prescribed injunction. He had acquired unmatched expertise in Quranic recitation. In his hospice, the slave girls chanted God's name while grinding corn. His insistence on the correctness of form brought him into confrontation with learned clerics and ordinary devotees.[15] His works, *Khulasat ul-Arifin* and *Al-Aurad*, enabled him to institutionalize the Suhrawardi order in south-west Panjab, besides striking a balance between Islamic Law and Islamic mysticism. In the first work, he treated human heart as the primary site for receiving divine illuminations through a regimen of prayers, spiritual exercises and pure intentions. In the second one, he designed the structure of remembrance of God (*zikr*), including prayers and Quranic recitations for different occasions.[16] Syed Jalaluddin Bukhari of Uch modified the ideological apparatus of the Suhrawardis. Returning from a seven years stay in the cities of West Asia, he established a seminary in his hospice, which attracted a large number of students, teachers and theologians. His curriculum was based on the twin foundations of knowledge (*ilm*) and actions (*amal*). He gave precedence to knowledge as it determined the legality of any action. At the outset, a novice studied Islamic jurisprudence (*fiqh*) according to one of the four schools, besides the Quran, Hadis and Arabic language. In the second stage, he was allowed to engage in action, comprising a variety of devotional exercises. As a result, the boundaries between Sufism and jurisprudence crumbled, while the respective roles of the Sufi and Alim intertwined.[17]

In the mystical discourse, divine love has been explained in terms of physical love. Baba Farid, employing sexual imagery, saw the seeker as wife and God as husband. If she failed to enjoy sexual union, she spent the night in loneliness. Her bodily organs, smouldering like a slow fire, twisted in shape and lost their fragrance. Pangs of separation drove her to insanity, though her passion was strong enough to overcome all obstacles. Fakhruddin Iraqi treated the seeker as a lover, whose heart reflected the Beloved's beauty. Even prophets and saints were not immune from love. The lover sacrificed his life for love like the legendary lovers of yore. In the game of love, the Beloved was a hunter, who shot a fatal arrow at the lover. The Beloved was a beautiful woman, whose sensuous parts forced the lover to lose his body, heart and soul. Love, as a quality of the Creator, underscored the unity of lover, love and beauty. Bu Ali Qalandar believed that the lover, viewing with the eyes of faith, saw God's beauty in all forms of creation. He must realize that God was also in love with him and, in fact, His passion was greater than his. Love raised the lover above binary distinctions and enabled him to unite with his Beloved. Shaikh Jamaluddin Hansavi, a distinguished disciple of Baba Farid, saw love as a fire that ignited with the fuel of passion and burnt in the breast of the lover. It epitomized three interrelated phenomena of affliction, hardship and exhaustion. An antithesis of reason, it pushed the lover into a sea of woes. His state was similar to that of Majnun, who was stricken with madness on separating from Laila. Left with no alternative, he resigned himself to the will of the Beloved. His patience was as effective as prayer.[18]

Baba Farid had a keen interest in musical sessions (*sama*) and mystical poetry. The Qawwals, aware of his passion, often visited his hospice to sing at gatherings. When a Qawwal was not available in Ajodhan, Baba Farid turned to passages on mystical love in prose and verse. In a letter from Qazi Hamiduddin Nagauri, a quatrain pointed to the inability of human faculties to appreciate the sovereign majesty of God and the incapacity of the eye to behold the beautiful face, even if it was unveiled. According to a sentence, 'This humble, weak and worthless beggar Muhammad Ata, who is the slave of dervishes from head to toe, is as lowly as the dust of their feet.' On hearing these words, Baba Farid was elevated to spiritual ecstasy and, thus, manifested his closeness to God. In his own verse, which was sent to Shaikh Badruddin Ghaznavi, he indicated a desire to spend his life in bestowing wonders, provided his heart was composed enough to praise the Lord. When Baba Farid was attracted to an impressive verse, it remained on his lips throughout the day, though he did not express the resulting turmoil in his interior. Sometimes, locked in the privacy of his cell, he recited Persian mystical verses on the loving devotion to God and the desire to live and die for Him. While humming such lines of poetry, he walked in the direction of the Kaaba and, jubilant in his ecstasy, turned back and bowed his head in the posture of surrender. However, he disapproved feverish jumps on such occasions, because bodily movements did not constitute dance. The Chishti indulgence in Sufi music roused the opposition from Muslim orthodoxy. A Qazi of Ajodhan, in his complaint to the theologians of Multan, alleged that Baba Farid attended musical performances in the mosque and even broke into dance. The theologians, learning that the man was Baba Farid, did not pursue the matter.[19]

Sufis were charismatic figures, who performed incredible deeds. The biographical accounts rarely failed to attribute miraculous powers to the Sufis. On the one hand, miracles lent legitimacy to Sufi lineages and, on the other hand, strengthened the faith of the followers in the spiritual exemplars.[20] Baba Farid enabled an oil seller to recover his wife, who had gone missing during a governor's raid on a village. He recovered a falcon for a huntsman and induced his Turkish master to give up cruelty. Acting at the instance of his sons, Baba Farid caused the death of an oppressive revenue officer. He cured a man of a serious ailment, so that his brother could continue his spiritual pursuit. He persuaded the rich grandson of Zafar Khan to maintain the family of a poor man with five daughters.[21] Shaikh Sadruddin Arif, who headed the Suhrawardi establishment of Multan from 1262 to 1285, functioned as a Sufi through his miracles. He weaned Ahmad Maashuq (the son of a merchant of Qandhar) from alcoholism through a sherbet and enabled him to evolve as a mystic. He made his 7 years old son Rukhnuddin Abul Fateh give up his infatuation for a deer and memorize half a section of the Quran every day. Through punishment, he forced a follower Shaikh Budh to abandon the task of land measurement and, instead, dedicate himself to spirituality. He blessed Maulana Qutbuddin Behram with a son Fatehullah. Shaikh Arif, after his death, appeared to Fatehullah in a dream and guided his Quranic memorization.[22] In Kaliyar Sharif, Shaikh Alauddin Ali Ahmad Sabir caused earthquake, fire and plague in order to teach a lesson to his detractors. Shamsuddin Turk Panipati provided an unending length of rope to the Delhi army besieging Chittor. Jalaluddin Panipati, in order to enable the peasants to pay their land tax, converted their iron tools into gold. Bu Ali Qalandar caused the Yamuna to recede 7 miles, as the fish had injured his legs during a penance.[23]

The Sufis, in their attitude to the state, varied from scrupulous distance to intimate coordination. The early Chishtis kept aloof from contemporary politics. Baba Farid, speaking prophetically, advised Sidi Maula to refrain from associating with rulers and nobles, as such a practice spelt doom for a dervish. He did not bless Ghiasuddin Balban's bid for the throne. In his eyes, the state did not have the power to help the needy. He regretted that Sher Khan, the governor of Multan, did not seek his help in warding off Mongol attacks and, thus, did not recognize his sanctity.[24] His lineal descendants, as we will see, reversed the principle. In contrast, the Chishtis of Hansi rejected the Tughluq overtures for political assimilation. In Multan and Uch, the Suhrawardis aligned themselves with the Delhi Sultanate from an early stage. Shaikh Bahauddin Zakariya supported Shamsuddin Iltutmish in a tussle against Nasiruddin Qubacha. He employed his spiritual power (1224) to defend Multan during a siege under Dorbei Doqshin. As an emissary of the governor of Multan, he negotiated (1246) the withdrawal of Mongols in return for a ransom.[25] His grandson Shaikh Ruknuddin Abul Fateh paid five visits to Delhi during the Khalji rule. He received seven lakh *tankahs* from Alauddin Khalji and distributed this sum among the needy. He presented the petitions of people to Sultan Qutbuddin Mubarak Shah Khalji and secured royal orders on each. He assisted Muhammad bin Tughluq in quelling the revolt of Behram Aiba Kishlu Khan. He interceded with the Sultan to save the inhabitants of Multan from a massacre. The Shaikh and his nephew received a grant of 100 villages for personal expenditure and maintenance of the hospice of Shaikh Zakariya.[26] Syed Jalaluddin Bukhari of Uch paid frequent visits to the court of Firoz Shah Tughluq. He secured the Sultan's approval on the petitions of the people. He also mediated between the Delhi Sultanate and the chiefs of Sind.

So long as Baba Farid was alive, the hospice at Pakpattan concentrated on performing austerities, training disciples, hosting visitors and distributing amulets. With the burial of Baba Farid inside the hospice, the complex began to evolve as a shrine (*dargah*). According to popular belief, the spiritual charisma (*baraka*) of the late saint survived in his tomb as well as those of his descendants. The celebration of his death anniversary (*urs*) institutionalized a number of rituals – tying of turban on the spiritual head (*dastarbandi*), musical sessions (*qawwali*), common kitchen (*langar*) and passing through the southern gate (*bahishti darwaza*) – that coalesced into what Eaton designated as 'theatre Islam'. The growing popularity of Baba Farid's cult, which emanated from the shrine, attracted state patronage. As seen above, Ghazi Malik, the long serving Khalji governor of Dipalpur, sought the blessings of Shaikh Alauddin (the grandson of Baba Farid), who foretold the enthronement of three Tughluq rulers. Muhammd bin Tughluq (r. 1325-51) bestowed the town of Ajodhan on the shrine. As a result, Shaikh Alauddin, who managed the land grant and came to be known as the Diwan, settled the pastoral Jat clans as sedentary cultivators and collected state share of crops on which the tax was levied in kind. The clans, participating in the rituals of the shrine and gaining access to theatre-oriented Islam, slowly converted to the new creed. The evolving political and religious bond was strengthened with a series of marriages between the males of Diwan's family with daughters of the clan notables. In this manner, the Chishti shrine of Pakpattan played the historical function of incorporating the local system of culture into a larger cultural system, having connected the rustic clans politically with the Delhi Sultanate and religiously with Islam.[27]

Political Turmoil and New Rulers

After the departure of Timur, the history of Panjab revolved around the rise of Khizr Khan. A tussle erupted between Khizr Khan and Mallu Iqbal Khan, with Panjab as the bone of contention. Mallu displaced Bahram Khan Turkbacha, the governor of Samana, who was a partisan of Khizr Khan. Mallu, having killed Bahram, imprisoned local chiefs such as Rai Daud, Rai Kamaluddin Muin and Rai Hinu, the son of Rai Juljain Bhatti. Khizr Khan, in a battle near Ajodhan (12 November 1405), defeated and killed Mallu. Daulat Khan, acting on behalf of Sultan Mahmud, displaced Bairam Khan Turkbacha, who had replaced the late Bahram. Khizr Khan, arriving in support of his ally, forced Daulat Khan to retreat to the Ganga-Yamuna Doab. In a significant move, Khizr Khan distributed *iqtas* among his partisans, giving Sirhind and neighbouring *parganas* to Bairam Khan Turkbacha, Samana and Sunam to Zirak Khan and Hissar Firoza to Qiwam Khan. He besieged the Sultan in Siri and Ikhtiaruddin in Firozabad. He occupied Rohtak, ravaged Mewat and occupied places in the Ganga-Yamuna Doab and environs of Delhi. Following the death (1412) of the Sultan, he consolidated his authority over his territories. He snatched the fort of Siri from the new ruler Daulat Khan after a siege of four months. On 6 June 1414, he occupied Delhi and inaugurated the Syed dynasty.[28]

Khizr Khan took steps to establish order in different parts of Panjab. He appointed Malik Abdul Rahim as the governor of Multan and Fatehpur. He placed under Prince Mubarak the districts of Firozpur, Sirhind and the *iqtas* of the late Bairam Khan Turkbacha. The kinsmen of Bairam, treating Sirhind as a patrimonial fief, killed Sadhu Nadira (the Prince's deputy) and took possession of Sirhind. They besieged Kamal Badhan, who succeeded Sadhu Nadira at Sirhind. Zirak Khan, the governor of Samana, forced the Turkbachas to withdraw into the hills and induced Tughan Rais Turkbacha to submit. An adventurer, posing as Sarang Khan, revolted in Bajwara and spread his tentacles to Ropar and Chhat. The combined forces of Zirak Khan, Tughan Rais Turkbacha and Sultan Shah Lodi pushed Sarang Khan into the hills. Tughan, as governor of Jalandhar, laid a trap (1420) for Sarang Khan and killed him. Tughan himself rose in revolt and, besieging Sirhind, ravaged the area between Mansurpur and Pail. Suffering a sharp reverse at the hands of Zirak Khan near Ludhiana, he fled to the territories of Jasrath Khokhar.[29]

Jasrath Khokhar, the son of Shaikha Khokhar, played a prominent role in Panjab for two decades (1421-42). Many times, he descended from his mountainous stronghold beyond Sialkot and plundered the plains of Panjab. Long back, he confronted Timur between Tulamba and Dipalpur, besides assisting his father in occupying Lahore. He was carried to Samarqand as a prisoner, while his father was put to death. Following a miraculous escape, he revived the Khokhar power by assisting the rebellion of Tughan Rais Turkbacha and intervening in the succession dispute of Kashmir. After the death (20 May 1421) of Khizr Khan, he plundered the territory of Rai Kamaluddin Muin near Ludhiana and pillaged the tract along the Satluj up to Ropar. He besieged Zirak Khan in Jalandhar and Sultan Shah Lodi in Sirhind. Sultan Mubarak Shah marched beyond the Satluj and faced Jasrath Khokhar for 40 days. The leading governors (Zirak Khan, Sikandar Tohfa, Mahmud Hasan, Malik Kalu and others) converged on the scene. Jasrath, while retreating across the major rivers, lost his men and material. The Sultan rushed in hot pursuit, while Rai Bhim of Jammu demolished the Khokhar fort of Tilhar. The Sultan, camping on the Ravi for a month (Decembrer 1421), took comprehensive measures to rehabilitate Lahore and appointed Mahmud Hasan as its governor.[30]

Within three months, Jasrath returned to Lahore and carried out attacks for five weeks. Shifting east to Kalanaur, he clashed with Rai Bhim. The provincial governors and local elements (Malik Rajab of Dipalpur, Sultan Shah Lodi of Sirhind, Rai Kamaluddin Muin of Ludhiana and Rai Bhim of Jammu) joined Sikandar Tohfa, forcing Jasrath to retreat. The Sultan, dissatisfied with the conduct of officers, transferred Sikandar Tohfa to Lahore and Mahmud Hasan to Jalandhar. Jasrath, keen to undo his recent setback, attacked Jammu and killed Rai Bhim. Joining hands with Shaikh Ali of Kabul, he ravaged Lahore and Dipalpur. Sikandar Tohfa advanced up to the Chenab without making any gain. Mahmud Hasan, holding the districts of Multan, Bhakkar and Siwistan, renovated the fort of Multan and forced Shaikh Ali to retreat to Kabul. After a gap of five years (1423-8), Jasrath bypassed Lahore and besieged Kalanaur. Defeating Sikandar Tohfa in a battle, he crossed the Beas and raided Jalandhar. The Sultan deputed Zirak Khan and Islam Khan, the governors of Samana and Sirhind respectively, to meet the challenge. Sikandar, joining his forces with Rai Ghalib Kalanauri, defeated

Jasrath near Kangra on the Beas. Jasrath left his spoils at Jalandhar and fell back on Tilhar. Mahmud Hasan was assigned Hissar Firoza in addition to Multan.[31]

During a span of four years (1430-3), diverse elements – a disaffected officer, a local chief and a foreign invader, viz. Faulad Turkbacha, Jasrath Khokhar and Shaikh Ali – became active and collaborated with one another. Trouble started with the death (1430) of Syed Salim, the governor of Bathinda. Faulad Turkbacha, a slave of the deceased, revolted at the instigation of his master's sons. Having defeated Yusuf Sarwar and Rai Hinu Bhatti, he established himself in the fort and prepared for a long siege. As the Sultan marched out from Delhi, the Panjab officers (Zirak Khan, Islam Khan, Kamal Khan and Malik Kalu) besieged the fort. Following the failure of negotiations with Mahmud Hasan, Faulad continued resistance for six months and invited Shaikh Ali from Kabul, promising a payment of 2 lakh *tankahs*. Shaikh Ali, having failed to profit from his incursion eight years earlier, arrived at the Jhelum to join with Khokhar notables (probably related to Jasrath) like Ainuddin, Abul Khair and Khajeka. He passed through Qasur and ravaged the territory of Rai Firoz Muin, forcing him to leave the siege of Bathinda followed by other nobles. A triumphant Faulad met Shaikh Ali and paid the promised amount. Still dissatisfied, Shaikh Ali abducted Faulad's family and plundered a vast area from Ludhiana and Jalandhar to Multan and Jhelum. He also succeeded in killing Sultan Shah Lodi, an uncle of Bahlol Lodi. Twice he penetrated (6-8 June 1431) the fortifications of Multan. With the arrival of Panjab officers such as Zirak Khan, Islam Khan, Kamal Khan, Yusuf Sarwar and Rai Juljain Bhatti, he met a disaster (7 July 1431), while retreating across the Jhelum.[32]

Jasrath, lying low for four years (1428-31), took advantage of Faulad's revolt and Shaikh Ali's invasion. Laying siege to Lahore, he captured Sikandar Tohfa and his followers. Shaikh Ali, returning to Panjab, targeted Tulamba (23 November 1431) and captured Muslim theologians, women and children. Faulad came out of Bathinda and killed Rai Firoz Muin, gathering numerous horses and goods. When the Sultan approached Samana, Jasrath raised the siege of Lahore and carried Sikandar Tohfa as a captive. Shaikh Ali lost interest in Multan and fell back on Bartot. Yusuf Sarwar besieged the fort of Bathinda, while the Panjab officers (Zirak Khan, Islam Khan Lodi and Kahun Raj) joined the Sultan at Panipat. In 1433, Shaikh Ali intended to attack the besiegers at Bathinda to relieve pressure on Faulad. Mahmud Hasan, marching to Bathinda, forestalled the move. Shaikh Ali overran the country from Seor to the Beas, attacked Dipalpur and occupied the fort of Lahore. Yusuf Sarwar failed to defend these places, while Mahmud Hasan's reinforcements forced Shaikh Ali to retreat. In January 1433, Sultan Mubarak Shah reached Samana and took the affairs of Panjab in his hands. Mahmud Hasan and Islam Khan Lodi joined the Sultan, while other nobles continued the siege of Bathinda. Sikandar Tohfa, holding the charge of Dipalpur and Jalandhar, went in pursuit of Shaikh Ali. The arrival of the Sultan at Tulamba forced Shaikh Ali to flee from his base in Seor. Amir Muzaffar, the representative of Shaikh Ali, paid a tribute to the Sultan and gave his daughter in marriage to him. The Sultan placed Jalandhar and Lahore, fiefs of Sikandar Tohfa, under Mahmud Hasan. The royalists, after a siege of four years, occupied the fort of Bathinda and killed Faulad. Delhi Sultanate, facing the opposition of Jasrath and Bahlol Lodi, tried to play them against each other. The two warlords, reaching an understanding, promised to refrain from interfering in each other's territories.[33] The Khokhar neutrality partly contributed to the rise of the Lodis to sovereign power.

The empowerment of the Lodi Afghans becomes understandable in the context of a distinct social structure and migration of Afghan tribes. The Afghans were a pastoral nomadic society, wherein kinship was the organizing principle of the tribes. Owing to increase of population and pressure of Ghilzais, the Lodi Afghans were driven out of Roh. Averse to agriculture and commerce, the Afghans combined pastoral nomadism with horse trade.[34] Malik Bahram, an Afghan merchant, took up a job under Malik Mardan Daulat, who was the governor of Multan during the end of Firoz Shah Tughluq's reign. His son Sultan Shah served under Khizr Khan, the next governor of Multan. Following his exemplary bravery in a military encounter with Mallu Iqbal Khan, he received the governorship of Sirhind along with the title of Islam Khan. In due course, Islam Khan raised a contingent of 12,000 Afghans, most of whom were his clansmen.

Though he had a number of sons, he chose his nephew Bahlol Lodi as his successor through a will. Bahlol imported horses from north-western lands and sold them to buyers in India, including the Sultan of Delhi. Once Sultan Muhammad Shah (r. 1434-43) paid Bahlol through a payment order drawn on a subdistrict (*parganah*) in Lahore. Bahlol employed force to collect the amount from a rebellious peasantry. Under the patronage of the Sultan, he came out of the class of merchants and entered that of nobles. Every year, he mobilized a growing body of troops for the Sultan in lieu of revenue assignments near Lahore. He increased his power through uniting the Afghan factions and looting merchant caravans. He assisted the Sultan in his tussle against the *wazir* and provided 20,000 troops against the Khalji ruler of Malwa. He received Sirhind in fief along with the title of Khan-i Khanan, enabling him to aspire for sovereignty. By 1443, he practically controlled the vast area from Lahore to Hissar Firoza.[35] Acting with patience and tact,[36] he displaced Hamid Khan, the *wazir*, and inaugurated the first Afghan State on 19 April 1451.

In the second half of the fifteenth century, two Suhrawardi saints, Haidar Shaikh (1434-1508) and Shaikh Yusuf Qureshi, became the rulers of Malerkotla and Multan respectively. Haidar Shaikh, trained under a descendant of Ruknuddin Abul Fateh in Multan, shifted to Malerkotla on the banks of Bhumsi. His blessings enabled Bahlol Lodi, the governor of Sirhind, to wrest the sovereign power in Delhi. As Bahlol ascended the throne, he married his daughter Taj Murassa Begum to the Shaikh and gave 69 villages in dowry.[37] The Shaikh, being an eminent Sufi and son-in-law of the Sultan, transformed the land grant into a *zamindari.* He formed matrimonial alliances with landed magnates. He married the daughter of Rai Bahram Bhatti, a *zamindar* of Kapurthala. He married his daughter Bibi Mangi in the family of a *zamindar* of Tohana. On his death in 1508, his dual role as a Sufi and *zamindar* was bifurcated among the offspring of his two wives. Shaikh Hasan, born of Taj Murassa Begum, became the spiritual head of the Sufi establishment. Shaikh Isa, born of the daughter of Rai Bahram Bhatti, inherited the landed estate. Shaikh Hasan's suit against the arrangement was rejected in the office of the governor of Sirhind. His sons, in frustration, killed the governor. The Delhi Sultanate, confiscated the estate, which was restored only in 1543. The descendants of Shaikh Isa, remaining neutral in the Mughal-Afghan conflict, formed alliances with the Rajput *zamindars* of central Panjab and took their daughters as wives. As loyal *zamindars* of the Mughal State, they maintained an armed retinue and collected land tax on behalf of the administrator (*faujdar*) of Sirhind.

Up to the middle of the fifteenth century, the Delhi Sultanate tried to maintain its control over Multan and, for this purpose, turned its military resources against Jasrath Khokhar and Shaikh Ali. This situation changed under the last Syed ruler Alauddin Shah (r. 1443-76). Owing to the pressure of the neighbouring kingdoms and internal challenges, the Delhi Sultanate was unable to appoint a governor in Multan. In this political vacuum, the inhabitants of the city and local *zamindars* persuaded Shaikh Yusuf Qureshi, a spiritual descendant of Shaikh Bahauddin Zakariya, to assume the reins of administration. The new ruler, by winning over local chiefs and recruiting fresh troops, gained strength and legitimacy. Rai Sehra, the Langah chief of Sewi, swore allegiance to Qureshi and gave his daughter in marriage to him. He attained access to the palace under the pretext of getting his retinue inspected and, employing a clever trick, ended Qureshi's reign of two years. Graduating from a tribal chief to a sovereign ruler, he adopted the Islamic name of Sultan Qutbuddin. He prevented the Suhrawardi establishment from playing any role in the Langah polity. Qureshi shifted to Delhi, where Bahlol Lodi received him with honour and gave his daughter in marriage to his son Shaikh Abdullah. The Sultan could not reinstate Qureshi in Multan, as his military expedition under Barbak Shah (Sikandar Lodi) and Tatar Khan Lodi was defeated at the hands of the Langah ruler Sultan Husain outside the Multan fort.[38]

Sultan Husain consolidated his power by forging alliances with local chiefs and Sufis. To the Baloch chief Malik Sohrab Dudai, he assigned the area from Sitpur to Dhankot. He received the allegiance of the Thattawa chiefs and, thus, gave Shor to Jam Bayazid and Uch to Jam Ibrahim. In order to erase the claims of Qureshi, the Langahs declared that the current descendants of Shaikh Zakariya were superior to Qureshi, while the Bukharis of Uch and Multan were nobler than Haji Abdul Wahab. However, a conflict erupted between Mahmud Khan (Sultan Husain's grandson) and his *wazir* Jam

Bayazid. Sikandar Lodi (r. 1489-1517), hoping to recover Multan, deputed Daulat Khan Lodi, the governor of Panjab, to resolve the issue. This officer, through mediation, notified Ravi as the boundary between the warring factions. The two regimes, in order to widen their support base, turned to the local chiefs. Mahmud Khan won over Malik Sohrab Dudai, while Jam Bayazid acquired the allegiance of Chakar Khan Rind. Jam Bayazid invited scholars and Sufis of Multan to settle in his capital Shorkot.[39] The local chiefs belonging to different tribes (Langah, Thattawa and Baloch) began to dominate the political stage in south-western Panjab independent of Delhi.

Babur planted the seeds of the Mughal State in north-western Panjab. Three tribes (Jud, Janjuhas and Gakkhars) inhabited the Sind Sagar Doab. The tribal chiefs, maintaining armed retinues, received a nominal levy based on the number of oxen and households. At times, there were violent conflicts among tribes and sometimes between two branches of the same tribe. When Babur entered (1519) the area, he expected the chiefs to pay homage and a symbolic gift. However, he did not ignore the complaints against Hati Gakkhar who, besides carrying depredations, had killed his brother Tatar Gakkhar and the Janjuha chief Malik Hast. Babur occupied the forts of Pharhala and Andraba. Since Hati remained elusive, Babur made peace with him through diplomatic exchanges. Babur treated the riverine tract on the Jhelum and Chenab in a different way. He traced his claim to Timur's successors, who had been in possession of Bhera, Khushab, Chenab and Chiniot. Dealing with village headmen (*chaudharis*), he imposed a ransom of 40 lakh *shahrukhis* and deputed his men to collect the amount.[40] Next year, he occupied Bhera and Sialkot, besides ravaging Syedpur (Aminabad). In his administrative arrangements, Babur maintained a balance between his own officers and his Afghan allies. Daulat Khan Lodi, dissatisfied with Jalandhar and Sultanpur, undid the arrangement. Babur, firming his control over Lahore and Sialkot, punished Daulat Khan Lodi. He marched across the Duns of Siwaliks and occupied a number of forts. With a victory (20 April 1526) over Ibrahim Lodi at Panipat, his sway was established over entire Panjab from the Indus to Yamuna.[41] In 1529, the Mandahars of Kaithal refused to accept the Mughal authority. The punitive action resulted in a massacre of thousands of Mandahars and the devastation of the area.[42] Ahmad Yadgar's chilling detail was similar to Guru Nanak's account of the Mughal atrocities on the people of Syedpur.

Guru Nanak, in his observations on the contemporary situation, condemned the Lodi government and Babur's atrocities. The times were dark. Truth had vanished and falsehood reigned supreme. Since Islam was ascendant, the Shaikhs became assertive and a new tax was levied on temples. Qazis and Brahmins ceased to perform their functions, leaving the Satan to hold wedding rites. The kings were cruel like butchers and ferocious like lions. The village headmen (*muqaddams*) were akin to hungry dogs. Owing to their oppression, they disturbed the sleep of the masses. The state functionaries inflicted wounds with their nails and licked up the oozing blood. If their conduct was judged in a higher court, their noses would be chopped off. Babur, having conquered Khurasan, terrorized Hindustan. Leading a marriage party of sin, he rushed from Kabul and forcibly demanded the tribute. In the battlefields, the Mughals fired guns, while the Pathans attacked with elephants. Millions of religious preceptors failed to employ their miraculous powers to stop Babur's advance. The Lodi rulers, losing their wits in revelries, could not eat or pray. As princes were cut to pieces, tall edifices were burnt. All signs of wealth (sports, stables, horses, chariots, drums, bugles, red uniforms and sword belts) were destroyed. In an unequal fight, a lion fell upon a defenceless herd of cattle. Dogs spoiled a priceless country. Women of diverse ethnicities (Hindus, Turks, Bhattis and Thakurs) lost their husbands. Since their marriage, they had lived in luxury. Their dwellings turned into cremation grounds. Their heads were shaved and dust was poured down their throats. Ropes were put around their necks, breaking their pearl necklaces. The Mughals, complying with royal orders, dishonoued them and carried them away.[43]

Mirza Kamran, a son of Babur and brother of Humayun, ruled over Panjab and Afghanistan for ten years (1530-40). The relentless Afghan advancement towards Lahore forced him to retreat from Panjab and settle in Kabul. Subsequently, the Afghan State faced tough resistance from the tribes of Panjab. Sher Shah (r. 1540-5), at the beginning of his reign, erased the Mughal stamp from this area. He gained the submission of prominent Baloch chiefs (Ismail

Khan, Ghazi Khan and Fateh Khan Dudai) who agreed to furnish an unspecified number of horses. The Gakkhars, owing to their long association with the Mughals, refused to submit. An Afghan army ravaged the Gakkhar country and killed the chief Sarang Khan Gakkhar. Following a limited success, the Afghan State tried to subjugate the chiefs of Multan. The Afghans, with some support from Chakar Khan Rind and Bakhshu Langah, launched a military operation against Mindu Baloch and Fateh Khan Jat, both of whom were captured and executed. The people were assured that land tax would be collected in accordance with the Langah practice.[44] In north-western Panjab, the joint Ghakkar-Niazi revolt attracted a ruthless punitive operation (1547-9) during the reign of Islam Shah. In spite of apparent military success and construction of massive forts in Rohtas and Mankot, the Afghan State displayed a pathetic lack of political acumen in dealing with the tribes of Panjab.

Strands of Spirituality

The Jogis represented an ancient spiritual tradition. Following the path of Patanjali, they placed eternal existence in the domain of annihilation. They aimed at uniting with the Absolute through control over psychological and mental processes. Gorakhnath was their principal leader, while Machhandarnath and Chauranginath were senior spiritual masters. Baba Haji Rattan, an incarnation of Gorakhnath, taught Jog to Prophet Muhammad. Some Jogis followed the tenets of Hinduism, while others observed Muslim practices. Mastery in Jog depended on eight principles of non-violence, truthfulness, celibacy, prayer, contentment, cleanliness and suppression of five senses. Of several veins emanating from seven levels of human body, three – right (*ida*), middle (*pingla*) and left (*susumna*) – were associated with sun, earth and moon. The biggest vein, running along the spine, split into two, one penetrating the right nostril and the other passing through the left. The Jogis held regulation of breath (*pranayam*) as the most exalted of all prayers. Gazing between eyebrows, a Jogi pulled in breath through the left nostril and released it through the right, uttering 'hin' and 'sa' without moving the tongue.[45]

During the medieval period, monasteries of the Jogis were found in Gorakhatari, Tilla Balnath and Jakhbar Jogian. At Gorakhatari (near Peshawar), a long cave led to an underground chamber which, owing to its narrowness, forced the visitors to crawl in. A group of Jogis, sitting in the midst of candles and incense, observed breath control. The place was maintained with land grants from the rulers and Hindus of the area. Tilla Balnath was perched on an isolated peak in the Salt Range. Apart from stores, residences and *samadhis*, there were temples dedicated to Shiva, Bhairava, Lakshman and Hanuman. In 1581, a community of 300 Jogis lived here. The novices, during a two-year apprenticeship, shared physical tasks. A distinction was made between senior and junior members. At sunrise and sunset, prayers were held with concerted sound of flutes and conches. An establishment of the Jogis flourished at Jakhbar Jogian, an obscure village in the upper Bari Doab. The complex embraced *samadhis* of former *mahants*, besides accommodation for the chief abbot, Jogis and pilgrims. While temples were dedicated to various Hindu deities, a small shrine enclosed a smouldering fire. The Mughal patronage was recorded in 18 documents pertaining to land grants.[46]

Abdul Quddus Gangohi (1456-1537), the most prominent Sabiri Chishti saint lived in Shahabad near Ambala. His mystical practices revolved around breath control (*pas-i anfas*) and prime recitation (*sultan ul-azkar*). He was intimately familiar with *Amritkunda*, which laid down techniques of breath control and purification of human body, with reference to body postures and *chakra* meditations. With a specific manner of breathing, a part of the vital spirit residing in the body was united with that pervading all nature. In his tract titled *Rushdnama*, Gangohi demonstrated the similarity between the terminologies of Jog and Sufism. The Jogic equivalent of the inverted prayer (*salat-i makus*) of the Sufis was a regressive exercise (*ulti sadhna*) involving a reversal of bodily functions. The Jogic state of equilibrium (*sahaj*), leading to ontological immortality, was similar to the Sufi ideal of subsistence in God (*baqa*). Gorakhnath's concept of absolute truth (*parbrahma*) was parallel to Ibn Arabi's Unity of Being (*wahdat ul-wujud*). Regarding breath control, Gangohi proposed the transformation of three different breaths moving upwards, downwards and emerging through the whole body. A practitioner was required to transform these three breaths into a single one, which subsequently turned back. The three corners (*trikuti*) stood for the junction of three cords (*ida*, *pingla* and *susumna*) that served as conduits for the three breaths. Sometimes, Gangohi conceived the junction as a penultimate circle above the eyebrows and, other times, situated it in the navel. Designated as the fundamental base (*muladhar*), it meant the crown of the head, which was the abode of brain and receptacle of seminal fluid. Owing to collection and heat of the breath, the seminal fluid turned into clear water and suffused through the whole body. As the body of the seeker became subtle, he received the illumination of divine mysteries and experienced the state of annihilation.[47]

The Qadiri order, starting from Uch, established its branches in Shergarh and Lahore. Muhammad al-Husaini (d. 1488) and his son Abdul Qadir Sani (d. 1533) developed the lineage from Uch. Besides obligatory prayers, they laid stress on contemplation (*muraqba*) in the interlude between two prayers. Shaikh Daud (d. 1574), who managed an extensive hospice at Shergarh near Dipalpur, laid emphasis on the recitation of creedal statement (*kalima*) and salutations in praise of Prophet Muhammad. In nightlong vigils, the Shaikh led loud chants on these sacred words. He gave lessons from Attar's *Mantiq ul-Tair* and Jami's *Lawaih*. On every Thursday and annual feast of Shaikh Jilani, the Shaikh distributed the entire stock of offerings. He commanded the devotion of Jat highwaymen, who operated between Shergarh and Lahore.[48] Miyan Mir (1531-1635), based in Lahore, mastered Ibn Arabi's *Futuhat-i Makkiyya* (Meccan Revelations) and *Fasus al-Hikam* (Bezels of Wisdom). He excelled in training disciples. On every day, he and a few companions searched out a secluded site in the city. Sitting separately under trees, they engaged in contemplation. They congregated at one place for obligatory prayers. He held that the three stages of spiritual endeavour – canonical law (*shariat*), mystical path (*tariqat*) and ultimate reality (*haqiqat*) – required the purification of the body (*nafs*), heart (*qalb*) and soul (*ruh*). In his view, divine union was attained through passion (*jazba*) by virtue of which God pulled the novice into His being.

Alternatively, he followed the path of mysticism (*suluk*) involving discipline and self-mortification (*riyazat wa mujahida*) under the tutelage of a mentor.[49]

Breath control (*pas-i anfas*) and prime recitation (*sultan ul-azkar*), as Gangohi had developed,[50] were assimilated in the Qadiri discipline. Miyan Mir, while teaching select disciples, associated these practices with four planes of existence – phenomenal world (*alam-i nasut*), imaginative world (*alam-i misal*), spiritual world (*alam-i malkut*) and realm of divine might (*alam-i jabrut*). His instructions for breath control noted the respective positions of body parts such as knees, hands, eyes, nostrils and fingers. The inhalation and exhalation through the left and right nostrils, while uttering the first part (*la ilaha illa allah*) of the creedal statement (*kalima*), required an incremental increase in the suspension of breath. In order to remove distracting thoughts, the seeker concentrated on the spherical heart (*dil-i mudawwari*) instead of the physical heart (*dil-i sanobari*). When he climbed to the final stage of his journey to the divine realm (*alam-i lahut*), he witnessed divine unity (*tauhid*) and unlimited realization of truth (*tahqiq*). As for prime recitation (*sultan ul-azkar*), it had come down from Prophet Muhammad and Abdul Qadir Jilani to Miyan Mir, who further handed it to a few disciples. It involved listening to a perpetual sound, which had been existing before creation without interruption. Prophet Muhammad, while contemplating at the cave of Hira, absorbed this practice and, seeing Jibrail, received the revelation (*wahi*) of the Quran. To him, the sound appeared like a boiling cauldron, buzzing of bees, clanging of bells and speech of angels. The saints, listening to this sound, attained immense power of will and spiritual delight. A practitioner, sitting in seclusion, directed attention to his ears and heard the sound in its increasing volume. Becoming subtle in his being, he plunged into the ocean of subtlety and absolute being.[51]

While the Sufis instituted breath control and prime recitation, the central districts of Panjab witnessed the emergence of Sikhism. In this context, a number of places – Kartarpur, Khadur, Goindval, Ramdaspur, Tarn Taran and Sri Hargobindpur – assumed importance. The Sikh Gurus belonged to non-elite Khatri families that were rooted in the rural areas. Guru Nanak (1469-1539), an argumentative teacher and gifted poet, earned unprecedented fame for his long travels to Assam, Lanka, Sumeru and Madina, besides his exemplary life at Kartarpur. The Sikh Gurus exercised the authority of nominating a successor and, thus, imparted continuity to a new belief system and social order. Interacting directly with their followers in congregational enclaves (*dharamsal*), they communicated their teachings in the form of verses that were sung in musical modes. The need to collect this authentic poetry necessitated the development of a new script, Gurmukhi. As the number of Sikhs grew, the Gurus deputed their representatives to spread their message and collect offerings. The Sikh scripture, as Guru Arjan compiled with a massive intellectual effort, contained the verses of first five Gurus, Baba Farid and Bhakti saints. This holy book was installed in Harmandir Sahib, which was constructed in the middle of a tank in Ramdaspur (Amritsar).

The Sikh Gurus rejected caste, race and lineage. In the True Court, people were judged on the basis of their actions, not their birth. All castes originated from the same seed, while all humans were crafted of the same clay. According to Guru Arjan, the Lord treated all humans as His children and preserved their honour without any discrimination. He declared that the saints belonging to depressed castes (Namdev, Kabir and Ravidas) had attained salvation through their pious devotion to God.[52] The Sikh scripture has given ample space to the anti-caste discourse, which pervaded the contribution of these saints. Sant Namdev exposed the Brahmins for ousting him from a temple and forcing him to pray behind the sacred structure. Visualizing God as an artisan, he treated the tools of his craft as vehicles for the dissemination of his teachings. Sant Kabir criticized the Brahmins for their dubious intellect, empty rituals and greed for wealth. For him, all humans emerged from the same divine light and were composed of the same material. He grafted his spiritual ideas on the craft of weaving, so that even the toilers understood them with ease. Sant Ravidas, hailing from the caste of tanners (Chamars), offered the vision of a alternative social structure obtaining in Begumpura. Populated and prosperous, it would be free from taxes, fear and restrictions. The Sikh principle of social equality acquired a practical shape in the pious congregations (*sadhsangat*). In these sacred spaces, the four castes merged into one. Among the Sikhs, a Brahmin could become the disciple of a Khatri. At the same time, the Khatris were made subordinate to the Jats, who formed the lowest rung of the Vaishyas. The Sikh warrior bands, while fighting against the Mughal State, comprised Jats, carpenters, shoemakers, barbers, washermen, confectioners and petty traders.[53]

The Sikh practice of social equality extended to women. Guru Nanak advocated unconditional acceptance of female biological processes, particularly menstruation. In procreation, a mother preceded the father. Through their union, the feotus was lodged in her womb. A child, endowed with little understanding, was attracted to its mother's breast and quaffed the milk. A man found the wife indispensable and, when she died, acquired another one. Since the kings were born from her, she could not be called inferior.[54] Throughout this reference, Guru Nanak referred to the woman as a vessel (*bhandu*), as he saw her as a cornucopia from which the entire creation poured forth. In the Sikh scripture, the validation of woman was advanced through the imagery of conception, gestation, giving birth and lactation.[55] Guru Nanak, in his composition entitled *Bara Mah*, came out in support of female sexuality. During a year, the changing seasons had a direct impact on a bride. She could not live without her spouse even for a moment. She kept on looking at His path. When she dissolved in Him, she became a chaste wife (*suhagan*). With her body and soul, she recited His name and sang His praise. When she took shelter at His feet, her body became pure and she obtained genuine peace. Since her Husband was away, she suffered the pangs of separation and her body was wasted. She only felt His presence in her interior. The spouse, returning from His sojourn, enjoyed her and imparted splendour to her bed. As she became jubilant, her life was placed on an even keel.[56] For Guru Nanak, a bride's sexual urge was not only conformed to nature, it was imbued with spirituality. The Guru, it is tempting to suggest, might have been familiar with the lives of Hir-Ranjha. Deeply involved in the problems of the contemporary society, he did not hesitate to side with the sufferers.

Akbar and His Opponents

Humayun, on his return from exile in 1555, defeated the Afghans at Dipalpur, Machhiwara and Sirhind. He appointed Mughal officers in the occupied areas. In spite of this success, the control of the Mughal State over Panjab was fragile and uncertain. Shah Abul Maali, the governor of the province, was guilty of mismanagement and disloyalty. The Afghan power was still substantive owing to the presence of Sikandar Sur in the northern hills and Hemu beyond the Yamuna. The Mughals, even after occupying the fort of Mankot, faced stiff opposition from the hill chiefs. On many occasions, they formed large confederacies to resist the Mughal expansion. Mirza Hakim, the autonomous ruler of Kabul, aimed at annexing Panjab to his dominion and repeatedly attracted the attention of the provincial administration. When the Mughal State introduced a series of reforms in the land revenue system, it met strong resistance from the Bhatti *zamindars* of Sandal Bar. Akbar (r. 1556-1605), undertaking intense military activity and deft administrative measures, attained a limited measure of consolidation for his kingdom. For over thirteen years (1585-98), he treated Lahore as the imperial capital and settled the larger north-western region. It was not surprising that Akbar should make a frequent appearance in Damodar's narrative.

Soon after the restoration of the Mughal rule, the new regime confronted a major challenge from the Afghans and local chiefs. The Mughals demonstrated their military power in the hills and secured the allegiance of several *zamindars*, including Raja Dharam Chand of Kangra. Akbar, defeating Hemu at Panipat (5 November 1556), recovered Delhi and Agra. Sikandar, with the support of some *zamindars* of Panjab, ravaged the plains and took shelter in the fort of Mankot. Akbar occupied the fort after a siege of six months and made a decisive intervention in the Gakkhar affairs.[57] Sultan Adam Gakkhar, aligning with Humayun, had overpowered the Janjuhas and brought the entire Gakkhar country under his sway. Akbar, in order to cut him to size, favoured his nephew Kamal Khan Gakkhar. He bifurcated the Gakkhar domain between Adam and Kamal. Adam was defeated in a Mughal attack and Kamal was recognized as the sole Gakkhar chief. Kamal, receiving a *mansab* of 5,000, served the Mughal State in Kabul and on the Indus. In addition to his brother, four of his kinsmen were enrolled in the Mughal service with military ranks. Akbar's alliance with the Gakkhars went a long way in deepening the Mughal authority in north-western Panjab. However, Akbar could not win over Chakar Khan Rind, the powerful Baloch *zamindar* of Multan, who maintained his autonomy in the face of Mughal ascendency.

Akbar, mindful of Sikandar's support base, intervened in the Panjab hills. Raja Takht Mal of Mau, who had assisted Sikandar, was put to death and his brother Bakht Mal was installed as the chief. In 1558, a Mughal campaign extracted a large booty from Jammu. In 1560, punitive measures were taken against Raja Ganesh of Talwara, where Bairam Khan had taken shelter.[58] When Akbar reached (1566) Lahore to check Mirza Hakim's incursion, a number of *zamindars* of northern districts expressed their submission and offered tributes. The death of Raja Jai Chand of Kangra in Mughal custody induced his son Raja Bidhi Chand to rise in revolt (1572). Husain Quli Khan, the governor of Panjab, occupied the forts of Dhameri and Kotla. Crossing a number of streams and cutting through a thick jungle, the Mughals snatched the fort of Bhawan and plundered the temple of Mahamai. The Mughal siege of Nagarkot could not be concluded owing to the intrusion of the rebel Mirza Ibrahim Husain. The Mughals negotiated a settlement with Kangra. The chief paid a tribute of five *mans* of gold in Akbar Shahi weight. A delegation of responsible persons was required to stay at the Mughal court until the delivery of the fort. Raja Birbal, who had received the principality in fief, was given a monetary compensation. Raja Gopi Chand agreed to appear before the governor of Panjab, while a Mughal garrison was placed in the fort. In the name of Akbar, the public prayer (*khutba*) was recited and coins of the chiefdom were struck.[59] The Mughal suzerainty over Kangra was a major step in the ongoing consolidation of the Mughal State in Panjab.

Mirza Hakim, Akbar's foster brother, ruled over Kabul. Failing to resist the pressure of Mirza Sulaiman from Badakhshan, he turned to Panjab. So long as he sought a temporary shelter, Akbar assisted him in recovering Kabul. When he tried to snatch Panjab from Akbar, the Mughal provincial officers fought him back. This was illustrated in Akbar's response to the three attacks from Kabul. In 1564, Hakim arrived on the Indus and sent his emissaries to Akbar and Mir Muhammad Khan, the governor of Panjab. In order to help him, Akbar sent the Panjab troops under the governor to Kabul. Besides members of the Atka Khail, Kamal Khan Gakkhar and several *zamindars* restored Hakim in Kabul.[60] After two years, Hakim entered Panjab and, ravaging Bhera, advanced to Lahore. The Panjab officers defended the fort, while the news of Akbar's march to Lahore forced Hakim to retreat across the Indus. Akbar deputed the Panjab officers to ensure a peaceful retreat of the Kabulis and give assurances to the peasantry of Bhera.[61] After a gap of 14 years, Hakim crossed (1580) the Indus at the head of 15,000 cavalry. Mirza Yusuf Khan, who held a *jagir* on the Indus, overpowered the Kabulis. Kunwar Man Singh, replacing Mirza Yusuf Khan, took charge of the areas on the Indus. As a strategy, Hakim was allowed to reach Lahore. Raja Bhagwant Das, Kunwar Man Singh, Saeed Khan Gakkhar and *jagirdars* of Panjab defended the fort. Hakim failed to make any headway and, learning of Akbar's arrival at Sirhind, rushed back to Kabul. The Mughal army, comprising Kunwar Man Singh, Madho Singh, Surat Singh and others established order in Afghanistan. Participants in the campaign included the chiefs of the Gakkhars, Janjuhas and Balochis.[62] Akbar, on his way to Kabul, marched through Kangra and Salt Range.

The Mughal State, in spite of imposing its authority over Kangra, faced renewed opposition from the hill chiefdoms. Raja Basu (r. 1580-1613) of Mau defied Akbar many times. In 1590, he joined a widespread rebellion involving sixteen principalities between the Satluj and Beas. The combined strength of the force was 10,000 horsemen and 100,000 foot soldiers. Zain Khan Koka, leading military operations from Pathankot to Kahlur, forced the chiefs to submit.[63] In 1592, Jammu and neighbouring principalities refused to participate in the Mughal expedition to Kashmir. The chiefdoms between the Ravi and Chenab rose in revolt. Shaikh Farid Bokhari and Husain Beg Shaikh Umari led the punitive action. The Mughals, occupying the forts of Jammu and Ramgarh, subjugated Jasrota and Lakhanpur. The Mughals pacified the rebellious tract between Jammu and Kangra.[64] In 1596, Raja Basu and some neighbouring chiefs revived the resistance. Though the Mughals demolished the fort of Mau, Raja Basu ignited (1602) another rebellion, which spread in the hills from the Beas to Chenab. When the Mughals besieged the fort of Jammu, it received support from the chiefs of Kangra, Lakhanpur, Jasrota and Mankot. The Mughals distributed portions of the unpacified area among their officers.[65] For thirteen years (1585-98), Akbar turned Lahore into the imperial capital and made it the base for settling the north-western region between Kashmir and Balochistan. Zain Khan Koka, during a decade (1586-97) of campaigning, suppressed the Afghan tribes beyond the Indus.

The Mughal polity recruited hundreds of officers, who were placed in a hierarchy of military ranks (*mansabs*) and paid through transferrable revenue assignments (*jagirs*). The state maintained a class of theologians (*ulama*) through land grants that were planted in the midst of traditional rural elites. It employed a large secretarial class trained in Persian, accounts and record keeping. From every subdistrict (*mahal*), it collected a vast statistical data on cultivated land, estimated revenue, magnitude of land grants, military resources of *zamindars* and castes holding *zamindari* right. In 1580, alongside the organization of twelve provinces (*subahs*), Panjab was fragmented into three such units. The province of Lahore comprised the area between the Satluj and Indus, while Multan embraced the arid plain beyond Bathinda up to Dera Ghazi Khan. The cis-Satluj tract was merged with the province of Delhi. Each province was provided with a set of officers such as *sipahsalar*, *diwan*, *bakhshi*, *mir adl*, *sadr*, *kotwal*, *mir bahr* and *waqia nawis*. The following table illustrated the strength of some landed groups in Panjab, with reference to their respective places of settlement, cultivated areas, estimated revenues in *dams*, castes holding the *zamindari* right and the sizes of their retinues.[66] This record pertained to the period (1595) when Damodar lived in Jhang Siyal on the Chenab and contemplated a narrative on Hir-Ranjha.

During the first decade of Akbar's reign, the Mughal State continued Sher Shah's revenue system, whereby a uniform rate of assessment was converted into cash on a single price list. From 1567 onwards, efforts were made to reform the system in accordance with local conditions. New revenue circles were constituted through

Mahal	*Bighas*	*Revenue*	*Castes of Zamindars*	*Cavalry*	*Infantry*
Panipat	568,444	10,756,647	Afghan, Gujjar, Ranghar	100	2,000
Rohtak	636,835	8,599,270	Jat	100	2,000
Sonepat	283,299	7,727,323	Afghan, Jat	70	100
Karnal	540,444	5,678,242	Ranghar, Chauhan	50	800
Jind	281,584	5,401,749	Salar, Rajput, Jattu	500	4,000
Hansi	836,115	5,434,438	Rajput, Multani, Jattu, Jat	500	7,000
Kaithal	918,025	10,688,630	Rajput	200	3,000
Thanesar	228,988	7,850,803	Ranghar, Jat	50	1,500
Banur	420,337	12,549,953	Ranghar, Afghan	700	3,000
Sirhind	828,458	12,082,630	Rajput, Bara, Khori, Dadah, Jat	1700	2,000
Ludhiana	43,469	2,294,633	Awan, Khori, Ranghar	100	700
Maler	103,444	260,583	Muin	100	500
Bajwara	12,363	2,425,813	Khoriwaha	30	200
Talwan	201,450	6,780,337	Muin	70	700
Chaurasi	96,330	5,463,913	Afghan	50	1,000
Sultanpur	101,865	4,020,232	Bhatti	200	1,000
Garhdiwala	58,083	2,670,087	Jat	20	200
Nakodar	78,731	3,710,756	Muin	20	1,000

Batala	515,479	16,820,998	Bhatti, Jat	200	5,000
Talwara	6,334	514,666	Bakkal	20	200
Pathankot	199,872	7,297,015	Brahmin	250	2,000
Qasur	259,456	3,915,506	Bhatti	300	4,000
Eminabad	515,675	24,853,006	Khokhar, Cheema	500	5,000
Pasrur	509,858	27,978,583	Jat, Bajwa, Telah & c	200	4,000
Bhalot	20,312	818,182	Minhas	100	2,000
Chiniot	154,154	2,806,369	Jat, Jabuhar	500	5,000
Sialkot	102,035	22,090,792	Jat, Ghuman, Cheema	500	7,000
Sodhra	121,721	7,096,710	Cheema	100	1,000
Goindwal	55, 069	1,253,957	Virk, Jat	50	300
Bahlolpur	170,607	3,830,575	Jat	100	500
Mangli	2,839	432,000	Minhas	400	2,000
Hazara	270,392	4,689,136	Jat, Khokhar	700	3,000
Attock	5,418	3,202,216	Khattar	1,000	5,000
Khushab	73,086	2,702,509	Afghan, Niazi, Isakhel	500	7,000
Shamsabad	26,664	7,034,503	Gakkhar	50	500
Makhial	9,320	834,000	Janjuha	100	1,500

grouping subdistricts with similar fertility and climate. Pertaining to ten years (1570-80), information was collected on cultivated areas, yields and prices. Based on these figures, revenue rates were fixed directly in cash for each crop. The system, officially termed as *zabt*, was applied to the vast plain from the Indus to Ghagra.[67] Yet, the land tax was collected through the intermediacy of *zamindars*. The reforms, taken together, had an adverse impact on the *zamindars*. On the one hand, they appeared to have suffered a reduction in their share of the produce and, on the other hand, their prestigious position in the rural society was undermined. The Mughal State, aware of the military resources of the *zamindars*, sought to coerce them into collaboration with local officers. The most important function of the military commanders (*faujdars*), entrusted with the charge of a district (*sarkar*), was to ensure that the *zamindars* duly paid the land tax of their domains, failing which they were chastized and even expelled. In this context, the rebellion of Bhatti *zamindars* becomes understandable.

Sandal and Farid, father and son, held a *zamindari* in the Sandal Bar (Rachna Doab). They did not accept Akbar's authority. They refused to pay the land tax and carried out predatory raids. They were brought to the Mughal court at Lahore and, at the orders of Akbar, put to death. Their headless corpses were hung at the city gate. Four months later, Farid's widow Ladhi gave birth to a son, who was named Dulla.[68] At the advice of astrologers and Pandits, Ladhi was chosen as a wet nurse for Akbar's son Shaikhu. Dulla and Shaikhu were brought up together at Pindi, the headquarters of the Bhattis. At the end of this period, Akbar advised Ladhi to educate Dulla, who could be taken in the Mughal service. Since Dulla fell out with the Qazi, he did not learn anything. Heading a gang of boys, he broke the pitchers of women fetching water. From Ladhi, he learnt the circumstances in which the Bhatti elders were killed. Dulla, declaring his revolt against Akbar, mobilized a retinue of 500 young men and embarked on a career of social banditry. He plundred the caravans from Qandhar, Bokhara and Kashmir. Akbar, suspecting Shaikhu of shielding Dulla, sent Mirza Nizamuddin to attack Pindi. Dulla rode to Chiniot to rope in his uncles and nephews. Nizamuddin destroyed Pindi and captured the women of Dulla's family. Dulla, on his return, defeated the Mughals and rescued the Bhatti women. Dulla came to Lahore with the Mughal cavalcade. At night, he died of consuming poisonous liquor.[69] According to another narrative, Akbar ordered the execution of Dulla in public, so that the resistance of Sandal Bar collapsed and the crisis of the Mughal State blew over. However, the hopes of Akbar were not realized. On Dulla's face, everyone saw fearlessness, pride and determination.[70] Since then the chivalry of Dulla has been celebrated in the annual festival of Lohri. Dulla has become a permanent symbol of resistance in the Panjabi folklore.

Shah Husain on Hir-Ranjha

Shah Husain (1539-99), the famous Sufi poet of Lahore, was born in a family of weavers. His spiritual genealogy was traceable to Abdul Qadir Jilani through a chain of Qadiri masters. During his youth, he offered prayers and undertook austerities, besides reciting the Quran and studying its commentaries. At the age of 36, he underwent a profound experience as his teacher recited, 'The life of the world is nothing but play and pleasurable distraction' (Quran 6:32, echoed in 29:64 and 47:36). As a result, he abandoned constraints of ascetic piety, legal rectitude and rational seriousness. Instead, he immersed in pleasure and retained an inward sense of pure devotion to God. He drank wine in public and, resorting to song and dance with a band of companions, walked through the streets of Lahore. Living in this state, he fell in love with the Brahmin lad Madho, whom he took as a disciple. Malik Ali, the Kotwal (police chief) of Lahore, threatened to punish Shah Husain for his unlawful conduct. A strange turn of events led to the cancellation of punishment and execution of the Kotwal. Shah Husain employed his miraculous powers and brought under his influence a large number of people, ranging from the Emperor and his nobles to the *zamindars* and peasants.[71] Shah Husain held that divine love could not be separated from physical love. Just as his love for Madho coalesced in his spiritual engagement, his narrative of Hir-Ranjha was rooted in his mystical discourse. His verses echoed with the female voice in general and sexual imagery in particular.

In the eyes of Shah Husain, God permeates all forms of creation. Sovereign in the universe, God enjoys autonomous power over His creatures. The path leading to God, being extremely hazardous, was comparable to crossing thousand of rivers and meadows. To gain access to God, the best course was to traverse the path of love under the guidance of a perfect mentor. A seeker, abjuring arrogance and adopting humility, turned his quest into a joyful experience. He erased the chasm between the outer and inner dimension of religion. Since God imbued every pore of his body, he preserved His name every moment and felt annihilated in Him. Essentially a traveller, he treated the world as an inn. Shah Husain distanced himself from contemporary Sufis, who maintained large establishments with their disciples and followers. Instead, he identified himself with the humble mendicants (*faqirs*), who lived in pious congregations (*sadhsangat*) and attached themselves to the Lord. For Shah Husain, the spiritual quest was similar to the married life of a young woman. On the eve of her wedding, she hoped for happiness from the love of her husband and, at the same time, felt sad at the impending separation from her relatives and friends. On reaching her husband's house, she tried to cherish every moment of life with him. Owing to the transience of her beauty, she employed every means to attract the attention of her husband. During separation from her husband, her body was shattered and a fire smouldered in her heart. The remedy of her ailment lay with her lover, who was a saintly physician (*sant tabib*). She could not withdraw from love, as the divine pen (*qalam rabbani*) had willed her choice. The woman, who slept in the arms of her husband, was hailed as a chaste wife. The one who did not stood cursed. The one who remained awake was fortunate (*vad bhagi*).[72]

Shah Husain, in a score of mystical poems, gave voice to the pain of Hir. The story of her love for Ranjha had spread in all directions. There was hardly a person who had not heard it. Hir, the daughter of a powerful *zamindar*, had fallen in love with a herdsman in service of the clan. She abandoned her high status and became a recluse (*bairagan*). She had taken this decision as a deliberate choice. She inflicted a great wound on herself. Bold and courageous, she did not care if one person or one lakh knew her preference. The people could do nothing except wag their tongues. She would continue with what she had started. She saw herself as the servant of her Sanwal, which was an endearing epithet for Krishna. Like a diligent maidservant in service of a saint, she performed all household chores. Lost in her thoughts about Ranjha, she had no control over her body and mind. When she was seen collecting the dried leaves of *pipal* in the jungle, the people felt that she had gone crazy (*diwani*). As they were not her confidants (*mehram*), they did not know that she had been struck with the arrow of love in her infancy. Even while lying in the cradle as a suckling baby, she writhed in the pain of love. The people saw her love only when it had grown up to maturity. Like an elephant, love was large, strong and fearsome. Ranjha, as its mahout, steered it on the path of love with a goad (*ankas*). Hir was like a moth that perished in the fire, but did not withdraw from the heat. She was reminded of the day when Ranjha, a complete stranger, walked in from Takht Hazara to Jhang Siyal. She sacrificed her life for this path as it enabled her love to take root. There was a dramatic change in her life. She abandoned spinning that she had learnt from her mother. Becoming sick of it, she threw away the basket of cotton rolls and spun yarn. One situation led to another – arrival of Ranjha, meeting between them, her withdrawal from a virginal status and her falling in love with a stranger.[73]

Since everyone knew about the love affair, Hir faced a number of questions from the people. They were keen to know the identity of her lover. Appearing almost suddenly, he began to serve the Siyals as a herdsman. In addition to caring for the buffaloes, he had fallen in love with his employer's daughter. Hir was upbraided for choosing a lover, who was socially inferior to her own elite status. Ranjha was a wanderer with obscure antecedents, while she was the daughter of a mighty landed chief. Love did not consider social barriers, but people did not understand this. Hir took up the cudgels on his behalf. She announced that Ranjha was the landholder of Takht Hazara. She and her friends belonged to the Siyals, a term applicable to both the clan and place, which constituted the social space of their love. She insisted on introducing herself as part of a group of girls, which was related to Ranjha in ways more than one.[74] She alluded to the relation between Krishna and Gopis. She did not say anything about Ranjha's parents, caste and clan. She was also silent about the circumstances in which he was forced to leave his village. For Shah Husain, any further reference to his antecedents was irrelevant to his narrative. Our poet has deliberately kept Ranjha in the background. His image of Ranjha was hazy, deceptive and mysterious. For him, he was merely a herdsman, who lived on the other side of the Chenab. Hir, who was in love with him and who rejected her marriage among the Kheras, yearned to unite with him.

Apart from Takht Hazara and Jhang Siyal, the Chenab was an important site in the quest of love. It figured in two mystical poems. Shah Husain has painted a vivid picture of the scene on its ferry near Jhang Siyal. Hir, supposed to cross the river to meet him, found the journey hazardous. The obstacles were numerous and insurmountable. She was forced to undertake it alone. No one was willing to accompany her. The river was deep, while the night and distance were long. Instead of a robust boat, only a rickety raft (*tulla*) made of bamboo sticks and dried grass was available. Differences cropped up between Hir and the boatman (*mallah*). She admitted having made a mistake, while the boatman was perfect. She could not figure out any door that could be knocked. What was worse, a number of lions inhabited the area around the ferry. These obstacles, taken together, made her task daunting. She was in two minds. At one moment, she felt that it was essential for her to go, as she had made a promise to Ranjha. Therefore, she made entreaties to the boatman. She saw the Chenab as a veritable worldly ocean (*bhavsagar*), which was vast and stormy. Only expert swimmers could cross it. On second thoughts, she abandoned her intention altogether. She felt guilty of breaking her promise. She could send a messenger to the other side of Chenab. If the messenger returned with news about Ranjha, she would give him a gift of her own rings. In her predicament, Hir desired to board the boat of the saints and take the oath of allegiance to them. The step, in practical terms, meant erasing her physical existence. She had to die while she was alive.[75] This was a standard mystical principle that demanded a withdrawal from the materiality of life.

Ranjha, while serving as a herdsman in Jhang Siyal, took the buffaloes out for grazing. He remained away during the whole day. Hir, unable to live without him even for a moment, searched for him in the moors and jungles. Often, she failed to locate him. In the evening, the buffaloes returned to the village, but Ranjha was not seen with them. Day and night, Hir was on his trail in the wilderness, crying out his name at the pitch of her voice. The thorns of acacia pierced her feet. In her exhaustion and desperation, she prayed to God to provide her the means to meet Ranjha. At this moment, she underwent a strange experience. On the one hand, she was unable to find Ranjha in spite of her strenuous efforts. At the same time, she felt that he was always with her. Her entire being was imbued with him. For her, he was both present and absent. Larger than life, he appeared to be the master of the two worlds, physical and spiritual. Despite his great power, he was negligent (*beparwah*) towards her. Such grievances did not erode the foundation of her love. She continued her firm attachment to him. She recited 'Ranjha Ranjha' so frequently that she herself turned into Ranjha and, ceasing to be Hir, she attained a new identity. She asked everyone to address her as Ranjha and not as Hir. Having undergone a complete transformation, she had become a new person. She had achieved her aim with the guidance of the saints, who had removed all doubts from her mind.[76]

Shah Husain has taken a keen interest in three interrelated developments – Hir's confession of love for Ranjha, her conflict with her parents and her rejection of the Khera boy. As seen above, the people of Jhang Siyal had come to know the affair. Hir's shocked parents could not tolerate her intimacy with their servant. In order to put an end to the relation and growing rumours, they started preparations for her marriage among the Kheras. Hir jumped into the fray and tried her best to forestall the marriage. Speaking bluntly, she urged her mother to refrain from mentioning the name of the Kheras. She had chosen the herdsman as her husband and, therefore, she would not even consider the Kheras. God knew the purity of her love. Seeing the arrangements of her wedding, Hir became rebellious. She did not expect any dowry or any other form of wealth from them. Every moment, she demanded that Ranjha be given to her, so that she was freed from the muddle (*janjal*). Disregarding her protest, she was forced to sit on the wedding mat and take the ceremonial rounds. She was utterly helpless. Her tragic fate had been inscribed in her destiny (*lauh qalam*). She beseeched her mother to reverse her fate if it were in her means. The Kheras pushed her into the palanquin, though their claims were false. She could not stop them, as she had neither the power nor any excuse. Ranjha had trapped her in the net of his love and, thereafter, left her in the lurch. This pain had pierced her heart. Her strings were in the hands of God. Yet, she would not accept the marriage.[77]

At Rangpur Khera, Hir's life was miserable. Separation from Ranjha wrought havoc on her body. Being young and immature, she was ignorant of the complexities of love. Her physical degeneration indicated that love could not be hidden. Without her lover, her nights became long and she was unable to sleep. Her body, shedding flesh, began to decay. Reduced to a skeleton, her bones crackled. Separation had struck deep roots in her. Like the knife of a butcher, it had penetrated her innards. Ranjha, acting like a sharp splinter, sank into the depths of her interior. Even the pliers failed to pull out the lakhs of needles. Only a confidant could pull them out with his kind words. Numerous Muslim theologians and judges, who had acquired tonnes of knowledge, delivered empty sermons to her. They failed to understand her malady. The thorns of separation, having settled in her thoughts, had driven her to madness. In her misery, she could not turn to anyone for solace. Her food, instead of providing nourishment, left an opposite effect. Her bread comprised of thorns and curry was made of sorrow. She employed her own bones as fuel in the hearth. The wounds on her body were unique. Only Ranjha could act as a physician (*tabib*) to cure her affliction. Instead of medicinal herbs, he would administer the potion of love, which could serve as an antidote to separation. If Ranjha appeared as a Jogi, she would become his female counterpart (*jogiani*). She would not mind if people were shocked at her transformation and ridiculed her as crazy (*kamli*).[78]

Diffusion of the Story

During the lifetime of Shah Husain (1539-99), the tale of Hir-Ranjha had spread as far as Sind. It was possible that the entire story was versified in Sindi. Alternatively, Sindi folklore might have commemorated some of its important episodes. Wandering minstrels, moving from one Sufi establishment to the other, played some role in diffusing the romance at the popular level. Shaikh Daud (1514-74), the famous Qadiri saint of Shergarh (tehsil Dipalpur, district Okara) developed a keen interest in the couplets from the life of Hir-Ranjha. He invited Valeya, a singer from Sind, to stay in his hospice (*khanqah*). On one occasion, he felt intoxicated on listening to a Sindi couplet, which is translated as follows:

I celebrate my joy at Ranjha's arrival to my house.
Qazis and *mullas* were not involved; I myself intensified my love.

Valeya explained that Hir herself had composed this couplet. She was elated when Ranjha came to her house. Raising a loud cry, she announced the event to the whole world. She took pride in elevating the level of her love. She did not allow anyone, not even the Muslim theologians, to interfere in it. Shaikh Daud, on hearing the explanation, declared that he had secured God's forgiveness for seven generations of Hir and Ranjha. He persuaded Valeya to sing this couplet for him in the peaceful environs of a neighbouring jungle. Feeling ecstatic at the mellifluous rendition, he wandered in the wilderness throughout the day. The Shaikh came under the impact of the couplet in the early stages of his life. During this perod, he was an Uwaisi and, therefore, received spiritual inspiration from the spirit of Abdul Qadir Gilani. The Shaikh, pleased with Valeya, wanted to reward him with some material benefit. Instantly, Valeya found the surrounding vegetation turning into gold. For some moments, he lost his consciousness and, on regaining his composure, expressed his preference for religious devotion instead of worldy gains. Twice a day, the Shaikh sent food for Valeya and his family from the common kitchen. He also provided a daily allowance for the needs of Valeya's children.[79]

Baqi Kulabi (d. 1579) reconstructed the story of Hir-Ranjha in Persian verse, though in a short format.[80] According to him, Hir-Ranjha had caused an uproar (*ghogha*) in Hindustan. His tale has overlooked many episodes and characters, besides failing to mention places such as Takht Hazara, Jhang Siyal and Rangpur Khera. He has also chosen to ignore the role of Ranjha's brothers, his stay in the mosque and encounter with a boatman on the Chenab. For him, Ranjha left his home on hearing of Hir. He directly went to Chuchak, who employed him to graze buffaloes. Hir met him through a nurse. When their love brought a bad name, Ranjha quietly left the town. Hir met him in a dream and persuaded him to return. Meanwhile, she was married to a man named Hussam. When the husband approached her, she gave him a beating. Thereafter, she returned to her parental home. Hussam went to bring her, but she refused to come with him. A distraught Hussam appealed to Shah Adli. The Qazi and Mufti assigned Hir back to Hussam. Hir reached the place of her parents-in-law only to fall ill. Ranjha assumed the garb of a Jogi and arrived on the scene. Hir visited the Jogi for treatment and found that the Jogi was indeed Ranjha. Hir again went to her parental home. Making soulful entreaties to her mother, she sought permission to live with Ranjha. Hir, facing a firm refusal, went away with Ranjha. After some time, Ranjha met a sudden end. Hir prayed for her death. A wide crack appeared in the earth and she sank into it. The lovers were buried in the same grave.[81]

Though Damodar composed his romance of Hir-Ranjha in the second half of the sixteenth century, it remained hidden from scholarly view for a long time. Its manuscripts managed to survive in parts of western Panjab where Damodar hailed from. In 1927, Bawa Ganga Singh Bedi brought out the first printed version of Damodar's work. This text was prepared on the basis of two manuscripts, both of which were traced to Jhang. Right in the beginning of this text, there were seven stanzas that were absent in the version that Jagtar Singh produced. In 1981, this scholar visited Multan (Pakistan) in connection with his doctoral research. A man named Bhagwan Das Miglani came to meet him. His parents had been killed in the riots of Partition. His sister had drifted to India with a convoy of refugees. Bhagwan Das had made many efforts to search her. Perhaps, he met Jagtar Singh in order somehow to contact his sister. In any case, he learnt the purpose of Jagtar Singh's visit. He revealed that he had a number of books and manuscripts in his possession. He invited Jagtar Singh to his house and showed his collection of literature. One of them was a manuscript of *Hir Damodar*, which was written in the Persian script and Nastaliq calligraphic mode. Jagtar Singh made an ardent request for the manuscript. Bhagwan Das refused to part with it owing to emotional reasons. His grandfather Khem Chand Miglani (son of Bija Ram Miglani) had inscribed it with his own hand in 1878. Bhagwan Das's father had preserved it with great care and, as a family legacy, it could not be given to anyone. However, he permitted Jagtar Singh to copy it.[82] The latter prepared a Gurmukhi version of the Persian script and, later on, added discussions on its literary aspects. In 2000, Punjabi University, Patiala, published it. The present study is based on this work.

NOTES

1. Economic diffrrentiation was a significant feature of rural society. The peasants did not claim proprietary rights over their holdings. Like semi-serfs, they possessed seeds, cattle and implements. They sold their produce to pay the land tax. The village headmen (*khuts* and *muqaddams*) were exempted from taxes and levied a cess on villagers. The rural aristocracy (*rais, ranas* and *rawats*), employing their military resources, resisted the early Turkish rulers and retained their position by paying tributes. In the early fourteenth century, the Delhi Sultanate subverted this hierarchy. For its needs, it created a new class of intermediaries (*chaudharis*) by abrorbing elements from the decaying rural aristocrats and headmen. By 1350, the ruling class saw the entire rural population (*riaya*) as divided into two classes, viz. the peasants and *zamindars*. The latter denoted a comprehensive category embracing all kinds of superior rights holders. Tapan Raychaudhuri and Irfan Habib, ed., *The Cambridge Economic History of India*, vol. I: *c.1200 – c.1750*, New Delhi: Orient Longman, rpt., 2004, pp. 57-9.
2. Ziauddin Barani, *Tarikh-i Firoz Shahi*, ed. Sir Syed Ahmad, Aligarh: Aligarh Muslim University, rpt., 2005, pp. 473, 479-80 and 483-4.
3. Surinder Singh, 'Rulers, Zamindars and Sufis: Probing a Triangular Model of State Formation', in *Situating Medieval India: Polity, Society and Culture*, New Delhi: Manohar, 2023, pp. 65-74.
4. Shams Siraj Afif, *Tarikh-i Firoz Shahi*, ed. Maulavi Wilayat Husain, Calcutta: Asiatic Society of Bengal, 1890, pp. 124-8; Ainuddin Ain ul-Mulk Mahru, *Insha-i Mahru*, ed. Shaikh Abdul Rashid, Aligarh: Aligarh Muslim University, 1959, Letter no. 11, pp. 20-1 and Letter no. 14, pp. 176-7.
5. Ziauddin Barani, *Tarikh-i Firoz Shahi*, pp. 567-71.

6. Yahya bin Ahmad bin Abdullah Sirhindi, *Tarikh-i Mubarak Shahi*, ed. M. Hidayat Husain, Calcutta: Asiatic Society of Bengal, 1931, pp. 145-57.
7. Ibid., pp. 157-64.
8. Sharafuddin Ali Yazdi, *Zafar Nama*, ed. Muhammad Ilahdad, vol. II, Calcutta: Asiatic Society of Bengal, 1888, pp. 46-172.
9. Khaliq Ahmad Nizami, 'Some Aspects of Khanqah Life in Medieval India', in *Studies in Medieval Indian History and Culture*, Allahabad: Kitab Mahal, 1966, pp. 85-6.
10. Shaikh Nizamuddin Auliya, recalling his training at Baba Farid's establishment, declared that nothing was achieved without hard penance (*mujahida*), which was superior to observation (*mushahida*). The former was an obligation for the sake of God. If it was directed against one's lower self (*nafs*), it ensured a high status on the day of resurrection. This moral was evident even in the nature of food. During the season of *delahs* and flowers of *kareel*, a disciple exerted himself to gather them. Baba Farid and his disciples ate them to satiation and, on such occasions, experienced the happiness of Id. When these were out of season, the companions were sent to the neighbourhood for circulating the begging bowl (*zanbil*). Hamid Qalandar, *Khair ul-Majalis*, ed. Khaliq Ahmad Nizami, Aligarh: Depatment of History, Aligarh Muslim University, 1966, pp. 85-6.
11. Khaliq Ahmad Nizami, *Religion and Politics in India during the Thirteenth Century*, New Delhi: Oxford University Press, 2002, pp. 243-5.
12. Fazlullah Majawi, *Fatawa-i Sufiyya*, Eng. tr. Julian Baldick, *Mystical Islam: An Introduction to Sufism*, London & New York: Tauris Parke Paperbacks, 2000, pp. 95-6.
13. Amir Hasan Sijzi, *Fawaid ul-Fuad*, Eng. tr. Bruce B. Lawrence, (entitled *Nizam Ad-Din Awliya: Morals for the Heart*), New York & Mahwah: Paulist Press, 1992, pp. 167-8; Amir Khurd, *Siyar ul-Auliya*, Delhi: Matba-i Muhibb-i Hind, 1885, pp. 117-18, 170.
14. Amir Hasan Sijzi, *Fawaid ul-Fuad*, pp. 140, 150, 181-3, 266; Amir Khurd, *Siyar ul-Auliya*, pp. 68-70.
15. Amir Hasan Sijzi, *Fawaid ul-Fuad*, pp. 251, 328.
16. Qamr ul-Huda, *Striving for Divine Union: Spiritual Exercises for Suhrawardi Sufis*, London & New York: Routledge Curzon, 2003, pp. 153-5.
17. Amina M. Steinfels, *Knowledge before Action: Islamic Learning and Sufi*

Practice in the Life of Sayyid Jalal al-din Bukhari Makhdum-i Jahaniyan, Columbia: University of South Carolina, 2012, pp. 63-77.

18. Brij Mohan Sagar, *The Hymns of Sheikh Farid*, Amritsar: Guru Nanak Dev University, 1999, Shalok nos. 30-1, p. 26; Fakhruddin Iraqi, *Kulliyat Fakhruddin Iraqi*, ed. Nasreen Muhtashim, Tehran: Intsharat Zawwar, 1392 AH, pp. 405-6, 415-17, 424-8, 440-1; Shah Sharfuddin Bu Ali Shah Qalandar, *Masnavi*, ed. Muhmmad Muslim Ahmad Nizami, New Delhi: Kutbkhana Naziriya, 1383 AH, pp. 23-5, 40-1; Jamaluddin Ahmad Hansavi, *Mulhimat wa Ahwal wa Asar*, ed. Sardar Ali Ahmad Khan, Lahore: Sang-e Meel Publications, 2005, pp. 20-8.
19. Amir Hasan Sijzi, *Fawaid ul-Fuad*, pp. 197-8, 252-3; Hamid Qalandar, *Khair ul-Majalis*, pp. 224-5; Amir Khurd, *Siyar ul-Auliya*, p. 505.
20. Three factors appeared to have induced the Sufis to associate with miracles. First, Sufism, in comparison to orthodoxy, was conscious of its defective theological foundations. Orthodoxy traced its basis to the Quran and Prophetic practice (*sunnah*), besides enjoying the support of the secular arm of the medieval state. Sufism, in order to compensate itself for what it lacked in reality, resorted to miracles. Second, Sufism took Islam to the masses and, while dealing with myriad problems at a personal level, left ample room for belief in miracles. Third, the accounts of miracles created an atmosphere to impress what was necessary and rational. M. Mujeeb, *The Indian Muslims*, New Delhi: Munshiram Manoharlal, rpt., 2003, pp. 120-1.
21. Hamid Qalandar, *Khair ul-Majalis*, pp. 87-8, 147-50, 182, 236-8.
22. Hamid bin Fazlullah Jamali, *Siyar ul-Arifin*, Delhi: Rizvi Press, 1893, pp. 129-30.
23. Surinder Singh, *The Making of Medieval Panjab: Politics, Society and Culture, c.1000 – c.1500*, New Delhi: Manohar, 2020, pp. 458-83.
24. Ziauddin Barani, *Tarikh-i Firoz Shahi*, p. 209; Amir Hasan Sijzi, *Fawaid ul-Fuad*, p. 327; Amir Khurd, *Siyar ul-Auliya*, pp. 71-2.
25. Khaliq Ahmad Nizami, *Religion and Politics in India during the Thirteenth Century*, pp. 269-72.
26. Hamid bin Fazlullah Jamali, *Siyar ul-Arifin*, pp. 140-1; Ibn Battuta, *Rehla*, Eng. tr. Mahdi Husain, entitled *The Rehla of Ibn Battuta: India, Maldive Islands and Ceylon*, Baroda: Oriental Institute, 1976, p. 97.
27. Richard M. Eaton, 'The Political and Religious Authority of the Shrine of Baba Farid', in *Essays on Islam and Indian History*, New Delhi: Oxford University Press, 2000, pp. 203-24.

28. Yahya bin Ahmad bin Abdullah Sirhindi, *Tarikh-i Mubarak Shahi*, pp. 173-80.
29. Ibid., pp. 183-90.
30. Ibid., pp. 194-7.
31. Ibid., pp. 198-202, 212-14.
32. Ibid., pp. 214-21.
33. Ibid, pp. 223-33.
34. Andre Wink, 'On the Road to Failure: The Afghans in Mughal India', in *Islamicate Traditions in South Asia: Themes from Culture and History*, ed. Agnieszka Kuczkiewics Fras, New Delhi: Manohar, 2013, pp. 272-4, 297-8.
35. Abdullah, *Tarikh-i Daudi*, ed. Shaikh Abdul Rashid and Iqtidar Husain Siddiqui, Aligarh: Aligarh Muslim University, 1969, pp. 3-7; Shaikh Rizqullah Mushtaqi, *Waqiat-i Mushtaqi*, ed. Iqtidar Husain Siddiqui and Waqar ul-Hasan Siddiqi, Rampur: Rampur Raza Library, 2002, p. 4.
36. According to a popular tradition, which Mushtaqi and Firishtah have recorded, Bahlol Lodi visited a dervish with his friends. The dervish asked if anyone was willing to purchase the throne of Delhi with 2,000 *tankahs*. Bahlol presented him 1,600 *tankahs* he had in his pocket. In return, the dervish conferred the kingdom of Delhi on the visitor. The friends of Bahlol made fun of him. Bahlol asserted that he had not made a bad bargain. If the prophecy of the dervish materialized, he would get precious jewels at the price of peanuts. If it turned out to be false, he would not suffer any loss, as it was always meritorious to serve a holy man.
37. Nawab Iftikhar Ali Khan, *A History of the Ruling Family of Sheikh Sadruddin Sadr-i Jahan of Malerkotla (1449 AD to 1948 AD)*, ed. R.K. Ghai, Patiala: Punjabi University, 2000, pp. 2-10.
38. Khwaja Nizamuddin Ahmad, *Tabaqat-i Akbari*, vol. III, Eng. tr. Brajendranath De and Baini Prashad, Delhi: Low Price Publications, rpt., 1990, pp. 788-95.
39. Ibid., pp. 795-805.
40. Zahiruddin Muhammad Babur, *Baburnama*, tr. ed. and annotated, Wheeler M. Thackston, entitled *The Baburnama: Memoirs of Babur, Prince and Emperor*, New York: The Modern Library, 2002, pp. 270-81.
41. Ibid., pp. 316-27.
42. Ahmad Yadgar, *Tarikh-i Shahi*, ed. M. Hidayat Hosain, Calcutta: Royal Asaitic Society of Bengal, 1939, pp. 125-8.

43. Manmohan Singh, ed., *Sri Guru Granth Sahib*, Text with Eng. and Pbi. tr., Amritsar: Shiromani Gurdwara Prabandhak Committee, 2nd edn., 1982, pp. 360, 417-18, 722, 1288.
44. Abbas Khan Sarwani, *Tarikh-i Sher Shahi*, ed. S.M. Imamuddin, Dacca: University of Dacca, 1964, pp. 165-8, 170, 183-6.
45. Abul Fazl, *Ain-i Akbari*, vol. III, Eng. tr. H. Blochmann and D.C. Phillot, Kolkata: The Asiatic Society, 2010, pp. 187-98; Mobad Kaikhusrau Isfandiyar, *Dabistan-i Mazahab*, vol. I, ed. Rahim Razazada Malik, Tehran: Kitabkhana Tahuri, 1362 AH/1983 AD, pp. 157-61; Veronique Bouillier, *Monastic Wanderers: Nath Yogi Ascetics in Modern South Asia*, New Delhi: Manohar, 2017, pp. 22-5.
46. George Weston Briggs, *Gorakhnath and Kanphata Yogis*, Delhi: Motilal Banarsidass, rpt., 1980, pp. 101-3; Zahiruddin Muhammad Babur, *Baburnama*, pp. 171-2; Father Monserrate, *Commentary of Father Monserrate*, ed. S.N. Banerjee and J.S. Hoyland, Jalandhar: Asian Publishers, rpt., 1993, pp. 113-15; B.N. Goswamy and J.S. Grewal, *The Mughals and the Jogis of Jakhbar: Some Madad-i Maash and Other Documents*, Simla: Indian Institute of Advanced Study, 1967, pp. 49-193.
47. Carl W. Ernst, 'Islamization of Yoga in the Amritkunda Translations', *Journal of the Royal Asiatic Society*, Third Series, vol. 13, no. 2, July 2003, pp. 217-20; Yusuf Husain, 'Haud al-Hayat: The Arabic Version of Amritkund', in *On Becoming An Indian Muslim: French Essays on Aspects of Syncretism*, ed. M. Waseem, New Delhi: Oxford University Press, 2003, pp. 63-74; Simon Digby, 'Abd al-Quddus Gangohi (1456-1537): The Personality and Attitudes of An Indian Sufi', *Medieval India: A Miscellany*, vol. III, Bombay: Asia Publishing House, 1975, pp. 46-9.
48. Abdul Baqi bin Jan Muhammad, *Maqamat-i Daudi*, Urdu tr. Khwaja Hamid Yazdani, Rinala Khurd: Syed Muhammad Mohsin, 2003, pp. 205-7, 252-5: Abdul Qadir Badauni, *Muntakhab ut-Tawarikh*, vol. III, Eng. tr. Wolseley Haig and B.P. Ambashthya, Patna: Academica Asiatica, rpt., 1973, pp. 80-1.
49. Dara Shukoh, *Sakinat ul-Auliya*, ed. Tara Chand and Syed Razazada Jalali Naini, Tehran: Muassasa-i Matbuati-i Ilmi, 1963, pp. 50, 83.
50. Prime recitation (*sultan ul-azkar*) was an advanced form of contemplation, wherein the seeker became oblivious of his physical existence and climbed to the state of self-anihilation (*fana ul-fana*) and subsistence in God (*baqa ul-baqa*). Under its impact, the seeker felt calmness of sleep. Alternatively, his body shook as alluded to in the

chapter on earthquake (*surah-i zalzala*) of the Quran (99:1-3). In this state of absolute truth (*alam-i malkut*), he secured knowledge of divine mysteries and heard a strange sound. His concentration on this sound enabled the seeker to attain salvation from his physical being, imbibe mystical knowledge and see divine light. This happened between his sleep and wakefulness when his senses were weak. The experience, difficult to describe, was recognized through symptoms. The moment was comparable to the experience of Prophet Muhammad in the cave of Hira. Muhammad Akram Barasawi, *Iqtibas ul-Anwar*, vol. II, ed. Muhammad Ehteshamuddin, Aligarh: Institute of Persian Research, Aligarh Muslim University, 2018, pp. 351-61.

51. Dara Shukoh, *Risala-i Haqq Numa*, Eng. tr. in *Sufi Meditation and Contemplation: Timeless Wisdom from Mughal India*, ed. Scott Kugle, New Lebanon: Omega Publications, 2012, pp. 137-45.
52. Manmohan Singh, ed., *Sri Guru Granth Sahib*, pp. 487-8.
53. Surinder Singh, *Medieval Panjab in Transition: Authority, Resistance and Spirituality, c.1500 – c.1700*, New Delhi: Manohar, 2022, pp. 291-337.
54. Manmohan Singh, ed., *Sri Guru Granth Sahib*, pp. 140, 473, 989.
55. Nikky Guninder Kaur Singh, *The Feminine Principle in the Sikh Vision of the Transendent*, New York: Cambridge University Press, 1993, pp. 30, 59.
56. Manmohan Singh, ed., *Sri Guru Granth Sahib*, pp. 1107-10.
57. Abul Fazl, *Akbar Nama*, vol. II, Eng. tr. Henry Beveridge, New Delhi: Atlantic Publishers and Distributors, rpt., 2019, pp. 76-81, 89-91 (hereafter cited as Abul Fazl); Abdul Qadir Badauni, *Muntakhab ut-Tawarikh*, vol. II, Eng. tr. W.H. Lowe and B.P. Ambashthya, Patna: Academica Asiatica, rpt., 1973, pp. 11-12 (hereafter cited as Badauni); Khwaja Nizamuddin Ahmad, *Tabaqat-i Akbari*, vol. II, Eng. tr. B. De, Calcutta: Asiatic Society of Bengal, rpt., 1996, pp. 222-3 (hereafter cited as Ahmad).
58. Abul Fazl, vol. II, pp. 261-2.
59. Abul Fazl, vol. III, pp. 51-2; Badauni, vol. II, pp. 165-6; Ahmad, vol. II, pp. 400-402.
60. Abul Fazl, vol. II, pp. 361-5; Badauni, vol. II, pp. 71-2; Ahmad, vol. II, pp. 289-90.
61. Abul Fazl, vol. II, pp. 407-12; Badauni, vol. II, pp. 89-92; Ahmad, vol. II, pp. 318-24.
62. Abul Fazl, vol. III, pp. 493-5; Badauni, vol. II, pp. 299-302; Ahmad, vol. II, pp. 544, 548.

63. Abul Fazl, vol. III, pp. 884-5.
64. Allahdad Faizi Sirhindi, *Akbar Nama*, Eng. tr. H.M. Elliot and John Dowson, in *History of India as Told by its Own Historians*, vol. VI, Allahabad: Kitab Mahal, rpt., 1981, pp. 125-9.
65. Abul Fazl, vol. III, pp. 1060, 1081, 1084, 1206-9, 1213, 1248-9.
66. Abul Fazl, *Ain-i Akbari*, vol. II, Eng. tr. H.S. Jarrett and Jadunath Sarkar, New Delhi: Oriental Books Reprint Corporation, 3rd edn., 1978, pp. 292, 299-301, 320-7.
67. John F. Richards, *The Mughal Empire*, New Delhi: Cambridge University Press, rpt., 2007, pp. 84-5.
68. Surinder Singh, 'Mughal Centralization and Local Resistance in Northwestern India: An Exploration in the Ballad of Dulla Bhatti', in *Popular Literature and Pre-modern Societies in South Asia*, ed. Surinder Singh and Ishwar Dayal Gaur, New Delhi: Pearson Longman, 2008, pp. 89-112; Surinder Singh, 'Revolt of Dulla Bhatti against the Mughal State: A Study of Oral Tradition and Modern Cultural Forms', in *Situating Medieval India: Polity, Society and Culture*, New Delhi: Manohar, 2023, pp. 139-62.
69. Kishan Singh Arif, *Qissa Dulla Bhatti*, ed. Gian Chand (titled *Qissa Dulla Bhatti Ate Us Di Bhav Jugat*), Amritsar: Ravi Sahit Prakashan, 1987, pp. 71-121; Ahmad Salim, *Tin Lok Vaaran*, Amritsar: Ravi Sahit Prakashan, 2015, pp. 30-54.
70. Najm Hosain Syed, *Sedhan, Saran Te Hor Lekh*, ed. Purdaman Singh Bedi, Ludhiana: Jaswant Printers, 2005, p. 142.
71. Mahmud bin Muhammad Pir, Haqiqat ul-Fuqara, Eng. tr. (entiled *Poetic Biography of Madho Lal Husayn*), Scott Kugle, in *Same Sex Love: A Literary History*, ed. Ruth Vanita and Saleem Kidwai, New Delhi: Penguin Books, 2008, pp. 165-77; Nur Ahmad Chishti, *Tahqiqat-i Chishti*, Lahore: Al-Faisal Nashiran wa Tajiran Kutub, rpt., 2000, pp. 324-31.
72. Kala Singh Bedi, *Shah Husain Lahori: Jeevan Te Rachna*, Chandigarh: SSB Publishing Company, 1978, Kafi nos. 16-17, 68, 112, 129.
73. Ibid., Kafi nos. 66, 87, 97, 116, 132.
74. Ibid., Kafi nos. 109, 162.
75. Ibid., Kafi nos. 73, 96, 98, 119.
76. Ibid., Kafi nos. 124, 132, 145.
77. Ibid., Kafi nos. 74, 78, 138.
78. Ibid. Kafi nos. 73, 93, 119, 145, 163.
79. Abdul Baqi bin Jan Muhammad, *Maqamat-i Daudi*, Urdu tr. Khwaja

Hamid Yazdani, Rinala Khurd (Pakistan): Syed Muhammad Mohsin, rpt., 2003, pp. 105-7.

80. Baqi Kulabi, as a poet, was significant enough to figure in Badauni's account of the poets of Akbar's reign. This man, originally hailing from Kulab, spent a long time in Hindustan. He was killed in the rebellion of Masum Khan Kabuli who, along with many prominent nobles, posed a big challenge to Akbar in Bihar and Bengal. It was not possible to know the side on which Kulabi stood. We do learn that Kulabi had a natural talent for poetry. In the few specimens of his Persian verses, he expressed his great suffering at the hands of a cypress like beloved, who had her eyes on gold and silver. It was hoped that she would recognize his worth when he was no more. Abdul Qadir Badauni, *Muntakhab ut-Tawarikh*, vol. III, Persian text, ed. Maulavi Ahmad Ali, Aligarh: Centre of Advanced Study in History and Publications Division, Aligarh Muslim University, rpt., 2018, pp. 194-5.
81. Jagtar Singh, ed., *Hir Damodar*, Introduction and text, Patiala: Punjabi University, 2000, pp. 29-30.
82. Ibid., pp. 72-3.

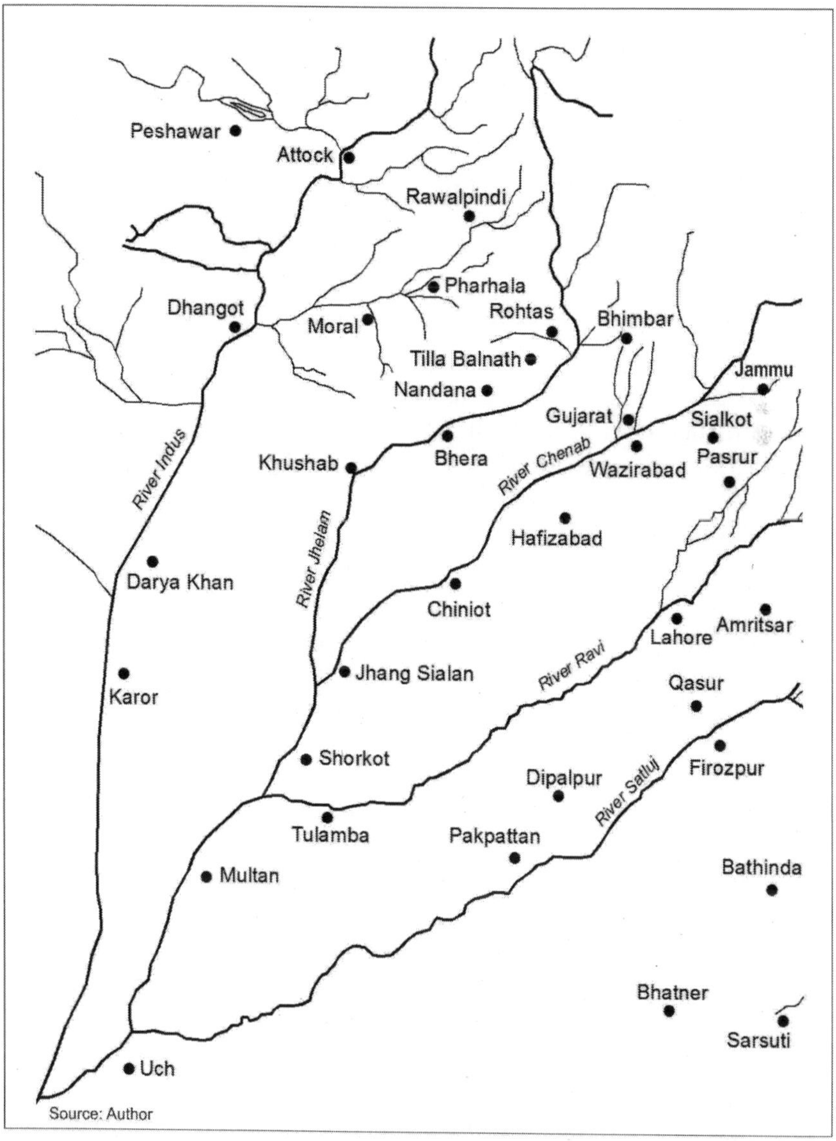

Map: Western & Central Panjab

CHAPTER 3

Translation in Prose

I, bearing the name Damodar and belonging to caste Gulati, arrived in the subdistrict of the Siyals. He deliberated in his mind to settle here. He entered the town of Chuchak, where the Siyals held the chiefship (*abdaleen*). He became happy on observing their ways. He established himself in this happy settlement (*vasti*). He met Chuchak and went up to Kundi. Chuchak gave him much assurance (*dilasa*), so that his sadness (*dilgeeri*) dissipated. Feeling comforted, he set up a shop (*hatti*) at the place. He lived among the Siyals, where happiness prevailed. With his own eyes, he saw the entire spectacle (*tamasha*), comprising lakhs of buffaloes and lakhs of cows. Since kingship was in the hands of Akbar, there was no excuse for opposition (*heel na hujjat*). Damodar asserts that four sons were born in Chuchak's house, which was imbued with immense joy. Greetings were received from many people. Chuchak, in his jubilation, distributed alms (*kharait*). A large crowd (*khalqat*) arrived at the site. The chiefship of Chuchak was praised because living was marked with prosperity. It was indeed a marvel that Kundi, in her old age, gave birth to a child. When Hir was born, O folks, no one could discern any blemish on her face. Wrapped in silk and fed on butter, she was placed in the lap of a nurse. Her face was so beautiful that every onlooker was impressed. Thus, Hir was born in the house of Chuchak. When she grew up, her feet did not touch the ground. Whoever looked at Hir, he was not able to lift his feet. On her waist, she tied a loincloth of five fibres (*panj tani*), while her torso was covered in a silken top. Damodar, on seeing the ways of Hir, resolved to construct a tale (*qissa*). He narrated what he saw with his eyes. He did not possess any virtue. A passion, arising in his mind, filled him with desire (*ummak*). From his mouth, he uttered what came into his vision (*nazr*). Everyone must hear the tale that follows.

Alliance between the Siyals and Kheras

At the outset, I must recite the name of the Lord (*sahib*), who has created this world. By detaching the earth and sky, He has forcefully lodged the moon and sun (*qamar khurshid*) in their separate orbits, so that the same shadow has been spread to every place. I, named Damodar and of caste (*zat*) Gulati, have put together this tale. Chuchak was the great master (*khawind*) of land. Which quality of his should I relate? As the lord of land and rivers (*bhuyin nai da sayin*), he competed with Akbar in his claims (*davey*). A large variety of materials – gold, silver, goods and treasure – flowed into his stores from the seven directions. The merits of his four sons, each surpassing the other, were talked about. Khan, Pathan, Sultan and Bahadur were not subservient to anyone. God, acting through a mother, conferred beauty on a new born. Look at the power of the Almighty (*qadir*). In His majesty, He played His own game, so that an order came down from the ultimate source. Let us see. The womb of Kundi sprouted in her old age. A mine of love (*khan ishq di*) was planted at Chuchkana. In the house of Chuchak, a daughter was born, leading to happiness all around. Washed clean and wrapped in silk, the baby was placed in the lap of nurses. As soon as she attained the age of two years, offers of betrothal (*kurmayian*) began arriving. When she was four, she came to speak the truth. At the age of six, she started doing meritorious deeds. At the age of eight, her fame spread to every door. At the age of ten, she brought the four rivers under her command. At the age of twelve, she attached her eyes with those of Ranjha.

Father and brothers, forming a resolution (*mata pakaya*), thought of giving Hir away in marriage. If they sent her to the land of the Pathans,[1] they would be able to extend their sway beyond the Indus. If she were offered to Akbar Ghazi,[2] they could acquire the right of assessing the land tax. They decided to stick to this resolve.

Meanwhile, the Siyals got together and, after mutual consultation (*maslat*), said to Chuchak, 'In your house, Hir has grown up. She has to be married somewhere. A daughter, being alien property (*mal paraya*), cannot be kept as such.' All the Siyals conveyed this. Chuchak replied, 'Brothers! You do not know that a letter has been received from the Kheras. The servants (*kammi*) arrived last night, but no arrangement has been made for them. No one went to inquire about them. The letter has not been read out. You cannot blame (*dosh*) me on any count.' The Siyals clarified, 'O Khan! There is no reason why we would not give away the daughter. A refusal is not proper (*munasib*). The divine plan has provided an opportunity for sealing a grand kinship (*sakka vadda*), which would be useful later on. All times are never the same for everyone, as bad times do come. Do not be casual. This moment does not brook patience (*tahambal*).'

Chuchak, withdrawing into the interior of his house, found that the resolution was acceptable. Returning to the village common (*sath*), he gave vent to his feelings. He summoned the Brahmins and, assigning the (visiting) Brahmin to them, directed them to provide hospitality (*khijmat*) to him. Similarly, the Doom was made the guest (*mijman*) of the Dooms.[3] Following the passage of eight days (*athohar*), Chuchak came to the village assembly. Meeting his clansmen, he discussed the matter of gifts for the messengers. A goldsmith was called. Receiving gold in his hands, he was asked to craft a necklace (*trag*). After offering congratulations (*vadhai*), the ornament was put around the Brahmin's neck. To each messenger was presented a set of clothes along with a horse (*jora ghora*). As soon as they received the complete attire (*siropau*), they were given a farewell. Chuchak placed the cloth of submissiveness around his neck. He asked the messengers to convey his humble message (*bahut aajazi*) to the Kheras, inviting them to come a hundred times.

The servants left the place and discussed what was in store. Having received one gift from Chuchak, they looked forward to another from the Kheras. However, if Ali managed to hear the news before their arrival, dust would be poured on their heads (*sir khak*). Their path, being inhospitable (*painda manda*), slowed their pace. The pressure of circumstances forced them to pick up speed. Ali, who was sitting in the assembly, carried worries (*fikr*) in his heart.

The servants, on meeting the Kheras, broke the news. Ali became cheerful (*khushali*) when they appeared in his view. He was imbued with happiness up to his head. While laughing, he asked for the exact message. Kheras, who were the lords of land and rivers (*bhuyin nayi de sayin*), converged on the scene. Fastenings of Ali's clothing snapped, as his body could not hold his joy. In his heart, he wished the drums to be beaten. He got the drums (*tamak*) in place. With happiness in his heart, he freely distributed the goods from his stores (*kothey*). He sent servants to invite his relatives. The Khans and their sons arrived. Sitting in council, the clansmen ate food and discussed plans for the future.[4]

Ali suggested, 'Listen. O Brothers! Let us deliberate on our choices. We cannot do with patience. We must activate our hands. We must leave for the Jhang of the Siyals in order to formulate a bright relation (*raushan saak*). There can be no laxity. Let us get ready quickly.' It came into everyone's mind to do as the Khan said. Horses – silver, grey, spotted and Arabi – were provided with tasselled strings (*gajgah*). The Arabi (*taazi*) steeds, with velvet pommels (*makhmal hanney*), broke into an energetic dance. As the Khans and princes assembled, the world came out to watch. The Khans, who were lords of the land (*bhuyin de khawind*), marched out carrying the entire baggage. They took along horses to be given as gifts, while the cash was loaded on camels. The entertainers – jesters, mimics, musicians and dancers (*bhand bhagatiye sarnai kanjariyan*) – were clad in their distinct attires. The Khans and Maliks overflowed with colours. They had summoned the beige leading horses, besides the spotted and black ones. Wooden slings (*behangi*) were placed on mules, while decorated camels completed the train. Accompanied by camels and ponies, the camp of the Khans also contained ornamented weapons. On this day, the earth could not carry its own weight.

Chuchak, on hearing the arrival of the Kheras, exercised restraint (*sanjam*). He had made available ghee, jaggery, sugar, grain and fodder. He summoned wine-bearers and balladeers (*dhadi*). Quilted coverlets and mattresses were spread in the lounge (*dalan*), which was given a plaster of clay. The lion like warriors, who were lords of the land and rivers, descended from their horses. Musical notes broke out in Indra's court (*indar akharey*),[5] as drums and pipes were played.

The mimics danced in full strength, while the dancing girls sang with gusto. Chuchak sent a chain of eatables, accompanied by new glasses and frying pans. Having eaten the food, preparations were made and the hosts escorted the *zamindars*. Meeting in the midst of affection and laughter (*muhabbat naley hass kar*), they locked their chests in warm embraces. Endowed with handsome physiques, the highly ranked sons of distinguished mothers, appeared as if the moon and sun were ensnared in the net of destiny. After inquiring their well-being (*khair*), they were warmly embraced and brought to the mansion. Reaching the hall, they dismounted, as people came out to see them. Great warriors, each surpassing the other, were lords of the land and rivers. Cups of wine flowed as the balladeers sang the tales of chivalry (*dhadi vaaran*). After the day was spent in eating, the time of night came. Following the bouts of play and laughter, the *zamindars* went to sleep. No one was sad.

Next morning, they were attired in finery from head to foot. The world came out to watch them. In the early morning, the lords raised their hands. Jesters and mimics, accompanied by beggars, leaped out into the open. Horses, along with blankets and silks, were ready to be gifted. The beggars, being pleased, sang joyful songs (*duayin mangal*) and gave blessings of safety. The guests did not intend to stay for the second night. Chuchak placed the end of his turban (*pallu*) around his neck. The clan of the hosts (*mel kutumb*) made preparations for all eventualities. Chuchak asked, 'O my relatives. Speak the truth. What should be given?' The clan, reaching common consent (*mata*), resolved to give a turban to each man and a coverlet to each beggar. A camel and an Arabian (*taazi*) horse was tied to pegs. They also decided to give a full set of gold-embroidered clothes from head to foot (*siropau sunehri*), so that they attained glory (*sobha*) in the world. As they sat in council, they ruled out any laxity in the matter. When the Khans, who were the lords of the land, sat down, there could be no grievance. The jesters and mimics danced, while scenes of mimicry were enacted. The people were delighted on seeing the dance alongside the playing of drums and pipes (*bheri te sarnayi*). The *zamindars* got up for the banquet. After eating, they got ready and asked for their apparels (*pehraye*). The Siyals were happy presenting garments to each person. Having stayed for a night, the Kheras were leaving in the morning. The world came out to watch. Chuchak, putting the end of his turban around his neck, declared, 'I have released my Arabi horses on the earth. I have earned many enmities (*vair*), forcing all my rivals to submit to me. This great Khan never lowered himself. It is only now that Hir has made me bend.'[6] Ali, holding the hand of Chuchak, replied, 'Hir is my honoured lady (*sahibiani*) and you are the lord of my head. I am exalted by what you have done. With what words can I praise you? I have sold myself to you without any price. I have no excuse (*uzar*) to offer.' Precisely at this moment, Ali clasped the hand of Chuchak. The Kheras, taking their leave, left for their home. The Siyals returned to their houses.

Both sides appeared in their best colours. Both invited the Dooms to sing at their doors. The whole world came out to offer greetings (*vadhai*), while joyful songs (*mangal*) were sung in every house. The new alliance, having satisfied the interests of everyone, filled the relatives with joyous illumination (*raushan saak savaye*). The mother of Hir, having summoned the girls, performed the ceremony of happy omens (*shagan*). Rice was boiled with buffalo milk and sugar puffs (*patasey*) were added. Kundi asked the girls to first put the dessert in Hir's mouth. Along with the first morsel, she gave a maund of gold as offering. As the Kheras returned to their mansion, they were welcomed with greetings. The mother, inviting all the lads (*naddey*), prepared a dessert of rice and milk. She gave the first morsel to her son and, offering a maund of gold to him, fulfilled her wishes.

Conflict between the Siyals and Sambhals

Hir, a girl aged 9 years and already betrothed, personified the light of spiritual excellence (*azmat ki rushnai*). One by one, she chose who ever pleased her and, thus, assembled her band (*aatan*). Who ever heard of her beauty (*surat jamal*) turned towards the group. In this manner, she collected 360 friends, who found favour with her. In a clear statement, Hir fixed (*sarishta*) the activities for every watch of the day. In the first watch (*pehle pehar*), they ate butter and bread. In the second, they chewed boiled grains (*ghunganiyan*) and rocked on the swings. In the third, they played in the moors and ate the hard melons (*rendi khakhari*). In the fourth, they bathed in the river, where the entire band converged. To this schedule of activities, Hir devoted her days. Brave as a tigress and drawn as a bow, she did not allow any fire to smoulder. Like a white tiger (*bagga shinh*) roaming in the jungle, she invariably rushed to the rescue of anyone crying (*dhrohi*) for justice. The Siyal girl shot arrows without a bow. Earlier, whenever Chuchak was present, only his name was invoked for help. Now, only Hir's name was invoked, as she had subjugated the entire land (*saari zimin nivayi*). She roamed in the jungle at the head of her retinue (*kattak*) and, acting as a chief, made the whole area tremble. There was a universal cry of approval for this daughter of Chuchak.

Noora, a Sambhal by caste,[7] got a magnificent boat (*berha ajab*) crafted for himself. Luddan, the son of a boatman (*mallah*), was summoned from afar.[8] The boat was assigned to him and a ceremonial turban (*siropau*) was tied on his head. He was happy in his heart, having won the approval of all. One day, a few *zamindars* came to see the boat. They were pleased to see it. After deliberating (*maslat*) among themselves, they asked Luddan to let them enter the vessel and examine it in detail. Luddan took them in and enabled them to gaze at the spectacle (*tamasha*). Noora, having learnt about it from someone, was filled with rage. He sent a Doom, conveying abuse (*gali*) in acute anger, to summon Luddan. Making sure that he did not run away, he was given hard blows even as no one intervened. Luddan, reduced to helplessness, became inflamed with bad temper. When he gathered his wits to reply, he stated, 'O Khan! You have failed to recall the day when you called me and held my chin. I am insulted. Hard times are on me. I have been pushed to the edge of my grave (*qabr kinare*). I am humiliated (*beizzat*) when old age has come over me and the time of my death has arrived.' Noora cried, 'O Jhinwar! Your gaze has risen to such insolence. You never asked me. Who were the ones allowed on board? You are so ignorant of the protocol (*adab*). I am so angry that I wish to kill you here and now. How can I let you go when you do not even repent?' Luddan began to reflect in his mind. Even if he had to regret, he would retaliate with his right hand. If he were destined to run away with the boat, he would do so at the first opportunity. It was better to die than to live a life of misery.

One day Luddan saw his chance. Noora had gone in some direction. At night, Luddan took the boat away and, thus, made the best use of the occasion. The traveller journeyed throughout the night and cried in the darkness, 'Is there any lord, the progeny of a noble woman (*rath sawani*), who will give shelter to me.' Hearing the cries, the *zamindars* fell silent and did not say anything. Why should anyone acquire fever and earn a fresh enmity. It was not proper (*munasib*) to provoke a clash and get one's men killed just in lieu of a boat. In view of Noora's name, no one was willing to offer passage to the fugitive. Luddan, in his mind, reflected on his condition. He had become a thief. No one had taken him in sanctuary. He wished to die by consuming poison (*mohra*). Though the utterly tired Jhinwar raised loud cries, no one offered him any protection. Sitting disconcerted (*darvar*) in the boat, he could not figure out where to go. Weary of exhaustion, he kept on screaming. Still no one came out with a remedy. He had become a thief of all *zamindars*. No one came forward to shield him. Luddan thought of leaving the boat and running away. In his bewilderment, he reached the subdistrict (*sik*) of the Siyals.[9] On the banks, he saw an enclosure as well as a commotion. Thrusting fingers into his ears, he cried like a cuckoo, 'Will someone, who is engendered by a noble lady, give me protection.'

As Luddan had run away from the Sambhals, no *zamindar* promised him safety. Hir, then present in the enclosure with her band, heard the painful cries. Having lost her calmness, she became alert (*chamkayil*). She felt that someone, in his distress (*dukhiara*), was seeking protection (*saam*) of the Siyals. Hir took the girls into her confidence. Seeing the boat from a distance, they went forward. As soon as the boat came into view, they charged at it and cried, 'O Hir! See the spectacle of what cannot be described.' Prancing like a young elephant, the entire retinue advanced. Hir asked Luddan, 'Who is crying out? Speak the truth (*haqiqat*). Have your companions died? Have you heard the death of someone back home? Are you carrying stolen cattle? Why do you scream? It is Hir who asks you. Who has forced you to flee?' The girl, in high temper, spoke with raised eyebrows. Luddan replied, 'O Girl! Listen to what I say in my lamentation. Noora, who belongs to the caste of the Sambhals, got a boat constructed. I, in my innocent childhood, was employed. No flower has ever been hurled at me. I was insulted when I became old and moved close to my grave. You are a big *zamindar*, the master of land. On seeing you, I came to you.'

Hir commanded, 'Tie your boat in our dock (*taang*). You are not short of anything. Who the devil is this Noora, the one who got the boat made? Park the boat and fix the pole. I have come to like this boat. Except I, the progeny of Chuchak (*chuchak jayi*), no one has given shelter to it.' Luddan pleaded, 'Call your brothers and uncles, both paternal and maternal. I place the yoke (*lajj*) of submission around my neck. Give me a rope and oar, so that I stay here. If the *zamindars* (Sambhals) come and, tying me, carry me away, you will lose your honour. O Hir! Inform your brothers, *zamindars* and father Chuchak.' Getting angry and raising her eyebrows, Hir exclaimed, 'Let the ancestors of Noora be cursed. Why are you so scared? I will kill them whenever they come here. No one can deter me if I hear of a raid. I will call my father and uncles only if the progeny of Akbar attacks.' Luddan said, 'My rope and honour are in your hands. You are not willing to rally anyone to your side. Do what you want. I have placed my dignity in your hands. They (Sambhals) will not rest without coming here. This is something you overlook. Take the rope of the boat. O Girl! Show your masculinity (*mardi*).' After the rope was flung and the pole anchored, the boat was tied. As this was done with their approval, the band of girls was happy. As and when they saw the boat, they laughed and bathed by its sides. Because of this, Luddan recovered his morale (*dhiraj*).

In the first watch, the girls ate bread and butter (*saag makhan roti*). In the second, they made merry on the swings and ate boiled grains. In the third, they played in the moors and ate hard melons. In the fourth, they entered the boat and, thus, made the Chenab a favourite resort. The girls, adopting these practices, spent the time of the day.[10] Whenever they heard anything good or bad (*changa manda*), they did not let any inkling out. The entire band, comprising mighty warriors (*bali bahadur*), was not subservient to anyone. Only the name of Hir was invoked for justice. A mean informer (*bakhlana*), having seen the boat, carried the tale (*markhayi*). In order to serve the thorny pangs of his stomach (*pet pajuti sool*), he informed Noor Khan in detail, saying, 'Listen, O Khan! Why have you tied the turban on your head. Your boat is in the possession of the Siyals, who have given orders for its custody.' On hearing this, the Khan fell into a rage. He called all the *zamindars*. He informed them that the Siyals had tied the boat in their dock. People who had seen it had returned with its proof. The Siyals wish to die and taste iron. They are thirsty for blood. They are getting ready to meet death and even lose their possessions. Noora made an accurate assessment of the situation. Falling into a fury and calling a Doom, he immediately sent a letter to the Siyals, writing, 'I know about the boat. Bind up Luddan and send the boat. He is our thief. Give a serious thought to this matter, failing which I am also coming.'

The Doom, carrying rancour in his heart, reached Jhang Siyal.[11] Chuchak, who was sitting in the village common (*sath*), gave blessings for his welfare. He asked, 'Where have you come from? Whither are you going?' The Doom did not utter a word from his mouth, but handed over the letter. On reading the letter, Chuchak became furious and declared, 'Since when have the sheep grown horns? How can Noora send you to us?' The Khans fell upon the Doom and delivered blows of the shoes (*chhittar*) on his face. The Doom, suffering acute pain, started crying. In fact, he was caught between the jaws at Chuchkana. The Khans pinned him down. The local Dooms displayed their power, while the victim's face was blackened and he was beaten with shoes. The tormentors threw taunts at the mother of Noora, so that the embarassed (*sharminda*) Doom fell on his face. On the third night, he returned to his master and fell into a bout of weeping, saying, 'O Khan! Look at my condition. Imagine what is passing in my head. My body is covered with blood (*ratt viratti*). This has happened to your servant. If I die, it will be great shame. Here, it is the mother who is dying.' On hearing this, Noora was outraged and began to wail. He summoned his men and asked them to make preparations without delay. Horses of different hues – black, brown, silver, grey and spotted – were saddled. In this manner 360 horses were mustered.

The Sambhals, crying 'Ali Ali' in their fury,[12] charged in great style. Just as the boat had pierced its way, the retinue (*lashkar*) covered its journey. Keen for an encounter, its intention could not be cooled. After covering a distance of six leagues (*kos*), it became thirsty for blood. The Sambhals stopped and, sitting in council, discussed their options. 'To leave the path and take to the moors. To snap the boat and drag it back. To bind Luddan in ropes and give him a severe beating. If the Siyals meet us, we will draw out our weapons.' Accordingly, they abandoned the road and went into the moors, forcing the birds to raise a clamour. Dust rose up to the sky, while the stars went out of sight. The earth was pounded in a manner that it could not bear the weight of the Sambhals. Luddan, on seeing the furious riders, turned pale. Thrusting his fingers into his ears, he raised frenzied cries, 'O Hir! That time has come. Your honour is at stake. You will meet the one who had the boat crafted and is its owner.' Luddan cried this out. The band of girls, rushing out of the enclosure, quickly moved to the moors. The rising dust masked the sky. Luddan, showing them the potential breakfast (Sambhals) for the crows, repeated that his dignity was in their hands. He wanted Hir to recognize the owner of the boat.

Hir and the girls went to their houses. They tied grey (*bhurey*) shawls around their bodies. In stealth, they secured double-edged swords (*sarvahiyan*) and picked the shields. Eager for a clash, they reached the boat in a moment. Luddan said, 'Daughter! The alien troops have come. You will not be able to stop them. At this very moment, call your brave brothers, so that they (Sambhals) cannot take the boat from you. Hirey! Pay attention to this, as I am being surrounded.' Hir responded, 'Go away from my sight, lest I should kill you first. We are keen to grapple. Why should I call my brothers? See the spectacle of the encounter. Watch how much do we attack. Girding up my waist cloth (*kachhota*), I will face the assault from the front.' Turning to her band, she exclaimed, 'O Girls! Listen. Let us agree to this plan. The alien sons (*puttar paraye*) of the Sambhals have descended. Let us face them from the front. The horses will crush our creepers, but we will strike head on.' Luddan, turning green and yellow, was ready to flee.

Hir, having mustered her army, came forward to confront the enemy. As the troops assembled from different directions, the contenders could see each other. On seeing the sight, the Sambhals, who all were valiant *zamindars*, stood astonished. Hir of the Siyals was thirsting for a clash. Noora, belonging to the caste of Sambhals, stirred his mare into action. Striking his heels inwards, the reckless Noora inquired about Hir. He drew his sword (*misri*) from its scabbard and, brandishing it, asked which one of them was Hir, who was confronting him. At this, Hir leapt ahead like a gazelle (*harni*) and stated, 'Are you blind? Have you been slashed and knocked down? You have not heard of me. I am Hir, born of Chuchak. I am ready to face you.' The two were locked in a duel. Noora, having pulled out his sword, aimed it at Hir's head. Leaping back, she defended the strike. Noora delivered a second blow, while Hir turned behind a mare. She shouted, 'Do not run away, O Jatta! Now it is my turn.' Hir, pulling out her scimitar, struck at Noora'a head. The blow was accurate and did not diverge from its target. It covered the earth with blood. Half of his body was entangled in the pommel (*hanney*) and half lay on the ground. It appeared as if a washerman had thrown a baggy trouser (*suthan*) over his cord.

Instantly, Hassi rushed forward, exclaiming, 'What calamity (*qehar*) have you committed? While you attacked, we just stood by. You did not do the right thing. Allow us to fall upon them and watch the spectacle. This is what everyone says. Hirey! If you are hurt, the entire band will be widowed (*randa*).' In reply, Hir said, 'Listen. Sister Hassi! This is not the proper way. To be a chief (*sikdar*) and still stand back. It will be a curse (*laanat*) on me. Life and death are not in anyone's hands. Whatever pleases God, it happens. Sister Hassi! I do not mean to hurt you at all.' Hassi remarked, 'Sister, you did not slight us. Watch the scene with your own eyes. To fight the alien sons is no joke. Living and dying went along with a person. Life cannot be relied (*bharvasa*) upon. A warrior is one who does not turn aside.' Hir said, 'Well done (*shabas*), Hassi. Your words are well spoken. The Sambhals came to attack us. The Lord has given us the opportunity. We are required to face the first clash. Sisters! How will you fare today? You must display such bravery that everyone praises you.' Hassi said, 'O Hir! Watch out our performance. An encounter has fallen into our share. They are men, while we belong to the caste (*zat*) of women. Whatever pleases God happens. Sisters! Stand up with determination (*hatth*), if you are bearing weapons (*loha*).'

Look friends. The girls are enacting a battle (*jang machaya*).

The (Sambhal) gentlemen stood and watched, while the girls were itching for a fight. They saw with their own eyes, as the girls stepped forward. All the girls drew their swords and turned their shields up. See the courage of the girls, who are attacking with the cries of 'Ali Ali'. The *zamindars*, with their hands on the bows, wished to clash. The ninth watch, as humid as the Arabian weather of Multan, indicated the onset of monsoon. The *zamindars*, with the plumes of their turbans fluttering like the dragonflies (*bhambiri*), filed in a line. Rearing to collide, they extended their hands to hold their weapons. The Siyals placed the shields over their heads. What a way to advance? Crawling on their chests like iguanas, they made an assault, crying 'Ali Ali'. Eager for a fight, they got together and charged. Arrayed in battle formation (*jamaati*), they were ready to die. Swords flew from all directions. Which quality can be stated? Corpses fell on the ground, while blood flowed on thighs and arms. It appeared as if the Jogins, without heads on their bodies, had come to drink blood.[13] The entire earth turned red like the lac (*alta*) dye in a wedding. The band of girls, owing to their keenness to clash from different directions, remained undeterred. They were eating iron just as someone consumed sherbet after stirring it. The warriors, crying, 'Strike strike (*maar maar*)', did not tire of fighting. Hir of the Siyals rendered twelve persons lifeless. Though eight girls lost their lives, they continued to attack. Thirsting to engage in combat, they did not think of detaching themselves from action. Saying 'Ali Ali', they pierced into the opposing ranks, giving no space for retreat.

The *zamindars* were tired, but not the girls. Leaping back, they caught the reins of horses. They fell back to a distance of two arrows and then charged from the rear. Hir commanded that no one would advance (*hora paya hukmi*). They must remain where she had positioned herself. Noora said, 'Listen, O Brothers! Let us not continue in this manner. If we are killed at the hands of the girls, it does not bring any glory to us. Let us go, leaving Luddan and the boat. It is not proper to fight any more.' Noora asked his men to pull the reins back. Hir, challenging in a loud voice, addressed Noora, 'You have come with a special purpose. Now, do not turn back. As we are eager to fight, I am going to charge.' Noora heard this, but did not act on it. The fairies (*hooran*), belonging to the Siyal clan, had appeared after splitting the sky. They consumed refined flour, wore silken clothes and fed on nuts. See the carnage of the Siyal girls, who were not afraid of dying. In accordance with the divine order, they shot arrows through their eyes and flew without wings. Noora, the *zamindar*, said, 'Listen, O Brothers! I speak for the brothers to hear. It is not proper (*munasib*) for us to fight, even as the girls are eager to do so. The Siyals are truly great warriors (*vadde bahadur*) and they are bent on clashing with us. Imagine those who had given birth to them through their wombs.' He spurred his horse and summoned his retinue. Hir also fell back and ordered, 'Cover your face with your clothes. Do not attack anyone. The bearded one has retreated. His face has lost all shame.' Saying these words, the daughter of Chuchak turned back.

The dead (Sambhals) were dragged and thrown into the river. However, the girls (who had lost their lives) were buried. For one watch, Saleti, while crying, held the girls in her embrace. Having faced the calamity, they came to the ferry, where the creepers were growing. Someone carried the sad news to Chuchak. As the Siyals kept on hearing, they also kept moving. They could not say anything. Nor could they think. Like monsoon clouds (*ghatt saavan*) collected drops of rain, the Siyal retinue (*lashkar*) kept on assembling. As numerous as the stars in the sky, they could not be contained in the moors. The brothers, all mighty warriors, were ready to fight for Hir. They said, 'Are your brothers dead? What did you do? We were not informed at all. We have learnt that the Sambhals descended here, but we did not get even a small inkling. Where have they gone? You must tell us. Speak the truth. Tell us the place where we ought to go.' Thus, the brothers initiated a discussion. Hir replied, 'Listen, Brothers, Khan and Sultan! Someone has told lies (*koor*) to you. Some hungry herdsmen (*bhukke chak*) arrived from somewhere. They laid their hands on the creepers. The girls ejected them without difficulty, so that even I did not see anyone. Whom shall I ask to tell you that Akbar had attacked me?' Having questioned all, the Siyals returned. Hir was left alone. Luddan's face retrieved its radiance. He offered his greetings (*salam*). It was good of her to push back the retinue (of the Sambhals). This brought freshness to his heart. As he abandoned his isolation (*sutak*), his heart got rid of all doubts.

In this way, Hir was born. In this way, she was betrothed. In this way, she played the game. In this way, the boat appeared. In this way, the moor figured. In this way, Hir was born and brought up. In this way, Damodar has stated all the facts (*haqiqat*). The tale is completed. Now, we compose the story of Ranjha.

Rupture in the Zamindari Household

Mojam, a big *zamindar*, was the lord of the land and rivers. A Ranjha by caste,[14] all the seven paths led to him. In his house was born Dhido, whose looks were bright (*raushan rup*). Bravo the mother of Dhido Ranjha. The world had not seen such mothers. The entire world came out to congratulate. Mojam held celebrations to welcome this light of spiritual excellence (*azmat ki rushnai*). When Dhido was 2 years old, proposals for his betrothal began arriving. When he was 4, the sun gave its glimpse. When he was 6, all came to see him. What a face and form (*surat shaql*) did he possess? Nobody could compete with destiny. Whoever saw him was gripped in his looks. Ensnared thus, he could not walk away. The brothers did not like the splendour (*tej*) of Ranjha. When Ranjha completed his sixth year, his mother died. Though the brothers became happy, their hearts were not at peace. After mutual consultation, they resolved to kill him and throw his body in the river flowing south. It was best for him to die, as they would be at ease. When Mojam discerned the unfavourable gaze, he could not rely on anyone. Throughout the eight watches, he kept him close to his chest, without trusting anyone. All this time, he kept an eye on Dhido. He treated him as a delicate rose from morning to evening. The enemies of Ranjha, acquiring a dominance (*ghalib*), desired to kill him. Tahir, Zahir and Jeevan decided among themselves (*mata keeta*) to kill the boy. The whole world comes to see him. Whom should he deny the entry? It would be difficult for them to get the chiefship (*sikdari*) if he was allowed to live. The brothers thought it proper to do away with the boy. The three resolved to act without any delay. Mojam, who managed to hear this, decided to guard (*chauki*) him. If any harm was done to his beloved boy (*lal*), he would be forced to cry till his hands were torn. Since he could not trust (*visah*) anyone, he abandoned his food and sleep. Then Mojam decided in his mind to find a match for Dhido. His mother had died. If his father also died, in whose lap would he be put? The brothers, with evil intent (*mandi niyat*), had decided to harm him. For eight watches from morning till evening, Mojam smouldered like smoke.

Yaqub Khan Waraich was a big *zamindar*. Mojam, owing to his constant anxiety, sent a Brahmin and Doom to him. Bending with humility and putting his turban end around his neck, he dictated a letter, keeping it hidden from the people. The servants got up and travelled for three days. On reaching Yaqub, they showered ample blessings (*asees*) on him. The Doom passed on the letter Mojam wrote. Not speaking from his mouth, the Doom just handed it over. After reading the letter, the Khan began to reflect. He did not say anything. He read the entire content of the letter, which was put into his pocket. Still reflecting in his heart, he went out and entered again. He summoned his clan (*qabila*) and got the letter read.[15] After it had been read, Yaqub said, 'Listen, my clan. All of you must sit and choose. These servants have come from Hazara. If kinship (*saak*) is to be made with Mojam, the servants must be treated with respect. Brothers, say what is in your minds. State the matter that is in your heart.' The entire clan spoke in one voice, 'Khan, you are our lord. If you do not know, then we will say something. If the messengers (*pacharu*) have come for Dhido, it is our good fortune (*bakht*). Mojam is demanding one daughter. If he says so, we would all give our daughters.' The servants, who were treated with dignity, were accommodated in the house. They were given red bedsteads (*ratta palangh*) to sit. They were hosted for eight days. Yaqub, after consulting his clansmen, got gold necklaces (*trag*) crafted. The ornaments were put around the servants, who were permitted to depart. Bidden farewell, they walked on their way.

When the servants entered Hazara, Mojam saw them. Hearing them, Mojam felt immensely content (*bahut razi*). Drums were installed. Goods were freely distributed from the stores for the benefit of the clan (*jamiat lashkar*). Tahir and Zahir, averse to the proceedings, became even more inclined to kill Dhido. If Mojam died and Dhido lived, they would surely loose the chiefship. Since they could not afford to lose the inheritance, they thought day and night of the strike. When Dhido mounted the horse, the birds stopped moving. The birds and rabbits remained still, because their feet were rendered motionless. If a man or woman saw him, they could not bat their eyelids. Big *zamindars* came to see Dhido. Mojam made up his mind to get him married. He would establish kinship with a big *zamindar* by putting Dhido in his lap. He was an old man (*zaeef*) inching towards his grave, whereas Dhido was faced with numerous evils (*bahut balayin*). An enmity within the house was like a spark in the cloak. It did not permit any laxity. Mojam exerted (*traddad*) himself to make arrangements (*uddam*) for the marriage and, for this purpose, agreed to hold the ceremonies, but with a difference. Making of a union was possible only at that particular moment. What will happen later on? Nothing could be said. In view of his anxiety about the onerous task, he assumed a complete silence. Mojam called a Doom and drafted a letter for the Waraichs. He asked for the knotted strings (*gandhin*) without any tardiness. He wished to see happiness while he was alive and, for this, Dhido had to be married. The Doom was sent along with the Brahmin.

Reading the letter, Yaqub gave assurances (*dilasa*) and made arrangements. He persuaded the servants to be patient and stay for the night. He gave the knotted strings and, sending his own servants as escorts, allowed the messengers to depart. He took all the measures and placed the drum. All the people came to know that Mojam had initiated a big event (*kaj rachaya*). In order to marry off Dhido, he was organizing the things on a grand scale (*vadda vistar*). On hearing this, every one became happy. The development appealed to everyone. Look at Mojam. He was giving shape to an elaborate celebration. Meanwhile, among the Waraichs, the *zamindars* sat to make choices. They said, 'O Brother! How this is to be done? Assign work to us. Do not hesitate. Laxity will not do.' The Waraich (Yaqub Khan), while playing a big game (*vaddi bazi*), made suitable provisions. As he enumerated the tasks, the entire humanity turned up. He sent formal invitations to his brothers and relatives. While collecting the material – ghee, jaggery, sugar, flour and grains – his mind lost its equanimity. Since the headache turned out to be as big as the head, the arrangement was equally extensive. He also sent a string of sixteen knots to the Ranjhas.

Mojam, in his mind, felt pleased. He arranged for provisions.

Sending servants to his relatives, he conveyed the essence of affairs. A drum was placed, while trumpets and pipes were played. Mojam was anxious to know the day when Dhido would be married. Here and there, the preparations were afoot. Dhido was placed in ceremonial seclusion (*mayian*). Mojam applied perfumed pastes and henna (*chiku vatna mehandi*) on Dhido. Mojam acted as both father and mother. Even this, the brothers found amiss. Since their intention (*niyat*) was bad, they had decided to kill Dhido. The boy was 10 years old. Which quality of his could be explained? A ring in the nose and danglers in ears, he had a golden bangle on his wrist. His long hair, with curled tresses (*zulf kundal*), appeared like little serpents.[16] Anyone who saw him failed to get up. All sisters-in-law, being in love with him, did not eat without looking at him. As they rubbed perfumed paste on him, they kept on emitting sighs. His face was like the moon, while his eyes burnt like flaming torches (*munh mehtab akhin balan masalan*). Which attribute of his could be described? How could such a son, produced by a mother, be praised?

When seven knots remained, the day refused to turn. The divine will, being inexorable, could not be averted. Mojam died. His grains were exhausted and his chapter was closed. The untainted (*nichhakka*) Dhido remained there as such. At this very moment, the brothers stopped the ceremonies of the marriage. In accordance with divine orders, the plunderers (*ghaniman*) had a field day. They took away the valuables, silks, carpets and whatever appealed to them. The state of Dhido was like the handle in the axe's mouth (*katth kuhare*). The brothers, after deliberations, formed a plan. They all agreed on separating Dhido. Their intention was bad and the decision dubious. God's will could not be averted. Whatever is in Dhido's lot will happen. The three sat weighing their options on the manner of killing Dhido. They could murder him in sleep, give him poison, choke his breath or slash his body and throw it in the river. In this way, they hoped to get rid of their anger. To begin with, they would separate him in the right earnest, so that no sin (*badi*) attached to them. Divide the property and goods (*milkh maal*) inside, besides the property lying in the seven directions. Then divide the garments and loincloths, so that no clue is left for inquiry. If he were subjected to this fate, they would not be sunk in sin. The brothers called Dhido, so that the shares were allocated. 'We would make four shares of the estate (*tarka*) belonging to our father and grandfather. The property, both inside and outside, must be demarcated (*farq o farq*). Owing to deceit ingrained in the hearts (*dil dagha*) of the brothers, Dhido's skin would be pulled out.

Dhido protested, 'Listen, Tahir. You are in the place of our father. I know nothing. I am a suckling child (*dudh vata*). My honour is in your hands. My fate is sealed. Inside you have one thing, but outside you give assurances. Your intention is not good.' Once Dhido understood the matter, his face turned pale. The brothers advised, 'O Youngman! Remove Mojam from your mind. Earn your livelihood like a Jat. To kill the weeds in your land, pick up the spade and hoe (*kahi vahola*). Dhido, come with us, so that we focus on work.' Raising the level of their stance (*uch madar*), the brothers implemented the policy of Chanakya.[17] Dhido argued, 'Brothers! Land is yours. Water is yours. You may take everything by division and subdivision. My hands are red (with henna) and so are my feet. How can I wield the spade. As Mojam died, all kindness (*muhabba*) disappeared. The Chenab is no longer my abode. Fate does not let me stay, while the tax collector (*muhassil*) is chasing me.'

From the north (*ubhi tarfon*), some travellers came to Jhang Siyal. They sat with us and initiated a discussion. Mojam was blessed with a son, who is the light of spiritual excellence. Hearing the praise of Dhido, our consciousness (*surt*) was elevated. Damodar, leaving the Jhang of the Siyals, went towards the north. After covering three stages, he arrived at Takht Hazara. He saw the village where Ranjha was born. On seeing Dhido, his heart was ensnared. Ranjha, with sadness (*udasi*) ingrained in his heart, could not stabilize himself. People of Hazara indulged in rumours (*chocho*), depressing Ranjha even further. See the action of fate. How God took away his bread and water (*dana pani*)? Damodar wished to walk with Ranjha. In every street, people sat together and discussed the matter. After the death of Mojam, Dhido was left without any support. First, he was separated and, then, forced to leave. In every lane, this is what was heard. Damodar, having joined his finger with Dhido, began to wander. After hearing so much from the people, we could not eat any food. Everywhere there was unseen land (*andithi bhuhin*). They wished to know where to go. However, Damodar's heart decided to travel south (*lammi tarf*). Ranjha, wearing fine clothes, showed a good face. With bangles in hands and danglers in ears, he wore a blue waistcloth. He wrapped around him a shawl of high quality (*uchi ambree*). People, seeing his youth (*jawani*), sank in sorrow. In Hazara, young girls and old women did not like whatever had happened.

Following the demise of Mojam, the wedding was stopped. This did not remain concealed. People, being fearful, did not say so. It was a great wonder. Whatever the True God ordained, only that happened. Inside every house, people complained (*gila*) against Tahir and Zahir. Just see. Only yesterday, Mojam died and today they decide to kill Dhido. In every house, it was said that Tahir had stopped the wedding (*kaaj rahaya*). From the peculiar ways (*lokachari*) of the people, Dhido managed to learn of the conspiracy. According to the voices emerging from Hazara, Dhido would surely be killed. The brothers, often huddled together (*maslat*), made only this resolution. Hearing constantly of the murderous plan, Dhido turned pale. He decided to run away with his life, as he did not want to die. Leaving his brothers, Ranjha came out of the house. A staff and flute in his hands, his heart was inclined to leave. Wearing a red turban and wrapping a shawl, he wore a blue waistcloth. A ring in the nose and danglers in his ears, his long curls emitted a murmurring sound. When Dhido left at midnight, he did not have any expenses (*kharch*) on him. Owing to the fear about life, he could not stay even if he wanted. Night and day, Dhido walked without putting his foot on the earth. Holding a staff (*khundi*) and flute (*vanjhali*) in his hand, he reached a mosque at night. Dhido settled in it for the night. As the girls went to fetch water, the Creator played a game. The daughter of Sardara sold herself on seeing Dhido. Precisely at this moment, a group of Jats (*jamaat jattan di*) appeared. The face of Dhido turned pale. They had come here too. His brothers might have sent spies to kill him. All of them sat together in the mosque and spoke to Dhido. They wanted to know where he was bound for. Dhido replied, 'Uncle! The fate is food and water. God had ordained this game. With the death of Mojam, all kindness was gone. The brothers conspired to kill me. For fear of life, I became a wayfarer (*rahi*).' Dhido explained that nothing was in his hands, as fate had forced him to walk away.

The girl, who was smitten, returned home with pain (*sool*) in her. She said, 'O Mother. Take this pitcher from my head, failing which I will throw it on the ground. A moon had ensnared me in the mosque. Will you not give me the bridegroom I have found? Otherwise, just place your hand on my head, so that I run away free.' The mother delivered a sharp slap on her daughter's face, saying, 'A young virgin (*kanj kuari*) should not speak thus. Why have you thrown away your honour? Just now, if your father and brother hear this, they will surely punish you. Born of my womb, you will not speak again. Your mother does not like it.' The daughter replied, 'If I discarded the veil from my face, this will be heard by one and then by one lakh. I am sold out without a price (*mul baghair*). This I have wailed for you to hear. As you deem proper, give him to me. It is through sheer luck that he has come into my hands. Otherwise, I will run away on my own, having abandoned all shame.' The mother asserted, 'Be patient. Let me go there. You have seen a mere slave (*gandh ghulam*). Let us find out. From which place the stranger (*pardesi*) has come? That is, the one who has ignited a passion in you. Listen, O Daughter. Let me go to the spot. I will ask for the information.' In this way, the matter of the girl proceeded further.

The girl was not lying. She was truthful in what she stated. He (Dhido) did not look like being born of a mother and father. How can a tongue praise him? The Jhinwar woman, who was sold out, could not move a step. If he were a bit older (*chukh vadera*), she would have tied him in marriage (*nikah*). Having lost her senses, she rushed to the Jats and spoke to them, 'Tell me. How is he related to you? Which one is your caste? To which caste the boy belongs? Where are you going? Brothers, speak the truth (*haqiqat*). I want to know this.' They replied, 'We are Jhinwars. This is our caste. We have come from the city (*garh*) of Multan and are going towards the boats of the Jhelum, as we wish to make money.'[18] The Jats, with deceit (*dagha*) in their hearts and tormented by hunger, resorted to such lies. The woman said, 'I give my daughter to your son. Brothers, we will be satisfied (*razi*). The knot will be tied tonight.' This decision was in the interest of the Jats. The Jhinwar woman was inclined to make them happy. On hearing this, the Jats were pleased. They pleaded, 'Bring sweetened bread and buffalo milk for us. We accept your daughter, so that now we are related (*sakke*) to each other. First you feed us and the task will be performed at night.' The arrangement suited both the sides.

Having said this, the woman returned to her house. Calling for sugar and ghee, she boiled vermicelli (*sewiyan*). She also picked up a pitcher of buttermilk, a smoking pipe and tobacco.[19] She deposited these items in the mosque. Placing her virgin daughter (*kanj kuari*) in seclusion, she applied perfumed paste and henna on her. The Jats said, 'Dhido. Come and share this food with us. It is due to our good fortune. Close the door. We told lies for the sake of our stomach. After eating, we will immediately leave. The Lord has granted this sweet morsel (*nivala mittha*), which is included in our good fortune (*naseeb*). Our path is difficult. We will cover it in small patches.' Dhido protested, 'I do not intend to go in for this marriage. What are you saying? It is better to go hungry than enjoying this hearty feast. I do not like this at all. You have grabbed the right of another (*haq paraya*) by telling lies. You have no fear of God. Hear me, uncle. I will not touch what is unlawful (*haram*).' At midnight, the Jats decided to march out. At the appointed hour, they ran away, so that no one knew anything about it. Dhido, with hunger embedded in his body, also left the place. The traveller embarked on a journey from the north to south.

Dhido, still in fear of life, kept on walking in silence. As he had come, so did he leave. This is what he did. He did not ask for food. He did not enjoy any allowance (*wazife*). He did not pour any buttermilk to drink. Let the fisher woman (*machhani*) take charge of her house. She will be wise to go to the mosque and see for herself. Let her pray for him, as he goes to meet his beloved in accordance with destiny. Leaving the path, he entered the wilderness (*aujhar*), so that no one pursued him. It was difficult to face the pangs of hunger and thirst. While going ahead, he started weeping. On the edge of his vision, he saw a habitation from a distance. Dhido was inclined to stay there, provided it pleased the Almighty. Forced by the demand of his stomach, he entered the habitation (*basti*). He hoped to put a morsel in his mouth. Seeing a housewife (*suani*), he requested, 'Give me a grass mat. I fell from above and lay prostrate on earth. I have nowhere to go. Dogs and recluses (*darvesh*) are not respected anywhere.' She replied, 'You may sit on the top of my eyes. I am your offering in four pieces. Without good fortune, guests do not descend. They bestow grace on us. For you, I am spreading a white mattress on a red bedstead (*ratta palangh*).' As it came into her mind, she took out flour for baking. The woman engaged herself in feeding Ranjha. When the master of the house arrived, he exclaimed, 'Without good fortune, the guests do not descend. They bestow grace on us.' Since this also was in the woman's heart, she took out flour for baking. Both extended a warm welcome. Dhido felt comforted. Sitting on the bedstead, he consumed butter, flour and buffalo milk. They served (*khijmat*) him in a proper way. He ate and drank to his satisfaction. They made him sleep on the red bedstead.

When Dhido woke from a sound sleep, the gentle hosts made inquiries. 'What is your caste? Which one is your clan? Which father had given birth to you? Without a dispute, the native place (*vatn*) cannot be abandoned. You have come in hard times. Tell us the reality of things (*kul haqiqat*). We have asked a question.' Dhido replied, 'If I had any antecedents or legacy, I would have told you so. There is no source or abode that are mine. I am from no place. I fell from above and lay prostrate on earth. I do not have any lord. I cannot speak of any mother or father. They have not been seen or heard anywhere.' The Khan said, 'If you are alienated from your home, you must say so. I will provide you with a camel, mare, mule, buffalo and cow. I will provide wells besides silting land (*sailabe banne*). I will give you all means of cultivation. If I have a sister or niece, I will tie you in matrimony.'[20] Dhido laughingly replied, 'You have imparted plenty of strength to me. You have given me honour. As for me, I have no abode. With your heart and life, you have done good to me. Blessings (*rehmat*) be on you, brother. Once I return from the pilgrimage (*ziyarat*) to the saints, I will settle in this place.'

As he had decided in his heart to leave, Dhido got up and, bidding farewell (*videya*), walked away. His destination was far away and his path was longer. He did not take any companion with him. That he arrived at the subdistrict of the Siyals (*sik siyali*) became a reality. He stopped at a riverbank, besides which the Chenab flowed.

The helpless one (*vichare*), as his heart so wished, sat on the bank. While reflecting, he took out his flute to play. A boat came within his sight. He was playing the Rag Bambiha. Panjpir,[21] sitting in the boat, felt much pleased on hearing the melody and felt like going towards the bank. As they focused their eyes, they saw the bank and brought the boat to it. Ranjha was amazed (*darvar*) at what he saw. The boat docked on the bank and Panjpir stepped out. A meeting (*majlis*) took place in which the five saints sat with Dhido. They took the complete details (*kul haqiqat*) of the story, which Dhido narrated. To their questions, Dhido gave answers. Panjpir felt satisfied. Ranjha played Rag Lalit on his flute, which the saints found pleasing.[22] With divine favour, each saint conferred a boon on him. They tied Hir to the lappet of Ranjha. Panjpir appeared to Hir in a dream and spoke to her. Twisting her ear and awakening her consciousness, they revealed, 'Always remember not to accept anyone else. This has come into the will of God. Listen, O Girl, what we state. We have tied Dhido to your lappet.' Making the matter complete and firm (*muhakam gal sampuran*), they offered milk to her. Instantly, Ranjha attained enlightenment (*rushnai*). Everything became visible to him. Ranjha, having sold himself, acquired his ideal (*var*) from the saints. As they departed, Ranjha saw them.

Development of Love

Dhido, having spent the night, woke up in the afternoon and decided to move towards the boat. He was in such a state that he walked like an intoxicated elephant. His complexion had become as ruddy as the cloth dyed in red colour. In this new state, he entered the boat. He saw Luddan standing in front of him. The Jhinwar was sold out on seeing Dhido, who instilled devotion in the onlooker. He exclaimed, 'O blessed son! Give the message. From where have you come? Where are you going?' Luddan asked these questions. Ranjha replied, 'Fate does not move backwards every day, taking us along with it. I am a wanderer (*sailani*), who is out to see. I do not have any relative to show. My only companions are a staff and flute (*khundi vanjhali*), which enables me to release the flow of music.' In this manner, Dhido met Luddan. Luddan did not implore much, so that Dhido readily agreed to play on the flute. A number of wild animals like tigers and leopards came to see the spectacle. Pythons and cobras, who could devour a bodily creature, were eager to see. Luddan, intoxicated without wine, emitted froth from his mouth. He wished to keep Ranjha with him. Luddan said, 'O blessed son (*barkhurdara*)! Say what I may give you. I will give you cattle, a buffalo and two women. First and last, these have come into your lot. I circumambulate (*ghol ghumai*) all these as an offering on you.' Dhido replied, 'It is better dying than begging. How can I beg? Buffaloes and cows are welcome to you. I have nothing to do with them. I am entirely pleased with you. I ask for nothing else. If you agree, uncle, I may lie on the bedstead (*palangh*) for a while.'

On hearing this, Luddan fell into silence and did not utter a word from his mouth. Ranjha kept waiting and looking. Speaking to himself, he said, 'Did I receive what I asked for? He (Luddan) does not speak. Nor utters anything from his mouth. He has not given any reply.' Having waited for long, Ranjha became angry and flared up, 'The world is false. Its people are false. It makes false promises. I am not inclined to beg. But, you are forcing me to do so. When I did ask, you are choked and give no reply. You do not let me sleep on the bed. How can you give me women and buffaloes?' Luddan explained, 'The daughter of Chuchak and sister of Pathana does what she pleases. When she sees you, she will kill you. Then you will know her. She has brought all the four rivers under her authority. Drawn like a bow, she moves about, ready for hunting. She does not fear Akbar at all. She has rendered the Mughals powerless.'

Ranjha said, 'I am not expecting any gain from anyone. Nor have I acquired any official document (*khat*). I have no claims on anyone. Nor have I ploughed an edge of the field. I am the master of the mat and fire. What do I care for the bedstead.' Speaking in this manner, he put on his shoes and left. A moment later, Luddan rushed after Dhido and picked him up in his lap. He said, 'I will be of use to Ranjha and, if I die, I will be a sacrifice for him. In my old age, I would have died if he had walked away.' Luddan brought him back to sleep on the bedstead. As the swing rose up, Hir saw a man sleeping on the bedstead. She leapt into the river, not caring to pick a float or raft. The band of girls (*aatan*) stood astonished, wondering at what has come into her mind. She fell from the sky like lightning and released from bondage like a gazelle. The girls prayed to the saints (*pirs*) to ensure that God might bring her safe to the shore. Still standing confounded, they could not understand what they saw. For any gain or loss, only she is responsible. One who is bound will not be released.

At this moment, the girls plunged into the river, where the waves bore them. Sometimes they submerged in water and sometimes their heads emerged, as all were expert swimmers (*taru*). When rendered helpless (*aajiz*) by the river, they appeared to sink. Crossing the river, they swam to the shore and landed an arrow shot from the ferry. At Hir's command, the girls broke and held some flexible branches. Taking vigorous strides, Hir advanced with measured steps. Twisting her hand, she wiped the sweat, which had appeared due to her anger. When will she attain her object of reaching the boat? From a distance, Luddan saw the arrival of the divine horde (*kattak rabbana*). As soon as Hir became visible, the Jhinwar turned pale. His tongue failed to respond. He could not figure what to say. He felt that his death was approaching. Hir, calling Luddan to her presence, asked, 'Listen, O Luddan. Do you wish to die? Have you come close to your grave (*qabr kinare*)? Is he a bigger *zamindar* (*ratth vadhera*) than me?' A terrified Luddan replied, 'He is a saint, who is equal to the expectations of his master (*ehu wali khasam da poora*). His words do not offend. He requested for sleeping on your bed. How could I refuse him? Had I refused out of your fear, something might have happened to you.' Luddan gave this explanation to Hir. She exclaimed, 'Luddan, with dead brothers, thinks it wise to build up a saint and then put him to bed.' The girls, falling upon Luddan without any break, delivered so many blows on him that he became half dead. Though his body was covered with blood, the desire (*arman*) of the girls was not satisfied. Ultimately, they pushed him into the river.

Hir commanded the girls to hit the person sleeping on the bed. He had been posing as a distinctive mark of the Siyals. As blows of the stick did not reach his body, their urge to punish dissipated. Hearing the commotion, Ranjha bared his face to show his moon-like forehead (*chanan vanna matha*). The girls were entrapped like the fish writhing without water. Ranjha leapt out of the boat and, landing on the bank, screamed. At the same moment, Hir jumped out and held his arm. All the girls also jumped out. Ranjha, on seeing the retinue, felt scared. As soon as he lifted his mantle, the girls were much pleased. Once Dhido skipped off the bedstead, the daughter of Chuchak went after him. She asked what he held in his armpit. Ranjha showed his flute and conch. Hir urged him to play just once on the flute. Ranjha adjusted the flute in his hands. What notes did he produce? A whistling sound emerged from the reeds, bushes and acacia. Wild beasts like tigers and leopards came for pilgrimage. They appeared to offer prostrations (*sajdey*) on the Id.[23]

Luddan saw that the band of girls was facing what he had gone through. From a distance, he shouted to Ranjha, 'Release the band from your hands. If you play another melody, how can we live? Put down the flute from your hand, lest anyone should die.'[24] Luddan located Hir in the battlefield and began to knead her limb. When she woke up, she declared, 'Uncle, I am your offering. I needed one like him. The one you brought to meet me. At this moment, I am giving two buffaloes to you. Sisters, let someone bring him here.' Luddan replied, 'If he was worthy (*laiq*) of your door, that is why I allowed him to sleep on the bedstead. I was tired of pleading (*minnat*) with him, but he would not be persuaded. You made it truly happen, though you did not see and left me half-dead. Listen, daughter Hir. A tight rope has shackled me.' Hir admitted, 'I am full of faults (*pur taqsir*) and devoid of virtues. You are the honour of this guilty one. If a son spoils something, the father does not disown him. With my scarf (*pallu*) around my neck and hands on my feet, I fall at your feet.' Luddan, while laughing, stopped her and made her stand up. Hir held Dhido and brought him to the bank along with her 360 friends. The Lord made this game. All of them – the band of girls, Dhido and Chuchak's daughter – sat on the bank. Their state was such that nobody spoke to anyone.

Hir of the Siyals cast secret glances. She drew lines on the ground. However, she did not say a word from her mouth. Within her interior, she was experiencing something. In her heart, numerous worries had settled. If the Creator is true, then the saints had bestowed Dhido in her lappet. Ranjha too felt something in his interior, but did not say anything. Looking downwards and focusing on the ground, he kept on digging the earth. Such was his state that he could not utter a word from his mouth. Guessing (*qiyas*) in his mind and reflecting in a truthful manner, he understood that the saints had tied Hir to his lappet. Then, a Siyal girl said, 'We must state our preference. Can any reliance (*visah*) be placed on breath? We must give up any negligence. It is not proper (*munasib*) for us to adopt patience (*tahamal*). Say, O Hir. If the matter materializes, one of us can bond with him.' The second girl stated her concern, 'How did you construct the issue. There is no honour in stating thus. At stake is the shame of all *zamindars* (*ratthaiyan*). Listen, O girl. Do not speak again. You have not put the things in a rational way. All of you are betrothed. Only I remain a maid (*kuwari*).' Viro, the daughter of a Doom, spoke with force. She said, 'You, the daughters of *zamindars* (*sau zadiyan*) have lost your honour. You cannot see the reality. He is a servant who carries weight (*gandh gahir ghulam*). None of you understands him. He does not match any one of you, the daughters of *zamindars*. Only I, a girl from the menial stock (*kamiani*), am an exception.'

Hir started crying, but did not say a word from her mouth. Her pain did not stop even while she sobbed. As her eyes flowed and weeping continued, she could not share her affliction with anyone. Only Hassi questioned her many times. She asked, 'For whom do you cry? Give us an answer. Girl! Should I have him beaten and expelled from here if he does not please you? How can we discern your sorrow (*vedan*) if you do not relate it? Without your speaking, your pain cannot be known.' Hir replied, 'Listen, O Hassi. What can I explain? No one can know my suffering? What can I say about it? It is a difficult story (*aukhi ehu kahani*). Inside me, there is deep agony. I cannot reveal it through speech. I swear by my father, I repent having met him. In this way, I regret meeting him. Only if I could bring back the days past, I could exercise my choice for a lover. What is going on in my interior must be expressed without speaking. I regret the days spent without Ranjha. I have extracted my heart for you. Be careful. Do not expose it to anyone. On his steps, place your steps, but without matching an eyelid with an eyelid. Right at this spot, I will die if he is made to leave. Let no one be alarmed. I place my life on your eyes.' Hassi promised, 'I will not blink an eyelid. I state this for you to listen. I will place my steps on his steps. I do not trust anyone. We will ourselves lead him to the path. If we see father and brothers, we will escape from behind.'

Hir made all the girls stand up and commanded, 'Get up and go to the swings. No one should sit here.' Hir was left alone. She made Hassi sit at a distance. She held Ranjha and brought him to the bedstead. Hir announced, 'Let no one call me Hir. Nor refer to me as Saleti (daughter of the Siyals). I have no caste nor am I linked to any lineage. I am dyed in the colour of the herdsman (*chake nal chaketi*). When was Chuchak my father and mother? When was I their daughter? I am tied to your lappet, if you accept this Jat girl.' While she spoke in this manner, her pride was broken. She became the dust of the earth without a bit of conceit. She had a scarf around her neck and hands on her feet, but love had aroused her intelligence. Just as the saints dyed Ranjha in red, Ranjha dyed Hir in the same colour.[25] Hir instructed Ranjha, 'Where there are trees – banyan, fig and *siris* – there is the ancestral meeting place (*sath babbani*). Walk slowly and speak sweetly. First, ask for water. Cover your face with the lappet of your turban. You should not speak much.'

Imparting this advice, Hir went ahead. She spoke to her mother, 'Mother, I have found a herdsman. Getting up every day, he will graze the buffaloes. Owing to his grace (*barkat*), the grass will not dry up. The buffaloes will not drop their calves. They will never be afflicted with foot and mouth disease (*rora*). Monsoon will bring plenty of showers (*savan vasan fuharey*). I have discovered such a herdsman. Now, it is up to your lot (*bakht*).' Ranjha came to Jhang Siyal and met Chuchak. The Khan was sitting in the village council (*sath*). Ranjha came and bowed his neck. All the Siyals asked, 'Brother! Where have you come from?' Ranjha, while bending, remained silent. They questioned again, 'O wayfarer! Give us the information. From which town have you come?' Ranjha replied, 'If you bear with me, I am going to give all news (*sandesa*). Hungry of stomach and rendered helpless by thirst, I have moved from one place to the other.' Chuchak called Hir and asked her to bring water. She stated, 'Father, milk remains unattended and butter uncovered. No one is with me. Many cats and dogs roam around. I cannot come. There are plenty of leftovers and sweet bread. There is no servant here. If anyone comes from outside, you may send him in.' Inside, Hir prepared sweetened breadcrumbs (*choori*), mixing sugar from above. She laid out the red bedstead and spread a white mattress on it. She placed ghee and sweetened bread, pouring cream on it. Ranjha was fed, while she stood with a fan in her hand. Placing one cotton roll above the other, Saleti performed a number of omens (*shagan*). With the shawl around her neck, she poured drops of buttermilk on her palm. 'As an iron nail fixed a hoe, I am your subject (*raiyyat*). Ranjhan, my shame is in your hands. I am your offering (*sadqeh*).'

Ranjha, getting up from the side of Hir, went to Chuchak, who asked, 'Where have you come from?' Ranjha replied, 'Without a dispute (*kajiya*), the native place (*vatn*) is not given up. My brothers gave me much pain.' Chuchak asked as to whose son he is. Ranjha stated, 'Takht Hazara of the Ranjhas. I have walked from there. Caste Ranjha, name Dhido and son of Mojam. After the death of Mojam, all the attachment (*muhaba*) was lifted. My brothers hurt me a lot. They formed a plan to kill me. I travelled all the way to you.' Chuchak offered, 'You did the right thing in coming to me. I will keep you on my eyes. I will give you camels, horses, buffaloes and cows. I will give you wells on riverine land (*sailabe banne*). I will give you ploughing as an occupation. You will sow yourself and reap yourself. I will not let the rulers (*hakim*) see you.' Ranjha responded, 'Gold, money, goods and treasure reach you from seven directions. You are able enough to give everything. Your actions never face any obstacle. Whatever I ask, you will give me. I have truly understood this. If you agree to take me, I will graze the buffaloes.' On hearing this, Chuchak fell silent, thinking, 'He is some incompetent (*nalaik*) person. Agriculture (*zamindari*) does not appeal to him. He approves the work of a herdsman. I am giving him a mare and a pair of camels. He does not accept these at all.' Chuchak, hearing the reply, began to worry in his heart. The Khan said, 'Listen, Miyan Ranjha. I give you some advice. I will give you a mare, a pair of camels and a full set of clothes (*siropau*). The work of a herdsman, grazing buffaloes and cows, is not good. I will send my son with you, so that you are escorted with dignity.' Ranjha insisted, 'I came with the hope of getting shelter (*saamein*) from you. I will not go back home. The streets and straws are my enemies. It is not proper to return.

Countless people eat from you. They do not face any shortage. Have no fears. Give me a staff (*khundi*) for grazing buffaloes.'

In order to deliberate, Chuchak called his clansmen and announced, 'The son of Mojam, having left Hazara, came looking at us. I was giving him a mare and a pair of camels. He does not agree at all. Speak, brothers. What should be done, except giving him buffaloes to graze.' They observed, 'You called us to this corner. You wanted to have a consultation (*maslat*). These days, we thought, you are going to conquer a town. Your beard has turned grey in the sun. You are handing the cattle over to a suckling baby. In your senselessness (*masti*), you are deliberately wasting the buffaloes.' Chuchak said, 'Brothers, I am tired of making excessive entreaties (*minnat bahuteri*). He does not come into my hands at all. He insists on grazing buffaloes. He does not favour anything else. Do not mistake him by looking at his face. He finds the work of a herdsman as suitable.' The clansmen agreed, 'Whatever he asks, we will do. Whatever happens, we will face. There are eighty-four herdsmen serving (*khijmat*) in your domain. Wherever there is a marsh in a pond, they dry it. Wherever a crack appears in an embankment, they fill it up. In this manner, any stigma (*kalank*) on their name is erased.' Turning to Ranjha, Chuchak said, 'We will give you the cattle. We will give you sweet food in the morning and evening (*mitha tukkar sanjh sabahin*). Compensating you in this manner, we make a vow. On the Thursday (*jummerat*), you will go with the buffaloes.' This is what Chuchak said to Ranjha.

The clansmen approved the decision, as the Khan framed it. Boiled milk and sweet bread of refined flour was brought. Chuchak invited Dhido and all the clansmen to take a morsel (*nivala*). As they sat to eat, Dhido showed his miraculous power (*azmat chak vikhai*). He quietly ate the first morsel. Then, becoming enraged, he shouted, 'O Khan! It is the cruellest of all cruelties. With no fear of the Lord, you did this to a destitute (*gharib*). It is very wicked of you. You have fed me the milk of a miscarried buffalo (*tarui*), which had dropped its calf.' On hearing this, the Khan was amazed. Look at his statement. Is he a spiritual master or a true saint? Did he state something acquired from the unseen world (*ghaib*)? Did he find this in a dream? Chuchak put Dhido to another test. He asked, 'Dhido.

How did you know that it was a miscarried buffalo? We are surprised on hearing this. Did you learn this in a dream? Did you perform a miracle? Did anyone reveal it to you? We have spent a lifetime among the buffaloes. We did not attain this ability (*atkal*). Tell us the way you discerned it.' The Khan made this query. Ranjha explained, 'The buffalo was in its third pregnancy. Its colour was reddish. Its forehead did not have any white mark. It dropped a female calf of six months. The herdsman had gone somewhere. It swallowed the placenta (*jer*) and suffered in the moors, while its master was absent. Since then, it was not mated anywhere. You made me drink her milk.' The Siyals felt that Ranjha was either a spiritual guide (*pir*) or a true saint (*wali sachava*) or a light of spiritual excellence (*azmat ki rushnai*). Without speaking and spoken to, he revealed his skill. All (Siyals) were satisfied. All became favourable towards him. They were confident that only he could graze the buffaloes. All the *zamindars* felt assured of everything. Everyone was in his favour. Hearing this, Chuchak celebrated (*shadi*) the occasion. He got the drum (*tamak dhol*) installed, saying, 'Listen, friends. Listen, brothers. I have acquired a unique herdsman (*chak navela*).' On hearing the drum, the world leapt out.

When Ranjha was seen anywhere, the entire world felt sorry. This *zamindar*, looking like the moon (*mehtab*), was entangled in some problem. The girls said that if he could be theirs, they would protect him with a shade over his head. They had acquired a bridegroom (*lara*) in the form of a herdsman. Ranjha, kissing his staff and driving the cattle, entered the moors. He dug a pit and, raising a platform, lighted a smouldering fire. He built a hanging bedstead (*jallar*) among the trees and, thus, made an arrangement for his stay. The other herdsmen, abiding by the orders of Chuchak, started making rounds of the newcomer. While doing so, they wondered at the decision of Chuchak. Since Ranjha was without any social base (*be-muniada*), they thought it better to kill him. They began by catching the cattle in a snare. When the day passed and evening (*tarkalan*) fell, there were worries. The Siyals, looking at the path, tried to figure out the cause of Ranjha's delay. Ranjha, descending from his station, called out to the cattle, so that his masters were not offended. He climbed on a shisham (*tahli*) tree and raised a melody. When he played on his flute, he touched wondrous notes. The wild animals – tigers, leopards and deer – converged for pilgrimage. Pythons, cobras and porcupines also fell in line. The buffaloes, hearing the sound, twitched their ears and stopped taking mouthfuls of hay. They felt possessed like the Gopis whom Krishna summoned.[26] There was no end to the assembly of buffaloes, tigers, leopards and deer. Leaving the station, Ranjha climbed down to the earth. He caressed the heads of tigers and, thus, offering much solace (*dilasa*), said, 'Brothers! Fate (*qismat*) has brought us to stay here for a few days.' The herdsman escorted the herds back.

The *zamindars*, tired of waiting, wondered at the cause of the delay. With the arrival of the buffaloes, a dust rose to the sky. They went inside the respective homes, while all the *zamindars* sat milking them. When they brought the pots, the herdsman displayed a miracle (*azmat chak vikhaye*). The buffalo, who normally demanded fodder, did not ask for it. The one, who had given birth to a calf, had no mind to feed it and yielded milk without ado. The one, who was recalcitrant (*khattar*), acquired an additional colour and stood still to be milked. When the *zamindars* saw this, they came to Chuchak. In Jhang Siyal, a common cry spread all over. 'We will not allow the herdsman to leave. As long as life (*hayati*) is relied upon, we will give him everything. He is a strong and perfect saint. There is no need to test the one who is already tested (*azmai azmeha*). Though the herdsman is true, we will not trust him.' When Dhido brought the buffaloes back after grazing, the herdsmen did not take it kindly. How could he go out at night when the tigers were out dancing in circles? How can he set his foot where the pythons and cobras were out to bite? All the herdsmen were united in their thoughts. At the time of evening prayer, Ranjha returned to the settlement. Weaving a magic on his flute, he called out to the cattle. When the buffaloes heard the true melody (*sarod sachava*), they felt like coming out. Dhido played the flute in a manner that the buffaloes were charmed. Breaking their mouth net (*muharak*) and losing their patience, they were keen to burst out. They broke the restraining ropes with force. They could not be controlled. How can the Gopis remain patient when Krishna was calling them? Dhido, moving with the cattle, brought them to the moor at a suitable hour. Making a station with twisted rope, he made a seat (*asan*) on it. He led the cattle into the interior of the wilderness (*aujhar*), where the vegetation was dense. The birds and beasts were happy with Dhido. The herdsmen sat together in council (*maslat*) and decided, 'We will kill him. At midnight when sound sleep takes over, we will throw his body in the river. If any force comes out from his side, we will face it. Since the herdsman has snatched our bread, we will remove this stigma (*kalank*) from our neck.'

The herdsmen, motivated by evil intentions, gathered their double-edged swords (*sarvahiyan*) and started sharpening these weapons. On a dark night and in the midst of a drizzle, they carried the armaments on their shoulders. The herdsmen, who served eighty-four *zamindars*, came to the moors. An advance party, sent to examine the situation, found that Dhido was sitting in contemplation (*dhiyan*). Taking out the swords from their scabbards, they attacked, crying 'Ali Ali'. They saw a large army of warriors, wearing black robes and mounted on black horses. They spurred their horses into action, so that the herdsmen fled from the scene. Many died in the battlefield, while some had broken arms. There was no one to provide them with water. Many had unfulfilled desires, as many were hit during their flight. The only one, who remained intact in body, was the one who slipped away all alone. The women, who were beating their chests in mourning (*siyape*), sat in council. Someone conveyed the entire details (*haqiqat*) of the incident to Chuchak. He sent someone to investigate if his herdsmen had picked the fight. At the same time, he summoned the herdsmen to uncover the episode first hand. The herdsmen stated, 'Dhido coveted our bread, so that we resolved to kill him. The mighty (*mahayen*) among us made an assault. From the front appeared an army of black clad warriors on black horses. Carrying their swords, they chased us. We decided to run away.' Thus addressing Chuchak, they asserted that this was what became visible. Chuchak was convinced (*nisha nihayat*) that Ranjha was blessed (*barkatvand*) and, since he had been tested, there was no need to test him any further. With every passing day, it became clear that Dhido was endowed with miraculous powers. The herdsmen, with their hopes shattered, did not have anyone to complain. They said, 'The herdsman has snatched our bread (*tukkar*). It is not in our fortune (*naseeeb*). Whatever was in our lot, we have consumed. How can we get our food again? It is futile to expect anything from Chuchak. Planting wood and growing grass remains in our lot. As for Ranjha, the moors belong to him. Himself he takes out the cattle and himself he brings them back. Even while sitting, he understands all about the moors, including its plants and reeds. All wild beasts, including tigers and cobras, have become his friends. Ranjha is a perfect saint, whom all places treat as a confidant (*mehram*).

Circulation of Gossip

After two months were spent in this manner, the gossip (*chocho*) began to spread. In the girls' common (*aatan*), Hir assigned a task to Hassi. Let her place crushed breadcrumbs (*choori*) in a platter and pour sugar over it. As the gossip reached the girls, they did not say anything out of fear. They felt that the Siyal girl (Hir) was a gone case, as she will not be her normal self again. She has been sold without a price. They must give her some advice (*matt*). It was after much thought that they brought themselves to speak. 'O Sister. Your affair has become public. When father Chuchak will hear this, no food will be cooked in the hearth. Becoming intimate (*ashnai*) with a herdsman, you are freely moving about with your unbound hair. Wise girl! Listen to the truth. Attaching yourself to a herdsman, you have made a mistake.' Hir replied, 'When I was a virgin (*kanj kuari*), I played with dolls. When I met my husband (*shauh*), I took the ritual rounds. No one else comes into my mind. I gained a perfect master (*kamil murshid*), so that I need nothing else. The boat and swings are for you, while Ranjha is my lord.' When the friends heard this, they fell silent. They were astonished at the brazen reply. How can fire remain concealed in cotton? Her very forehead has given birth to love. How can it be hidden? This is indeed a wondrous play (*achraj khel*). The gossip spread across Jhang Siyal and then through the entire world. In every place arose a discussion around the ruin of Chuchak's daughter. Becoming intimate with a herdsman was the worst of all calamities. As the gossip circulated, Chuchak did not know anything about it. In the eighty-four villages of Chuchak, nothing else was talked about. Everything – streets, straw and birds

– offered the same testimony (*ugaahi*). The people complained that Chuchak's daughter has been spoilt. Everyone was saying that she must be strangled to death.

When two or three days passed, nothing remained a secret. There was a commotion (*ghogha*) in the world about the fall of Chuchak's daughter. The entire town had no fear of speaking about it. The people became equally insolent (*be-adab*). Surprisingly, the scandal did not reach the house of Chuchak. One day, early in the morning, Chuchak came out to get an embankment (*banh*) dug out. He had summoned all the town's inhabitants, who were put to work. All the servants (*kammi*) were engaged in the task, so that nobody said anything. Until now, the Lord had not removed the curtain of Chuchak. An anger rose among the tribe (*qabila*). The women of the rival families (*sharik*) came to the *zamindar's* house in Chuchkana and, meeting the daughters-in-law, carried the news further. The entire group of rivals came. None of the women showed any fear. The daughters-in-law spoke to Hir's mother, 'Mother! Listen to what we have to say. We are conveying our anguish. Whether living or dead, we are silenced on hearing of the affair. Have you lost your senses? You are knowingly giving your assent. Listen, O Mother. It is not proper (*munasib*) that the clan (*zati*) should be stigmatized.' In response, the mother asked, "What do you say? Has Chuchak earned a fresh enmity (*vair navela*) during these days? Has someone looted merchandize (*saudagari*)? Has the search (*khoj*) led to our house? Has someone come to tell us that a death has occurred in my parental home? Speak, O Ladies. Has Akbar come out in hot pursuit?' The women argued, 'We have not heard of any death in your parental home. No track has led to your house. Since Akbar has no cause to be offended (*ranj*), he has not come in hot pursuit. Here, the wedding band (*shadiyane*) is playing, but you have not heard anything. Listen, O Mother. The one who is born of your womb has ignited a tall flame (*alamba*).'

The mother (Kundi) said, 'Ladies! Get up and go to your homes. You have given me an extraordinary wound (*phatt awwala*).' She rubbed her hands and shook her neck. Bringing her hand to her forehead, she declared her intention of consuming poison (*mohra*) and dying right there. What solace did she get from life? In her old age, her daughter had inflicted a stigma (*dagh*). The women sat in council and discussed their next step. When Hir returned, they would make her understand, without revealing the secret to anyone. They would protect the parents (Chuchak and Kundi) in old age, without stretching the matter. They would wait for Hir in the girls' common. When two watches of the day came to an end, Hir came there. The sisters-in-law, calling her many times, made her sit. Two of them greeted her, saying that they sacrificed their life for her. The third said, 'We have heard that you are intimate with the herdsman. Confirm it for us.' Saleti, getting angry, exclaimed to her sisters-in-law, 'You must hear good or bad with wisdom. What wrong did you see in me? By opening the bundle of opposition (*khilafatai*), you have raised the heat of my frame. It is not proper for the Khans to speak without seeing.' They said, 'Your father is a hawk. Your paternal relatives are white falcons and your brothers are buzzards. Your mother, like a flying crane, is a sacrifice for you. You are a small falcon of a sister-in-law. Do you have any sense? O wise daughter! When will you understand? Whose daughter are you and whose daughter-in-law? Who raised you and increased the estate?'

There was a big uproar (*shor*) among the Siyals and, with every passing day, it grew to a peak. The sisters-in-law, while speaking without restraint, quietly called in their mother-in-law and asked, 'O Mother! When it was the turn of Hir, why did you give birth to her? By cutting the umbilical cord around her neck, you have given birth to an inferno.' On hearing this, Kundi wept tears of blood and exclaimed, 'Do not say more. We have forced our rivals to bow before us. Now I am prostrate with my face down. If I knew I am giving birth to an inferno from my womb, would I not have cut her throat?' The woman of the *zamindar*, sunk in deep pain, kept on crying. Hollow in her mind, she secretly called Hir and said, 'Listen, daughter. In my old age, I gave birth to you from my womb. Should I live or die? Should I cut my throat or swallow poison? You spoilt daughter. I am devastated.' Hir replied, 'Listen, O Mother! May your sons live long. How did you get a fever? What have you seen of me? I am without any fault (*be-taqsir*). How do you level false allegations? I am innocent. I am a virgin, who knows nothing of intimacy.' In this manner, Hir fully deceived Kundi, the woman (*mehari*) of the *zamindar*. 'Listen, O Daughter! You are a suckling baby. I sacrifice my life for you. Whose daughter are you and whose daughter-in-law? As they (Kheras) are lords of land and water, they control all routes from the seven directions. They compete with Akbar in their claims (*dawa*). At least sometimes, you must understand. O wise daughter! This is not proper.' Hir countered, 'Listen, O Mother! Who has told you so? He (Ranjha) is an alien son (*putt paraya*). He came here through his fate. There is no honour for him. All address him as herdsman. The Siyals do not show respect to him. Listen, O Mother! I tell you that I am not to blame (*dosh*) in all this.'

'Listen, O Hir! You have done well. Where have your qualities led? In every house, people talk about you. The sister-in-law is crying. Soon, your brothers will hear it. If the herdsman were to die somehow, we will be ruined. Only if he had not come here at all. From where did he come? An arrow of enmity has struck us.' Hir replied, 'Listen to me, O Mother! I am telling you. Who will make you understand? You are sitting with a mouthful of rice. Do not defame an alien son. You are so naïve. Be wise. They will comprehend who are capable of doing so. Only they, who have given birth to sons, will understand this pain.' Striking her forehead, the woman of the *zamindar*, said, 'The string has been pulled. I have understood the notes from your statement.' Getting up, full of anger, she began to cry. Then, she did not speak. Owing to the onset of bad times, she seemed to be losing her senses.

One day, Chuchak came out. He intended to get an embankment dug to channelize water. He summoned the entire town (*qasba*) and assigned work to everyone. A crude person (*gawar*) said to Chuchak, 'O Chuchak Khan! Your days pass suitably well. No one has ever disgraced you. But, your daughter has drawn a line over you.' Hearing this, a knot developed in Chuchak's stomach. Wearing a frown on his forehead, his face turned pale. Nobody could figure out the cause. Leaving the hall, verandah and living room, he withdrew to a cellar (*kothi*). If the mistress of the house cried, it was not an empty matter. The woman, entering the place, spoke to the Khan with a smile, 'Why are you sad (*dilgeer*) and silent? Why did you come inside? Which sorrow has consumed you? Has anyone offended you?' The woman asked these questions from Chuchak Khan. With a pale face,

Chuchak lamented, 'My stomach is torn. Who will tie a bandage? To whom shall I narrate? The matter cannot be described. Nor can it be seen. If I say it from my mouth, it will only stick to my forehead. It is better to die than live this kind of life. I wish to eat poison. With what face can I speak?' Kundi asked, 'Did you earn a new enmity on your head these days? Have the thieves looted a caravan? Has the track (*khoj*) led to the Siyals? Has an enemy (*ghalim*) inflicted some evil? Has King Akbar embarked in hot pursuit. Your state is not normal as before. You have come in a strange condition.'

Chuchak replied, 'I have not brought any fresh enmity on my head. No track has led to our house. I have not offended anyone these days. I have not nurtured any evil intention. Nor has Akbar come in hot pursuit. O Mother of Hir! If you had not given birth to her, who would have shot arrows at us?' Kundi said, 'May the children of our enemies die. Curse them who have given currency to this matter. For eight watches, I remained worried at this calumny (*badi*), which people have cooked up. You heard it only today and withdrew into the cellar (*hujra*). But, I have been hearing this every day. May the children of our enemies die, as they have given fever to your frame.' After complex exchanges, Kundi developed a spirit of trust and persuaded Chuchak to sit down. She argued that an allegation cannot be levelled without seeing. The father and brothers, without seeing, cannot throw an accusation at a virgin. Admitting that her words were true, Chuchak came out. A fire (*atish*), burning inside Chuchak, could not be extinguished even after trying to do so. Inside his mind, he kept on wondering about the mode of inquiry. Throughout eight watches of the day, he walked to and fro in exasperation. His face acquired a yellow hue (*zardi*). Chuchak, even though a Khan, did not know what to say or do.

In his perplexity, Chuchak summoned Kaido and pleaded, 'Do not be cross (*nabar*) with me. You are also the progeny of our parents (*ma peyo jaya*). You go from house to house. Have you also heard of something? Say it, brother. Speak the truth. Did you see anything?' Kaido said, 'O nobleman (*syeada*)! What have I seen? Why was she begotten from the womb? Why did the *zamindar's* woman, who became productive in old age, not strangle her? Curse the women who give birth to such daughters. This is what I saw and heard. Ashes have fallen on your white head.' Chuchak said, 'Listen, O Brother. I sacrifice my life for you. I make a request to you. Go to the moors and collect the facts (*haqiqat*). Come back and tell me. We do not know why she goes to the moors. In the name of the Lord, do not oppose (*nabar*) me. I am in great trouble.' Kaido said, ' Listen, O Nobleman. Have you lost your senses? What service do you assign to me? Even Akbar cannot overpower her (Hir). You want me killed. If she were to see me, she would not spare my life. Why don't you go yourself?' Chuchak, while weeping, became tired of making entreaties. Putting the turban around his neck, he said, 'Brother! Go as you deem proper. To me, you are my father and mother. Do not be hostile to me.' Kaido insisted that his words did not make any sense. Chuchak, with his turban around his neck and hands on his feet, requested Kaido to be on his way immediately.

Seeing the pain of his brother, Kaido walked to the moors. Hiding himself, he sat down and did not utter a word. While he sat waiting in his concealment, the time of Hir's arrival came. He observed the proceedings of the union. Hir, carrying a bowl of sweetened breadcrumbs (*choori*) on her head, offered her salutation to Ranjha. Kissing his feet, she picked up dust and rubbed it on her face and forehead. While she stood in front of him with folded hands, he asked her to bring the milk, so that he was able to eat the food. She picked up the pot and left. Kaido, availing of the opportunity, came out to beg. He asked for alms (*bhikheya*) in the name of Allah. Dhido treated him with respect and offered him the sweetened breadcrumbs. Almost immediately, Kaido carried it to Chuchak. 'Listen, O Siyals. You, who have daughters, should not keep them under any circumstances. They should be drowned in the rivers or their heads should be separated. (Showing the content of the alms, he continued) Since everyone cannot have enough share, you must taste only with your fingers. You eat the coarse corn bread (*dhoda thapi*), while the herdsman eats this fare.' Chuchak picked up the sweetened breadcrumbs and brought them to his wife. He taunted, 'You with a dead father! This is what he (Ranjha) plunders. We have never eaten it. If the herdsman eats such stuff, there must be a lot of affection for him.' Kundi, while picking up the small pieces and shedding tears of blood, put forward a defence, 'Since the girls had made a vow (*mannat*) to Khizr,[27] they had put extra ghee in it. I had myself prepared the sweetened breadcrumbs. The girls selected this day to make the offering. Ashes be on his (Kaido's) head. He appeared from somewhere. They did not give him any alms. He has performed this deception (*dagha*) to heat up your frame.' Chuchak had doubts (*guman*) about his wife's explanation. The matter did not leave his mind. He came out of the house and, sleeping in the village assembly, kept on worrying. Which bandage can bind a torn stomach? In utter desperation, he struck his forehead and waved his hands.

When Hir returned with the pot of milk in her hand, she discovered the footprints of Kaido. She asked Ranjha if someone had come there as it appeared. Surely, it was a spy (*janjus*), who had left the marks of a trembling heel. She left the place in order to find out. Hir figured out that this was the work of Kaido. He had breathed fresh air into the flame (*alamba*). Earlier, there was some curtain (*pardah*) over the affair. But, he had awakened the sleeping people. In every home, the gossip regarding Hir was exchanged, so that the sentiment had settled among the Siyals. Hir saw the fire (*muata*) her uncle (*taya*) had ignited. She could not restrain herself. Becoming enraged, she picked up a burning twig and set fire to his hut, which was reduced to cinders. Someone informed Kaido of the occurrence. Hearing this, he came to the site and accused Hir of burning his abode (*takiya*). He cried, 'O Daughter Hir! What have I done? You have burnt my hut. A lamb, which was tied to the peg, has been roasted. Add to it the egg-yielding hen, utensils, spoon, needle box and overcoat. Burnt alongside was a rosary, necklace and prayer mat (*tasbi seli te mirgani*). You have burnt the hut of a grocer (*hatt pasari*). Which of the goods can I retrieve?' Hir replied, 'Uncle! What have I done as yet? I will inflict even more on you. I will not spare your beard and a single hair on your head. One by one, I will pull them out. I will crush at its base the only leg, which is still intact. I will drink your blood. I will not let you live. I will kill you here and now.'

Kaido explained, 'May his children die. The one who summoned me. I did not know anything. He (Chuchak), putting his turban around his neck, made repeated entreaties and sent me to the moors. What have I to do with it? Listen, your ladyship (*sahibiyani*)! Why are you angry? Daughter, this deliberate destruction of my hut is a sufficient lesson (*nasihat*) for me.' Hir said, 'What you wished, you have done on my head. What will I do on your head? Uncle, where will you escape? The wood is in the mouth of the axe. Where will you run away from me?' In these words, Saleti made her uncle understand. Kaido admitted, 'If Mughals become my enemy, I would be released by turning a mendicant (*faqir*). If the *zamindars* become my enemy, I will be released by becoming their supporter. If the whole world becomes my enemy, I would put my turban around my neck. From your enmity, I will not be worthy of living.' Hearing this, Hir made up her mind not to spare Kaido. She threatened, 'Where will you go after escaping from me? Chasing you, I will kill you here and now. Since you have dared to pick up a fight with me, I will slash your head at night.' Kaido pleaded, 'O Hir! The dead have ample space. For the living, there is none. I will go to Rajoa Syedan, where I will set up a fire. I will find a place to which no one has a claim. I will settle there. Where your enmity (*vair*) exists, I will not be able to stay there.'

Hir Resists Patriarchal Oppression

The matter kept entering Chuchak's mind. 'How can I speak about it. It cannot be told to anyone. Can I establish it in my interior? I will go there and see with my own eyes. I will not reveal the secret to anyone.' Chuchak decided to himself probe the case. One day, exactly at noon, Chuchak went there. Ahead both were sleeping on the station (*jallar*). What shall he do? On seeing them, he turned back. He felt ashamed. Having seen the reality (*haqiqat*), he called out to them. After the Khan had made many calls, only then both of them heard. When Hir woke up, she was surprised. She awakened Ranjha. 'Get up. Why are you sleeping? The father has come upon us.' As Hir walked away, Ranjha rushed into the moors. Again and again, Chuchak called for him. Ranjha listened but remained silent. He heard great anger in the moors, but did not give any answer. Instantly, he smeared mud on his body. When Chuchak was tired, Ranjha called out. He came and met Chuchak, who asked, 'You herdsman! Why did you not speak? While yelling, my throat became hoarse. You did not reply. You heard, but deliberately kept silent. You are putting my life in danger.' The Khan did not relent. What words (*sukhan*) did he speak? Ranjha explained, 'A young buffalo (*jhoti*) was caught in the mud. I could not hear. When I pulled it out from the front, its rear was struck. When I pulled out its rear, its front was struck, while I kept grappling with it. O Khan, I could not understand anything. As soon as I heard your last call, I immediately came to meet you.'

Chuchak alleged, 'O Herdsman! The way you pull out buffaloes. I have heard everything.' Chuchak, in his rage, struck Ranjha hard with a cane. 'Return to us the charge of the cattle. Go away with your honour.' Saying this, he delivered a second blow of the cane on Dhido. Ranjha started crying and his blood oozed out. He protested, 'I have not sold off any buffalo to swallow up the money. I have neither milked the buffaloes nor drunk their milk. Come and take charge of the cattle. Come to the enclosure. Take the buffaloes and cows into your custody. O Khan! If you snatched away the herd, you have not snatched away Hazara.' Chuchak ordered, 'Bring the cattle and hand them to me. Brother! Go to Hazara. Taking pity (*taras*) on you, we employed you. But you broke into our house. There is no place for you here. We dismiss you.' Ranjha, putting on his shoes and making a preparation, became a wayfarer (*rahi*). Ranjha played on the flute to call the cattle. What melodies flowed from him? All wild animals – tigers, pythons and deer – came to pay their homage (*ziyarat*). None of the animals and birds lagged behind. Hearing the notes, the buffaloes came rushing. How could the Gopis be patient when Krishna called them? Ranjha said, 'O Khan! Take charge after counting. I am not carrying off anyone with me.' Chuchak, hearing a few melodies (*sarud*), fell into an intense ecstasy (*masti*).

Ranjha picked the staff and flute in his hands. Wearing his shoes and laying the blanket on his shoulders, he became a traveller. While he was walking away, the cattle went along with him. Chuchak cried (*hora*) to make them stop. The more he turned them back, the more they moved away. They did not stop when attempts were made to do so. The Khan, tired of pushing the cattle, walked with greater speed. Ultimately, broken with fatigue, he put his turban around his neck and tried to placate the herdsman. The Khan said, 'You are upset because of the blows I delivered. For me, you are like a brother to our Khan and Pathan. If a father punishes his son, the matter does not interest any *zamindar*.' In this manner, the buffaloes were turned back. Once again, Ranjha came to the moors and so did the cattle. Chuchak, by giving consolation (*dilasa*) and making entreaties, appeased Ranjha. Though Chuchak left the moors and returned home, he brought back some old worries (*chinta*). The entire clan (*qabila*) came to know of the entire situation. Chuchak spoke to himself. 'With what face shall I see them. What shall I tell the brothers? Whatever was heard turned out to be true. Not an iota (*ratti*) of it is false. I kept testing (*ajmaye*) in my own way, but the herdsman turned away the buffaloes. What shall I speak of the hapless Hir? The herdsman has even succeeded in swaying my buffaloes.'

The Khan came home in a miserable state. He called his wife and made her sit. God had shown with the eyes what was heard as gossip. The one who was born out of her womb had gone out of her hands. It was just as if yesterday had turned into today. In their old age, they had earned this income (*kamai*). Then, two noble persons sat in council (*maslat*). What can be done? They had been deprived of their honour. Should they mix some poison and drink it. They must do immediately what they should. They should not show any laxity. They must be anxious and not patient (*tahambal*), so that a dam is quickly raised to stop the flow. Instead of a hundred twists, they would fix only one knot and overlook any other action. This is the only right step. There is no alternative. This will be given a practical shape. Any delay is not proper (*munasib*). They will rush with the wedding knots (*gandhi*). Today itself, Hir Siyal should sit for the wedding rounds (*lavan*). Chuchak, with deep concern, held deliberations at home. 'Listen, O Wife! It will not do without holding the function (*kaj*). The more is the laxity, the more will be the trouble (*khuwari*). How our faces have been blackened? I have done my best to cover up (*kajmai*), but Hir is bent on making it public.' The Khan, acting secretly, summoned the servants and assigned different tasks to them. He distributed the material among them. He gave gold to one, pearls to the other, cloth to another, sugar to one and flour to still another. Chuchak secretly instructed them to go about their work.

In Jhang Siyal, the gossip flared up. 'Chuchak is making preparations for the wedding.' How can truth remain concealed? The people were a witness (*ugaahi*). Whoever spoke did not say anything else. Everyone said that Chuchak was marrying off Hir. Kundi, speaking to Hir, said,

KUNDI: Listen, daughter! I am a sacrifice for you. I am speaking for you to hear. Having bloomed in youth (*jobanvant*), you roam around in the moors, even as you have been made a beloved. Jhang is talking about you. In every house, there are no other topics. O Daughter! Only blackness has come to us. O wise daughter! We are marrying you off.

HIR: O Mother! Those who recognize the truth (*haq*) know. Listen, wise mother! We are absolutely new and without blame. Our hearts are not attached to anyone else. Water has flowed to merge with water. Nothing remains. Listen, O Mother! Who has fixed this relationship (*kurmai*)? The truth must be told.

KUNDI: What great excitement was there at your betrothal? You can only presume (*guman*). We searched for the best. No one is comparable to the Kheras. For them, there are lakhs like us. They have no scarcity. Listen, daughter! I speak the truth, while you are not aware of it.

HIR: Listen O Mother. Great are the Kheras, whom you have praised. Those who adhere to pure love (*pak muhabbat*) are not given any consideration. To hell with the Kheras, whom you praise at my face. I sacrifice my head to those, who treat the conjugal bond as true (*sach suhag sachava*).

KUNDI: Listen, daughter. I sacrifice myself for you. Who can make you realize? He came in a discarded state all the way from Takht Hazara. No one was willing to employ him as a herdsman. You are the only one who praised him before us. But, we were made to fall flat on our face. Your father did not approve of it. All the *zamindars* would have felt relieved if Ranjha had been killed.

HIR: Listen, mother. You are the mother of Chuchak's sons. Who can make you understand? Sitting with your mouth full of rice, you should not slander the alien son. Saying such things behind the back is not proper (*munasib*) for someone who has herself borne sons. If God is kind to you, it is not proper for you to disgrace others.

KUNDI: You do not have mercy (*mehar*), while privileging the herdsman over your own brothers. Instead of cutting the umbilical cord, I should have cut your head. People have two daughters in their houses. Wise daughter. Are you the divine army (*kattak rabbani*) to have intimacy with a herdsman?

HIR: Mother! Whom are you trying to convince? I will not succumb to pressure. Ranjha has entered every pore of mine. You are snatching me by force and giving me away to the Kheras. When I jump off the wedding mat, then you will understand. Hir Siyal only cries in the name of Ranjha. I am madly in love (*dard diwani*) with Ranjha. My clothes have become wet with my tears. If I unite with Ranjha, only then I will fulfil my desire for life (*shauq hayati*). Those who do not adhere to truth are too worldly to comprehend the path of love. Who has fixed this marriage?

KUNDI: Daughter. Your father has fixed the marriage. Being intoxicated with youth, you do not restrain yourself. You have stained the honour of the clan. By your intimacy with the herdsman, you pierce through the jungle at night. Yet, you do not remain silent.

HIR: Just as the flowers flutter in the garden, I live by gazing at Ranjha. Becoming a gardener, I place him in the necklace around my neck. I found him in the boat and he subjugated my heart. In the eyes of the world, I became his auspicious wife (*suhagan*).

KUNDI: This kind of husband is not accepted anywhere.[28] You have no shame in forming intimacy with a herdsman. We are helpless, as the claims of the Kheras are sealed. May Ranjha die.

HIR: Mother! If you confer Ranjha as my husband, every day will become auspicious for me. Ranjha is my charming beloved (*dilbar yaar*). Let him live in this world and religion. The Khera is worse than a fake coin (*kasira*), while Ranjha is valued at one lakh. He has been inscribed in my lot.

KUNDI: This can happen only if the parents approve the relation. The great clans have formed a bond, as written in the destiny. You should not act in haste. We have kept the herdsman away from this. You must remain agreeable to the Kheras.

HIR: If you keep the herdsman away from me, I will cry in pain. I will not be able to digest the food (*tuam*) if I do not see my lord (*shauh*). Each moment of mine will be as long as a year. I will take six months to bat an eyelid. Only the True Lord will unite us.

KUNDI: We have already sent the wedding knots to the Kheras, fixing the wedding day. Whether sitting or standing, we are looking towards their path. As we are their slaves, they will not give us any postponement (*mohlat*). The Siyals are busy in making arrangements. Listen daughter. Many disputes will arise. The whole world will be making inquiries. We are *zamindars*, the lords of the land (*zimin de khawind*). We do not tolerate the weight of even the flowers. We have a big reputation in the town (*qasba*). On our head is the responsibility of all homes and hearths. People have three daughters each in their houses. For me, you are a basket of burning coal (*chhajj angaran*).

HIR: Mother! I discovered my mentor (*pir*) a long time back. I make it clear to you. Listen to me with attention. My proposal is worthy of acceptance. Give up your claim with humility. What else can be explained? I am sold without my breath, as I have discovered my mentor.

KUNDI: Daughter! When did you discover this mentor. He was merely grazing our buffaloes every day. Whom are you trying to convince by repeatedly referring to him as your mentor? The world is conveying its complaints to us. Our face is blackened. We are disgraced in the world. People curse us. Since your father gives you the advice (*nasihat*), you must understand it in whatever way you can.

HIR: O Mother! When I organize a feast for Ranjha, I myself husk the rice. If there is a minor lapse, Ranjha does not eat the food. Only the one, bearing pain in her heart, is able to appease Ranjha with her entreaties. If he remains true until the end, I will also remain attached to him.

KUNDI: Daughter! The claims of the Kheras are sealed. They would not forgo them. O wise daughter! See the reality. You must snap all ties with Ranjha. We cannot think of anything else. Who will marry you other than the Khera? You must try to understand and keep your faith intact.

HIR: False relations never turn out to be true even if they are formalized a hundred times. There were no Adam and Eve at the site, where our betrothal took place.[29] The great saints of the Lord (*vadde vali sadiq sahib de*) announced our betrothal. Mother and father must reflect, as they do not have any knowledge.

KUNDI: Daughter! You will be ashamed in the end, if you try to stretch the matter. Kheras, being the virtual wrath of the Lord (*qehar jawal sahib de*), will not spare you. By authority (*hukmin*), they will take you away even if they have to fight. We will be ashamed (*nilaj*). One should not give birth to daughters, who disgrace their lineage.

Chuchak initiated the joyful festivities and placed the drums. Hearing of the wedding, the entire world jumped out. They congratulated the chief's wife, as they approved of the proceedings. The number of beggars was so large that they could not be accommodated in the space. When Ranjha and Hir were sitting in the moors, they heard the sound of the festivities. Ranjha asked, 'Hir! Has someone allocated the work of the wedding? Or is it a betrothal? Or is it a religious rite (*sunnat*)? Or is it associated with an ancestor?' Hir explained, 'It is not any special day. It is neither anyone's wedding nor a betrothal. It is neither the celebration of a union nor the commemoration of an ancestor. There is a commotion in the settlement. Gossip is circulating in Jhang Siyal. If you say that I will bring any news from the Siyals, I have no mind to do so.' Ranjha said, 'I am not a herdsman of long standing. I am also born of the *zamindars* (*rathan da jaya*). When I came, you captured my heart and I came to be known as a herdsman. I am roaming around and suffering, as I receive blows of the cane. The name of my father has been disgraced. Hirey! Tell me your reality (*haqiqat*). What is coming into your mind?' Hir replied, 'Listen, lord! You are a perfect master (*kamil murshid*). Since I am helpless (*aajiz*), do not test me. I have fallen at your feet. Do not go anywhere after leaving me. Give me love, which is pure and true (*pak muhabbat sachi*). Do not deceive me. Listen, Ranjha! I will die at your feet.'

Ranjha asked, 'We are hearing the arrival of the marriage party of the Kheras. Let us see what happens. Who will take care of my honour when you are tied to pre-wedding ritual (*maiyan*)? The whole world will be after me. From whom will you ask about me? What will be the situation the day you are married?' Hir said, 'You have given me a unique wound (*phatt awalla*). To whom do you marry me? Let the Kheras go to hell (*khawan khasman*). I cannot figure out what you say. You are asking something from me. You are testing me. I have renounced the Kheras. My heart is devoted to reciting (*zikr*) your name.' Hir got up and, returning home, worried in her mind. In the house of Chuchak, the drums were beaten and the sound was heard. The girls were singing, while flour was ground. Numerous crafts were being practised. Hir thought, 'Who will go with the Kheras? Let him (Ranjha) not ask me. If you hear anything, O Ranjha, come to take me away.'

Proceedings of the Marriage

The marriage procession of the Kheras comprised of relatives, all of whom had been invited. Horses – white, grey, spotted and golden – held up their necks that were decorated with tufts of colourful strings. The pommels and saddles were decked in velvet. The marriage procession of the Kheras looked exceedingly impressive. Ponies meant to be gifted walked along. What can one speak of fabrics such as waistcloths and sleep-covers? Cash was loaded on camels and Kashmiri ponies. If these were not sufficient, what else could be demanded? The leading horse (*kotal*), provided with trappings, moved with banners. Jesters, dancers and singing girls (*bhand bhagatiye aur kanjariyan*) raised melodies in the air. Drums and clarions were played, while hawks and falcons were flown. This day, whatever was seen, the earth could not bear its weight. When Chuchak learnt that the Kheras had arrived, he began to exert himself. Flour, rice, ghee and sugar were made available. There was no limit to grains, quilts and mattresses. The two *zamindars* (Chuchak and Ali) were not inferior to Akbar in any manner.

The Siyals called a council (*maslat*) to decide on the invitation for the oil ceremony. If Hir was not clutched with the hands, they would be disgraced without reason. Since she was moving about, all ready to resist, how could they be saved? How could she be sent away as a captive bride? In a collective decision (*mata*), the Siyals were convinced that Hir would not come to the site of the marriage rituals. Where she sits for eating her food, they would conceal her brothers. When she finishes a hearty meal and gets up to wash her hands, she would be overpowered and confined to her room. Accordingly, three brothers and four maternal uncles came in and hid themselves. Butter, buttermilk and buffalo milk were brought. Sugar was mixed in. After eating, Hir asked for water. Her mother helped her in washing hands. As soon as she got up, the brothers laid their hands on her. Crying for help, Hir said, 'Brothers! You do not have any sense. Let no one touch me. Where you have to take me, I will go myself. You should not touch me. In the name of the Lord's will, I will speak and you must listen to what I say. Brother. Do not touch my body, as Ranjha has touched me with his hands (*mainun hath ranjhete laye*).' With due authority, Hir was confined in the room, otherwise she could not be sent away after marriage.

Chuchak ordered, 'Kundi, bring poison (*zehar*). Give it to her at night, so that she dies. In her place, let the daughter of Khan be married immediately.' Everyone agreed to this, provided there was no delay. Poison (*mohra*) was brought and kneaded in the flour. It was mixed into finely ground flour, butter and buttermilk. Kundi cooked the food well and, making Hir sit, fed it to her. She ate her fill and thereafter, gave her answer, 'Listen, mother! You placed me in the pre-wedding ceremony, while the brothers were sitting concealed. It was good that I came of my own and they did not lay their hands on me. You gave me a full dose of poison and, thus, defiled my purity. Poison does not affect those who digest it with the help of perfect love (*kamil ishq*).' Acting on authority, Hir was confined inside, but not before she raised an outcry, 'Hassi, my true friend! Come and see. Whose I am? To whom do I belong? If this is what pleases the master (Ranjha), I accept out of regard for him.' Saleti, in the grip of aliens, wrings her hands and shakes her neck, 'O simple mother! You have brought henna. Whose hands are you going to colour (*dast rangesi*)? I have one heart, which I have given to Ranjha. What will you give to the Kheras? I am not the Balochi's camel, who bows at door after door. Ranjha will not leave me. Who will go to the Kheras?' As dense clouds rain on the mountains and water flows down to the low land, Hir was separated from her spinning circle (*trinjan*) and put through the pre-wedding ceremony. 'Friends! Rub the paste (*cheeku*) on me, as my arms are in your control. For people, this is the practice. Mother, for me, it is a funeral rite (*muhkane*).'

The herdsmen cornered Ranjha, 'O herdsman Ranjha! The Kheras have arrived. What happiness they show? From whom will you eat sweetened breadcrumbs and butter? Hir is being married. You snatched the cattle from us. What we will inflict on your head? Rest assured (*khatir jama*). We have heard that you will be killed here.' Ranjha said, 'Listen, brothers! I do not have any knowledge. Fate has entangled me. I have stayed here only so long as my livelihood (*rizq*) has made me do so. I will go after leaving the Siyals. I have not prepared any document (*khat*).[30] What have I done? I have not ploughed the boundary of any field.' They said, 'You have detached (*udasi*) your mind only when the master is sending Hir away. Earlier, you were not inclined to go, as you were consuming milk and cream. We cannot penetrate your interior to see the trouble you are in. They will severe your head (*sir kapsaini*) if you give flame to the fire.' Ranjha replied, 'Listen, brothers! You prefer to indulge in hurling abuse (*gaali*) and picking a fight. Do whatever you feel like. You have caught me as one without roots (*be-muniyada*). Being the one without any excuse, I cannot advance any argument. My heart has burnt. If the Kheras have snatched Hir from me, they have not taken Hazara away.' The herdsmen argued, 'You have fattened your body by eating sweetened breadcrumbs. You do not suffer from any adversity. Throughout the eight watches, you moved around in carefree intoxication (*almasti*). When you were called, you never responded. Now, herdsman! You have come into our grasp. You are in for punishment. This rootless one! How does he argue?' Ranjha protested, 'Brothers! I am making an earnest request (*arz*) to you. But, you are inclined to kill me. Now, my heart is focused on Hazara. Who will release me from here? I stayed wherever my fortune (*qismat*) brought me. Brothers! Listen. If I take anything from here, you can snatch it from me.'

In her pre-wedding rites (*maiyen*), Hir raised a clamour. Taking erratic sighs, she kept on crying. Food and water became unlawful (*haram*) for her, as her husband imposed fasts on her (*rozey khasam rakhaye*). What joy did she experience in the moors? Now, who will feed her? How can she eat when the master (*murshid*) himself restrains her? Inside, the brothers saw her condition. 'Who shall we marry off? Our shame (*lajj*) does not remain, notwithstanding our attempt to conceal? All the *zamindars*, who were summoned, unanimously resolved to kill Hir at night. Since there are many daughters in Chuchak's house, another will be placed in the oil ceremony. This cannot happen. We must weed out this stigma (*kalank*) from our neck.' The entire clan and tribe (*kul qabila*) were pleased at this. All, including four maternal uncles and three brothers, took a collective decision. All wanted Hir as dead, showing no mercy (*taras*). The bridal string (*gana*) was tied on the hand of Pathana's daughter. In the evening, the Khan (Chuchak) came to the venue of the oil ceremony. Chuchak called Hassi and, sitting in a corner, made her understand. 'Sleep at a distance from Hir, as we have resolved to kill her. Be alert lest you should be killed.' Hassi said, 'You have done well having resolved to kill Hir. Without this, your prestige does not remain. You do not allow her to live. Father! You have removed this obligation from your head. You should not neglect this matter. In the name of the Lord, may the Khan remain safe (*salamat*). But, you must kill me first.' Hassi, turning to Hir, said, 'Listen, Hir! Your father and brother called me out. They explained to me that they are going to kill you. Therefore, while remaining near, I should sleep at a distance from you. They came specially to say this to me. However, they did not give me the reason for the same. Make no mistake, they will attack you.'

Hir said, 'Whom are they going to kill? Hassi! It does not matter to me. False shoots and straw ropes are fundamentally incapable of binding. What do these rootless ones know? Why do they intend to kill me? How can one die when Dhido is the protector (*sayin*)?' At midnight, when all were in deep sleep, the maternal uncles and brothers entered with the intention of killing Hir. In the front, the warriors in black attire and mounted on black horses, stood as guards (*chauki*). Pulling out their swords from the scabbards, they went in hot pursuit. The assailants fell on the ground and their jaws became locked (*dandan*). There was no one to pour water in their mouths. The wife of the *zamindar* started wailing and shed tears of blood. She poured water to separate the jaws. All the while, she clasped them to her chest and kept on crying. With fire in the front and a wall in the rear, the thorns were up for destruction. Chuchak and others looked like wads of cotton facing a fire.

A large marriage party of the Kheras arrived, emitting colours of victory in plenty (*rang hambhiri*). There were Turki, Tazi and Irani horses, besides camels and Kashmiri ponies. The velvet (*makhmal*), which adorned their forelegs, hind and saddles, hung down in fullness. A delightful marriage party (*janj sukhiri*) came for the marriage of Hir Siyal. The *zamindars* descended in a garden, while the drums played and emblems shone. As soon as the drums received the first strike, the world came leaping. They included young girls, old women and young maidens. In fact, no one was left out. Damodar saw with his own eyes (*main ditha akhin*) the impending end of Ranjha. Hir, while weeping, raised a clamour. 'The marriage party has come and the entire world is happy. I, deprived of brothers (*nibhrai*), keep on suffering. The horses neigh and the revellers shine, but my end is near. May their children die who have pushed me into this ceremony.' Chuchak sent sweets (*halufa*) that the servants brought. Let the people see. The entire world, including all the villagers, turned up. The relatives, both by blood and marriage, came along with many others. As numerous as the shades of a tree, there was no limit to them. Veils of flowers hung from the heads. Full sets of apparel had been prepared. The bridegroom was decked in a gold threaded saffron suit (*sunehri siropau*). The husband of Hir drew applause, as all eyes focused on him. The world came out to see the bridegroom.

On hearing about it, Dhido, recollecting the memories, felt like taking a look. If the whole world has come leaping, he should not knowingly stay back. He would go and see the husband (*khasam*) of Hir. It was difficult for him to resist. As he approached, he saw a bunch of girls. Seeing them, he turned back. The girls exclaimed, 'Look at Ranjha. The lover of Hir has come.' Ranjha, afflicted with a severe giddiness (*jhoona*), collapsed on the ground. The sharp stump of a tree pierced his foot, so that a plenty of blood started flowing. It was not in his fortune (*nasib*) to see the marriage party, which came for Hir. In his anxiety to see the marriage party, Ranjha thought of sitting on a lofty place. He called an ox (*sandha*), so that he would ride it and see everything. He did accordingly. The ox, seeing the burning torches, began to freely run around. The herdsmen of Chuchak, present in front of the Kheras, were performing their duties. As Dhido moved around, he performed the pilgrimage (*ziyarat*) of every person. Vasava Khan, on seeing Dhido, inquired about him, 'Who is this young man with a blanket? From where has he come? Brothers! Tell me.' The Khan asked in this manner. The herdsmen gave a reply, which was heard, 'He came all the way from Takht Hazara in a desolate (*rulda*) condition. The Khan (Chuchak) took him in his service. Hearing of the marriage party, he turned up to see it.' The herdsmen spoke thus. As Ranjha removed the blanket, his exceptional beauty (*rup sawaya*) came into view. Vasava Khan exclaimed, 'He is a perfect saint of the Lord. Nothing was shown to you. He appears as the light of spiritual excellence (*azmat ki rushnai*).[31] His enemies (*harifan*) have struck an arrow at him. Appearing as the recipient of the ultimate divine favours (*nur inayat*), he is under the protection of saints. He is the perfect one, who has concealed himself.'

The herdsmen began an altercation with Ranjha, saying, 'Why did you bestow your glimpse (*darshan*)? It was good of you to be hidden. You have manifested (*zahir*) yourself. On what business did you come here?' Until now, Ranjha was being pushed around and everyone was quarrelling with him. He wrapped a tight bandage on his foot and turned back. A Doom girl (*doometi*), having spotted him, reported to Hir, 'O Hir! I saw Dhido from the back of the house.' Instantly, Hir came running and met him. What words (*sukhan*) did she speak? Putting her scarf around her neck, she touched his feet and cried, 'Dhido Ranjha, my lord! Why have you imprisoned (*bandi*) me?' While embracing him, she caressed his body with her hands. Ranjha replied, 'A snake has bitten me and my foot is in a bandage. Do not touch me. What is my relation (*saak*) with you?

I am going to Hazara. You will go and live with the Kheras. From whom will I claim my dignity? Here, we shared many a laughter. Henceforth, I will embark on my jouney.' Hir pleaded, 'Dhido! You are the lord of the entire earth (*kul zamin da khawind*). Only you have constructed this play (*bazi*). Why am I, full of flaws, put to trial? As a sacrifice, I circumambulate around you (*ghol ghumai*). What is my fault (*taqsir*)? I must know. Why I have been thrown in a prison? My perfect master (*kamil murshid*)! You are my only refuge. I have no other place to live.' Then, Hir was dragged into the house, while Ranjha went to the moors. Owing to the pain of separation (*dard firaq*) and a pale complexion, he did not say anything. He played on the flute and, expelling his bitterness, raised a soulful melody. What a mourning (*matam*) flowed from his mouth!

A Brahmin came to perform the rites (*reet*). Carrying the wedding thread (*mauli*) in his hands, he said, 'O wife of the chief! First, call the girl. I have looked in every place. The Khans are looking forward to me, so that the suitable time does not pass.' Along with the Brahmin, the chief's wife (Kundi) walked in. The Brahmin, while conducting the rite, announced, 'O daughter Hir! I am telling you. May the lord increase the wealth of those who give the offerings (*vel*). And this also includes the mother-in-law and father-in-law. Since your purposes are good, I make the auspicious omens (*shagan*) for you.' The mother beseeched (*minnat*) Hir not to say anything. Hir asserted, 'I have one heart, which Ranjha has taken. Mother! I do not have another one. Another man will not touch me. Nor will an alien (*mahram*) do so.[32] I have acquired a perfect master. I do not need anything else. Let him perform the omens. I will not recognize anyone else. I belong to Ranjha and he is the lord of my head.' Then, Hassi was despatched to the moors to bring Ranjha. The chief's wife told him that he will tie the first wedding thread. As soon as Ranjha showed his face, a light was emitted from the sun. Hir got up and fell at his feet. She placed her long scarf (*pallu*) around her neck and stated, 'Tie it wherever you wish. Since I am without any ego, I do not make any demand. I, the simple one (*nimani*), know nothing except the perfect master (*murshid sayin*). Throughout the eight watches, I contemplate (*dhiyan*) only you, without wasting a single breath. Since nothing is in my control, make me dance in accordance with your wishes.' The

Brahmin asked the chief's wife, 'Who is he? Tell me. I have found all the facts (*kul haqiqat*). Why do you force her to marry? O chief's wife. I have heard so much gossip that I learnt without asking. I have seen with my own eyes what I had been hearing.' The mother, luring the Brahmin with a bribe (*vaddi*), drew a curtain over the matter. She allowed the Brahmin to depart and then escorted him. While she was busy in the cover-up, everyone declared, 'She (Hir) is gone.' When will Hir be put in the palanquin?

The *zamindars* sat on the wedding mats (*khare*). So did the Khan (Sahiba). The Qazi directed, 'Bring the girl, so that I may bind her in the matrimonial bond'. Uncles, brothers and chief's wife came to bring her. Hir anticipated a disorder (*khallal*) in her life. She warned, 'Brothers! Do not touch me. I will go on my own. My uncles and brothers are not intimate with me. The only exception is my lord Dhido.' Saleti wrapped a shawl around her and went ahead, but only to see the proceedings herself. She sat on the wedding mat, knowing that it will do no harm to her. The Qazi said, 'Listen, daughter Hir! Do you need a representative (*vakil*)? From whom, except from your representative, shall I take your consent. This is a condition of the Shariat. Do you accept (*qabool*) the son of Ali? Speak so that everyone may hear.' Instantly, Hir gave her reply, 'O Qazi! I am neither dumb nor deaf, who would need a representative. I am present, sitting and visible. Take my answer as such. You ask me to speak to the people. Here, let the world hear. Ranjha has been conferred on me as a blessing (*mubarak*), just as Khera might be for the mother.' Hir, with her mouth choked, was not permitted to speak. They said, 'Let us go. Let us go.' The brothers, using force, turned her around and made her stand for the wedding rounds (*lavan*). She cried, 'Father! What will you achieve by using force, when the shawl (*loyi*) has been removed from my face?' She went inside, where arrangement had been made for sleeping.

After performing the requisite ceremonies, the Khera was brought in. Putting his foot on the bed, he woke Hir up and made her sit. She exclaimed, 'Who is it? Who is this Khera?' She delivered a hard slap (*tamacha*) on his nose, so that his teeth were damaged and blood started oozing. His brain (*maghz*) went into a spin and his heart was filled with guilt. As his pain intensified, he declared that he would die if Hir was to hit him a second time. With his teeth wrecked and bleeding, the Khera howled. Hir, while crying, complained that she had been touched by one who was not intimate (*na-mehram*). The Khera, in order to save himself, tried to use his wits (*aql*). He said, 'Whom did you slap? Named Ranjha and wearing a black shawl, he walked up to this place. Since I was attracted to him, I followed him to be able to see. On account of Ranjha, I came to this misery.' On hearing these words, Saleti clarified, 'I make myself an offering. If I slapped you by mistake, forgive me for this sin (*gunah*). Putting my head covering around my neck and hands on my feet, you are the shame of this inept one. You are also born of my mother and father. There is no difference (*tafawat*) between us. Where did you see him? I ask you. I make myself a sacrifice for you. He is the joy of my eyes, my confidant (*akhin da sukh mehram mainda*). You must tell me. I look forward to his path. While I shoo away the crows, my body is uneasy. I sacrifice myself for you, O Brother! Tell me where is Ranjha?'

Khera said to Hir, 'If you order me, I will search for him. Being heedless, Dhido may still be there.' Hir replied, 'Get up, brother! Look for Ranjha. Shall I come along with you?' Khera, in order to save himself, slipped away. He went to the place where the marriage party had descended. Everyone wanted to know what transpired during his night with Saleti. All of them asked, 'She is known to be unique (*anokhi*). What happened to you? You must tell us.' He sat down and revealed the facts, saying, 'Brothers! Listen to me. The girls played a vicious trick (*chaag*) on me. They put out all the lamps. Ahead of me was tied a restive mare (*pabban ghori*). I was totally unaware. Father! Look. The mare kicked with her hind legs, giving me bleeding teeth.'

Departure of the Khera Marriage Party

Having spent the night, the Kheras woke up at dawn and raised their hands in gratitude. They started giving gifts of camels, horses and ponies, besides waistbands and thick wrappers. They gave away plenty of goods and cash. Still, they desired to give more. The *zamindars* ensured that the servants were satisfied. As food was ready, the servants came to invite the Kheras. The Khans arrived and, partaking of food, felt satiated. When they sat in the lounge (*baithak*), cups of wine (*sharab*) were circulated. The Khans asked for more. While the *zamindars* got intoxicated, Chuchak got up and walked in. He had the cots laid out. Articles of the dowry were displayed. Ornaments of inlaid gold, in great variety, were placed. The servants brought in pans of two maunds each and these were duly weighed. Silver-plated furniture, including bedsteads and chairs, were woven with golden thread. Apart from three silken suits, the dowry included bedspreads of woven silk. The ornaments were high in price. The bracelets looked impressive. The golden receptacle for holding antimony (*surmedani*) was studded with precious beads. The drums, made of silver, surpassed the ancient workmanship. Mountains of food came into view. People had arrived from all the seven directions. What can one describe of the scene? Every member of the marriage party was given gold-woven clothes from head to foot (*sirpau sunehri*), besides the gift of silver white vessels. Damodar saw with his own eyes that whoever observed the scene came forth in praise. The Kheras called the servants to pick up the dowry. All the goods (*asbab mohkami*) were firmly tied up. The entire baggage of the camp (*derah*) was packed, while the Kheras decided to depart. Damodar narrated what God willed him to say.

The Kheras, having tightened the ropes of the goods, prepared to leave. They bade farewell (*vida*) to the relatives. As night drew near, the Khera felt like dying. He was able to save himself the previous day, but felt anxious about the unfolding of the present. At night, he went to Hir and made an excuse. He said, 'I sent for Dhido. Listen, Hir! I specially went to the moors and called out to him. Has he not come here?' Look at the wisdom (*aql*) of the Khera, who tries to save himself. When a watch of the night remained, the beat of the drum signalled the departure. The young men, who were lords of the land and rivers, tightened their waistbands. Drums of silver hung from their pommels, while golden amulets shone on their arms. A velvet sheet (*uchhar makhmali*) was laid over the palanquin. Studded in gold, it stood at the door. In the privacy (*khilwat*) of a meeting, the Khans (Siyals) sat with Chuchak, discussing, 'How can she be put in the palanquin, while a big calamity lies ahead (*qehar qahari*)?'

Noora, speaking from the depth of his heart, suggested, 'Tie her mouth and push cotton into it. We must do this. We should signal the bearers (*kahar*) and leave quickly (*shitab*). We should do away with the farewells and, thus, save (*kifayat*) time.' Chuchak did not agree to the plan, because he did not wish his men to be killed. Jani advanced his idea with force, 'Listen O Khan! Tie her arms behind her back. There will be some commotion (*kukara*), but the marriage party will not know anything. Giving a signal (*shaarat*), push her into the palanquin. There is no other solution.' Chuchak agreed that this should be done. Sinking into sorrow, he started crying. Investing great effort and making ardent entreaties (*bahuti minnat*), he sent for Kaido and pleaded, 'I have put my turban around my neck. Do not be in opposition (*nabar*) to me. It does not matter if you have adopted the divine path of renunciation (*faqr rabbana*). You are born of my mother and father.'

Kaido taunted, 'What a game have you played? You violator of a daughter (*dhee para*)! You do not have any sense. How many footmen will you send? How many coolies will you send to lift the luggage? How many cots and baskets will they carry? How many bearers will be deputed for the litter? Place the drum on Ranjha's head and let him go along, so that the stigma (*kalank*) is washed away.' There were rumblings to the effect that Kaido had settled the matter. A Doom was sent to the moors to bring Dhido. On entering the place, the Doom called out aloud. Ranjha, angry at the yelling, asked, 'Who are you looking for? Speak out the facts (*haqiqat*). Do you need someone in place of a bull?' The Doom replied that he had been deputed to carry the drum on his head, because Hir was not willing to go. Ranjha got ready and, picking up his goods and leaving his abode (*derah*), emerged in a moment. A drum (*tamak*) was placed on his head and he was made to sit besides the palanquin.

Just then, the Khera arrived on his mare. Kundi said to Hir, 'Listen, fortunate (*sabhrayi*) daughter! I sacrifice my life for you. Sit cheerfully in the palanquin. The entire marriage party is watching, with its gaze fixed on you. Get into the palanquin, as your mother sacrifices herself for you.' Hir retorted, 'Why don't you enter the palanquin? You, the sigh of Chuchak! I will stand to see the spectacle (*tamasha*) if God puts you in the litter. You, the eater of children. You have given us a huge trouble. May your brothers die. You are an agent of death. Go away and die. I am immensely angry.' Kundi responded, 'For whom are you not going? We are sending him (Ranjha) along with you. Get up and see for yourself.' The mother asked her to make sure. Hir confirmed that it was the herdsman Ranjha, whom her mother had sent along with her. Instantly, Hir became willing to go. She exclaimed, 'After treating me badly, you have done well in the end. You have given Ranjha to be by my side. I am happy. Everything is flowery (*khushali gulnari*). Like travellers (*musafir*), I am getting up to leave. Mother! God has taken away my daily bread (*rizq*).' While Hir was seen off, the entire humanity (*lokayi*) wept. She said, 'Mother! I sacrifice myself for you. Please, acceed to a request of mine. I am afraid of making it. Confer a kindness (*neki*) on me. I put my head covering around my neck. Let Ranjha sit in the palanquin, which the bearers will carry.' Kundi assured, 'Daughter! Do not be hasty. Be patient. You will not be satisfied with looking at him with your eyes. What will you gain if he sits besides you. We are never satisfied with the fragrance of flowers. What if we touch them with our nose.' The mother, using arguments (*sukhan*), tried to make her daughter understand.

Hassi, while looking at Hir, started crying, 'O Hir! With your separation, there is no life for me. The boat and moors will devour us. Seeing them empty, we will die. The True Lord (*sache sayin*) has imposed a cruel parting on us.' Hir replied, 'Hassi! This disjuncture is harsh indeed. I will not be able to return. Where will I see the moors and friends? Whose desire will make me stand? Hassi! Owing to your yearning (*sikk*), this humbled one (*nimani*) will keep on crying. What does life offer to us among unknown people?' Hassi continues, 'Your life has meaning, as you are in love with Dhido. I am forced to live in a deserted Jhang Siyal. Henceforth, there is neither Dhido nor you. God has inflicted an unkind break on us.' The words of Hassi made the entire girls' common (*aatan*) cry in unison. Hir, weeping without control, said farewell (*videya*) to her friends one after the other. She admitted, 'I ruled in the moors on your support, while I was carefree (*albeli*). Having separated from your flock (*daar*), I am a solitary crane (*koonj*). Now, only the Lord is our companion (*beli*).' The girls replied, 'May the Lord be with you.

Now, you are leaving us. Where is Hir? Where is Ranjha? Where is the parental street (*babani gali*)? Where is the boat? Where is the ferry? Where is the *pipal* tree?' Hir said, 'Due to your separation (*vichhora*), I will die of my solitary state. Hassi, I sacrifice myself for you. I am leaving the girls' common and my attachments – boat, moors, *pipal*, swings, Luddan, father and brothers. I am leaving for an unknown place. There is no possibility of my return. I am being deprived of all support. Neither father nor mother will be there.' As Hir was given a farewell, the girls common and the courtyards began to cry. So did the trees, acacia and birds. The girls, by turns, embraced Hir. The mother cried and, pulling at her stomach, did not speak. The chief's woman felt that she should have given Hir to Ranjha. Everything in the natural vegetation – trees, leaves, bushes and reeds – wept. Among the humans, the old and young wept in the seven directions and cried, 'Saleti should not have left in this manner, because there was no oppression (*sitam*) in Jhang Siyal under her rule (*raj*).'

The bearers carried the palanquin, while Ranjha carried the drum. On the way, the inhabitants came out to bid farewell. Whoever saw the scene began to cry. The people raised a clamour. The departure of Hir made the entire world cry. The Kheras, carrying the palanquin, did not meet anyone. As soon as the mother appeared to bid farewell, the bearers interrupted their journey and she said, 'Listen. Daughter! You understand enough. I inflicted sorrow on you, while your brothers are helpless. We did not allow you to stay here any longer.' Hir responded, 'O Mother! Do not give false assurances (*jhoothe lare*). These are superfluous. I know what is transpiring in your interior. While I am leaving Jhang Siyal, you continue to pour burning coals on me. Stop giving false guarantees (*dilasa koora*), as I will leave on my own.' Sisters and sisters-in-law came to bid farewell. Even the nurses and nannies started crying. A huge clamour (*jhingar*) of wailing rose up. Hir said, 'Listen. O Mother! A daughter speaks to you. You do not know. I have become a guest, who is a traveller. What a game did you play, making me sit with a husband? I hand Jhang Siyal over to you, as I move on.'

The Khans dismounted from their horses, so that they could bid farewell. From the two sides, men and horses met in accordance with their ranks. The *zamindars* were warriors endowed with chests as big as houses. How can the faces of the young men be praised (*sifat*)? Damodar stood right in the front, so that he is able to describe the scene of farewell. Chuchak, in order to formalize the occasion, put his turban around his neck and declared, 'I had my first feud (*vair*) against the Chaddars, a hundred of whom were made prostrate at my feet. I had my second feud against the Nahars, while no one dared to complain. I have never bowed before anyone. Now, it is only Hir, who has made me bend (*nivaya*).' On the other hand, Ali assured, 'You are my lord and Hir is my honoured lady (*sahibiani*). Since you have given Hir to me, I will not accept any servant (*goli*) from your house. What you did has raised my stature. I do not have words enough to praise.' He bent down to touch the feet of Chuchak, who held him midway in the gesture.

The Kheras covered one stage of the journey. A thorn in the breath troubled them. How could they injure Ranjha, so that they fulfilled a desire of their heart (*dil arman*). Ranjha must be killed on the spot. It was not proper to spare him. A big enemy had been caught in their shawl (*bukkal*). Filled with rage, they struck at the drum. They shouted, 'Break his neck. He deserves to be killed. Till then, we will not have a bit of ease (*asaish*).' Apart from poking him with sticks, they kicked him on his ankles and heels. They were inclined to kill him. They tried to figure out the way in which he was to be slain. They did not have any metaphor (*tashbih*) to match their intention. The Kheras, traversing on the path, reached an elevated site. A watch of the day remaining, they dismounted. Cow dung cakes were stacked nearby. Flour was kneaded and, preparing sweet breadcrumbs (*choori*), they ate their fill. The *zamindars*, having tied their horses to pegs, sat down. They asked for the sweet breadcrumbs and directed a wise nurse (*siyani dai*) to feed Hir.

Since Hir had been crying all through, she had not eaten anything. Immediately the woman brought the victuals to Hir and said, 'Listen. O Hir! The father-in-law has sent this.' Hir, with a frown on her forehead, said, 'Nurse! What have you brought? Mine own have become aliens. Though they were my protectors, they did not show any mercy (*mehar*). Eating breadcrumbs and taking water, let them die. What relation (*ashnai*) do they have with me? I do not have anyone, neither father nor mother.' The nurse ate half of the *choori* and brought the other half to Dhido. Putting it on his hands, she told him that Saleti had eaten half and she had sent the other half for him. Ranjha got up and received the *choori* in both hands. As soon as he took the first morsel, he put it down, complaining, 'By reversing the truth, you have made me break my fast (*roza*). A curse (*laanat*) on you. Speak, O Nurse. You told a lie. It does not have the fragrance (*mushk*) of Saleti.' The nurse, resorting to another deceit (*dagha*), brought the *choori* to Hir and said, 'Daughter. Ranjha has given this half to you and has put the other half in his mouth.' Hir, who was hungry, took the name of the Lord. The one born of Chuchak sat down to eat. Filled with anger and sorrow, she alleged with raised eyebrows, 'Nurse! A curse on you! If you ask, I will break this bowl on your head. You dared to break my fast. You have kept a part of the *choori* for yourself. The fragrance of Ranjha is not there.' The nurse ate the *choori* and did not speak any more.

The marriage party stayed for the night and, when the day dawned, they left early in the morning. Placing the drum on Dhido's head, the travellers left for their destination. Joining in a conference (*maslat*), they began to discuss the matter of killing Dhido. Ranjha saw that the Kheras were taking Hir away. Having received blows on his bare body, he could not stop his tears from flowing. How could he retrieve Takht Hazara, while enduring the cruel protection of the Kheras? He could not share with anyone the pain, which was residing in his chest. Hir fired the first salvo, 'O Khera! You are a villain since antiquity (*qadimi bhaira*). Why do you have a broken hand? Ranjha has been knotted with my knot (*gandh gandhenda*). Only now, the string of the valuable necklace (*naulakha haar*) has broken. What will come into your hands? Have you not been deceived forever? You have merely killed our truth, using the hand of superior power.' The Kheras, joining hands with one another, came to beat Ranjha, pushing him into the net of their punishment. His entire body was drenched in blood. They did not show any mercy (*taras*). Whoever came forward had the advantage of fresh breath and clenched his teeth in rage. As the enemy was in their grip, they tried to fulfil every wish (*arman*) of theirs. Ranjha protested, 'Listen, friends. In the name of the Lord, why do you unlawfully (*haram*) attack me? Pick up the sword and cut my neck off. My condition is bad. With no compassion, you hold me again and again. Friends! Fear the wrath (*ghazab*) of the Lord. You are inflicting injuries on me.'

The *zamindars* collectively took a decision on the manner of killing Ranjha. With a sword, they would cut-off his neck and, thus, remove the stigma on their name. The entire world would hold them in contempt (*khuari*). They must do away with this censure (*malamat*). Whenever Ranjha came into their view, their eyes started burning. Just kill him and throw him in the river. Ayat Khan, who did not approve of the plan, argued, 'Don't do any such thing. The herdsmen of Chuchak are accompanying us. He should not be killed in this manner. If we carry the sin (*badi*) on our head, our honour (*lajja*) does not remain with us. Let us put him in the river along with the buffaloes and kill him by drowning.' A boat came and the *zamindars* embarked on it. Their hearts were filled with rage. Without any further delay, they pushed Ranjha into the river. There was no place in the boat. As Ranjha was shoved in, they liked the action, because he would quickly die. He could not be allowed to go alive with them. Hearing this, Dhido begged (*arz*), 'You are unlawfully killing me. If you are angry, it is my bad luck (*kubakhti*). You are not lawfully chopping off my head. You should not have earned enmity with me in such haste. What are you doing? Surely a redressal (*dawangir*) will be demanded from you. That is why you are not striking me.' The Kheras slapped Ranjha, because he was not moving in the way they wanted. Assuming authority over him, they ordered him to first enter the river, as the sunshine was ascending on their path. When he would be shoving the buffaloes through the river, then they would let him speak of his state.

Ranjha, while incessantly crying, remembered the spiritual guides (*piran*) and complained, 'I did not ask for Hir. You have yourself bestowed her on me. What a calamity (*qehar*) have you inflicted on me? First, you made me climb up to the upper storey room and, then, you pulled the ladder away.' Overtaken by his sorrow, Dhido started crying. Without any delay, the five saints showed their presence. They said, 'Dhido Ranjha! Why do you cry in your sorrow? We ourselves brought punishment on you, though your pain has reached its excess. Without this, you would not have become illumined (*raushan*). It is we who have got you punished.

Enter the river, as we have assumed the responsibility of your safety.' The buffaloes, were put in the river, while the waves carried them. Ranjha was pushing them ahead of him. He was reminded of his first meeting with Hir. It all happened in the river, where they fell in love with each other. Digging out the old painful memories (*dukh puraney*), sighs of sorrow escaped from his mouth, as if they were being narrated to Hir. Ranjha, taking out his flute, started playing a melody (*sarod*) on it. Living beings of the waters – turtles, crocodiles and others – gazed out of water. The oars fell from the hands of the boatmen, because they became unaware of their bodies. As the horses and members of the marriage party experienced ecstasy (*masti*), the boat went towards the south. By the afternoon, it touched the shore.

The members of the marriage party went to their respective houses. Saleti was made to wait in the garden. News reached the house of the Kheras, while congratulatory messages (*vadhai*) spread across the world. The womenfolk – mother-in-law, sisters-in-law and other relatives – got together. All of them came to undertake the ceremonies (*reet*). The mother-in-law, peeping at Hir, brought her forehead to touch that of the bride. Failing to bear the splendour (*jhavar*), she could not say anything. She praised the beauty of Hir, whose looks showed an excess of brilliance (*rup sawaya*). As soon as Hir showed her face, her mother-in-law sold herself out. She picked a morsel of *choori* and put it in Hir's mouth, saying, 'In the name of the Lord, Saleti, eat it. I am preparing the auguries (*shagan*) for you. Eat it with cheerfulness and let me fulfil my desire. My sense of renunciation (*vairag*) has not worn off. I sacrifice myself for you.' Hir replied, O Woman! How will you understand? Whom are you feeding the *choori*? I cannot swallow even a clove. To whom are you offering food? I do not feel like eating at all. Why have you raised this clamour? Why do I not eat? That will happen only if Ranjha sits with me.'

Hearing this, the chief's wife (*mehari*) was enraged. Instantly, the nurse revealed, 'Last night, everyone was given *choori*. The herdsman did not get it. The matter has come into Hir's mind and she is saying the same thing.' In the presence of the chief's wife, the nurse tried to twist the matter. When the chief's wife's tried to offer the second morsel to Hir, the latter did plain speaking, 'O Woman! To whom are you trying to give *choori*? Whom are you trying to feed? I happily ate only in the moors. Now you are breaking my fast. If you bring Ranjha to sit with me, I will make you understand everything.' All the Khera women arrived to play the game of 'Ring in Buttermilk' (*lassi mundari*). Hir clarified, 'Either Dhido Ranjha will play or I will smash the teeth of the Khera. Ranjha is the bridegroom of Hir. Let all the friends join in congratulating (*mubarak*) me.' The Khera women announced that Hir had refused to give her consent (*ammana*). A lot of commotion arose. Gossip spread among the people. The chief's wife got up and, deciding to cancel the ceremonies, declared, 'Let a beautiful face be put in the furnace (*bhatth*). She is speaking foul words from her mouth.' The chief's wife, brushing her clothes, withdrew herself from the last part of the wedding rituals. She spoke to her husband Ali, 'May your children die! What a relationship (*saak*) did you make? You do not know her at all. Even the wild animals like tigers do not confront her. The fierce creatures (*jarvane*) are scared of her. Putting an end to our comfort, you have ruined our condition. Everyone is terrified of her. How can you explain this?' Hearing this Ali became angry and declared, 'We will kill this herdsman. Kill him, drag him and throw him in the river. The stigma will be lifted from us. Let us kill Ranjha today itself. This is the only way proper for us.' Ali summoned his kinsmen and brought them to a unanimous decision. The Khans, angry at the situation, supported the order. A Doom girl, who overheard the proceedings, went to her mother and narrated everything. On hearing this, Dhido began to fear for his life and decided to leave the place. At night, he shoved the buffaloes into the river and swam across. At dawn, he emerged on the other side of the bank.

As Ranjha's mind turned to the palanquin, pain flowed from his heart. Pouring fistfulls of dust, he tried to erase the rising tension in his interior. He shifted his anger to his flute, so that the dryness was transformed into greenery. On hearing the melody, a large band of girls (*trinjan*) came out. They asked, 'O Stranger (*pardesi*)! What news have you heard? Has anyone died? Have your buffaloes been taken away? Have your goods been plundered? Why are you in this condition?' The girls questioned in this manner. When Ranjha saw the spectacle (*tamasha*), pain returned to him. He replied, 'What do you ask from an ill-fated person? Today my cargo (*khep*) was lost to plunder. Devoid of any foundation (*bemuniada*), I am in no condition. I have no place to take shelter (*luh*). My body is suffering from fever without a fire. I feel like dying at this spot. For me, there is nothing except darkness. For you, all is bright.' One Doom girl correctly figured out the things and said, 'Yesterday afternoon, the bands played when the marriage party of the Kheras arrived. All the Doom girls (*doomayan*) got together and rushed to beg for the presents (*vadhai*). I saw with my own eyes. He carried a drum (*tamak*) on his head.' The girls, accurate in recognizing Ranjha, offered, 'If you allow us, we make a request. We will make a shelter (*goel*) for you. This place is similar to the one in the moors. You are the same Ranjha and we are the same girls. We will raise fresh love (*nautan ishq*). If you agree, we will make an effort (*uddam*).' Ranjha replied, 'If anyone can live without life, I will be living while dead. How will I live? There is no life in me. My soul roams after Hir in a state, which I do not know. If anyone can live without life, I will be living without Hir.' The herdsman, keeping the buffaloes ahead of him, decided to leave. He entered the moor following the buffaloes. Though he tried hard to detach (*udas*) his mind, the pain rushed out in a flood. He touched his forehead to his old platform (*jallar*). The place was desolate. A distressed Dhido lighted a fire besides a bed of straw (*sathar*). Kissing the place, he climbed on to the platform and allowed a sad melody to flow out of his flute.

On hearing the notes, all the girls converged at the site. They wore a variety of clothes. Some wore a coverlet with borders, while others had stripes. Having lost all awareness of their bodies, they found themselves in a state of wonder (*hairat*). In what different modes did they come? Though they had suffered a big separation, they came back within a moment. How could they be patient? It was as if Krishna was calling his companions (*gopiyan*). On meeting Ranjha, they shared the suffering of their separation (*vairag*). 'In which dispute (*kaziya*) you were entangled? You returned ahead of others. A number of servants went along with the marriage party, but none of them has showed up. Which imbroglio did you face? You returned in this sad state.' Ranjha narrated, 'When we covered the first stage of the journey, I carried a drum on my head. They repeatedly struck me on my head. All of them subjected me to severe torture. By the time we reached midway, I was half dead. I tolerated what God made me tolerate. Listen, Hassi. When we reached the ferry (*pattan*), they resolved to kill me. The Kheras conspired to put an end to my life. This is precisely what they did. By pushing me into the river, they would have drowned me. They nurtured this evil intention. None of them accepted what I said. There was no mercy in their hearts. None of my wishes proved effective. Hassi! I was tired of making appeals. Left with no excuse (*sarpar*), they put me into the river. There was no raft, no boat and no ferry. I could not see the bank on the other side of the river. I was just thrown into it. I was utterly helpless. There was no shelter or any other such support. Taking the buffaloes along, I entered the river and God brought me safe to the shore. Thereafter, I was dragged into an enclosure for buffaloes. The girls came and told me that the Kheras had decided to kill me. They clearly heard this. As I was pushed out, I entered the river and faced the night in water. This is what happened to me. Hassi! I know nothing about Hir.'

Hassi said, 'Listen, Miyan Ranjha. It is good that you have come here. Let the Kheras be consigned to a furnace (*bhatth*). And so too the reputation of the Kheras. It is only you, who came and showed your face. We are delighted to see you. Life has acquired fresh splendour. You must stay here, as God has brought you here.' Ranjha replied, 'Listen, Hassi. How can I stay here? I have no strength (*quwwat*) in me. If anyone can live without life, you may ask me to live. Hir crowds every nerve and pore of my body (*rag rag rom hajum*). Her memory is inscribed on every spot here. All the girls appear like the stars, but the moon of Saleti is not there.' Hassi pleaded, 'Listen, Ranjha. We make a proposal (*arz*) for you. Let us sit and decide. The same moor and the same boat. We will make an abode (*goel*) for you. You are the same Ranjha. We are the same girls. A new love (*nautan ishq*) will sprout. If anyone speaks about you, we will dig out his eyes. You will stay here according to your wishes. With the headcovering around our necks, we plead.' Ranjha explained, 'Hassi! I will not be able to stay here without Hir Siyal. It is not proper (*munasib*) for me to settle at Chuchkana. My daily bread (*rizq*) has shifted to Takht Hazara in accordance with the power of the Almighty (*qudrat qadir*).' Hassi pleaded, 'Miyan Ranjha! If you leave this place, we will also go with you. You have extracted the life out of us. How are we going to live? Death is better than such a life. We will cry throughout eight watches of the day. Our living here has become impossible.'

Ranjha appreciated the plight of the girls, who will not stay even if made to. How could he give them advice (*nasihat*)? The more he tried, the more they stepped forward to face him. Ultimately, he agreed to stay in accordance with their desire (*razae*). However, this was not possible because they did not trust his words. Hassi said, 'Listen, Dhido. Every day, we will be worried (*fikr*) about you. We are helpless (*aajiz*) and full of sadness. You do not realize this. Either you take us along with you or we will go with you. Dhido! You must be clear about it. Otherwise, we will keep you with force.' The girls did not believe (*visah*) that Ranjha would stay in the moors. They could not rely on him. Nor would he be able to delude them. Only if they could feed him something, they would be more confident (*nisha nihayat*). If he promised something, they would rest assured (*khatir jama*). The girls exerted themselves to arrange food for him. Some of them went to bring *choori*, while others made him sit after effectively surrounding him. The girls handed him the flute, so that he raised a melody. As soon as the girls swooned (*moorchha*), Ranjha put on his shoes and walked away.

Returning to Takht Hazara and Facing the Waraichs

Ranjha reached Takht Hazara and met his brothers. He met his paternal (*pekayan*) family, though it did not tolerate him. While repenting, he asked himself, 'I made a mistake. For what purpose did I come there?' Though he felt disturbed, he detached his mind (*chit udasi*). He spoke to Tahir (eldest brother) with a smile, 'I have not come here for the division of property (*mal*). I was engaged in mendicancy (*faqiri*) for twelve years. Now, I have come to see the country (*vatn*). On coming here, I did not ask anything from you. Nor did I raise any demand (*suwal*). What will you lose? You do not speak cheerfully.' Tahir replied, 'We have been turned upside down. Did you go to the Siyals to dig wells? Did you go there to build a castle? You have blackened the face of Mojam. You called yourself a herdsman. A curse (*laanat*) on your being alive. In fact, you should have died there.' Ranjha explained, 'I am a mendicant (*faqir*) and you are Tahir Khan. I do not make any claims (*dawa*). Taking your name, I came to my native place. This is the result (*natija*) of my visit. I feel fully assured that no one belongs to anyone?' Ranjha did not like what his brothers said. Tahir complained, 'What shall I say to you, Dhido? Nothing has remained a secret. When we hear that you go with the buffaloes as the herdsman of Chuchak and when we hear that you follow the marriage parties carrying a drum on your head, I enter a state where I cannot choose between living and dying.'

The sisters-in-law came and asked Ranjha, 'We put our head-covering around our neck and hands on our feet. Tell us. For the one you became a mendicant (*dhuan kitoi*), what kind of a girl is she?' Ranjha felt that he must leave, as it was not proper for him to keep sitting there. He replied, 'What shall I say? What do you ask? I do not like your words. Do not bring Saleti in your minds. I feel like dying. Being fearful, I do not even emit a sigh, lest she should disapprove of it. Only a strong heart contains a sigh.' Ranjha's friends arrived and each one of them embraced him. They announced, 'We will put up a thatch and spread out a mat. We will fix a hedge all around. We will place pitchers of water and two smoking pipes (*chillam*). We will lay down (*bisat*) these things. They made this arrangement a reality.' All of them sat in the village common (*dara*). Everyone liked it. Day and night, they sat in meetings (*majlis*). The experience turned exceedingly beneficial. Day and night, they kept on sitting, with shawls thrown over them. They did not eat or drink. With the arrival of Dhido, the entire world shared in the delight.

Yaqub Khan Waraich heard that the son of Mojam had appeared. The Waraichs formed an assembly (*mela*) in order to leave for Takht Hazara. The *zamindars* covered the distance in one stage. On the other hand, Tahir and Zahir sat in council and considered the options before them. Yaqub said, 'O Khan! We have heard with our own ears that your brother has come. Mojam, in his turn, had rightfully produced him. He (Dhido) raised the reputation of the lineage (*kul*) by being called a herdsman. Listen, gentlemen! All the eminent men (*mahajan*) have come to discuss the matter.' On hearing this, Tahir became upset. After reflecting, he declared that they would give a jerk to the edge of the garment, as the plaintiff (*muddai*) had come to Hazara. The brothers and Waraich got together and, forming a body, came to the village common. Ranjha, on seeing them, felt disturbed. (Yaqub Khan) Waraich, addressing Ranjha, said, 'When it was your turn, Mojam died. He had not cut your head off. You rushed to do things that were improper (*nalaiq*). If you had not turned up like this, the name of your brothers would not have been removed.' Dhido replied, 'Listen, brothers. What is in your minds? You speak harsh words (*sakht zaban*). State the claim (*muda*) for which you have appeared. I am not at fault (*betaqsir*), but you use bad words. However, I will ignore them. Why don't you clearly reveal your purpose (*matlab*).' Yaqub alleged, 'Do we have no business with you? We have not come here to see your face? In our own interest (*garz*), we came to Hazara. Mojam had entrapped us. Either you marry or snap the relation. Give an answer. We have not come for your pilgrimage (*ziyarat*).' Dhido asserted, 'Go. You may marry where you wish. I do not make any claim (*dawa*). The lords of land and rivers cannot be the masters of mat and fire. You may come here again and again till I return. Still there is no claim between you and me.'

The *zamindars*, having taken the witness (*shahid*), got up to leave. They were detached (*udas*) from the situation. They tightened the straps and made preparations to be travellers again. Tahir grabbed the reins and took them away. He made an effort to stop them for meals. Tahir and Zahir asked the Waraichs to mount only after taking the meals (*tukkar*). Jeevan Khan, a brave warrior (*bahadur sura*), put the shawl around his neck and declared, 'We are not new to each other. We are relatives since long (*chirokey sakkey*). We are intertwined like ropes.' Jeevan, continuing in the same vein, said to the Khans (Waraichs), 'O Khans! Listen to what we say. We and you are in kinship with each other. In the past, there have been many alliances (*saak*) between us. We are intertwined like ropes (*une su vaan niayin*). O Khans! Here is the son of Tahir. Let the work be done at this spot. If this is not done, there remains no honour (*lajj*) in our relationship.' Yaqub Khan Waraich responded, 'Listen, sir. Earlier too, we were given assurance when you betrothed your brother. We came and saw you (*didar*). Now, you state this. We did not wish to return in this way. As if we got any happiness earlier.'

The Khans (Waraichs) put forward this reply. Jeevan again argued, 'If one has died or went mad (*mua te kamla*), we must not chase him. Let him perish in the furnace. Do not chase him. Let us leave him at that. We are not new. We are in kinship for long. We are intertwined like ropes. There is an intimate mix-up (*gadvad*) between us. Where is the need to examine it?'

From here and there, the *zamindars* (Ranjhas) organized the marriage. As the drum was installed, they gathered provisions such as flour, jaggery, sugar and grain. Seeking the auspicious hour (*changi sayet*), water was poured into the flour. The Brahmin, carrying the knotted string (*gandhi*), was made to rush. They brought in a variety of horses that were silver, grey, double hued, red and swift. Velvet ornamentations were hung from their necks, forelegs, loins and saddles. The turbans were studded with plumes, while drums were provided on two sides of the pommels (*hanne tabalbaz*). The *zamindars* looked impressive. What sons the mothers had produced? The marriage party of the Ranjhas was ready and it marched out for the ceremony. Dressed from head to toe (*siropau*), their pride matched the storerooms in size. Someone advised Tahir to take Dhido along with them. He too was the son of their mother and father (*ma peyo jaya*). It was not proper to leave him out. Tahir, leading the clan (*kul qabila*), went to placate Ranjha. 'My brother! Get up and come along with us.' Holding Ranjha's hand, Tahir beseeched (*minnat*) him to avoid any laxity. When the friends held Ranjha and raised him up, he replied, 'Listen, Tahir. It is not proper for me to accompany you. The entire loss will be yours. You do not understand. You do not see. What will I do there? The entire world will be coming. There will be talking. Damage will accrue to you (*ghata sab tusahin*). Tahir and Zahir. This is not expedient (*munasib*).' Tahir insisted, 'If you will not come, the entire marriage party will stay back. If you accompany, everyone will be satisfied (*razi*). After all, we are also going with you. You have descended from our paternal side (*pitriya*). You are like a father to your nephew. Dhido, get up. May I be your offering. If you are offended (*ruttha*), we will appease you.'

The Ranjhas arrived along with the Waraichs. The world came out to see. As the warriors dismounted in the garden, the youngsters brought refreshments (*halufe*). Food was cooked. The *zamindars* were fed. Preparations were made. From the girls' common, the members rushed out to watch. On seeing the guests one by one, they felt happy. In particular, they had their eyes on the bridegroom. As soon as they saw Dhido, they were infatuated (*mohiyan*) at the spot. Virtually sold out, they did not have the courage to make an inquiry. A friend of Dhido revealed the fact, 'This is Dhido, the one who is separated (*katratta*). Have you not heard?' On hearing this, the girls were surprised and could not utter anything. Seeing his face, they were captivated. One of the girls stepped forward and, moving up to Ranjha, asked, 'O Mendicant (*faqira*)! What is your name? Tell me. I may be mistaken about you. Are you the brother of Tahir?' Ranjha responded, 'How do you ask me?' After being bewitched thus, the girls came back from there and raised a clamour, 'She is the most unfortunate (*kubakht*) girl. We have just seen the one who was first betrothed (*mangenda*) to you. We are just sold out.' They came to the pre-wedding ceremony and joined the bride. The girl, while crying, wailed aloud, 'Come and show him to me. Let Saleti be sacrificed. I must fulfil my desire (*armaan*). You should console (*dilasa*) me until I see him. Help me take a look at him. My urge (*chau*) is supreme. My yearning (*virag*) must be erased.' The girls went to Ranjha and told a lie, 'Get up. The mendicants are calling you. Come and receive messages from the masters.'

Ranjha, on hearing the mention of mendicants, left the marriage and his brothers. Once brought inside, the matter was stated to him. As soon as he entered, he appeared as the light of spiritual excellence (*azmat ki rushnai*). The girls pulled him down and, making him sit in the centre, formed a circle (*ghummar*) around him. What thoughts emerged from the fiancée? All the girls spoke of her great pain. The fiancée, on her part, was experiencing convulsions (*chhik pajuta*) in her interior.

GIRL: What is my fault (*taqsir*)? I am the one whom fortune has ruined (*bakhton tatti*). You have abandoned me. Every day, I have been drawing lines (*aunsi*) on the ground, so that someone will unite us. Do not be in opposition (*nabar*) to me. I am dying. I do not have any defect. Which sin (*gunah*) did you see in me? Give me an answer.

RANJHA: I do not know anything. I am unable to earn a living (*khatt*). I have not learnt anything. How can one push the daughter of another (*parayi jayi*) into hardship? Such a thing is not proper for me. I have never done any labour (*mehnat*) with my hands. From whose house will I feed her? I have rightly understood that I have no strength (*quwwat*).

GIRL: Among the Siyals, you had vigour in plenty. You destroyed the name of your father. You had no shame in grazing buffaloes. Nor any shame in carrying a drum on your head. When Hir went away with the Kheras, then your mind brought you to Hazara. When my turn came, you have assumed the name of worthless (*makhattu*).

RANJHA: Such jeers (*tahne*) do not leave me. Your strictures (*ulame*) against me are harsh. I have understood myself. No vigour has remained in me. If I push in someone else's daughter, it does not bring any credit to me. I cannot lift any load, as there is no stamina in my body.

GIRL: When you lived there, you were quite satisfied (*razi*). You pleaded (*tarle*) for Hir, but she did not come into your hands. When the herdsmen reduced you to misery (*aajiz*), then detachment (*udasi*) sank into your heart. You became worthless when you lost Hir.

RANJHA: Bibi! Do not ridicule me. You have deliberately raised a false quarrel (*koora jhagra*). Leave my lappet (*pallu*), lest anyone should come from outside. There is nothing to give and nothing to take. All your clamour is of no avail (*kook nikkami*).

Ranjha, being truly distressed, spoke angry words.

GIRL: Why do you speak in anger? I live in perpetual stress (*nit andesa*). Throughout the day and night, I intently watch the road. In this state, I weep. Though I am overflowing with youthful beauty (*joban ras matti*), my hair have changed colour. If you are chasing someone else's right (*haq paraye*), why should I surrender my right?

RANJHA: I am not your right (*haq*). I have no aim (*matlab*) to pursue. You have trapped me through deceit. You have no shame. Outside, the people, including my brothers, will hear everything. This is not good on your part.

Ranjha stated the above. Just then, Tahir, who was asking for the way, walked in. When he saw the gentleman (Ranjha), he was taken aback. His eyes betrayed his feelings. He exclaimed, 'Outside it is refusal (*nah*) and inside it is acceptance (*razi*). I find it quite gratifying. Get up, Dhido! Sit on the wedding mat. The legal husband has been apprehended.' Ranjha explained, 'I swear by the Lord (*sayin di saunh*), brother Tahir. I did not know anything. Through deception (*dagha*), they brought me in. How do I know that, mentioning the name of the mendicants, they had laid a trap (*fahi*) for me? Brother Tahir, I speak the truth. She is born of my mother and father.' When Tahir came inside, Ranjha got himself released. Since his mind was fixed on leaving, he ran out. Having extricated himself, he thanked God. Instantly, he put on his shoes and sped away. Once Ranjha reached the village common, he began to exercise caution (*avdaani*). He had neither any intention nor any memory. Yet, providence pushed him into a trap. His complexion was pale and his state was bad. For this reason, he was grateful (*shukar*) to God. After three days, the marriage party of the Ranjhas came back.

Suffering of Hir in Rangpur Khera

The tale (*qissa*) of Ranjha has reached its completion. Now, the matter of the Kheras is to be written. Inviting relatives and brothers, the Kheras got together and began to make proposals. They brought Hir after marriage, but only attained affliction (*zehmat*). Ali asked them to put forward some solution (*maslat*). The *zamindars* sat to consider the options before them. 'If we quickly kill Hir, this only will make sense. How can our honour (*lajj*) remain intact if we show any laxity. Nothing suits us except removing the stigma (*kalakh*) from our face.' The chief's wife intervened, 'Khans! It is not proper to kill her. How can we kill the daughter of Chuchak? You are mistaken in making this suggestion. You said that you cannot take a bitch of his house. Khan! Have you forgotten? It does not behove you. What a plan (*mata*) have you recommended? There is no one near the place, where you store the grain. Sehti will be her neighbour (*hamsai*). She must stay there. It is a large area and the rooms are isolated. Let someone escort her there. Keep her there only.' This decision was arrived at.

Hir was brought and placed in the bungalow (*haveli*). No one was seen around. She was made to sit on a broken stool and a torn mat. Sitting with truth and patience (*sidq saboori*), her food was only desire (*sikk ahaar*). She became the neighbour of Sehti. While sitting, she kept on crying. Frequently, she got up to gaze at the path and shoo away the crows. She asked, 'My confidant (*mehram*) Ranjha! Speak the truth. To whom do I belong? I am the one who is ruined. Distances have been created between us. I am dying in my search for you. Like a fish without water, my body is restless. Better than this life is death, which will make me free (*farigh*). My sighs bring out tears.' Hir is seriously considering the possibility of death. 'You are the shame of this lost one. Without Dhido, there is no life for me.'

For Hir, the desire for Ranjha is like raw mercury (*kacha paara*). Her decaying body was writhing like fish without water. Her interior kept on smouldering and then got extinguished. Her state cannot be described. She cursed with her mouth, but she could not think of any remedy. She drew lines (*aunsi*) on the walls and drove the crows away. She placed her hands on her forehead. A fire has reached her mat (*sathar*), as her enemies (*harifan*) shot arrows at her. Ranjha has pierced every pore of her body. Only he will apply the medicine. 'O Mother! I will stay in the manner my perfect guide (*kamil murshid*) wishes to keep me.' The state of Hir has become inverted. She is imbued with Ranjha, but no one is familiar with her condition. Whom should she address as Ranjha? She has herself become Ranjha.[33] Ranjha belongs to Hir and Hir belongs to Ranjha. There is not even a bit of difference (*ratti faraq*) between them. Without each other, their life cannot be described. Without Ranjha, it is not possible for her to have any endurance (*dhiraj*). Her heart beats and chest trembles. When will the lovers meet? They are physically separate. In Hir's heart, there is no difference. She keeps on driving away crows. God has ordained that she must consume pain. This is what she does.

Reduced to misery in her bondage (*bandi*), she cannot narrate her woes to anyone. She is all alone. There is no one besides her. At whom should she gaze? It is Ranjha who resides in her eyes. Outside her eyes, she cannot see anyone. If she dies while waiting for Ranjha, she will become acceptable (*qabool*) to God. (She reflected) 'I have made longing (*sikk*) for you as my food. I eat and drink it. The pain of Ranjha is my earning. This has been conferred on me as my provision for the day. If I narrate my woes to anyone, no one pays attention to it. I have understood that my pain will go only with my death. When the moon rises, the whole world sees it. In contrast, my moon is far away. I keep my eyes fixed on the path and, all this while, I shoo away the crows. My longing for you is my food (*tosha*), which I am bound to consume. Sooner or later, my lord (*khawind*) will turn his heart towards me. After all, he is the honour (*sharm*) of this humbled creature. When the moon rises, the whole world sees it. But, I remain ignorant of it. There is happiness among the people, while this lonely one keeps on pining (*jhora*). He gave me all assurances (*dilasa*) in the moors. Why do you not think of me? If I die gazing at your path, I would have performed Haj at this very place.[34] I am imprisoned in a cell, while you know nothing about it. The people who burn me with their air, it is they who wish to put their arms around my neck. They have no shame in putting me into their house. How can I live with the Kheras? It is like making cotton put up with fire (*atish rooyi niayin*).' In these circumstances, Sehti inquires from Hir, who states:

HIR: Listen, Sehti! Pain has consumed me. My mother wronged me. No one has ever made any contact with me. I have no mother or father. To whom shall I convey the agony of my heart (*dil di vedan*)? Only the sufferer knows it. Shall I live or die? As I cry, my state is miserable.

SEHTI: Listen! Your face gives the proof (*ugaahi*). There is no need to inquire. A fire burns inside you. A curse keeps on killing you. O Girl! Tell me the facts (*haqiqat*). Why do you conceal this fire (*agg chhapayi*)? Hir of the Siyals. Speak up. I make myself a sacrifice for you.

HIR: Sehti! Do not chase me. I have become helpless (*aajiz*). My mother, father and brothers have erased me from their memory (*visraye*). With whose support can I speak? Who has given birth to me? Sehti, tell me. Shall I die or live? My eyes are given to excessive crying (*ronde nain sawaye*).

SEHTI: There is a unique desire (*chaat awwali*) inside you. I have come to know. How many batches of swimmers, who have consumed the herb of love, got drowned? The addiction (*amal*) never goes out of the bones. Their lives are spent in crying. I have understood the pain (*ranjish*) that the Lord gave you.

HIR: You may have understood it. Sister! It is a futile discussion. No one knows this. Nor anyone has seen it with the eyes. We came to this world, but our life has been wasted. No one is a relative. What do I need to understand? I have sunk in suffering.

SEHTI: Listen, Hir! You are an honourable woman (*sahibiyani*). How can you deny? Your eyes give clear testimony. From whom do you conceal? No one has been able to hide it. May your love remain alive for ever (*ishq salamat*). You are absorbed in love. Still you are not willing to admit it. Listen, Hir of the Siyals. How are you being tossed about in the river of love? Siyali! One, bearing a longing for this world, shows a green colour. Those, who long for the Lord (*sikk sayin di*), are red roses. They display distinct features. Yellow adorns one who longs for a man (*sikk manukh di*). Hir! You have a longing for love. Why do you try to hide it?

Sehti grew tired of making entreaties (*tarle*). Yet, Hir did not come around. How can Sehti draw out the secret (*bhed*) of Hir? Otherwise, Hir would wither away. Sehti felt, 'She does not tell me her condition. Instead, I will tell her of my state. If she does not come into my hands, I will relate everything to her.' Sehti went somewhere in her village. On returning after three days, she enacted a deceit (*fareb*). Thrice she fell on the ground, so that Hir exclaimed, 'May the Lord keep you.' Ultimately, Hir asked Sehti, 'Listen, Sehti! Did a fairy scare you? Did a demon (*deo*) appear before you? Has a ghost (*bhoot*) tormented you? Is there a shadow (*saya*) over you? Did you fall down from a horse? I do not know anything. May I be your offering. Tell me. Let me know something.' Sehti replied, 'The one, who is my lover lord (*sahib yar*), is not visible. Bahman Ramu is the comfort of my eyes (*akhin da sukh*). I am sold out to him. If I do not see him today, I will not be worthy of living. Listen, Hir! What can I tell you? What does it hold for me?' While hearing this, Hir became more and more excited (*chamkayil*). It came into her mind that Sehti could support her love. Saying, 'May God keep you,' Hir picked up the fan. She pressed the feet of Sehti and realized that her disease (*rog*) was the same as it was stated. She said, 'Listen, Sehti! May I be your offering? How will you show him to me? What sort of lover (*piyara*) is he? Let me have his vision (*didar*). You will not lose anything if he is shown to me. I have a keen desire (*shauq*) to see him, lest I should live for only a few days.'

Sehti explained, 'If I find him, I will bring and show him. Right now, he cannot be found. I will get my head cut-off and distribute sweets if I see my beloved. Listen, Hir! I make myself your offering. I will give you what you ask for. The doomsday (*akhir*) of which we hear has come on me.' The more did Sehti dig out her pain, the more did Hir become eager (*shitabi*) in her pursuit. With every passing moment, she felt happy (*khushali*) as if a sleeping organism had awakened in her. She continued to fan Sehti and massage her with a lotion. A spark was ignited in her frame. She nurtured an ardent desire to see Bahman Ramu. When Sehti came around, she summoned the Bahman. In order to ensnare Hir in a net of deception (*fand fareb*), she did not send anyone for him. Instead, he was brought in and shown at night. Emotion welled up in Hir and she prayed, 'O Lord! Ease my difficulties if it pleases the Almighty (*qadir*)'. When the Bahman would come to meet Sehti, the hapless Hir watched. Whenever the two were happy in their union (*milan*), Hir peeped through the window. She became a perfect confidant (*mehram*) on seeing their love (*yari*). In fact, she became an emissary (*raibari*) on seeing them in this manner. When Sehti was not present, the Bahman came to the place. He would go after leaving his message with Hir, who passed it on to Sehti. If Sehti went to her parental house, Bahmneta (Ramu) still came. Hir conveyed to him the messages of Sehti and made him fully understand. This is how Siyali performed the role of an emissary. For a long time, she served as a confidant (*mehrami*), so that there was no veil.

SEHTI: O Girl, Hir! You have given me happiness. I would yearn for the right messages, if you had not offered your confidence. You must relate your own affliction, as I do not keep a veil from you.

HIR: His name is Dhido. He is a Ranjha. I am sold out to him. A precept (*nasihat*) of this kind cannot be given except to a confidant. Only a confidant can know. An excessive pain of love (*vedan qehar ishq*) is overflowing from my organs (*lingin*). This separation (*faraq*) can be corrected if you send for him (Ranjha) and bring him here.

SEHTI: You were wrong in failing to reveal the secret. I am worried for you. Your body, which is like the sandalwood (*chanan vanni dehi*), is going waste. O Girl! In order to take this pain away from you, I will send Ramu. You have done a great wrong, O Hir. I grew tired of inquiring about it.

HIR: What is past is gone. Sehti! Now I am dying. Get up and see. You should not be cautious (*tahambal*) any more. Bring the lord of my head (*sir sayin*). Sehti! Bibi! I am your offering (*sadqa*). I may return to the world.

Sehti got up and sent for Ramu. She said to him, 'Go to Takht Hazara. You should not delay even for a moment. Narrate all her suffering. Like the love that has grown (*preet vyapi*) between you and me, the same has happened between the hapless Hir and the herdsman.' The Bahman, in order to leave, gathered his feet. Ramu said to Hir, 'Give me your message along with some token (*nishani*). It is impossible for me to wait, as I have taken the calamity (*musibat*) on my head. My affliction (*peer*) is the same as yours.' Saleti got up and came to give the message.

Hir explained, 'A beautiful bed (*palang suhava*) in the boat. He arrived from somewhere and was sleeping on it. He made me a disciple (*murid*) in the boat. I am his offering. He should assure me his sincerity and strong faith (*sabat sidaq aqida mohkam*). Tell my lord that I am full of faults (*auganhari*). Let him forgive me for my sins (*bakhsh gunah*). The dense shisham and the bald fig. It is there that we committed ourselves (*bol kitoyi*) to each other. On my head, the hair flew in full pride. On his head, a tuft grew long. Those who are dying rely only on life. Do I suffer from a misfortune (*kambakhti*)? The perfect master (*kamil murshid*) did not pay any attention to his disciple. Tell him to see what has happened to me. I am burning in separation (*firaq*). I am enduring a severe oppression. I am pining to see his face. The one, who has been ruined in love, may die of her affliction. With folded hands, I will enter the grave, while reciting the name of Ranjha. Just like the love (*preet*) between Dasrath's son and Sita. Also, like the love between Nand's son and Birkhbhan's daughter.[35] The love between him and me is similar. This is known to the whole world (*kul lukai*). Listen, my lord Ranjha. You are the master of my head. Get up, Ramu. You must reach your destination in the morning. I am dying. Sehti has ignited a sleeping fire. It has set me aflame. Ramu Bahman! Your journey is necessary. May you be under the grace of God (*karam ilahi*)! Ramu Bahman, brother. You must reach Hazara.'

The love of Hir percolated into the limbs of Ramu. Clenching his fists, he set out without taking any expenses. In view of the long distance, Ramu recited the name of Ram and initiated his steps. By the time the day dawned, he had covered 40 leagues (*kos*). On entering a village, he cooked his food. Having decided not to eat at the hearth, he packed the half cooked food (*adh pakki*) in his bag. He kept on walking at a rhythmic pace for four watches of the day, as if he had grown wings. By late evening (*nimashi*), he had covered 80 leagues. He entered a village as it was the time for taking meals. He got it cooked while standing, because he had still to walk (*chalanhara*). He did not sit at all. He faced the night and, when the dawn broke, Hazara came into his view. Ramu entered Hazara and stayed in a house of the Brahmins. He was asked the full facts (*kul haqiqat*). Ramu gave suitable replies. He stated that he was going to Kashmir for some work, but did not reveal the truth. This was what he said. Then, he asked, 'How are the rulers (*hakim*)? How are the rains? How are your chiefs (*sardar*)? How are your crops? This place has been enjoying plenty of peace (*bahut asudiyan*). I heard that Mojam was a good *zamindar*. Tell me about him. How are the sons of Mojam? Tell me about them.'[36]

A Brahmin of Hazara stated, 'All the three sons surpassed one another. They are not worthy of reproach. The crops are as good as the times. So are the rains. There was a lot of prosperity (*chokhi barkat*) during the time of Mojam. Even now, the situation is not bad. The fourth son of Mojam is a master of the mat and fire (*sathar dhuen da sayin*).' On hearing this, Ramu began to reflect and then asked, 'The three sons of Mojam are good. Where did the fourth one go? Did he leave his native place (*des*) and become an alien (*pardesi*). Where did he set up his fire?' Ramu posed this question to the Brahmins. The Brahmin of Hazara replied, 'The fourth son of Mojam did not go anywhere after leaving. Earlier, he lived among the Siyals till Hir did not marry. When she was married among the Kheras, he returned here.'

On hearing this, Ramu got up and came out of the village. He saw some boys (*neengar*) at play. He inquired about the village common (*dara*). Saying, 'We will show you uncle (*taya*),' one of them began to lead and another went alongside. In this manner, Ramu came to the village common. Here he made a seat for himself. He spent the entire day looking around. He did not get an opportunity to speak to anyone. He became weary of watching. When the day came to an end, the evening came on. Some people came and others went away. Ramu kept on sitting, intent on observing. Appearing detached, he walked on all the four sides. He did not know the purpose of continuing his presence at the site. He wondered when the people would go away from there. He did not feel at ease. He felt worried inside. Owing to the increasing tension, he did not feel like eating and drinking. As his anxiety could not be erased, his apprehensions kept on mounting. With the onset of the evening, all the people went to their homes. Ramu walked in. Coming near Dhido, he spread his mat. Ramu looked left and right, but did not see anyone. He felt eager to speak. He did not utter a word, lest anyone should hear. He looked towards the town (*shehr*), making sure that no one was coming. Ranjha, in his heart, tried to figure out the direction in which he (Ramu) would go. When the time for sleep arrived, Ranjha asked him, 'Friend (*beli*)! From which side have you come? Where will you go? With whom do you have a purpose (*matlab*)? Whom are you asking for? Brother! With what purpose are you sitting here? Tell me what is in your heart?' Ramu merely said that he was going to stay there. As the night descended, Ranjha said, 'I shall go to inform the village (*vasti*). An arrangement must be made early for your sitting and staying. If you do not have the provisions like flour and clarified butter, then I must inform someone. It will be difficult when it becomes dark.' This is what Dhido said.

Ramu said, 'Where shall I go? Listen to the facts. I have come for you. Hir has sent me to you. Take the messages I am offering.'

Hearing this Ranjha quarrelled with Ramu, 'This matter cannot be talked about. I do not know what you are saying. I do not know anything of Hir.' Then Ramu spoke, 'Is this your answer? The new boat and the boatman Luddan. When you saw its face, you occupied it. The River Chenab and the ferry (*pattan*) of Chuchkana. O Ranjha! I went and saw everything. You took rest on the bedstead.' Ranjha said, 'Friend! The boat, the Chenab and Luddan. I have not heard of these. Who went and who came? My livelihood is fixed here. Ramu Bahman! You are in error. I am not Ranjha. What do I know of Hir?' Ramu pointed out, 'Dhido! Take the second message, which I am stating to you. The canopied shisham and bald fig (*chhatti tahli te landa pipal*). You have stayed there. You grazed buffaloes in the moors and Hir would come to meet you. Sitting on the platform (*jallar*), she fed you sweetened breadcrumbs. These are the messages I am offering.'

Ranjha, collapsing down and falling on his feet, said, 'Brother! You have seen her with your eyes. Is she well (*sahi salamat*)? State the facts (*haqiqat*). Tell me about the one born of Chuchak. My very life is a matter of faith. I will not hesitate to die. Speak out the facts, as my end is drawing near.' Ramu replied, 'There is neither a drop of blood nor a bit of flesh on Hir. It is something that cannot be described. She does not die. After dying, she revives and lives again. She burns and then extinguishes. She will live only as long as I delay. Listen, O Lord (*sahib*)! When I return, she will not be alive.' Dhido Ranjha clenched his fist and, putting an amulet (*trag*) around Ramu's neck, said, 'Ramu! You must reach early in whatever way you can. I am also following. O Hir! See that I am coming. On seeing Ramu I have become alive.' While preparing to leave, Ranjha detached (*udaas*) himself from the place. He burnt down his hut in the village common and broke the pitchers. At midnight, he departed. It was no longer possible to stay. In the end, he would reach Saleti, lest the Lord should end her life. Owing to his ardent passion (*sikk*) for Hir, it was necessary for him to meet her. It came into his mind first to go to Tilla. When he completed the first stage (*manzil*) of his journey, he arrived at the Jhelum.[37] When he completed the second stage, he had climbed the mountain. At the end of the third stage, he reached the Tilla. As soon as he saw the place, he resolved to pay his obeisance (*didara*). There could be no delay in this. Having inquired about the path, he reached the abode of the saints (*maqam piran*).[38]

Experience at Tilla Balnath

Ranjha, arriving at the monastery of the spiritual preceptor, benefited from a vision (*darshan*) of Sidh Bagai. The Jogi asked Ranjha, 'From which country (*kehre deson*) have you come? Tell me the facts (*haqiqat*) about yourself. What is the purpose (*manorath*) of your coming here?' On seeing Ranjha's face, the Jogi was enamoured. Yet, he asked his questions. Ranjha, putting a cloth around his neck and lowering his head, declared, 'Baba! Of which high state (*jah*) shall I speak? I have come to meet you. There is no land (*ja muqami*), which I can call mine. Nor am I born of anyone. Confer your blessings (*thapna*) on me.' Sidh Bagai said, 'Your bearing is curious (*chal ajaib*). Why do you wish to be a Jogi? You appear to be overtly fastidious (*hushnaq*). Jog is not suited to you. You have eaten the bread your mother cooked. Why do you enter the path of Jog?' On hearing the Pir, Ranjha started crying and pleaded, 'I have come into your refuge (*sharni*). Whoever was favoured with your kindness (*kirpa*), he was able to swim across the world. Even Gopichand and Bharthari took Jog. What about a poor (*gharib*) one like me?'[39] Having come to the Tilla, Ranjha fell at the feet of the master, who explained, 'Living in Jog is extremely distant (*khara dureda*). How can you know these matters? Enduring in the path of Jog is difficult. Its secrets are hard. Our bounties comprise begging food and sleeping on the mat (*mang khana te sathar sauna*). Yet, I will give Jog to you, provided you give truthful answers to my questions.'

Ranjha stated, 'Takht Hazara is our place (*vatn*). I am born of Mojam. When I was struck with misfortune, I left my home and came to the subdistrict of the Siyals (*sik siyalin*). A daughter in the house of Chuchak was nice. She is named Hir. Seeing her, I was sold out (*vikana*) to her. She ensnared my heart. When she was married in the country (*des*) of the Kheras, I got involved in a dispute (*qaziya*). Since I could not think of any place, I came into your protection (*saam*).' When Ranjha narrated this, the Jogi was surprised. He summoned his disciples and, making them sit, asked them to offer some advice (*maslat*). He told everything about Ranjha, including his name and caste. He did not hide anything. The Jogi sought an answer from his disciples. On hearing this, the disciples said, 'He is not fit (*laiq*) for Jog. He has not told you anything unknown. The herdsmen have already narrated this. You are the master of the Tilla. For you, there is no dearth of disciples.' In fact, they clarified that things did not work out in this manner.

The Jogi got angry and rebuked the disciples. Declaring that Ranjha appeared to be of good lineage (*aseel*), the Jogi delivered his sanction with a pat. As a result, Ranjha became the light of spiritual excellence (*azmat ki rushnai*). In a moment, he got up from his seat and fell at the feet of Sidh Bagai. As he had climbed up to the Tilla, the master placed Hir in his lappet. Ranjha pleaded, 'Ahead of me, even the straw of the streets is my enemy. Ask me with your tongue to go and give me your mandate (*thapi*). This heart does not stay in peace. I am required to work in alien lands and alien waters.' From here and there, they fell at the feet of each other. Receiving the authorization from Sidh Bagai, Ranjha made up his mind to leave. He appeared in curious clothes. Clad in saffron (*bhagva ves*), he rubbed ash (*bibhoot*) on his forehead and put large rings (*darshan*) in his ears. He walked away and camped (*derah*) on the bank of the river. First, he came to Hazara and, from there, turned towards the south (*lammi tarf*). Passing through Chiniot,[40] he appeared in Alipur. On the fourth day, he appeared in Jhang Siyal.

Ahead, the crop of millets (*juari*) was ripe. The girls were perched on the platforms (*manhiyan*). The maidens (*kuari*), after getting married, had already left for other places. The remaining, while sitting on platforms, were shooting stones from the catapults (*khabbani*). Inside, they were pining (*jhora*) away. At this moment, Ranjha entered the subdistrict of the Siyals. The first girl, rising up with a start, began to say, 'The peacocks, partridges and hawks are screaming. The cuckoo is singing melodies. The cool breeze has cooled the body, while the buffalo does not move her mouth. If the Lord correctly ordains, Ranjha has set his feet today.' The second girl gave out the message, 'Sister! I am telling you. The chest has unconsciously become cool. The peacock has been squeaking since morning. Owing to the impact of the breeze on us, happiness (*khushali*) has penetrated every pore. Sister! It is true. This is not an empty indication.' The Siyal girls, each on her own, sat down to reflect (*fikr*). Today, the moors are wearing bangles (*choora*). The trees offer such a testimony (*ugahi*). Their bodies, owing to anxiety (*kahal*), are activated. Leaving aside the millets, they turned to inspect Ranjha. All the Siyal girls began the search. They went to every place. They searched at the wells, riverside belt (*sailabe banhe*), ponds and water channels. They searched the grasses, reeds, acacia and, in fact, every spot. Weary of the search, they could not trace Ranjha.

Again, the Siyal girls began their search. What a mode of searching? Like the servants of the king, they employed their hands to do the job. They explored the moors and areas beyond, without showing any laxity. It appeared as if the plants too were lending a hand in the search (*agola*). Again and again, the girls felt anxious and, therefore, turned their mind to the search. They failed in the effort because Ranjha could not be seen at all. Even after a rigorous search across the moors, he was not seen anywhere. At last, the girls saw a Jogi. Acting in unison, they surrounded him and said, 'We wish to ask you. Your work is to perceive (*bujhna*). Let us see if you can tell us. Out of the two (Hir and Ranjha), whom are we going to meet? We are living in renunciation (*viragi*). If we meet anyone of the two, we will give you a share from the first harvest (*laap*) of millets.' The Jogi turned the beads of his rosary, but did not say anything. Putting the beads to his nostrils, he smelt them and repeatedly touched them to his eyes. Appearing to be absorbed (*matvari*), he searched for something in the beads. In his mind, he was formulating some deceit (*dagha*). Again and again, he raised his finger and pointed towards the north. The girls asked him, 'Are you blind? Are you dumb or deaf (*gunga dora*)? You do not say anything from your mouth. Is he a wise Jogi? How does he roam about with his mouth covered? Are you a magician (*sahri*)? Why are you silent? We are unable to figure out. We are desperate. Quickly speak to us.'

Again, the Jogi took the rosary in his hands and turned the beads around. With anger, he made signs (*sharat*), but did not speak at all. The girls said, 'We will give you a harvest of millets. Why don't you decipher the auguries (*savan*)? Tell us the truth. Give us messages.' Still, the Jogi continued to shake his hands. Ultimately, the girls offered tidings (*sunehe*), 'A Jogi came from afar. A breeze came upon us from the north. Did you not experience the fragrance (*mushk*)? We have seen him and correctly recognize him.' No one could reckon this. Hassi clarified that he was not any Jogi. It was Ranjha, who had himself arrived there. All the girls, having accurately recognized him, went ahead and clasped him. They correctly identified Dhido, though he did not speak. Some clung to his feet, some to his hands, some to his legs, some to his arms, some to his front and some to his back. Still others just gazed at him. What a way of greeting him? They appeared as if demanding alms on a festive occasion. They asked about his suffering and related the facts about themselves. While doing so, they cried and sighed. 'Listen, lord (*sahib*)! You have forgotten (*visaar*) us. We did not come into your mind. After becoming a Jogi, you did not pay us a visit. We are the same band of girls.' Taking hold of him, they brought him to the place, where there was the shisham and fire. Separated for long, they dug out the travails and spoke of detachment (*vairag*). Making Dhido sit, they pulled out the old pain. In this long meeting (*majlis*), they expressed their concerns for Ranjha. They agreed with what he said.

HASSI: With your orders (*hukm*), we propose this, provided it pleases your mind. The band of girls asks you to stay here and make a thatch (*goel*). The same boat and the same moors. The band puts a shawl around its neck. Stay here, as it suits us.

RANJHA: Listen, Hassi. How can I stay here? My heart is not attached to this place. Without Hir, there is complete darkness (*kul hanera*) and nothing is visible. Hir abides in every nerve of mine. I do not have any other relationship (*ashnai*). I am going to the Kheras, if it pleases the Lord. What do you say? O Hassi.

HASSI: Dhido! Listen to a request (*arz*) of ours. Where will you go? You are the same Ranjha and we are the same girls. Why don't you agree to our plea? We anxiously waited for you. Now you do not intend to stay here. Otherwise, the band of girls will go with you.

RANJHA: Listen, Hassi. Putting my life at stake (*sir rakh tali*), I came to Hir. Wherever she is, my desire (*taangh*) is towards her. True, now I came on my own. Here, my wishes have no effect. Only God makes me move. Wise Hassi! How can I stay? Hir Siyal has ensnared my heart.

HASSI: If you intend to leave, take us with you. The moors are inclined to swallow us. It is difficult to live with this separation. You are not (the same) Dhido and Hir is not with us. You may go wherever you like. You may not stay. What will happen if you torment us?

RANJHA: Listen, Hassi! How can I stay here? The moors will swallow me. My honour is merged with Hir. How can I stay without her? Just once, I wish to see Saleti. This is what my heart desires. Speak, Hassi. Without seeing her, I am not able to bear this separation (*vairag*).

HASSI: Take us along with you. We will not stay here. Just as you take your pain (*peer*), you must appreciate ours in the same way. You ask us to stay. Sir (*miyan*), how is it possible when you do not stay. Living here has become very difficult (*aukhera*). You must take us with you.

When the girls realized that Ranjha would not stay there at all, they saw it as the declaration of his verdict. They cannot accompany him. Fate (*qismat*) had played this game. The girls called for sweetened breadcrumbs and a milk bowl (*choori chhanna*) for Ranjha. They urged him to play a melody (*sarod*) for them. Hassi conveyed their request to him. Ranjha picked up his flute (*bambiha*). What a melody (*raag*) did he raise! Animals, birds, lions and the spotted ones came to see the spectacle (*tamasha*). The Siyal girls, in their amazement, lost their senses, as if someone had made them drink wine (*sharab*). At this moment, Ranjha put on his shoes and sped away.

The Jogi in Rangpur Khera

The village of Sehti was pleasant (*suhava*). Ranjha reached there. The locality was prosperous (*chokhi thor giraun*). On seeing the country, Ranjha was deeply impressed. Ahead, the town of the Kheras was three leagues away. It appealed to his mind. The place could not be avoided. He was not bound to give anything in writing. After due reflection, he set up his fire (*dhuan*). He sat down on the riverbank and arranged his seat (*aasan*). Making up his mind, he picked up a spade and then looked for fire. Queen (Rani) Sehti, who was sitting ahead, saw him. She felt that the sun had descended on earth. She picked up the fire without asking anyone. She was surprised to see him. In order to ignite the fire, she moved forward and faced the Jogi. She asked, 'What did you lack to become a Jogi? I am putting this question. Face like the moon and eyes like the flaming torches. What youthful looks (*jawani*)! Like a person showing his back to go away. I am like a mother who gives birth.' Sehti wanted the Jogi to tell her, as she is an offering for him. The Jogi said, 'I fell from above and lay prostrate on earth. I am no one and I have no place. I have no abode. Nor do I have any asylum (*na koi luh na takiya*). Which matter shall I describe? A dervish, who begs at the door, does not get any respect from anyone. If I had any antecedents or any future (*agga na pichha*), I would have told you so.' Sehti said, 'A mighty recluse (*faqir*) and a great ascetic (*tapassi*). This is how you appear to me. Jogi, I make myself your offering.' She picked up the fire with her own hands, saying, 'I feel content at your appearance (*darshan*). Your arrival has come into our lot (*bakht*). Where was your sainthood (*faqiri*) when you got Luddan thrashed?' Ranjha, feeling enraged, overturned the fire and asked, 'How do you blame a mendicant? We do not like this.' Sehti, with great effort, fixed the fire again and asked, 'Where was your sainthood when you carried a drum on your head?'

Dhido, becoming indignant, overturned the fire again. 'You speak bad words (*mande sukhan*) for us. My mind is anguished. How does this verbal abuse affect us? What if someone utters disparaging words?' Ranjha, full of fury, threw the fire away. Sehti made him sit and admitted, 'O Mendicant! I am in error, having said bad words. Listen! May I be your offering. Without any fault (*betaqsir*) of mine, you are angry with me and rebuked me. Where was your sainthood when you offered sweetened breadcrumbs to Kaido?' Ranjha exclaimed, 'Who are you? Tell me the facts (*haqiqat*). You have uncovered my affliction (*rog*).' Collapsing on his feet, Ranjha felt that she was revealing whatever happened to him in the past. He pleaded, 'I have come into your sanctuary (*saam*). You are speaking the truth.' Sehti said, 'Listen, Dhido. Hir is in my house. She has related to me the entire secret (*bhet*). She told me all the facts, including the manner in which you fell in love. Dhido Ranjha! Rest assured (*khatir jama*), for we had sent the Bahman.' She provided him with much comfort (*dilasa*). On hearing these words, Dhido wept a lot and, putting his shawl around his neck, admitted, 'So, you have summoned me. All my honour (*lajj*) is in your hands. Sehti! You must be steadfast in upholding my honour. I am your offering.' Sehti said, 'Listen O Dhido! Your honour is my responsibility. I have shamed 900 turbans of my paternal relatives (*pekayan*).[41] Spend the night here. You may go at dawn. Set up your fire on the banks (*kadhi dhuan*). Sit here in silence. Do not show yourself to anyone.'

After spending the night, Ranjha got up and came to the Kheras. On the bank, he sat in a distinct posture (*aasan*), without exposing himself to anyone. While sitting, his body became uneasy on account of the pangs of separation (*firaq*). Early in the morning, he came to light the fire. When he focused his eyes, he saw that Hir Siyal was sleeping. Without a drop of blood and without a bit of flesh, her hands were twisted and her neck trembled. There was a black stool and torn mat (*kala kira te trutta trada*). Hir was sleeping on her side. As Ranjha watched, Hir lay there, having fed on suffering. Sitting on her palms, she pulled her hair. To whom could she relate her misery? Sunk in the stupor of an opium addict (*posti*), she was afflicted with worries about Ranjha. While crying and driving the crows away, she asked, 'Dhido! Tell me. To whom do I belong?' There is no one who could unite her with Ranjha. The Jogi, in order to beg (*bhikheya*), raised a demand from Hir, 'Give me alms. I have come to this place. I am hungry. The intensity of hunger has made me vulnerable (*aajiz*). I have come especially (*uchecha*) for this. Give alms to me.' Thus did the Jogi state. Hir said, 'May your children die. What shall I give you? What alms shall I offer? In my helplessness, I cry day and night. I cannot see and hear anything. First, I yearn and, then, I sigh. This is what I eat and drink. If you ask for alms, I can give you only hunger, if you wish.' The Jogi said, 'Why will you offer hunger in alms? I can see plenty of grain such as lentils, corn and millets (*maanh juwar cheena*). Why don't you put these as alms. Give me grain, so that I go from here. Hunger has inflicted immense torture on me. Give alms (*kharait*) and let me eat to satiation. May the Lord fulfil your desires.'

Crawling on her chest, Hir moved like an iguana (*goh*). The Jogi gave a lot of blessings (*aseesan*), as Hir got up to give alms. With great difficulty, she brought a handful of millets and asked the Jogi to spread his shirt (*jholi*). Ranjha began to think of a way in which the millets could be spilled. The Jogi deliberately spilled the millets. He kept on repenting while trying to gather the grain. Hir, picking up a quarrel, asked the Jogi to get up and leave, lest she should pour dust into his lap. The Jogi sat there, but Hir did not approve of it. Hir, feeling drowsy like an opium addict, looked up again and again. She threatened, 'Get up, Jogi. Why do you sit here? I am extremely angry. Even in this state, I will hit you with a stone, if you keep on sitting with this casualness.' Still the Jogi did not speak, but kept sitting with his face covered in a shawl (*bukkal*). Whenever Hir looked up, she found the Jogi sitting there. She spoke again, 'Get up, you mendicant (*faqira*). I will hit you with this stone.' Picking a stone, she raised her hand, threatening, 'What an adamant posture (*dharna*) the Jogi has adopted. Your father must be a wanderer.' While Saleti quarrelled, she felt a distant fragrance (*mushk*). She stated, 'Jogi! Shall I give more alms?' She rightly presumed (*guman*) that it was Dhido Ranjha, who had arrived. She sprang up and, full of excitement, had a vision (*darshan*) of Ranjha with her own eyes. Ranjha gave the right response to her.

JOGI: Why have you become green and yellow? Tell me your sorrow (*vedan*). If God Himself wills, I will provide you with a remedy. Which malady (*ranjish*) has afflicted you? Explain it to me. I will make you better, if it pleases the Lord.

HIR: You are sinking into a swamp. Stop this noisy chatter on my head. Why are you concerned about others? Bring your own affair to fruition. My own calamity (*qehar*) has ruined me. Do not harass me to this extent. Jogi! Turn off your back forthwith.

JOGI: Tell me of your pain. I ask you to explain. I will give you packets after duly binding them. You will swallow them with hot water. What is your distress (*vedan*)? You must relate all to me. With promptness, I will give you packets, so that you are cured.

HIR: Your ears have not suffered any abrasions, while the ash does not suit your body. I have recognized you. O Jogi! Stop your whizzing sounds. Your hands and feet are gleaming. You are like the moon of the fourteenth night (*hathin pairin ujla chaudas sanda chann*). Open your eyes and show me. Agree to what I say.

JOGI: I came from the remote land of Bhutan and, rolling down from the hills, landed in Multan.[42] I am a Jogi for the last seven generations. You have erred in your presumption (*guman*). Human beings are of various kinds. Do not let any doubt settle in your mind. Relate your malady, so that the Lord relieves it.

HIR: Listen! You sinking Jogi. Do not tinker with my affliction (*rog*). A match (*jamki*) smoulders in my interior, while a flame burns without oil. Do not uncover any tale (*baatri*). Do not pierce me with a spear. If you wish to eradicate my disease, do unite me with the herdsman. This rope does not suit your waist and this ash (*bhibut*) does not suit your forehead . Why did you leave your home and, thus, depart from your dwelling (*derah*)? Endowed with radiant hands and feet, you appear to be a delicate lad (*ahl malook*)? I have rightly conjectured. Your fame has spread in the towns.

JOGI: I started from the town of Narvar and tumbled down to this place. My body was mingled with ash, which was also poured into my hair. Give me alms (*bhikheya*), so that I leave after offering my parting salutation (*adesh*). A dispute (*qaziya*), which destiny had decreed, has come before me.

HIR: Rings have been pushed into your ears. Explain this to me. You have got your ears split, while the blood did not horrify you. Why didn't your mother die on the day you left your home? O Jogi! Speak the truth to me.

JOGI: I walked from the country of Kirana and rolled down to this place. I am a Jogi for ages. Do not understand and speak falsehood. Why did you err into this deception (*bhulave*)? Tell me. You must relate the entire matter, which is inside you.

HIR: You are not a Jogi. You must be a secret paramour (*chor yaar*) or a highway robber (*bat pal*). You have deceived women (*rannan thagiyan*). You have tricked children. You tell lies. You do not speak with caution. If you are a true Jogi, open your eyes and show me.

JOGI: Sidh Bagai has bound my eyes (*akhin badhiyan*). Only he will come and open them. My mentor (*guru*) has forbidden me from opening my eyes and casting a glance. Which delusion has trapped you? Speak the truth from your mouth. Relate the entire pain, which has afflicted you.

HIR: At night, you assume this garb and, in the morning, you announce this to me. You do not have the bag and horn in your hands. You have resorted to a clever trick (*hunnar*). You have adopted the garb of mendicancy (*faqr*) in order to cheat women. Where is the bowl of equanimity (*khappar bhugat da*)? Yet, you have put on a guise.

JOGI: Birds and dervishes do not carry their expenses (*kharach*) with them. Those who rely (*takiya*) on God are assured of their bread (*rizq*) forever. I have come to beg alms from you, wearing the garb (*bhes*) of a Jogi. Otherwise, you may just refuse, so that I depart after offering a salute.

Hir said, 'If you are not Ranjha, then I will die.' Saying this, she collapsed and fainted. As the Siyal fell into a swoon (*dandan*), there was no one to pour water into her mouth. The Jogi, who cried the tears of blood, resolved, 'I must leave after closing the matter. She must be told now, lest she should die.' Panjpir arrived and, acting internally, informed Hir, 'It is Dhido, who has come, wearing the garb of a Jogi. You must get up and meet him. You must be alert (*khabardar*).' Then Hir got up and revived the dramatic manifestation (*bahur kare pragta*).

HIR: Which Jogi has bestowed you the mandate (*thapna*)? Which Jogi has given you his teachings? Your hands and feet are radiant. You are delicate and goodlooking (*ahl maluk sunikh*). Wearing the garb of a Jogi, you roam around, offering greetings in the name of the formless (*alakh*). From door to door, you beg. You eat what you get as alms (*mang khaven tu bhikh*).

JOGI (to himself): With these very hands, you gave me rice dessert (*kheer*) to eat and buffalo milk to drink. Sitting together, we exchanged our thoughts (*maslat*). Let Hir listen to the one who is deprived. In the moors, you gave me all assurances (*dilasa*). Why do you hesitate now? When a calamity (*vakht*) has fallen on me, you refuse to recognize me. I am the same Dhido Ranjha.

HIR: Where is your native place? Which is your country (*vatn*)? On which river do you reside? Tell me this. Which Jogi has given you his authorization? Now, you have come after getting your ears bored. O Jogiya! Let me know your antecedents.

JOGI: My place of birth is Takht Hazara, where the River Chandal (Chenab) flows. Sidh Bagai has given me his blessings. He is the spiritual guide (*pir*) at the Tilla. I endured the strong waves and pierced through the thick forests. Focus your eye and recognize. I am Ranjha and you are Hir.

Hir flew towards Ranjha like a hawk (*baseen*) and stuck to his neck. She stood holding his shirt and felt his body with her hands. It was as if the hands of the earth were trying to discern the sun and moon. Has Ranjha really come? It may not be a dream. As she cried tears of blood, her pain was laid bare. The sky turned black owing to the sighs of the afflicted ones. The sparks flew out of her body and, like the stars, reached up to the sky. Both of them wept, as the separation (*virag*) refused to dissipate. Hir said, 'It is she (Sehti) who provided the means (*vaseela*). Her name is Sehti. Listen, lord Ranjha! I will be content (*nisha*) if I somehow introduce you to her. She shared my pain. How can I show you? As night approaches, I will stay with Sehti. You should sit at the riverbank. You must go early, lest anyone should carry the tales. Big enemies (*vadde ghalim*) are opposed to our lives. They are inclined to kill us.'

The Jogi went to the riverbank, where he established his mat and fire. Covering his face and head, he assumed a distinct posture.[43] On the third day, Sehti came and, looking at Hir, exclaimed, 'Today, your colour is not visible. Your condition is not the earlier one. Brave like a tiger, you sit and shoot arrows.' To Hir, Sehti put a question. Hir replied, 'Owing to your grace (*sadqah*), I am becoming fresh day by day. Since Ramu conveyed the news of Ranjha's arrival, my face acquired its radiance (*lali*). Today or tomorrow, I may have his vision (*didar*) and my mind will be illuminated (*mat rushnai*). Sehti Rani! Because of this reason, I look better.'

Sehti said, 'Listen. You may be able to beguile others. Can you do the same to me? As soon I saw you, I understood your sorrow (*sinjati vedan*). You are deliberately trying to mislead me. Hirey! I am fully aware of all the facts (*haqiqat*) about you. How can your work be done? You are trying to hide your stomach from me, your midwife (*dai ton pet chhupendi*).' When Sehti stated this, Hir Saleti was filled with fear. She explained, 'Mother (Bibi)! Someone, with his face and head covered, came to ignite the fire (*dhuyin melan*). Because of your fear, Sehti Rani, I did not call him. With the same gait and the same body, he appeared to me.' Sehti responded, 'He did come, Hirey. It is absolutely true. I must tell you. Keep quiet. Do not say a word from your mouth. No one should be able to see. Your fire has been extinguished. Now, it has afflicted me. Listen, Hir! For your sake, I have brought shame on 900 turbans.[44] Listen, Hir! Nothing else will serve the purpose. First, we will quarrel. Each and every abuse (*gaal*) that I hurl at you, the same should you throw back at me. We will quarrel till the end, so that all the people converge. Listen, Siyali! This is what will succeed. Today, we will make this effort. When Sehti got up at dawn, she was full of anger.

SEHTI: We are not bonded slaves (*gand ghulam*) of anyone. You have brought in a new daughter-in-law after marriage. What a revenge (*nivatta*) you have taken! She is a strange girl (*kuri anokhi*). Siyali! You must seek the kindness (*khair*) of God. Everyone laughs at you.

HIR: Do not speak the wrong words to me. You are such a mean person (*kamini*). Of which great father are you born (*vadde peyo di jayi*)? You dare to utter such words. O Girl! Do not dare to speak to me again. See, the way you jump around. Who are you to admonish me?

SEHTI: Sisters! You are good neighbours. You ask from Hir. We are not bonded slaves, who could have married her through deceit (*dagha*). We employ so many servants (*kammi*) like her father, who cannot be counted.

Sehti was filled with anger up to the brim.

HIR: You call yourself the daughter of a big father. You have no shame. Comparing my father with your servants, who cannot be counted! I have been sitting here for the last thirty-five months. No one came to look at me. The entire courtyard (*vehra*) must listen. In the name of food (*tukkar*), they did not even make an offering.

SEHTI: O Girl! To whom should we make an offering? You have raised a revengeful act (*nivatta*). You are a mean bitch (*kamini kutti*), who has raised this wrangle (*siyapa*). My father has humbled many like your father. What an exalted girl came into our hands! What a great reputation (*jass bhalera*) did we acquire?

HIR: Who are you? Just a vain woman, who is prancing about. How dare you praise your father? The Khera is of no use. We have seen your exalted father, who has been described as a rich man (*daulatvand*). The only thing that came to me from your house is a torn mat.

SEHTI: If a torn mat has come to you, no one can be blamed for this. Gold and silver flows to my father from the seven directions (*satte pahin*). We do not reckon the likes of your father and grandfather. In the walls of my father, gold is embedded in the mortar (*kandhi gil sona*). However, we do not make it known to anyone.

HIR: Neighbours! Do justice (*nyaye*) from what you have heard. They claim to have gold in the mortar of their walls. Is it of any use to others? A curse be on a woman like her. Such a thing does not behove you. I did not put on your ornaments for any sufficient period. In fact, you have taken away what I received from my father.

SEHTI: This is not false. What she says is true. I am going to the assembly of my father and grandfather. I will get for you all the gold and pearls (*sona moti*) that are yours. If you intend to cohabit (*vassan*), I will go there just now.

Sehti, pretending to be angry, did not put on her shoes and left forthwith. Acting in anger, Rani (Queen) Sehti came to her father and exclaimed, 'We did not get the daughter of Chuchak. We married a mere slave girl (*goli*). O Father! What a calamity (*qehar*) did you bring? No one cared to look at her. Give her whatever she got from her father, as she has agreed to cohabit (*hir vassan te aayi*)'.

On hearing this, Ali got up in indignation. He sent all the materials – ornaments, gold, silver, bags, utensils, buffaloes, cows, bedsteads, mattresses and blankets – that could be enumerated. Inside and outside, so much of wealth could not be contained. Then

Saleti stood up and took the custody of all the stuff. At some place, she arranged the bags. At some place, she put the boxes. At some place, she spread out the bed linen. She decorated the entire space, arranging the utensils, goods, mattresses and blankets. Placing the goods in their respective places, she herself fixed the pegs. Sehti, following Hir to the spot, gave her assurance, saying, 'If you wish, I will get you some more items. Anything that comes into your mind?' Sehti herself was very happy, as the time for cohabitation drew near. On that day, the Kheras received felicitations (*vadhai*). Hir herself did the cooking. She herself kneaded and she herself baked. Laughingly, she walked across the courtyard. Her feet hardly touched the ground. She was swimming without water (*pani bina tare*). It was as if the wings had grown on her sides. Hir herself cooked, but distributed the food secretly.

After two or three days passed in this manner, Sahiba arrived, having put henna (*mehandi*) on himself. His gaze fell on Hir Saleti, who was sitting in the front. Leaping like a gazelle (*harni*), she went up to Sehti. On seeing a breathless Hir, Sehti was shocked. Sehti asked, 'Hirey! Have the fairies given you a fright? Did you see a demon? Did a ghost harass you? What a state you are in! Your face has turned pale and your eyes have become twisted. There is no strength (*quwwat*) in you.' Sehti, while giving her a message, exclaimed that she was in a bad condition. Hir replied, 'No fairy has given me a fright. Nor has a demon harassed me. No ghost has troubled me. I am not under any spectre. I do not suffer from any colic pain (*sul marora*). No one has tormented me. I got up and ran away, because I saw someone who is not intimate (*be-mehram*) with me.' Immediately, Sehti got up and picked up a fight with her brother, saying, 'Brother Sahiba! You did something bad (*manda kito*) in coming over here. Now, you must get up and leave. You will come in only when I tell you to do so.' Sahiba got up and left without waiting for a moment. When the Khan went to his house, Hir appeared at the site. Standing outside, she did not set her foot inside. The walls were plastered and cots were washed. She got the coverings of the quilts removed and got them washed. Once the interior was thus purified (*pak kitoi*), Hir put her foot inside.

The two, remaining inside, held a meeting (*majlis*). Sehti said,

'Girl! Let us make our choice. We must formulate a plan (*mata*). It has come into my head. The Lord has put our shame around my neck.' Since a huge burden is on her, there is no rest for her. She said, 'Hirey! Grind some turmeric (*haldhar*) somewhere. Both of us will go out. We will enact a deception (*fareb*) and we will inform Ranjha about it. Come and do as I say. Carry this bowl to the edge of the field. If Ranjha comes into your hands, only then call me.' They came to the edge of a sesame field (*banne tillan*). Hir was made to lie flat. The turmeric, which was in the bowl, was rubbed on Hir. A needle was pierced into her ankle, so that blood started oozing out. Sehti cried that a cobra (*bisiyar*) had bitten Hir. On hearing the cries from a distance, the herdsmen, along with buffaloes and calves, rushed to the site. They asked, 'Daughter! Tell us. What has happened? Your hair is in disarray.' She replied, 'Why do you inquire about my state? Just take a look at Hir. Go together and convey this. Go to the village. What are you looking at? Brother! I saw with my own eyes. A cobra, three yards long and black of colour, bit her. Go and inform Ali. There should be no delay.'[45] Precisely at this moment, a number of people went to give the information. Raising a tumult, they informed the village (*basti*). The daughter of Chuchak suffered a snakebite, forcing the world to leap out. If there was any Khera in the village, even one of them was not seen. All the women, without any limit, turned up. The more they saw the sting on Hir, the more they cried. The hair of the women were spread around, while the men shouted in alarm. Sehti, raising mournful cries, lamented, 'This is the profit (*kamai*) we have earned. A cobra has bitten her when she was on the verge of cohabitation.'

Ali, having summoned his horsemen, framed an announcement (*hukara*). 'Do not leave any healer (*mandari*), wherever he is found.' Sehti said to her father, 'You must listen to what I say. Father! Once, a calamity (*qaza*) struck our village. A snake had bitten a washer man, cobbler and weaver. The eyes saw that the three were dead and, therefore, they were ready for burial. A Jogi, emerging from somewhere, revived all the three.' Ali said, 'Daughter! What is the appearance of the Jogi? How can he be contacted? If someone has any information, he should come forward and tell me. If someone informs me, I will myself go. Or, someone can bring him here.'

Sehti replied, 'Yesterday, I saw him. God willing, my memory will not fail me. He had covered his face, forehead, hands and feet. He does not show himself. Let someone go into the village and look for him. Perhaps, he may be located. Father! It will be our good fortune (*bakht*) if someone brings him here. Right at this moment, he will revive the Siyal girl. He has been living at the ferry (*pattan*) for a long time. People have seen him.' However, they went again to ascertain the facts. It was confirmed that they had seen him. The *zamindars*, putting shawls around their necks, went there. No one was left behind. Ali, accompanied by the leading men (*mahajan*), reached the site. With all humility, he stated, 'Lord (*sahib*)! Listen to our supplication (*arz*). We received the daughter of Chuchak, though we deserved only a slave girl (*goli*) of their house. We have not been able to pay the debt (*qarz*), which has accumulated on our heads. We continue to carry it. We implore (*minnat*) you to come with us just once, lest the girl should be wasted.'

The Jogi turned and, sitting still, did not give any reply. Though they were tired of making requests, he did not turn towards them. In which ever direction the Jogi moved his face, the Khan also looked thither. The *zamindars* became weary of the repeated exercise, while the Jogi did not give any response. Ali and his companions got up to leave. He said to Sehti, 'Daughter! We are weary of requesting the Jogi, who has not come around at all.' On hearing this, the women (*kul zanana*) surrounded Sehti, who explained, 'Father! The Jogi remains in a perpetual state of absorption (*almasti*). He is absolutely heedless (*be-parwah*) of the world. If it pleases him, he may favour (*mehar*) us. All of you must fall at his feet. Father! The lions have their own sense of honour. In fact, they are imbued with it.' Queen Sehti, with a shawl around her neck, said to the Jogi, 'The lions preserve the honour of women, without turning away. You are an ancient spiritual master (*sidh pir puratam*). The honour of the weak ones is in your hands. We have not seen her (Hir) to our satisfaction. Our sense of separation (*virag*) has not dissipated. Come, O Mendicant (*faqira*), so that the girl is not wasted.' The Jogi declared, 'What is this to us? Why should it make us get up? The world is a false shadow (*koora saya*). The living organisms are perpetually engaged in biting one another. However, they do not make any proclamation in the world (*jag dhandora*). Which of the numerous incantations (*mantar*) shall I employ? A cobra has swallowed the entire universe.'

For the sake of Sehti, the Jogi got up and came along with the congregation. As he moved forward, a clamour of 'Let us go' (*hallo hallo*) arose among the people. Young girls and old women, rather the whole world, came out to see the spectacle (*tamashe*). There was no limit to the number of people (*beshumar khalqat*), who had gathered. The Jogi came to the place, where the Siyal was lying on her face. Sehti, exposing the victim, identified the spot where the bite was seen. As soon as the gaze of the Jogi fell on Hir, he withdrew on his reverse feet, declaring, 'It is not any of the known breeds such as cobra, krait, viper or stone crusher. It is the handiwork of a crowned cobra (*khadi choti vale bisiyar*). It will be difficult for me to relieve her of the poison.' Sehti said, 'Listen, O Lord! You are a perfect spiritual master. What are you telling me? We have seen your abilities when a cobra had bitten three persons. You came for their sake and revived them in the basement (*bhora*). Since she is still breathing, she has not died. You cannot delude us.' The Jogi replied, 'Bibi! She will require a herculean effort (*vaddi mehnat*), including the recitation of a large number of incantations (*mantra*). What is needed is a solitary house (*ikkala kotha*). No one should be able to peep through it. One person, who cries a lot, must be there in attendance (*khijmat*). If a treatment of forty days (*challiha*) is undertaken in a perfect manner, then the victim can be handled.' Again, a chorus of 'Let us go' was raised. A cot was brought in. Carried quickly on the head, it was brought to the house of Sehti. As the Jogi entered it, all the doors were bolted. Look friends! Sehti has fulfilled her promise (*ahd*).

Meeting of Hir and Ranjha

Sehti said to them, 'Laugh, play and enjoy yourself. There is no shortage of anything. If I die, I will be of use to you as an offering. O Girl! Give a hundred thanks to me, as I have united two souls that were pining for each other. In accordance with the order (*hukam*) of lord Ranjha, I will cook what is to be eaten.' Sweetened breadcrumbs (*choori*) were crushed. Buffalo milk was mixed with rice dessert (*kheer*). Sehti also prepared thick buttermilk (*ghati chhah*) and offered dried dates and variety of fruits (*chhuhare meve*). Eat, drink and enjoy. Sehti was their offering. As they sat to eat, Sehti stood fanning them. Sitting together, Hir and Ranjha touched the food with their hands. It was after a long gap of thirty-five months and nine days that God made them eat food. After eating and drinking, they enjoyed laughing and playing. In this manner, Hir Saleti acquired the moment of happiness. In the midst of peals of laughter, they played on the bed (*hasan khedan manje utte*). The extent of their joy crossed all limits. It was obvious that there was no need to describe it. Inside their minds, the spark (*jamki*) of unease kept on smouldering. Their actions would be put to scrutiny. At the moment, they had no clue about the manner of this reckoning. Sometimes, they became pensive in reflection and, at other times, they burst into laughter. In their heart of hearts, they were in a bliss. The Lord had enabled two souls, who had suffered the pangs of separation, to unite. Their faces acquired radiance (*lali*). Masters of love, their faces looked like the moon and their eyes burnt like torches (*munh mataab akhin balan mashalan*). This was an exact revival of the days when they were just Hir and Ranjha. Their happiness, which crossed all barriers, cannot be described. Having stitched love and passion (*mehar muhabbat*), they sat with arms around each other's neck. The sense of inner separation was lifted, as love attained a fresh hue (*nautan ishq*).

Eight days passed in this manner. The wife of Ali, accompanied by a number of people, came to the house of Sehti. Knocking at the door, she called out in a loud voice. Sehti, running from inside, came out. Her mother said, 'Daughter! Give us news about Hir. The mother makes herself an offering (*ghol ghumai*).' Sehti said, 'Listen, mother. What should I say? The Jogi has been standing for eight watches (*athe pehar*) without putting his foot on the ground. Holding peacock feathers in his hand, he recites incantations, while remaining hungry and thirsty. Saleti, while lying on the bed, breathes with difficulty. But, she has not turned her side.' Ali said, 'Listen, daughter Sehti! We are not doing any work. For eight watches of the day, our eyes are fixed here. We have forgotten all other tasks. Send us a message as soon as you see a change in her condition.' They came out and Sehti went inside.

Sehti said to Hir, 'Listen, O Hir! Speak the truth (*haqiqat*). How many lies shall I tell? How much shall I run on the wall, only to fall down in the end? It is true that I have united two souls (*sikde ruh*), who were longing to meet. You must eat, drink and enjoy. I am saying this to you. Listen, Saleti! Even if I die, I will be of use to you.' Eating *choori*, clarified butter, jaggery and sugar, they made a union of love and happiness. Experiencing contentment, they sat on the bed and, while laughing, conversed with each other. They were one soul and two bodies (*hikka ruh ate doe jusse*). The stern God had brought them together. On the eighth day, the Kheras gathered and came to the site. Ali, accompanied by the womenfolk (*zananah*), reached the outer portion. Since they cried in a loud voice, Sehti was able to hear. When she heard the arrival of her father, she was filled with excitement. While both (Hir and Ranjha) shrank back, Sehti opened the door. 'Listen, daughter! Give us some news. Everyone has become restless (*kalval*). Throughout the eight watches, our eyes are turned to this place. Do you see any change? Tell us so that our spirits are lifted. At the moment, we are not at ease (*khatir jama na koi*). O wise Sehti! What is happening inside?' Sehti replied, 'Listen, father! What shall I tell you? In came lakhs of snakes that were brown, black and spotted. Whoever came in turned back. The Jogi did not pay any attention to them. The field has not been conquered, though she (Hir) shows some change.'

Sehti went inside and, bolting the door, spoke to the two (lovers), 'A fire is burning on my head. How shall I put it out? How shall I pass through this edge of the sword (*khande dhar*)? I cannot figure out any solution? You must eat, drink and enjoy yourself. If I die, I will be of use to you.' Ranjha replied, 'Sehti! Our shame is around your neck. We have neither any support nor any prop (*luh na taqiya*). Since you know the best, you must uphold our honour in accordance with your promise (*bol*). In the street, even the straw is our enemy. We do not have any friend. Your hands are on our necks. No one else is ours.' Sehti said, 'Listen, O Herdsman, the drinker of buttermilk (*chhah piyaka*). You do not have any sense. You did not enable Hir to climb the mountain. Nor did you help her cross the Indus.[46] Instead, in a wretched condition, you kept on wandering in

Jhang Siyal. What a game (*bazi*) have you laid out? While revolving all the time, it came on the heads of this hapless one.' Hir said, 'Do not stand in opposition (*nabar*). I am your sacrifice. We have no other shelter. Sehti! You are our father and mother. Our shame is on your neck. We had torn it. You have sewn it up in the way you know best. We have no one else.'

While withering away and experiencing the pain, the third installment of eight days came to an end. A call was given to the people. There was a knock at the door. All inhabitants of the town (*kul qasba*), including the chief's wife and menfolk, reached the place. No one remained behind. Sehti came and opened the door. In order to make the inquiry, all the people joined together, 'Tell us, wise daughter Sehti! Do you see any change?' Sehti replied, 'Lakhs of snakes – brown, red, yellow and black – kept on coming. The Jogi, while reciting the same incantations, did not set his foot on the ground. Father! The snake who had stung your daughter-in-law has not shown his face yet. Listen, father! Hir has turned her side. I offer a hundred congratulations.' Sehti, closing the door, met the lovers at that very moment. Both of them, Hir and Ranjha, started weeping, because the time of reckoning was fast approaching. Sehti said, 'Laugh, play and enjoy. I am your sacrifice. If death comes to me, you should not stop playing.' Every day, while sitting inside, they ate to their fill. However, they kept on worrying. The fire in their interiors did not dissipate. They put their hands on their foreheads. As the time (*muddat*) drew near, they considered a number of plans. Failing to think of a viable solution, they sat down in sadness. Sehti, in an attempt to console (*dilasa*) them said, 'Dhido! I say this to you. O Herdsman! If it were in my power, I will bind you in marriage today itself. If it were in my means, I shall not do anything less. O Herdsman! Even if I have to die, I will send Hir along with you.' Ranjha said, 'Sehti! I offer my head as an offering to you. I will not hesitate in removing it. Who can pay back your kindness (*neki*)? We will never be able to compensate you. You have assumed a task. You must fulfil the same. We are a burden on your neck. We are absolutely helpless. We have no remedy (*chara*).' Sehti said, 'You should play, laugh and feel happy. I have taken upon myself this obligation (*ahd*).

There is no place for thrift (*sarfa*) in living and dying, particularly in case of those, who carry death on their head. Dhido! If our time has come to an end, it is impossible to put a stay on death. I, a sacrificial goat (*bali bakra*), have been of some use to you.'

Day and night, all three were perturbed as the duration neared its end. Sehti advised, 'Keep your cool. Do not be impatient. Eat well. I am your offering. We cannot say anything of the days that are stipulated. There is not a moment (*sayet*) of ease.' On the eighth day, everyone came to inquire. When the call came, Sehti heard it and came out. A number of people – the father and the tribe (*qabila*) along with paternal and maternal aunts – reached the site and asked, 'Did you see any difference? Did she ask for food or water? Daughter, speak the truth. Did anything come into your view?' Sehti replied, 'O Mother! Listen to what I say. I saw something strange (*achraj*). A black snake, with another one riding on it, appeared. The Jogi holding the foot of Hir, placed it before the snake. You must be congratulated as Hir moved a little. Father! Come after a week in order to give Hir a bath. You must celebrate this joy. Many felicitations (*mumarakh*) to you, as we are feeling alive. You must arrange for music (*shadiyane*), because Hir has been released (from her affliction). The Lord has done a favour to us. She has truly recovered, well and safe (*sahi salamat*). You must think of distributing alms (*kharait*).' On hearing this, Ali remarked, 'It is good that Saleti has been released. Felicitations to us.' He started making preparations. He got the drums (*tamak dhol*) in place. As the stores were opened, the entire world came to receive alms. The Kheras appeared to have acquired an extra colour (*rang savaye*).

Sehti said to Hir, 'Hirey! Listen. One week remains. What shall we do? I am tired of telling lies (*kur bulendi*) that have no foundations. What will happen in the near future? I do not have any clue. The end, which was anticipated, has arrived.' When five days had gone by, Sehti announced, 'I did for you whatever I could. Whatever was in my power, I offered that. Be ready to make a breach (*sanh*) in the wall. This is what has appealed to me.' The three of them agreed to this plan (*mata*). Sitting all night, the three made a breach. Now, they were ready. Sehti said to Ranjha, 'O Herdsman!

If my will had prevailed, I would have married (*parnai*) Hir to you. How will you energize your feet? You must fly away like the birds. Listen, lord Ranjha! This is what I tell you.' Interrupting herself, she stated, 'You should make preparations. At dawn, you should commence the journey, without stopping anywhere. Whatever is in store for us, I will be left to see. Now, you and I are in the protection of the Lord.' The lovers, bidding farewell (*vida*) to Sehti, embarked on the first stage (*manzil*) of their journey. In accordance with the divine will (*qazayin*), they stepped over the root (*mool ulanghi*) of a bush and, as a result, returned to the same spot again and again. All night, they kept walking like the oxen of an oil presser (*teli bail niayin*). When the day dawned, they were exhausted and called out to Sehti. When they narrated their experience, Sehti got up and, acting with wisdom (*siyanap*), filled the breach with a bunch of twigs. She asked, 'Hirey! How did you jump over this bush. It sprouts rather quickly. However, it must have been trampled under your feet.' On the second day, they journeyed to their full capacity. They alternated between running and sighing. During the four watches of the night, they walked with stealth. When they had covered a distance of 15 leagues (*koh*), the night ended and the day began.

Both hid themselves in the moor. They ate the food (*tosha*), which they carried with them. During the four watches of the day, they kept on sitting and did not show (*zahir*) themselves. With the onset of darkness, they got up and started walking at a fast pace, as if they had grown wings on their sides. On the third day, Ali arrived for the bath of Hir. The singers (*doomniyan*), carrying pitchers of buttermilk on their heads, were singing songs. The women and gentlemen were distributing alms along the path. As the songs were heard from here and there, the Khera (Sahiba) raised his hands. With dances here and verses there, a large number of people came out. Sehti had dragged her cot up to the door. On hearing the tumult, she assumed a complete silence and did not utter a word. Mother and father, while standing outside, felt terrified. Perhaps a cobra (*nag*) had bitten Sehti. Though they banged the door, Sehti did not give any response. A boy, made to climb over, peeped inside. Sehti was found sleeping at the door. When her palms and soles were massaged, she woke up. As soon as the latch was removed, there was a clamour inside and outside. When the door was opened, everyone entered. The *zamindars*, including the father and sister-in-law, declared, 'We have come to give Hir a bath. You walk ahead and we will follow you. Let us pour water on her body.' A large number of people were standing outside. All of them were anxious to see. Sehti spoke to her mother and father, 'Baba! Today, when I fell asleep, an intoxication (*masti*) overtook me. Inside and outside, this place was full of snakes. A poison rushed into me. Owing to this intoxication, I slept for three days. I am feeling drowsy (*allas*). Since I was sleeping outside, I know nothing about Hir.'

An entire world came inside. Everyone was feeling concerned. When they saw nothing, they conjectured that he (Jogi) had run away after tearing the wall. Soon, a cry went up. When they saw the breach, all of them shouted. They understood that the Jogi was none other than the herdsman (*chak*). The *zamindars* burnt in rage. They realized that he could not be anyone other than the herdsman. As they saw the total act of deceit (*kul fareb*), they prepared themselves right there. They said, 'Brothers! Reach there. There should be no delay (*tahambal*). Fix a pole in the ferry (*pattan tang lagahin*).'[47] All turned towards Sehti in order to inquire, 'O Sehti! Listen. When did you see them leaving? In which direction shall we go? Let someone tell us. We cannot be patient. We have already put saddles on the horses.' As mother and father asked Sehti, she pointed her hand towards the north (*ubhe hath bujhaye*).

The horses were fawn, black, silver, grey and spotted. Getting ready, they rode with the keen desire of killing the Jogi. They were thirsting to drink the blood of his liver. While they were searching, they encountered a few travellers (*pandhi*) and said, 'A young man along with a girl. Brothers! Did you see them?' The Kheras asked them to speak the truth. Replying with confidence, the travellers declared that they did not see anyone on their way. Turning the horses, the armed retinue (*lashkar*) pulled back. Galloping through the wilderness, the Iraqi horses did not stop even a bit. They covered two stages (*dumajla*) of the distance, though they kept on making inquiries. All of them suspected (*guman*) that the fugitives might have been there. The *zamindars*, on seeing another group of travellers, said, 'In appearance, the Jogi looks decent. He has a woman companion (*hamsai*). We have been searching for both of them. Brothers! Give us some clue (*sandesah*).' In this manner, they investigated the matter. They asked, 'Who are you looking for? State your purpose (*matlab*). Brothers! Why are you asking questions? One is a sun and the other is a moon of the fourteenth, both appearing as the light of spiritual excellence (*azmat ki rushnai*). We saw a lot of love and affection (*het muhabbat*) between them. They had their arms around each other's neck. On seeing them, our entire group (*kul jamaat*) was captivated.' On hearing this, the *zamindars* were inflamed and lifted the reins of their horses. As they rode at a medium pace, they encountered a bunch of girls. The *zamindars* stopped to question them. The girls said, 'O Khans! We saw that the man was enamoured of the woman. We were sold out on seeing Hir.'

On hearing this, the pursuing horses became brisk in lifting their feet. As their hooves struck the earth, they seemed to be speaking. As a result, the stars were covered in the sky. Hir and Ranjha, on seeing them, stopped in their tracks, as they could not bear the heavy burden. The arrival of the Kheras meant that they would become food for them. Ranjha said to Hir, 'O Hir! You must kill me somehow. If they kill me, they will do so in a cruel manner. In view of the old enmity, they will inflict a slow torture. In this forbidding terrain of thick wilderness (*aujhar vaderi*), they will kill me after a steady torture. If I die at your hands, I will be grateful.' Hir replied, 'You are my lord (*sahib*). I am your slave (*bardi*). Do not put me to test, as I am powerless. The powerless do not have any solutions. You are doing what is happening to you. In fact, it is you who have done everything that is unfolding. You are deliberately hiding this from me. O Lord! Does anyone have the power to touch you?' Ranjha said, 'No, Hirey! We have reached in the midst of difficulties. The alien sons (*puttar paraye*) have arrived. Soon you will see them raising their hands on me.' As the lovers were distressed in this wilderness, the bloodthirsty Kheras arrived on the scene. When the lovers looked up, the grazing horses came into their view. Their hearts became fresh and they took vigorous steps forward. They saw that the powerful *zamindars* (*khan vadhere*) had come for the hervesting of lentils (*maanh kapavan*).

In the Protection of the Nahars

Hir and Ranjha, having observed them from a distance, rushed towards them. On seeing them, they put shawls around their necks. Hir spoke out, 'I am the daughter of Chuchak from Jhang Siyal. Ranjha is my husband (*haq*). Please listen. I am his sacrifice. Chuchak, employing force, married me to the Khera. When I left with one whom I recognized as my husband, Ali mobilized an army. Listen, O Lords! Since I am surrounded in difficulties (*aukhi rudhi*), I came into your sanctuary (*saam*).' Ranjha pleaded, 'I am Dhido, the son of Mojam, hailing from Takht Hazara. I devoted my life to Hir and, at my door, set up the fire of a mendicant (*dar te dhuan*). Having failed to uphold the honour of my mother and father, I came to be known as the herdsman (*chak*). When I walked away with my rightful wife towards the south (*lamme*), Ali came out with an army (*kattak*). I have no support or asylum. Every straw, having become my enemy, has turned up to take my life. You are *zamindars*, the lords of the land (*rath zamin de khawind*). Seeing you, I rushed up to you. As I am surrounded in difficulties, I came into your sanctuary.'

(The Nahar chief offered) 'Come and sit in our protection. This is what pleases us. By using my authority (*hukmi*), I will keep you even at the risk of my head. I have taken this responsibility on my head. Even the dogs in our protection do not leave. You are the offspring of *zamindars*. We have decided to put our head at stake in the face of an army (*lashkar*). I will not hand you over even if Akbar marched in.' The Khans gathered their weapons and harnessed their horses. They committed themselves to lay down their lives. They became ready for this, declaring, 'Brothers! What hands will you display? We have assumed the enmity of others (*vair paraya*). Why should we not die? The son of Mojam and the daughter of Chuchak have come into our protection.' As an advance party (of the Kheras) appeared on the road, an army marched from that direction.[48] After offering a salute (*salaam*), they met the Khans (Nahars) and asked them if they had seen a Jogi along with a woman. The Kheras inquired this from the Nahars. The latter replied, 'No, we have not seen them. Neither in the front nor in the rear. They did not come here. We have been sitting here for long. So far, we have not completed the harvesting of lentils. Move forward and look at the road. Ahead, you may inquire. We are sitting in the moors, occupied in our work. We do not tell lies.'

The Kheras stated, 'Brothers! Listen. You are not telling us what we wish to know. We are tired and helpless. They (Hir and Ranjha) are speaking through your eyes. We have not digested the sugar that we consumed. Why do you mix poison in it? Brother! Tell us in all cordiality. Otherwise we will take the iron in our hands.' The Nahars replied, 'They did come here, even if they did not. We have nothing to fear. Sitting on dead trees, we are not sparrows who will fly away. Even the dogs in our protection are not returned. Here, the *zamindars* have come to us. If your army appears to be large (*kattak vadera*), our smaller one will soon attract more men.' Pulling out the swords from their scabbards, they rushed in from here and there, crying 'Ali Ali'. While they became thirsty for blood (*ratt trihaye*), the corpses fell here and there. The Kheras, extremely anxious to clash, did so. The Nahars, who were not deterred, fell upon their opponents. Crying 'Ali Ali', they again attacked. The two sides did not show any hesitation. As the bodies grappled, both sides were filled with vehemence. The corpses fell on their heads, as no one wavered. Nine Kheras and five Nahars were killed. As both sides called for support, the reinforcements (*vagaar*) jumped into the fray. It was brave of the Nahars. They were committed to fight. Their ardour could not be put into words. The *zamindars* were still inclined to clash. The enthusiasm was seen on both the sides. In this encounter, five Kheras fell down and three Nahars lost their lives. Heads were crushed like the breaking of pitchers. This is something, which cannot be stated. The uproar of the Nahars reached their village. Nothing remained a secret. The entire land turned red like the lac dye (*alta*) at weddings. I, named Damodar, was hiding (*chhapp khalota*) where there were two plants and a reed.

The true Syeds of Rajoa were going in a palanquin (*doli*). On hearing the cries and shouts (*kukara te lalkara*), they rushed in. They saw that the Kheras and Nahars were fighting and, while doing so, they were raising a tumult. As it was seen, the Syeds intervened and brought about a disengagement (*hora*). Separating the combatants from here and there, the Syeds made them sit.[49] They said, 'Speak up. Why are you fighting? Why are you getting killed? We are asking you. Why don't you tell us? Friends! Speak up. Why have you assumed this enmity (*vair*)?' The Khera (Ali) stated, 'Lord! Please Listen. We are saying this. Taking along all resources and mediators (*vasile*), I got the bridegroom married. There, we heard a lot of gossip (*chocho*). But, nothing was stated from the mouth. Taking the bride (*muklava*), we came back and made him (Ranjha) carry the drum. Lord! He was brought there. However, he ran away and assumed the garb of a Jogi. Though she (Hir) was hale and hearty, she was falsely shown as bitten by a snake. Using a clever artifice (*hunnar*), she was made to lie inside. He, disguised as a Jogi, came and deceived everyone. He made a false excuse of organizing a forty-day retreat (*chillah*). Making a breach (*sanh*) in the wall, he took away the virgin (*bilga*). After hearing this, I rushed after him. Lords! You must ask the Nahars, who are sitting here. Why did they give him protection?' This is how Ali narrated his tale of woe. Immediately, the Nahars spoke out, 'There is no difference (*tafawat*) between them (Hir and Ranjha). They came from somewhere and fell into our protection. Even the dogs in our protection are not returned. Do the *zamindars* have no honour? It is not proper to surrender them. Such an act will blacken our faces. We have got our youths killed, though we did not get anything out of it.'

The Syeds declared, 'Both the *zamindars* did evil (*manda keeta*). You got the youths killed. You have been into this business of killing. How can one make you understand? Kot Qabula is twenty-two leagues from here. You must fight a legal battle there. Whichever side the Qazi adjudicates, that person will take the woman.'[50] Brothers! 'Let us go' (*hallo hallo*) happened. This appealed to everyone. The Kheras and Nahars met each other, so that the sadness (*dilgiri*) was removed from their minds. Noise reached the village. After this, the army (*fauj*) of the Nahars arrived. When the story of the episode was heard, as many as sixty Nahars came mounted. From here and there, the entire world walked together. They brought the Kheras into the village and provided food (*tukkar*) to them. Hir and Ranjha, who were in hiding, were brought in. Hir spoke to the Kheras. What words did she utter? 'Ali! You have no shame. You have come after mustering an army. Having lost your honour, you do not feel ashamed (*sharminda*). With what face have you marched. All praise (*shabash*) for the Nahar *zamindars*, who gave us protection.' Hir made Ali listen to these words. Ali said to Ranjha, 'You have been conspiring from behind. It is not in our power. If we ever get an opportunity, we will drink your blood. Now you have wrapped yourself in a shawl. We will eat your flesh raw.' In response, Ranjha did not say a word. Hir said to Khera (Ali), 'O Khera! You must go away. You are an evil since time immemorial (*qadimi bhaira*). Why do you shout at my Ranjha? Who is this mean Jat (*kameena jatta*) to admonish us? I will burn the faces of all the Kheras. How dare you speak in our presence? A curse be on the entire clan (*kul zat*) of the Kheras. You are quarrelling with my Ranjha.'

The arrangement of stay was made in the village. The high and low arrived. Seeing an isolated house (*kotha hikk ikkala*), both the lovers were accommodated there. The Kheras, being offended, asked as to why Hir was allowed to stay with the herdsman. Nahars explained the matter to the Kheras. The Khans stated, 'Brothers! We have allowed them to be as they were seen (*jikar nazrin aayi*). When they met us, they had their arms around each other's neck. We did not see them separate. It is not proper to disjoin them. Such an act will not be acceptable. Since we found them together, we will not keep them apart.' The Kheras demanded, 'Your act is not proper. You should send Hir to your women's quarter. You are also *zamindars*, the masters of land and lords of rivers (*rath zamin de khawind / bhoyen nayin de sayin*). The whole world knows that he is an old thief (*chor chiroka*), who has been chasing her. Shall we live or die? Shall we consume poison?' The Nahars replied, 'Brothers! We will not separate them so long as we can. What is it to us? How can we ask them? We cannot inflict any pain (*ranj*) on them. You are yourself going to Kot Qabula in order to pursue the legal issue (*jhera jheran*). Whoever gets her, we will provide our support to the decision.'

All the Nahar girls came to see Hir. As they kept looking at her, they were sold out. Even after seeing her to their hearts' content, they were still desirous of seeing her. The women (*zanana*), getting together, showered praise on her. Food reached the house. Ranjha was woken up. When the girls saw his face, mouth and forehead, they were impressed (*pasind*) with him. The girls said that he was the most appropriate one for Hir. The Lord had rightly made this arrangement (*sayin sabab banaya*). The girls, having met Hir, felt inspired. In fact, they lost their power (*quwwat*). All the men and women were captivated. All of them said to the Kheras, 'What a calamity (*qehar*) you have inflicted? You mustered an army and, running in their pursuit, you led such a big search (*khoj*). Hir does not suit you. She is a beautiful match for the Jogi.' The Kheras became weary of listening to all this. At night, the food was served to them. During the night, they felt acute stomach ache (*soolan sall*). In the morning, they felt better.

Having saddled their horses, the Kheras made preparations to leave. All the Nahars came along with them. After the horses were made ready, they left for Kot Qabula. The Kheras asked the Nahars, 'Where are you going? You must truthfully tell us.' They replied, 'We are your rightful companions (*sathi sahi*). We are coming along with you.' The Kheras asked them the purpose of their journey. The Nahars explained, 'It is not proper for us to leave them in your hands. You may kill them on the way. However, we are bound to be compassionate towards them. We will present them where the judge, jurist and administrator (*qazi mufti hakam*) are found. When the Shariat speaks, we will hand over Hir.'[51] As the Nahars left, the Kheras accompanied them. In fact, the people made them go.

The lovers, wrapped in shawls and with faces covered, were made to walk in the front. As the people ran ahead of the horses, the Khera (Sahiba) wailed, 'Hir has employed a stratagem (*chaale*) to get the herdsman'. Hir shouted, 'You wretched Khera! May your face be burnt. I make myself an offering for Dhido. When the Lord distributed love, nobody conveyed a share to you. You are merely a string of the churn (*lar utla madhani*), which is useful only for rotation. Do not speak again. You wretched Khera. Your father is a wavering turncoat.' The Khera, while going along, lamented, 'May you neither live nor die. You bitch of a woman. You are a keep of the herdsman. You go about fornicating to the hilt (*kardi rajj haraam*). Today, the mother of the herdsman has died.' The Khera conveyed these abusive lamentations to Hir. However, Hir retorted, 'Where was the Khera when love was being distributed? Either you could not gain an entry or you lost the way. The contemptible Khera failed to get any response from this daughter of Chuchak (Chuchakani).' The Kheras, employing their power (*hukami*) knocked down Ranjha and grabbed Hir Jatti by her arm. The Nahars, while trying to stop the Kheras, said, 'This is not proper. Men should not argue with women. You must feel ashamed. Ahead, you will face each other. Only a little distance is left. You must remain quiet till Kot Qabula.' Hir cried, 'Ashes on the head of the Kheras if they dare to say anything to me. On my head is the true perfect master (*kamil murshid sacha*). He is my husband and I am his wife. From the beginning to the end, he is my lord I searched for and found. Ranjha is my true lord. Let ashes rain on the heads of the Kheras.'

After the fruitless argumentation, they reached Kot Qabula. With the evening prayer (*nimashan*), they entered the town. The Kheras parked their horses in the stables. The prisoners (*banduye*) were surrounded, while I (Damodar) helped them to sit. Next morning, justice will be done to both sides. After eating, all the *zamindars* slept. Next morning, they had to appear at the court (*adalat*). The two lovers slept surrounded in a circle. When the morning arrived, they were woken up. The Kheras said, 'Get ready, you thieves. We are going to present ourselves at the court'. When they entered the court (*kachehri*), they remembered the Lord. The gossip spread in Kot Qabula, as someone conveyed the news. They had been hearing of the daughter of Chuchak from Jhang Siyal. Accompanied by the herdsman, she had come to Kot Qabula to argue her case. A large number of people had come to see her. The judge (*qazi*), jurist (*mufti*), governor (*hakim*) and recordkeeper (*qanungo*) were sitting. The people of the town (*qasba lok*) also entered the court to observe the proceedings. The Kheras and Nahars, both placing their trust in God, arrived at the site. The Qazi directed the case to be stated in accordance with the Shariat.

Ali, filled with anger, was the first to state the petition (*arz*). He said, 'There is a lot of debt on our head on account of Chuchak's daughter. We held the marriage in the proper manner. There were rumours about the herdsman. There, we did not become aware of it. Listen to the details. I placed a drum on his head. Now, we have brought him here. Acting with stealth, she was shown as if bitten by a snake (*chori sapp laraya*). As a result, she was made to lie inside. He, becoming a Jogi, came as a healer (*mandri*). He made a breach in the wall and ran away with her. Ask the Nahars as to why they gave protection to them.' The Nahars stated, 'What we state does not have even a bit of falsehood (*koor na bhora*). There is no difference between them (Hir and Ranjha) from the facts. We were getting the lentils harvested in the moors. They came from somewhere. As they narrated the full facts (*kul haqiqat*), it became a question of honour (*lajja*) for us. We do not even return the dogs in our protection. Do the *zamindars* have no honour? The person, who has betrothed her, will take her. We have no interest (*matlab*) in the matter.'

Debate between Hir and the Qazi

QAZI: O Hir! Lady of excellent qualities (*guni gahire*)! Listen to the order of the Lord. This Ranjhan, of whom you are so proud, is the husband of someone else (*haq paraya*). You have shamed (*sharminda*) your father Chuchak. You have wasted the respect (*adab*) of your brothers. The proclamation (*jag dhandora*) has spread in the whole world.

HIR: Listen, Qazi.[52] This heart will not waver. What game (*bazi*) do you play? The love between me and Ranjha is very old (*nehu chiroka*). It began when the Lord created the world (*khalqat saji*). God has tied marriages of the hearts (*nikah dilan de badhe*). Qazi! What will you tie? You dispense justice on the basis of the Shariat. However, you have not tasted your share of love.

QAZI: Listen, O Hir! Lady of excellent qualities! You have come to quarrel. Ultimately, the truth will prevail and falsehood will not endure at all (*koor na mule taghe*). You are married among the Kheras. The whole world heard it. Listen, daughter Hir. How can love match up to the Shariat?

HIR: Listen, O Lord Judge! Tell us about matters that are truthful (*sachaviyan batan*). Those who forbid the lawful (*halal*) are doing what is unlawful (*haram*). A curse on the tribe of such people. I will not leave the lappet (*dawan*) of Ranjha even if I am pushed to the essence of low castes (*satt sanaatan*). You take justice rather lightly, because you do not understand the mysteries of love.

QAZI: You infidel (*kafiriani*)! Do not indulge in sacrilege (*kufr*). You speak to me of illicit love (*ishq haram*). You have a longing (*chetak*) for the herdsman. You have affixed a stigma on your tribe (*zati dagh*). Girl! I will enter your name in the punishment. You do not speak in the proper way (*na maqul*). Wise girl! You must understand what you state, lest you should weep when punished.

HIR: If I am punished because of truth, nothing will please me more. Sir, judge! You do not give proper weight to the fact that a daughter was born to you. I am present before you. Nothing remains concealed. If I enter the grave while I am living, you must quote a similar precedent (*rivayat*).

QAZI: Listen, Hir! When your father married (*parnai*) you off, the world came in the marriage party. You infidel! You should not die while living. Nothing remains hidden. If you deny, you will be thrashed in public. I have become angry. You ill-starred one (*kubakhti*)! How can I accept your statement as true? After all, you have intimacy (*ashnai*) with the herdsman.

HIR: Listen, O Qazi! You dispense justice. You know nothing about the case. You are doing only what pleases you. Those who are allured by illusion (*maya*) will be guilty of infidelity (*kufr*). That Hir belongs to Ranjha is known to everyone.

QAZI: Listen, O Hir! Lady of excellent qualities! The world has heard everything. You were married to the Khera. Your father married you off. The Kheras spent a lot of money and they brought a large number of people. You are afflicted with love (*ishq*). Yet, you dare to make statements. You have discarded all shame (*sabho sharm gavaya*).

HIR: You should not say such a thing. It does not behove you. You must fear the true God. This may not happen to a daughter born to you. The rule of Akbar Shah is quite strong (*raj vadera*). It has granted the judgeship (*qaza*) to you. Listen, Miyan Qazi! I am also the daughter of *zamindars* (*rathan jayi*).

QAZI: If your father is a big *zamindar* (*rath vadera*), you did not feel a bit of shame. Whatever happened to you in your parental home, you were made to go with the Khera. Hirey! You have done the most shameful act (*vaddi besharmi*). In a stealthy manner, you ran away. It will be good of you to go with honour. Otherwise, I will send you by force (*napp dasahen zori*).

HIR: Qazi! You are acting in haste. You do not fear God. My rightful husband is this Ranjha. All the people know this. Taking bribes (*vadhi*), you violate our rights and, thereafter, you show us the book (*kadh kitab vikhayin*). O Qazi! What justice are you delivering?

QAZI: Hirey! Girl! You are a shameless woman (*ran besharmi*). You accuse us of bribery. Discarding the lawful (*halal*), you have adopted the unlawful (*haram*). Your nose and ears will be cut off. You do not accept the Shariat of God, but repeatedly bring in the herdsman. You speak without decent manners (*be-adab alayen*).

HIR: The nose and ears of that person should be chopped, who is engaged in a secret intimacy (*yari chori*). Second, the nose of that person should be slashed, who usurps the property of another. Ranjha is mine and I am Ranjha's. Another marriage (*beya nikah*) is not possible. O Qazi! I have never seen the Khera, though I keep hearing about him (*kanni peya suninda*).

QAZI: Listen, Hirey! You have been married for three years. (During this period) You have been living with the Khera. This (Ranjha) is the herdsman of your father. All the people know it (*jane sabh lukai*). Starving and dying, he has again turned up and you eloped with him (*nass sidhai*). Why did you take this extreme step (*att chayi*)?

HIR: There (Rangpur Khera), I spent thirty-five and a half months. I did not eat the salt of the Kheras. Except this scarf (*chiri*) of my parents, I did not wear any three-piece suit (*trevar*). I will swear by any oath, which you wish me to take. I did not allow the Khera to approach my bed (*kadi manjhe pas na laya*). If my face looks radiant today, it is because Ranjha has shown his face.

QAZI: The Shariat states that Ranjha is a thief, who made the breach. He is an old thief (*chor chiroka*), who has been chasing you. All the people bear witness (*ugahi*) to this fact. The Khera is your rightful husband (*haq*). Why should he let you go? Throwing away your husband and enjoying a paramour (*yar manesi*). Hirey! How is it possible?

HIR: Miyan Qazi! Listen to the whole matter. I have understood my mandate (*sanad*). The love between me and Ranjha is very old (*nehun chiroka*). Then, I was a suckling baby (*dudh vati*). I would writhe in the cradle. No one could describe or understand my agony (*vedan*). Who is Chuchak? Ashes on Ali's head. I have recognized my own substance (*apni vast sinjati*).

The Qazi, filled with excessive anger, ordered Hir to be tied with ropes. She, standing with her body tied, bent her back (*kand nivayi*). Three times, a whip was cracked on her back, so that blood started oozing. She would not die of this beating, though her name was included in the punishment. She would not be able to live if Ranjha were subjected to torture. A hundred thousand people were listening. The entire world had come out. Every day, they had been hearing about Hir and Ranjha. Now, the Lord had shown them to the world. Whatever the governor asked, Hir gave suitable answers. Then, the Qazi put questions to Hir.

QAZI: Listen, O Hir! Whose daughter-in-law are you? Whose daughter are you? As masters of land and rivers, they link their lappet (*pallu*) with Akbar. I have great regard (*adab*) for them and, therefore, you will not be thrashed. Hirey! How much can I make you understand? Do not waste yourself.

HIR: O Qazi! What greatness have you seen (in Chuchak and Ali)? Tell me and show me. They are so great that gold and silver flows to them from seven directions. I consign all these goods into the hearth (*chulhe vich ghatan eh vastu*). Don't you know this? Listen, O Qazi! To me, everything appears desolate if Ranjha is not there.

At this point, the Qazi took the rope in his hands and got Hir's arms tied behind her back.

QAZI: Just say, 'I am the daughter-in-law of the Kheras (*main nuh khereyan di*)'. The whole world knows this. I will not release you till you do not bear witness to this. That you are not dying fills me with anger. How much favour can I confer on the Khans?

HIR: O Qazi! Listen to my petition. This is an undescribable story (*akath kahani*). It is earlier than the divine tablet (*lauh qalam*).[53] It predates the highest sphere and the empyrean throne. At that time, water was not visible. There was no time, earth, sun or moon. One light dissolved into another light (*joti jot samani*). Since then, I swear by the Lord, I had sold out to Ranjha. If there is anyone from those times, I will present him as a witness (*shahid*).

The Jogi was presented before the Qazi, who asked, 'You were a herdsman of Chuchak. When did you adopt Jog? You appear as the big bastard (*vadda harami*) of a herdsman. What a garb you have put on?' As Ranjha was held, his arms were tied behind his back. He said, 'O Lord! If there is an intimate (*mehram*), he would understand this way of life. If someone speaks, he is not relied upon. If someone explains (*sukhan*) it in detail, even then he is not believed in. Listen, O Qazi! The tongue has been sealed (*mohar zaban karin*). This is a difficult story (*aukhi ehu kahani*). The sign of a mute person, only a mute one can understand.' The Qazi, having made up his mind, ordered Ranjha to be whipped.[54] His arms were raised up in preparation of the punishment. Hir, who was watching this, leapt forward and clasped (*jaffa*) him to her chest. As efforts were made to pull her away, the people started laughing. Hir cried, 'In the name of Lord's justice, stop me if you can. Give his (Ranjha's) entire punishment to me. But, do not beat him. Even if his full punishment is inflicted on me, I will be sharing only half of it with him.' Awwal Fatta said to the Qazi, 'Honourable Judge, listen. Why are you getting them beaten? Just catch the Siyal and give her to Ali. Why are you causing this embarrassment (*sharminda*)? Where is the need to call for a witness? You already know everything.' As such, Hir was seized and handed over to the Kheras. The Kheras, having grabbed Hir, took her in their custody. She was put ahead of the horses. Some used stones. Others wielded the stick and still others employed their legs to beat her. One who was fed on milk and brought up on butter (*dudh nipuni makhan pali*) came into the hands of the frightened ones. I (Damodar), while standing, saw what was inflicted on Saleti.

Hir was pulled with a rope, which was tied around her waist. Still, she confronted Ali, 'Listen, Ali! I make myself a sacrifice for these blows, because I am receiving them from Ranjha. I give my head as an offering to him (*sir sadqah*). You must rightly listen. O, you brutish Jatt (*siyyada jatta*)! I am not supplicating before you.' The more she spoke, the more did the Khans beat her. Though her body was covered with blood (*ratt viratti pinda*), no one intervened to stop them. Her hair got mixed up with dust. Saleti, who could not be restrained, continued to hurl invectives. She said, 'Listen to me. You brutish Jatt! Do not have any misunderstanding. I am full of faults and shortcomings (*pur taqsir main auganhari*). My spiritual preceptor (*murshid*) is beating me. I have the support of a mentor like Ranjha, whose moves cannot be discerned. All this is the handiwork of Ranjha. You must know that Ranjha is making you do this.' As Hir kept on speaking, the Kheras kept on beating her. They did not show any laxity in the use of stones, sticks and slaps. Dragged with a rope, her clothes were torn as if entangled in bushes. However, the Kheras did not show any mercy to her. She clarified, 'Listen, Ali along with your son. You are inflicting a great punishment on me. The mentor, whose dog is being beaten, will take note. What if I have been humbled. He will preserve his own honour. Listen, Ali. Now, Dhido will not spare you.'

Justice through Supernatural Means

A fire broke out at the gate of Kot Qabula. Raja Adli, owing to his dependence on money, did not deliver justice (*adl*). The water was poured but it turned into oil. Fire arose from all the gates. The people of Kot Qabula raised shrill cries. The entire town became a blazing inferno. The people sought an answer (*lok jawab karenda*). They appealed (*dhrohi*) to the judge and governor to explain the burning of a prominent town. They said, 'If Akbar questioned you, what answer will you give?' The entire town came out with this appeal. As time passed, all the inhabitants of the town came out. The entire town, being extremely agitated, raised a cry in unison. While the fire kept on moving a step ahead, the people said that the Jogi had filed his suit (*jogi parcha laya*). The judge and jurist were amazed at the work of nature (*qudrat*). The congregation, with folded hands, marched to the Jogi. Everyone pleaded, 'Forgive this crime of ours. We will send an army to bring the Kheras back, if you put out the fire.' When Dhido raised his hand, the fire receded and the army passed through.

The Qazi declared, 'Listen, friends. We pronounced the judgement on the basis of whatever became manifest (*zahir ditha*). Who knows the matters of the Lord? God has delivered the justice. In accordance with prudence, the right to Hir belongs to the person, who puts out the fire.'

The entire congregation said to the Qazi, 'What a calamity (*qehar*) have you inflicted? Saleti is the right (*haq*) of the Jogi, but she was given to the Khera. The Jogi showed immense patience. That is why all this happened. Damodar claims that he saw this with his own eyes (*akhin ditha*) when the people raised a cry. The army was dispatched to seize the Kheras, so that they did not advance any further. Everyone, falling at the feet of the Jogi, supplicated (*minnat*) before him. Addressing the authorities, they demanded, 'You had thrown away the shoot (*bumbal*) earlier. Now is the time to earn some praise (*sobha*).' As the fire abated, the people offered their blessings (*asisan*). The army caught up with the Kheras and announced, 'You are being summoned again. Let us go quickly. There should be no laxity.' The entire community (*lukai*) was smouldering (in anger). Ali stood astonished at the arrival of the strong army. Hir discerned that the herdsman had shown his miraculous power (*azmat chak vikhai*). Saleti speedily turned back, not allowing the horses to come near. Tying up her loincloth (*kachhota*), she started running. What strides did she take? She reflected, 'The Lord has preserved the shame of the person, whose slave girl I am (*bandi bardi*).' The contingent reached Kot Qabula, but the fire did not give them any passage. The army said to Hir, 'Listen, O Hir! When we were coming from that side, the Jogi enabled us to pass through.' The troops asked the manner they could enter the town. Hir stood in front of the fire and, using her hand, removed the heat (*hathin tau hataya*). In this way, she assisted the army to pass through.

The Qazi explained to Ali the manner he interpreted the law, saying, 'I delivered a judgement on the basis of what became manifest (*zahir ditha*). But, no one knows the hidden mysteries (*batin baat*).' He also stated that the person, who would extinguish the fire, would take Hir as his right. Ali admitted, 'Jogi is the furnace and Hir is the fire. But, we are dying without death. We must go from here, as we cannot stay any longer. All the aristocrats (*kul mahajan*), whose death is imminent since the origin of life (*azal*), are burning.' Having seen the fire, the Kheras were overtaken by a sense of detachment (*udasi*). People of Kot Qabula said, 'Listen, O Chief (*sayyiada*)! Where are you going? At the outset, we will burn you. You brought a calamity (*bala*) to the town. How can we let you leave? Come with us. Since we are fellow travellers (*hamrahi*), we will sit here and burn together.' In view of the widespread panic, everyone looked towards the Jogi. Then, the Jogi stood up and, folding his hands, brought his eyes together. Putting the shawl around his neck, he appealed to the saints (*piran*), 'Shower your kindness (*mehar*) on the entire town and put out the fire'. Instantly, the fire subsided, while Ranjha made the people bow (*lok nivaye*).

The Kheras, who were foul and filthy, were beaten and expelled. The Kheras, having marched in after mobilizing their forces, did not look back owing to their humiliation. The people came to the Jogi and said, 'We are your slaves. We entreat (*minnat*) you to settle here.' The people fell at the feet of the Jogi, who had shown his miraculous powers. The entire world, including the judge and jurist, made supplication before him. Putting shawls around their necks and hands on their feet, they said to the Jogi, 'You have shown great miraculous power (*azmat bhali vikhayi*). Hir is your rightful wife.' Hir joined the Jogi. From Kallar Kot to Kot Qabula, the fragrance of musk spread up to the gate. Adli Raja recognized the delivery of justice. The crane was united with the hawk. With the walls of sandalwood and the strong scent of musk, the rose flowers flourished and bloomed. As the musk spread into the town, every heart was freshened up. All the people (*sabha*) fell at the feet of the Jogi, deeply impressed with his display of miraculous power. The entire world, including the governor and judge, came to pay their respects (*ziyarat*) to the Jogi and reiterated, 'First, thrash and expel the Kheras, so that they are not seen again'. The Kheras were banished. Their vigour was wiped out, while ashes were poured on their heads.

In 1529 Bikrami era, Hir and Ranjha were united with each other. God brought all the wrangles to an end. The kingship (*patshahi*) of Akbar was on the ascendant with every passing day. The lovers, giving their blessings (*asisan*), came out of the town. The inhabitants (*raiyyat*) of the town, putting shawl around their neck, requested, 'O Lord, Ranjha! Kindly stay on. Here we will set up new halls (*dalan*) for you, besides whatever you say.' They replied, 'Bid us farewell. We will go from here and set up a house.' Damodar claimed that he saw with his own eyes, as they went towards the south (*lammi tarf*). When they had travelled three leagues, I (Damodar) was also with them. Five riders, wearing black robes, arrived from invisible realm (*azghaibon*). Caressing the heads of both, they were inclined to kiss their heads, saying, 'Listen, O Hir! Without all this, you would not have become enlightened (*raushan*).' Having said this, they went into hiding somewhere. Once gone, they never came again.

The tale of Hir has been completed. No love has ever been equal to it (*iss samm ishq na koi*). As the lovers took love upon themselves, they carried it to its logical fruition. This was known to the three worlds. I, name Damodar and caste Gulati, wrote what I saw (*ditha so likhioyi*). Having left Rajoa, I have settled among the Siyals.

NOTES

1. The Afghans (Pathans) had a long association with India. Besides long distance trade, they served in the armies of Delhi Sultanate and rose to the rank of nobles. The formation of Lodi and Sur kingdoms gave a fresh impetus to Afghan immigration to India. Afghan colonies appeared in the towns of Indo-Gangetic plain. Ludhiana acquired its name from the Lodis. In the Mughal province of Lahore, Afghans held *zamindaris* in the subdistricts of Jalandhar, Chaurasi, Thandot, Jalalabad, Khushab and Hazara Qarlugh. West of the Indus, the Afghan tribes, particularly the Yusufzais inhabiting the Swat-Bajaur region, did not accept the Mughal authority and disrupted the Delhi-Kabul trade route that passed through the Khyber and Peshawar. During the mid-1580s, the Mughal military operations under Zain Khan Koka established a semblance of order in the disturbed area.
2. Marriages between Muslim rulers and Hindu princesses were entered into for sealing politicial accords. Firoz Shah Bahmani married a Vijaynagar princess, while Yusuf Adil Shah married a sister of Mukand Rao Maratha. Rao Maldeo of Jodhpur married a daughter to Sultan Mahmud of Gujarat and another to Islam Shah Sur. Haji Khan Pathan, a ruler of eastern Rajasthan, married the daughters of Bharmal of Amber and Rao Maldeo of Jodhpur. For Akbar, such marriages were part of a broader policy of firming political alliances with powerful chiefs. He

married a daughter of Hasan Khan Mewati, while her younger sister was married to Bairam Khan. While returning (1562) from Ajmer, Akbar married a daughter of Bharmal. In 1570, he married a niece of Rai Kalyan Mal of Bikaner, besides daughters of Rawal Har Rai of Jaisalmer and Chandersen of Marwar. In 1584, Prince Salim married the daughters of Bhagwant Das of Amber, Raja Udai Singh of Jodhpur, Rai Singh of Bikaner and Bhim Singh of Jaisalmer. Prince Danial was married to a granddaughter of Rao Maldeo of Jodhpur. Satish Chandra, 'Mughal Relations with Rajput States of Rajasthan: The Foundations', in *Mughal Religious Policies: The Rajputs and the Deccan*, New Delhi: Vikas Publishing House, 1993, pp. 17-30.

3. The Brahmins outnumbered all castes except the Jats and Rajputs. Reaching a maximum where people were entirely Hindus (hills, submontane areas and Yamuna tract), they decreased gradually from east to west, disappearing in the western plains. Their functions and position being sacerdotal, they were consulted on omens and auspicious dates, besides officiating at ceremonies. The Doom was a Hindu name, while Mirasi was Muslim and Arabic. Apart from serving as genealogists for agricultural castes and outcaste tribes, they also performed as musicians and minstrels. They were assigned a low social ranking. Interestingly, both the Brahmins and Dooms were seen as notorious for their greed. Denzil Ibbetson, *Panjab Castes*, Patiala: Languages Department, Punjab, rpt., 1970, pp. 215-18, 234-5.
4. Among the Muslims of Panjab, the customs of betrothal varied from place to place. In the pre-betrothal negotiations, which the boy's family initiated, a group of men visited the girl's house. When both sides were satisfied with the suitability of the match, a day was fixed for the betrothal and token gifts (money, rings and sugar) were exchanged. The girl's side, deputing a delegation of servants, sent for the boy a Tika comprising a horse, a camel, a gold ring, clothes, cash, sugar puffs and dried dates. The two families began to associate. On an auspicious day, a party from the boy's side went to the girl's house. The betrothal comprised invocation of blessings (*niyat khair*) and recitation of prayer (*dua-i fatiha-i khair*). The two sides exchanged congratulations and customary gifts. Immediately after betrothal, the boy's relatives went to the girl's house with gifts for her. At the festivals, including the two Ids and Shab-i Barat, the two sides exchanged sweatmeats, clothes and cattle. H.A. Rose, *A Glossary of the Castes and Tribes of the Punjab and North West Frontier Province*, vol. I, Patiala: Languages Department, Punjab, rpt., 1970, pp. 803-13.

5. Indra was the god of thunder, who overcame drought and darkness, bringing water and light. He was also the god of warfare and used thunderbolt as his weapon. The world of Indra was filled with Siddhas, Charans, Apsaras, Gandharvas, Brahmarishis and other deities. As celestial plants and fragrant air marked the Nandana grove, his grand assembly (*sabha*) boasted of a richly adorned court, glittering chariots and enchanting music and dance. Roshen Dalal, *Hinduism: A Alphabetical Guide*, New Delhi: Penguin Books, 2010, pp. 164-5.
6. Damodar was referring to the ancient horse sacrifice (*ashvamedha*), which was undertaken to assert a king's paramountcy, particularly in the later Vedic period. A horse, after purificatory rituals, was anointed with the king's name. It roamed freely at the head of an army. The king claimed the territory it passed through. He fought against anyone who dared to catch the horse. After a year, the horse returned to the capital. In a grand ritual, involving ruling elite and priests, the horse was sacrificed and its flesh was consecrated to the gods. According to a scholaraly view, the sacrifice, besides legitimizing the king's power, ensured procreation owing to a focus on the king's wife. One of the most striking features was the transfer of material resources to and from the king. He appropriated wealth from chiefs, kinsfolk and priests. It was spent on elaborate rituals, gifts to important visitors, presents to priests and food to all participants. Kumkum Roy, *The Emergence of Monarchy in North India: Eighth-Fourth Centuries* BC *(As Reflected in the Brahmanical Tradition)*, New Delhi: Oxford University Press, 1994, pp. 119-24.
7. Sambhals have been listed as a clan of Muslim Jats in Montgomery district and engaged in agriculture. H.A. Rose, *A Glossary of the Tribes and Castes of the Punjab and North West Frontier Province*, vol. II, Patiala: Languages Department, Punjab, rpt., 1970, p. 351.
8. Jhinwars were included among menials who worked as watermen, boatmen and cooks. They made baskets, dug wells and cultivated water nuts. They were known as Jhinwar in east Panjab where they were largely Hindu and as Machhis in west Panjab where they were mostly Muslim. The Jhinwars (Machhis) were most numerous in central and western districts of the province, which were traversed by the great rivers and where they assisted in agricultural labour. Machhi women served as midwives and nurses. Besides supplying water in houses and at social functions, the Jhinwars carried palanquins and other burdens. As true village menials, they received customary dues for their services. Denzil Ibbetson, *Panjab Castes*, pp. 303-6.

9. In the late Sultanate period, there was a hierarchy of administrative units comprising *vilayat*, *shiq*, *khitta* and *iqta*. The term *shiq* was applied to Multan, Dipalpur, Samana and Hissar Firoza. A unit under the crown lands (*khalsa*) was placed under a *shiqdar*. His functions were to maintain peace and order, to help the revenue collectors (*amils*) in collecting the land tax, to provide military assistance to *amils* against the rebellious *zamindars* and *muqaddams*, and finally to look after the land grants to scholars, Syeds and saintly persons. Iqtidar Husain Siddiqui, *Some Aspects of Afghan Despotism in India*, Aligarh: Three Men Publications, 1969, pp. 140-3; Iqtidar Husain Siddiqui, *History of Sher Shah Sur*, Aligarh: P.C. Dwadash Shreni & Co., 1971, pp. 96-118.
10. In stanza number 67, Damodar seemed to repeat the daily schedule of the girls, which had already been laid out in stanza number 37. This repetition could be attributed to an oversight on the part of the poet. However, there was one difference. Earlier, the girls spent the fourth watch in bathing at the Chenab. Later on, they spent this time inside the boat.
11. The towns of Jhang and Maghiana stood 2 miles apart. The Chenab flowed at a distance of about 3 miles to the west. During hot season, the Kharorah branch of the river ran past both the towns. Its 3 miles long fine avenue of trees and handsome masonry bathing steps (*ghats*) added a peculiar beauty to the neighbourhood. The country around was well-wooded and fine gardens abounded. An inundation canal, leaving the Kharorah branch of the Chenab near Jhang, passed around Maghiana and emptied itself into the same branch aftrer a course of five miles. Maghiana lay on the egde of the highlands, overlooking the alluvial valley of the Chenab, while the older town of Jhang occupied the lowlands at its foot. *Imperial Gazetteer of India, Provincial Series: Punjab*, vol. II, Calcutta: Superintendent of Government Printing, 1908, pp. 217-18.
12. Ali bin Abi Talib (598-661) was the cousin and son-in-law of Prophet Muhammad. Married to Fatima, he was the father of two sons Hasan and Husain, besides two daughters Zainab and Umm Kulsum. He was one of the first converts to Islam. A mighty warrior, he led armies during the evolution of early Islam. In particular, he distinguished himself in the battles of Badr, Uhud, Khandaq, Khaibar, Jamal, Siffin and Nahrawan. The Sunnis acknowledge him as the fourth caliph. The Shias regard him as Prophet's successor and first in the line of Imams. Several Sufis saw him as the fountainhead of Islamic spirituality. Ali was admired as the epitome of bravery, generosity, learning, justice

and piety. For these attributes, the Muslims, cutting across regions and eras, invoked his name while facing heavy odds, particularly in warfare.

13. Aghoris were a sect of ascetics known for their abominable practices. They ate human flesh and filth, using human skulls as vessels. They were associated with Tantric rights of Shaivas, the worshippers of one of the forms of the Mother Goddess. They smeared their bodies with ash from funeral piles, wore strings of human skulls around their necks, wove their hair into a matted braid, clothed heir loins in tigerskin and carried a bell that was rung incessantly. Found largely in eastern India, they wandered from one pilgrim centre to the other. James Hastings, ed., *The Encyclopaedia of Religion and Ethics*, vol. I, Edinburgh: T and T Clark, 1967, pp. 210-12.
14. According to the records of late nineteenth century, the Ranjhas were a tribe of Rajput status, chiefly found in eastern uplands of Shahpur and Gujarat between the Jhelum and Chenab. In small numbers, they had crossed both rivers into the Jhelum and Gujranwala districts. For most parts, they were returned as Jats, except in Shahpur. They might be described with accuracy as of Jat status. However, they were Bhatti Rajputs. In Gujarat, they claimed a Qureshi origin as descendants of Abu Jahl, the Prophet's uncle. Following the death of Abu Jahl's son, they migrated to the Kirana Bar. But, they retained many Hindu customs. Subsisting mainly on agriculture, they were peacable and well disposed section of population. Denzil Ibbetson, *Panjab Castes*, p. 148; H.A. Rose, *A Glossary of the Tribes and Castes of the Punjab and North West Frontier*, vol. II, p. 323.
15. In 1593, the Gujjars complained against the oppression of Waraich Jats, who held the *zamindari* of Sialkot, including Gujarat and Aminabad. Akbar (travelling along the Chenab on his way to Kashmir) accepted the petition and, separating the villages under Gujjar *zamindari* from Sialkot, reorganized them in the new subdistrict (*parganah*) of Gujarat. Here, a new fort and town was established. Muhammad Amin, the *karori*, supervised the changes. Still the Waraichs held two-thirds of Gujarat, while the remainder was in the hands of Gujjars. In the nineteenth century, the Waraichs were one of the largest Jat tribes, holding 170 villages of Gujarat district. Crossing the Chenab in Gujranwala, they held a tract of 41 villages. Almost entirely Muslim, they retained all their tribal and many of their Hindu customs. Sujan Rai Bhandari, *Khulasat ut-Tawārikh*, Persian text, ed. M. Zafar Hasan, Delhi: G. and Sons, 1918, pp. 412-13; Denzil Ibbetson, *Panjab Castes*, pp. 114-15.

16. In the orthodox Muslim circles, long hair were frowned upon. Shaikh Bahauddin Zakariya castigated a scholar from Bokhara for his physical appearance. This man was held guilty of maintaining two snakes, i.e. curled hair and loose ends of his turban. Upset at the admonition, the scholar got his head shaved in the presence of the Shaikh. The Shaikh's companions shared the attitude of their mentor. Some of them walked out of a feast on seeing a man with curls. Shaikh Nizamuddin Auliya disapproved the narrow rigidity of the guests. Amir Hasan Sijzi, *Fawaid ul-Fuad*, pp. 313, 327-8.
17. Chanakya, also known as Vishnugupta and Kautilya (290 BC – AD 300), was believed to have been a friend, counsellor and prime minister of Chandragupta Maurya. Born and probably educated at Taxila, he began his career as a physician. He was said to possess the wisdom of a serpent and knowledge of obscure arts. The word Kautilya meant crookedness and treachery. The name might conceal the identity of a school of political philosophers, who earned the approbrious title for the doctrine they taught. Owing to Chanakya's Machiavellian and malevolent genius, the Mauryan Empire became the best-governed but oppressive state. His *Arthashastra*, though totalitarian and secular in tendency, advocated ruthless and cynical statecraft. Many scholars have condemned its ferocious criminal code and depravity of moral standards. Benjamin Walker, *Hindu World: An Encyclopedic Survey*, New Delhi: Indus (Harper Collins), 1995, vol. I, pp. 540-2.
18. The group of Jats, posing as Jhinwars, were based in Multan. According to their claim, they were travelling to the Jhelum, so that they could profit from the boats. If they were speaking the truth, they had been travelling north from Multan along the course of the Chenab. They might have met Ranjha somewhere near Chiniot. Ranjha, having fled from Takht Hazara, did not have any specific destination. Desperate to save his life from his brothers, he was walking south along the Chenab. The old town of Jhelum was located on the left of the Jhelum. During the Sikh rule, it occupied a settlement of boatmen with nearly 500 houses. An important timber depot, it collected logs that were floated down from the Kashmir forests. A good deal of boat building was carried on. In Damodar's time, the Jhinwars of Multan might be travelling to Jhelum and, purchasing boats for their livelihood, returned on their new vessels via the Jhelum, which flowed west of Multan. During the British rule, Jhelum became a prosperous entrepot of trade. *The Imperial Gazetteer of India, Provincial Series: Punjab*, vol. II, p. 153.

19. Tobacco, originally arriving from the European islands, became common in Mughal north India. Physicians recommended its smoke in certain maladies. Some wealthy persons also began to smoke it. The farmers, with an eye on profits, began its cultivation in preference to other crops. During Akbar's reign, its use spread among all classes including nobles, scholars, mystics, crooks and destitutes. As it became the first gift of hospitality, it was regarded as more important than food and beverages. People sucked at the same pipe, disregarding all social distinctions. Its bad effects on health became apparent. Worse than all intoxicants, it was the cause of several diseases. Besides blackening the complexion, it undermined virility and intelligence. A friend of drunkards, it turned the tongue away from divine remembrance. Sometime in the early seventeenth century, Jahangir ordered provincial governors and local administrators to ban the sale of tobacco. In spite of the public punishment of violators in the city of Lahore, it was impossible to suppress its use. Sujan Rai Bhandari, *Khulasat ut-Tawarikh*, pp. 454-6.
20. Cultivation of land demanded a massive input of labour, time and energy. In a single year, there were two major crops, Rabi and Kharif. The prepration of soil needed several rounds of ploughing that were accompanied by levelling and fertilizing. Before sowing, the seeds required a special treatment to check disease. Besides major cereals and commercial crops like sugar cane and cotton, a variety of vegetables and fodders were grown. After harvesting, the grain had to be treated for preservation until the next crop. Hamida Khatoon Naqvi, *Agricultural, Industrial and Urban Dynamism under the Sultans of Delhi 1206-1555*, New Delhi: Munshiram Manoharlal, 1986, pp. 15-18.
21. The cult of Panjpir was widely spread from the Indus to the Bengal delta. Since it was popular among lower sections of the Hindus and Muslims, its origin could be traced to pre-Muslim indigenous source. Sometimes the cult was centred on a single shrine with five domes and other times separate individual shrines were found alongside a single tomb. The quintet of five saints did not provide common names, as the pantheon varied with geography, ecology and culture. Some have traced the cult to the five Pandava brothers. Sunni Muslims included the names of Prophet Muhammad and four pious caliphs, while the Shias preferred five holy personages (*panjtan pak*) Muhammad, Fatima, Ali, Hasan and Husain. In Rajasthan, we come across Ramdev, Harbu, Mallinath, Guga and Pabu, though an Ismaili exemplar could

also find a place. In central and western Panjab, there was a curious admixture of Hindu and Muslim figures, besides Guru Gobind Singh. A votary describing himself as Panjpiriya implied his indifference to the identity of saints and indicated his own roots in lower social orders. According to a study on the Panjpir shrine at Abohar, five saints of Uch were believed to be buried with their wives. H.A. Rose, op. cit., pp. 572-3; Asim Roy, *The Islamic Syncretistic Tradition in Bengal*, New Jersey: Princeton University Press, 1983, pp. 213-14; Dominique Sila Khan, *Conversions and Shifting Identities: Ramdev Pir and the Ismailis in Rajasthan*, New Delhi: Manohar, rpt., 2003, pp. 89-92; Yogesh Snehi, 'Historicity, Orality and the Lesser Shrines: Popular Culture and Change at the Dargah of Panj Pir at Abohar', *Sufism in Punjab: Mystics, Literature and Shrines*, ed. Surinder Singh and Ishwar Dayal Gaur, New Delhi: Aakar Books, 2009, pp. 402-29.

22. The Indian music was notable for a wealth of *ragas*, multitude of scales, subtle refinements and manifold rhythmic modes. The world *raga* denoted colour or atmosphere. Theoretically, there were thousands of *ragas*. Practically, only a few hundred were known, while most artists performed about a dozen. A *raga* consisted of a fixed number of notes that were presented in an ascending and descending scale, possessing five or seven degrees. The tone material of a *raga* remained unchanged, forbidding modulations from one scale to the other. Besides musical features, each *raga* has extra-musical features like taste (*rasa*), personification, pictorial representation, magical properties and fixed performance time. It was believed that Raga Dipak caused fire, Mallar brought rain and Kedar cured diseases. Walter Kauffman, *The Ragas of North India*, Calcutta: Oxford and IBH Publishing Company, 1968, pp. 1-13.

23. In Islam, there were two great festivals. Id ul-Azha (feast of sacrifice) was celebrated on 10 Zilhijja and marked the culmination of the annual Haj. It commemorated Abraham's willingness to scarfice his son, whom God substituted with a ram. Muslims assembled in an Idgah, where the Imam delivered a Khutbah and sacrificed a sheep. The Muslims, returning home, sacrificed an unblemished animal. Of the three portions of the flesh, each was reserved for the poor, relatives and the family. Id ul-Fitr (feast of breaking fast) marked the end of Ramzan and sighting of moon. After distributing alms (*sadqah*) among the poor, the Muslims assembled in the Idgah, where the Imam recited two cycles of prayer and delivered the oration. The gathering

exchanged Id greetings. On returning home, they devoted themselves to making merry and distributing gifts. Festivities lasted three days.

24. God created five means (hearing, sight, taste, smell and touch) for acquiring knowledge. Four of them were situated in special organs, while touch was diffused in the entire body. Hearing was superior to other faculties as it ensured obligatoriness of religion and truth of apostles. Hearing recitataion of the Quran was most delightful to ears, while poetry generated different opinions. In an Arab tribe, a slave's sweet voice drove camels to run at full speed carrying double loads. In Khurasan and Iraq, hunters beat a brass basin to still the deer and catch them. In India, people went out in the open and, singing with a tinkling sound, lulled the deer into a trap. In Rum, physicians cured the sick with a specially invented stringed instrument, caliberating its duration of time to the intensity of disease. Anyone who said that he found no pleasure in sounds, melodies and music was either a liar or hypocrite or he was not in his right senses and was outside the category of humans and beasts. Ali bin Usman Hujwiri, *Kashf ul-Mahjub*, Eng. tr. Reynold A. Nicholson, Delhi: Taj Company, rpt., 1982, pp. 393-407.

25. These lines of Damodar were similar to the understanding of Ibn Arabi on the subject. The latter conceived a triad of God, man and woman, wherein man yearned for his Lord, who was his origin and in a similar vein woman longed for man to whom she belonged. For Ibn Arabi, the relation between God and man was parallel to the affinity between man and woman. The love with which God beheld man was manifested again in the love with which man beheld woman. The most profound union was the one between sexes. Man's annihilation in woman was total at the moment of consummation and, therefore, he beheld God in her. Shuja Alhaq, *A Forgotten Vision: A Study of Human Spirituality in the Light of the Islamic Tradition*, vol. I, New Delhi: Vikas Publishing House, 1997, p. 224.

26. Gopis were herdswomen, many of whom left their homes, children and husbands to dally with Krishna on the Yamuna. Imagining holding Krishna's hand, they engaged in a circular dance, which probably aimed at promoting fertility in cattle and plants. It was believed that Krishna multiplied himself many times and danced between each pair of Gopis. This idyllic picture of divine Krishna with Gopis symbolized the abstract relation of the deity to his devotees. It was a drama perpetually enacted in the heart of every votary. Margaret

and James Stutley, *A Dictionary of Hinduism: The Mythology, Folklore and Development (1500 BC – AD 1500)*, Bombay: Allied Publishers, 1977, p. 101.

27. Khwaja Khizr was venerated in large parts of Asia, though with diverse forms, rituals and purposes. In the Islamic world, traditions link him with Alexander the Great, Hazrat Musa, Mehtar Iliyas and Imam Ghazzali. He was conceived as standing on a fish, wearing a green apparel and keeping a long white beard. He was also known as Khwaja Khasa, Durminda, Dumindo, Zinda Pir and Bir Betal. Those associated with water, particularly Jhinwars and Mallahs, were devoted to him. In east Panjab, he was seen as a Hindu God of water. His worship comprised burning lamps, feeding Brahmins at wells and releasing little rafts of sacred grass in village ponds. All over Panjab, he was worshipped before travelling through water, descending into wells, repairing Persian wheels, protecting villages from floods and fixing prices in markets. The devotees made offerings of goats, cooked meat and porridge. Hindu women pleased him to procure sons, while Muslim women propitiated him 40 days after bearing a child. H.A. Rose, *A Glossary of the Tribes and Castes of the Punjab and North West Frontier Province*, vol. I, pp. 562-5.
28. During ancient times, eight types of mariages were noted. Under *brahma*, a father gave in marriage a well-adorned daughter. Under *prajapatya*, a man and woman jointly performed sacred duties without prior consent of woman's father. Under *aarsha*, a husband subsequently regularized the marriage by presenting two cows to his wife's father. Under *daiva*, a girl was given away to the officiating priest inside a sacrificial altar. Under *gandharva*, the lovers married secretly. Under *asura*, a girl was given away in exchange for a bride price. Under *rakshasa*, a woman was abducted while she was sleeping or intoxicated. The first four could become lawful with the apparoval of woman's father. The latter four became lawful only with the approval of both parents of the woman. A marriage contract was revoked if a sexual defect was discovered in one of the two partners. If marriage was arranged with a groom and, married to another through deception, it was invalid. Kautilya, *The Arthashastra*, Eng. tr. L.N. Rangarajan, Gurugram: Penguin Books, 1987, pp. 363-4.
29. Adam was regarded as the first human and prophet. His banishment from heaven along with his wife Eve figured thrice in the Quran (2: 34-9, 7: 19-25 and 20: 117-24). God ordered the two to dwell in the garden of heaven, where they would not suffer hunger, thirst and heat.

They were free to eat anything except from a specific tree. The Satan, acting through deception, lured them to the tree of immortality and an unperishable kingdom. The two disobeyed God and ate from the forbidden tree. Becoming conscious of their nakedness, they began to sew leaves to cover themselves. They expressed their repentence before God and begged for forgiveness. God banished them to a place on earth, where they could enjoy for a while. They would live there, die there and brought forth from there. According to the moral of the story, whosoever followed God's guidance would not go astray. One who did not, he would lead a miserable life and rise up blind on the day of resurrection. Seyyed Hosein Nasr et al., ed., *The Study Quran: A New Translation and Commentary*, New York: Harper One, 2015, pp. 23-5, 413-15, 805-6.

30. The word *khat* may be traced to village headmen (*khuts*, *muqaddams* and *chaudharis*), who were noted for their wealth, power and autonomy. *Muqaddam* is an Arabic word meaning the leading or first man, who was the headman of a village or group of villages. Barani used *chaudhari*, a Hindi word, as equivalent of *muqaddam*. However, *khut* is a non-Hindi word. Its first and last alphabets are Arabic or Persian. When it fell into the hands of persons ignorant Persian, its form changed. The nearest Persian word to it is *khat* or deed by which the *khut* might have undertaken to collect the revenue from villages that government placed under his charge. Alauddin Khalji, through a series of agrarian reforms, sought to erase the distinction between the privileged *khuts* and underprivileged *balahars*. Mohammad Habib and Khaliq Ahmad Nizami, ed., *A Comprehensive History of India*, vol. V: *The Delhi Sultanat 1206-1526*, New Delhi: People's Publishing House, rpt., 1982, pp. 356-7.
31. Damodar has frequently used this word for Ranjha to assert his spirituality. Here, it was not Damodar but a complete stranger, a prominent member of the Khera marriage party, who used this word. Vasava Khan reached this conclusion by merely looking at Ranjha and the strange spectacle of Ranjha taking rounds on an ox. Ranjha did not wish to be recognized and, therefore, concealed his face in a blanket. This would insulate his beloved Hir from unwelcome public comments. Inadvertantly, the blanket slipped a bit and revealed Ranjha's beauty. The glimpse was enough to attract the attention of the gathering. In particular, it roused the jealousy of the herdsmen, whose view of Ranjha was opposite to that of Vasava Khan.
32. Among the Muslims, a distinction was drawn between *mahrams* and

na-mahrams. The former denoted individuals forbidden to one another on the grounds of consanguinity and affinity, fosterage and some special cases. All others, called *na-mahrams*, were those with whom marriage was permissible. Women were kept in seclusion (*pardah*) to keep the *na-mahrams* out of their view. Elderly patriarchs feared that people of the opposite sex, outside the degrees of prohibition, might go wrong through mutual contact. As a result, they might contract a marriage tie independent of the will of elders and perhaps prejudicial to the bigger interests of the joint family or village community. Much emphasis was put on the spotless moral character of the woman and, more importantly, her public reputation for chastity. This was identified, in the long-run, with living in seclusion (*pardah*) and without possibility of meeting a *na-mahram*. Kanwar Muhammad Ashraf, *Life and Conditions of the People of Hindustan*, New Delhi: Munshiram Manoharlal, 2nd edn., 1970, pp. 174-5.

33. It was a concidence that Shah Husain expressed the same sentiment in a identical language. In one of his mystical poems, Hir states, 'Continuously reciting the name of my beloved, I have myself become Ranjha. Let everyone address me as Ranjhan Ranjhan. No one should call me Hir. The husband, whom I was looking for, I have searched him out. Says Husain! On meeting the saints, all my doubts have been removed.' Kala Singh Bedi, *Shah Husain Lahori: Jiwan ate Rachna*, Kafi no. 132, p. 387.

34. Pilgrimage (*haj*) is one of the five pillars of Islam. All Muslims were required to perform it at least once in a lifetime. Preparations involved arranging for dependents and settling debts. The rite consists of a journey to Mecca and, over the next seven days, a series of rituals reminiscent of an event in Abraham's life. At the outset, the pilgrims placed themselves in a specific apparel denoting inviolable state (*ihram*). On eighth Zilhijja, they made seven circumambulations (*tawaf*) of the Kaaba in anti-clockwise direction. Then they hastened (*say*) between two pillars and drank the water of *zamzam*. On the ninth, they assembled in the neighbouring plain of Arafat and stood in supplication to God. On way to Mina, they stopped at Muzadalifa and picked 49 or 70 pebbles. Next day, they arrived in the valley of Mina and threw seven pebbles at the obelisk denoting Satan. They sacrificed an animal on the Id ul-Azha and, during the next two days, threw the remaining pebbles at Mina and undertook another round of the Kaaba. None of the rituals were performed in congregation.

Abdulkader Tayob, *Islam: A Short Introduction*, Oxford: Oneworld Publications, 2006, pp. 98-108.

35. Love of Radha and Krishna is depicted in art, music and literature. It is described in human terms to reveal a divine mystery, which is beyond human comprehension. Besides the *Gita Govinda*, it has been narrated in later texts, including the Puranas. Krishna was identified with Vishnu and Radha with Lakshmi. Radha, the daughter of Brishbhan and Kalavati, was born in Gokul near Mathura. Krishna, as a child and youngman, lived in the Braj area around Mathura, where Gokul and Vrindavan were located. He played and danced with the Gopis, who were the wives and daughters of cowherds. Radha was his favourite. After meeting Krishna, she became devoted to him with heart and soul. Since she was married to someone else, her love was beyond the ordinary. She represented an ideal devotee, who constantly seeks and desires God. Roshen Dalal, *Hinduism: An Alphabetical Guide*, p. 321.
36. Damodar has composed the section on Ramu's mission with great skill. It was imbued with suspense, uncertainty and risk. At the same time, it contained valuable evidence on medieval society, particularly the modes of travelling and communication. To understand Ramu's task, it was imperative to recall that the Brahmins, as professional messengers, acted as emissaries among landed clans and, along with Dooms, carried out negotiations on matrimonial alliances. The travellers, on way to their destinations, could spend a night in a village. As per social customs, they stayed in the house of members of the same caste. During conversations, important information was exchanged. When the villagers were not engaged in work, they assembled in the village common and discussed matters of common interest, promoting a sense of social cohesion and local identity.
37. The Jhelum rose from a source in Tibet. It passed through Srinagar, the capital of Kashmir, and lent luster to its charm. On its banks, there were several gardens, buildings and walkways. Bridges had been built at a number of spots. Below Kashmir and near Pakhli, the Kishanganga joined the Jhelum. From here, it flowed to Dangli, the headquarters of the Gakkhars. Meandering through Mirpur and the town of Jhelum, it met the royal highway and, at this point, acquired the name of Jhelum. Thereafter, it passed through places such as Girjhak, Nanadana, Shamsabad, Bhera, Khushab and Khurdkhana. Near Jhang Siyal, it merged with the Chenab. Sujan Rai Bhandari, *Khulasat ut-Tawarikh*, p. 78.

38. Tilla Balnath, standing 3,242 ft above sea level, is an eastward continuation of the Salt Range. Rising rapidly from the Bunha torrent, the hill culminated at this point. According to tradition, Gorakhnath settled here in the Treta Yug and trained disciples like Balnath and Bharthari. The monastery, enclosed within a wall, was perched on the top of a hill. There were temples dedicated to Shiva, Bhairon, Lakshman and Hanuman. On a lower level, there were storerooms and residences of the Mahant and other Jogis. Attached to the main enclosure was a cowshed and, to its south-west, were a large tank and numerous *samadhis*. A cave has been named after Bharthari, while a stone slab marked the spot where Ranjha was initiated. During the seventeenth century, thousands of Jogis and innumerable devotees assembled here on special days, particularly Shivaratri that was associated with Mahadev. Sujan Rai Bhandari, *Khulasat ut-Tawarikh*, pp. 75-6; *Imperial Gazetteer of India, Provincial Series: Punjab*, vol. II, p. 159; George Weston Briggs, *Gorakhnath and Kanphata Jogis*, Delhi: Motilal Banarsidas, rpt., 1982, pp. 101-3.
39. Gopichand and Bharthari occupied an important place in the Jogic tradition along with Gorakhnath, Machhandarnath, Jalandharnath and others. In the Indo-Gangetic plain, extending from Panjab to Bengal, wandering minstrels sang their tales. The pattern of their stories was similar. Both were kings who turned Jogis, so that they were perceived as a single unit. Gopichand was said to be the king of Gaur, while his maternal uncle Bharthari was the elder brother of Raja Vikramaditya of Ujjain (Dhara Nagar). In Rajasthani folklore, the two paired as immortal companions, who composed devotional hymns to a formless God and wandered across the earth. Women, figuring in different roles (mother, wife, sister and low caste female magicians), claimed a crucial role in the tales. The protagonists, in different ways, parted from their wives to pursue higher goals. Ann Grodzins Gold, *A Carnival of Parting: The Tales of King Bharthari and King Gopi Chand as Sung and Told by Madhu Natisar Nath of Ghatiyali, Rajasthan*, New Delhi: Munshiram Manoharlal, 1993, pp. 57-70.
40. Situated on the left bank of the Chenab and 52 miles north-east of Jhang town, Chiniot was the headquarters of a tahsil of the same name in the Jhang district. A very old town, it was perhaps identified with Sakala, the capital of the White Huns. It boasted of a handsome mosque, which was built by Nawab Saadullah Khan Tahim, the governor of the town under Shahjahan. It had a shrine dedicated to Shah Burhan, who was revered by the Hindus and Muslims alike. The

country was well wooded and its scenery attractive. Famous for brass work and wood carving, its masons were said to have been employed at the Taj Mahal at Agra. A local mason was the architect of Golden Temple at Amritsar. In early twentieth century, Chiniot had houses of excellent brickwork. They mainly belonged to Khoja traders, who had business dealings with Amritsar, Calcutta, Bombay and Karachi. *The Imperial Gazetteer of India, Provincial Series: Punjab*, vol. II, p. 217.

41. Sehti meant to emphasize that Hir's elopement was not merely a revolt against Hir's husband and parents-in-law. Instead, it was a revolt against the entire Khera clan, which had sealed the Khera-Siyal matrimonial alliance and organized the Sahiba-Hir marriage. Sehti proved right because, the Khera clan saw Hir's elopement as a collective affront. Immediately, it mobilized itself to retrieve its honour. This was done through a long chase to catch the lovers, pitched battles with the Nahars and litigation in the Qazi's court. Though Sehti did not say so, Hir's action was also a revolt against the Siyals. If the Siyals were close by, they would have sided with the Kheras.

42. Multan, situated between Tulamba and Uch, stood on a mound 4 miles from the left bank of the Chenab. Around 1400, the Ravi seemed to flow past Multan, joining the Chenab 10 miles lower down. The city was located on the Delhi-Qandhar transcontinental trade route. It served as the most prominent centre of the Suhrawardis. Its governor, practically independent of Delhi, blocked the intrusion of the Mongols and Qarlughs. Ibn Battuta has left an account of his experiences in Multan. Ain ul-Mulk Mahru, the Tughlaq governor, revived its economy through canal irrigation, agrarian expansion and land grants. The Lodis failed to bring Multan under their sway. Rai Sehra, the Langah chief, founded a local dynansty in Multan. Sher Shah undertook extensive military oprerations in Multan to subjugate powerful local chiefs. Even Akbar could not impose his authority on Chakar Khan Rind, the famous Baloch warlord who was active in Multan.

43. The term posture denoted a way of sitting and repeated dynamic physical movements. In the first half of the second millennium CE, texts on *hatha-yoga* advocated a more complex posture, so that *Hathayogaparadipika* of the fifteenth century described fifteen *asanas* of which eight were not seated postures. In Panjab, Alexander the Great encountered naked ascetics, who assumed numerous postures while sitting, standing and lying. Jogis practised postures for three purposes – (1) as a stable base for breath control, *mantra* repetition

and meditation, (2) to acquire ascetic power (*tapas*) and (3) to attain therapeutic benefits. *Bahr ul-Hayat,* the sixteenth century Persian translation of *Amritkunda,* noted 22 complex modes of sitting as prerequisites for various types of meditations. The eighteenth century *Jogparadipika* held that 84 postures had therapeutic benefits, though all required the Jogi to gaze between his eyebrows or at the tip of his nose. James Mallinson and Mark Singleton, ed., *Roots of Yoga*, UK: Penguin Classics, 2017, pp. 86-92.

44. Sehti's statement finds resonance in the medieval historical experience as recorded in oral tradition. The landed clans, employing internal cohesion and violent means, controlled pieces of land for their survival. Using same methods, the clans imposed patriarchal control over their own members and kept the neighbouring clans at bay. The clans acted as a body to meet internal and external challenges. In Damodar's narrative, the landed clans (Siyals, Kheras, Waraichs and Nahars) acted as a body in war and peace. In the Mirza-Sahiba tale, the Siyals and Chanddars saw the elopement of lovers as a collective insult. To retrieve their honour, they killed the lovers following an instant chase. The Kharals, in retaliation, decimated hundreds of Siyals and destroyed the Siyal domain of Khiva.
45. King cobra (*Ophiophagus hannah*) was the largest poisonous snake in the world. Specimens were 4 m long, while the longest was 5.58 m. Its two fangs, 10 cm long, bore three smaller upper teeth behind them. Agile and excitable, its head grew to the size of a man's hand. In threat posture, its body was raised up and nasal openings emitted a hissing sound. Its large venom glands produced a huge quantity of poison. Fatalities from its bites have been recorded in India, Burma and China. The effect of a bite varied with the victim's metabolic reaction and the degree to which the snake was excited. Ten minutes after the bite, the victim suffered severe dizziness, besides impairment of vision, respiration and reflexes. Unless treated with anti-venim, the victim died in 15-60 minutes. H.C. Bernhard Grzimek, ed., *Grzimek's Animal Life Encyclopaedia*, vol. VI: *(Reptiles)*, New York: Van Nostrand Reinhold Company, 1975, pp. 415-18.
46. The Indus separated India from Kabul and Zabulistan. Some researchers traced its source to Qalmaq. Passing through Kashghar, Tibet, Kafiristan, Kashmir, Pakhli and Damtur, it reached the domain of the Yusufzais. Below Attock, it joined some tributaries of the Nilab and Kabul. Here, its channel was narrow and the flow violent. On the western bank, the boats capsized on striking the rock of Jalaliyah.

On the eastern bank, the fort of Attock stood along with attractive buildings and official bungalows. At this point, the Indus met the Lahore-Kabul highway. South of Attock, the Indus flowed along the hills of Khattak and entered the plains associated with Sambhal Afghans. After irrigating Multan and Baloch tracts, it merged with the five rivers of Panjab and assumed the vastness of a sea. Travelling through Bhakkar and Siwistan, it entered Thatta and ultimately fell into the sea at Lahri Bandar. Sujan Rai Bhandari, *Khulasat ut-Tawarikh*, pp. 78-9.

47. It was difficult for anti-state rebels to escape through Panjab. The state merely ordered its own fiefholders (*jagirdars*) and superintendents of roads to block the ferries. Similar orders were given to local *zamindars*, who exercised complete control over the ferries. The *zamindars* warned the boatmen about official orders. They fortified the banks with their retinues that did not hesitate to attack the fugitives. Since the boatmen lived under the patronage of the *zamindars*, they refused to provde their services to the fugitives. The boatmen could not be allured with the offers of money. Once the *zamindars* had taken initial steps, the state officials found it easy to tighten the defences. As soon as the state succeeded in capturing the fugitives, it rewarded the loyal *zamindars* with chunks of land. These inferences have been drawn from the manner in which Prince Khusrau was captured (1606) on the Chenab with the joint operation of *zamindars* and Mughal officers. Nuruddin Jahangir, *Tuzuk-i Jahangiri*, vol. I, Eng. tr. Alexander Rogers and Henry Beveridge, Delhi: Low Price Publications, rpt., 2009, pp. 66-7.
48. The internal cohesion within landed clans was traceable to the evolution of the *zamindari* right. In the early stages, a clan, loosely organized under a chief, wandered in search of land. Acting as a body, it brought virgin land under cultivation and settled a village. If it encountered a settled village, it used force to oust the existing clan and established its sway. The process, according to Irfan Habib, recurred until the dominion of the victorious clan crystallized into *zamindari* right. The factors of caste and force, so effective in the process, continued to be useful in defending its land against neighbouring clans and facing increasing pressure of the medieval state. In addition to these factors, a clan relied on internal solidarity to survive a variety of exigencies. Damodar, an acute observer of contemporary society, has given a cogent account of the Siyal-Sambhal and Khera-Nahar conflicts.
49. Syeds were regarded as the descendants of Prophet Muhammad

through his daughter Fatima. Owing to this, every Syed was supposed to be brave, truthful and pious, besides possessing every other noble quality. The Mongol ravages forced a large number of Syeds to migrate to Hindustan. They received land grants from the Sultans of Delhi and exaggerated respect from the Muslims in general. Beyond the meridian of Lahore, they formed large proportion of population, being the largest of all in the Salt Range and Pathan frontier. They constituted a smaller element of population in the eastern half of Panjab. As landowners and cultivators, the Syeds were known for their incompetence. Kunwar Muhammad Ashraf, *Life and Conditions of the People of Hindustan*, pp. 100-1; Denzil Ibbetson, *Panjab Castes*, p. 222.

50. It would be instructive to look at medieval Western Europe which, faced with endemic violence, evolved ways to reduce it. Broadly speaking, the legality of blood feud was recognized. Yet, the church tried to curtail violence by invoking the horror of bloodshed, while the traditional notion of peace played its part. The authorities drew a distinction between lawful reprisals and plain brigandage. Sometimes, they tried to limit the number and nature of wrongs that could be expiated in blood. As they grew stronger, they tried to forestall private vengeance by suppressing flagrant offences or crimes perceived as violation of peace. Above all, they laboured to bring hostile groups to reason and sometimes compelled them to conclude treaties of armistice or reconciliation under administration of courts. Marc Bloch, *Feudal Society*, vol. I: *The Growth of Ties of Dependence*, Eng. tr. L.A. Manyon, New Delhi: Aakar Books, rpt., 2019, p. 182.

51. The Islamic Law, known as the Shariat, was built on four roots. These were the Quran, Prophetic traditions (*hadis*), collective opinion of the community (*ijma*) and analogical reasoning (*qiyas* or *ijtihad*). To these elements, some scholars were inclined to admit custom (*urf*), particularly as justification for rulers to introduce secular enactments. During territorial expansion of Islam after the four pious caliphs, hundreds of schools of jurisprudence arose. Prominent among them were Hanafi, Maliki, Shafi and Hanbali. The first laid emphasis on analogical reasoning, the second on Sunnah and collective opinion, the third on collective opinion and the fourth on Prophetic tradions. After the formation of these schools (*mazhabs*), later scholars confined themselves to interpretation and adherence (*taqlid*), so that the gate of analogical reasoning was closed. Khaliq Ahmad Nizami, *Religion and Politics in India During the Thirteenth Century*, pp. 39-41.

52. Every town of the Delhi Sultanate, irrespective of its dimensions, had a Qazi. The central government, acting through the head of religious and judicial affairs (Sadr us-Sudur or Qazi ul-Quzat) appointed him. A Qazi was inedependent of the governor. In early stages, his function was limited to settling disputes. Later on, his jurisdiction was considerably widened to embrace management of the properties of orphans and lunatics, execution of testamentary dispositions and supervision of lands granted to the religious elite. He maintained streets and prevented encroachments on thoroughfares and open spaces. He took charge of contested properties. Local governors and officials assisted him in maintaining the dignity of law and bringing wrong doers to their senses. Ishtiaq Husain Qureshi, *The Administration of the Sultanate of Dehli*, New Delhi: Oriental Books Reprint Corporation, 1st rev. edn., 1971, pp. 158-62.
53. It was believed that God had ordered the inscription of tablets that enumerated divine decrees for humankind and events of the future. This phenomenon has been twice recorded in the Quran. God informed Moses (7:144-54) that He had written for him the tablets containing exhortations concerning all things along with their elaborations. Moses, angry at the idolatory of his own people, threw the tablets away. Following his repentence, Moses retrieved the tablets that laid out guidance and mercy for the believers. Another verse (85:21-2) noted the location of the Quran on a preserved tablet and indicated the uncreatedness of the Quran, which God guarded from any change.
54. According to Surah al-Nur of the Quran (24:2-20), a adulterous man or woman (not married to each other) was to be flogged with 100 lashes, provided there were four witnesses to the act of fornication (*zina*). Those who failed to bring four witnesses were to be flogged with 80 lashes. A husband could level the charge against his wife through his own five successive testimonies. In our case, the Kheras did not press the charge of adultery against Hir as they did not have four wirnesses. The Qazi, even in the absence of four witnesses, appeared to have held Ranjha guilty of adultery and awarded him the punishment of 100 lashes. Damodar, uninterested in legal complexities, was silent on the specific charges against the lovers, leaving room for speculation.

CHAPTER 4

Analysis of the Narrative

Damodar has told us little about himself. In the last stanza of his narrative, he noted the bare minimum about his life. Named Damodar, he belonged to the Gulati caste.[1] He hailed from Rajoa Syedan (a village near Chiniot). For unstated reasons, he left this place and settled among the Siyals.[2] We come across a few more facts in the controversial section ahead of the prologue. Without mentioning Rajoa Syedan, he referred to his arrival in the subdistrict (*shiq*) of the Siyals. Having reflected in his mind, he decided to settle here. He entered the town of Chuchak, where the Siyals held a dominant position. The place, having lakhs of buffaloes and cows, was in a buoyant state. The chiefship of Chuchak earned praise for the prevailing prosperity. Damodar felt happy on observing the ways of the Siyals. His first step was to meet Chuchak and his wife Kundi. Since Chuchak gave him a lot of assurance (*dilasa*), his depression was removed and he established a shop there. Damodar has hinted at the circumstances in which he migrated from Rajoa Syedan. Before leaving his original home, he faced some difficulties. After deep thought, he decided to search for greener pastures. He looked for a fresh start in life and suitable means of livelihood. Though confused and apprehensive, he found that Chuchkana was a pleasant place and the Siyals were generous patrons. Without any complication, he went into the protection of the Siyals. He might have identified himself with Ranjha, who was forced to leave Takht Hazara due to the hostility of his brothers and, after a series of adventures, slipped into the protection of the Siyals. In any case, the beauty of the infant

Hir ignited a desire in Damodar's mind and induced him to compose the story of her life. Since he did not possess the abilities of a poet, he merely narrated what he saw.[3]

We can draw a few inferences from the introductory section, even if its authenticity was doubted.[4] Damodar, leading a comfortable life and feeling reasonably secure, began to take an interest in his immediate surroundings. He was breathing in a cultural landscape imbued with the story of Hir-Ranjha. He learnt that Hir, a daughter of the Siyals, fell in love with the herdsman Ranjha. She rejected her marriage among the Kheras and, enduring numerous trials, united with her lover. With every passing day, Damodar discovered new facts. As his curiosity increased, he decided to narrate the story in the form of a romance (*qissa*). This was possible only if he was able to fill some gaps in his knowledge. Since the Siyals were understandably reticent about a rebellious daughter, Damodar decided to tap alternative sources of information. He visited a number of places such as Takht Hazara, the Nahar domain and Kot Qabula. He met a number of old people who were intimately familiar with episodes in the life of Hir-Ranjha. This experience made Damodar so confident that he claimed to be an eyewitness to some crucial occurrences. His claim was designed to lend authenticity to his narrative. However, his stance created a major contradiction in chronology. On the one hand, he asserted that Hir and Ranjha, after overcoming many hurdles, finally united in Bikrami 1529, which coincided with 1472 AD, i.e. the middle of Bahlol Lodi's reign and three years after the birth of Guru Nanak. On the other hand, Damodar claimed that he lived in the times of Akbar (r. 1556-1605) and the story of Hir-Ranjha also occurred in the same chronological frame. In fact, he has gone to the extent of claiming personal presence at the following moments in the story.

First, Damodar saw the beauty of the infant Hir following his settlement in Jhang Siyal. Second, he met a few travellers from the north and, learning about Dhido's superlative attributes, went to Takht Hazara. He met the handsome lad Dhido, who was depressed at the cancellation of his marriage and separation from the joint household. When Dhido left the village, Damodar accompanied him for some distance.[5] Third, Damodar saw the marriage ceremony of Hir, Ranjha's agony at his loss and departure of Hir's palanquin for Rangpur Khera.[6] Fourth, Damodar saw the armed conflict between the Nahars and Kheras while hiding behind some bushes.[7] Fifth, Damodar was present at Kot Qabula during the climax of the story. He helped the lovers to sit in a circle of the warring clans.[8] He was a witness to the punishment of the lovers, public protest against the Qazi's verdict and humiliation of the Kheras. Finally, he accompanied the lovers for three leagues when they departed for the south.[9] From the above statements, we find that Damodar has claimed to be present only at the beginning and end of the story. He was entirely absent when the Hir-Ranjha love progressed in the face of patriarchal opposition. Even during the six occasions when Damodar was present, he did not play any active role in the event. Nor did he say a word to the persons present. He preferred to be a silent observer, who was mentally involved in the proceedings. The structure of his narrative is visible in the following ten parts.

Part	*Sequence of Episodes*	*Stanza Nos.*
1	Birth of Hir; proposals for her betrothal; alliance between the Siyals and Kheras; visit of the Kheras to Chuchkana to seal the betrothal; procedures, rituals and festivities	1-35
2	Conflict between the Sambhals and Siyals over the boat and boatman; Luddan takes shelter with the Siyals; the Siyal girls under Hir defeat the Sambhals.	36-106
3	Rupture in Mojam's household; matrimonial bond between the Ranjhas and Waraichs; enmity of Ranjha brothers force Dhido to leave Takht Hazara.	107-81
4	Ranjha meets Panjpir and Luddan on the Chenab; Ranjha falls in love with Hir; Siyals employ Ranjha as a herdsman; the affair ignites opposition; fixation of Hir's marriage with Sahiba Khera.	182-387
5	Hir's strong resistance to the marriage; proceedings of the wedding; suffering of Ranjha; departure of Hir for Rangpur Khera; the Kheras torture Ranjha.	388-516
6	Hir shocks the Kheras with her resistance; Ranjha returns to Takht Hazara; revival of the Ranjha-Waraich alliance; isolation and humiliation of Ranjha.	517-97

7	Pangs of Hir at Rangpur Khera; compact between Hir and Sehti; Ramu travels to Takht Hazara with Hir's message; Ranjha becomes a Jogi at Tilla Balnath and reaches Rangpur Khera.	598-704
8	A sham fight between Sehti and Hir; Hir suffers a snakebite; the Jogi undertakes a 40-day treatment of Hir; the lovers meet and elope.	705-837
9	The Kheras chase the lovers; the Nahars provide protection to the lovers; battle between the Nahars and Kheras; intervention of the Syeds of Rajoa; the contenders travel to Kot Qabula.	838-900
10	Trial in the Qazi's court; debate between Hir and Qazi; whipping of Ranjha; Hir restored to the Kheras; fire in the town and public protest; reversal of verdict; union of lovers who leave for south.	901-63

Functions of the Landed Clans

A Persian history of Jhang Siyal coincided with the past of the Siyals. The Siyals, as a landed clan, claimed a descent from Punwar Rajputs, who originally belonged to Dharanagri. One of their branches relocated to Jaunpur. Siyal, the son of Rai Shankar, migrated to Panjab in the early Sultanate period. He converted to Islam at the inspiration of Baba Farid (1175-1265), who predicted a Siyal settlement between the Chenab and Jhelum. Siyal married Sohag, the daughter of Bahauddin Khan Mengan, a prominent landholder of Sahiwal. He was blessed with three sons named Bharmi, Kohli and Mehni. In due course, the sons headed three distinct clans named after them. After a sojourn in Sialkot, the Siyals migrated to the south-east of Jhang on the Chenab. They dug wells in an arid tract and settled as cultivators from the mounds of Kachh to Munger. The Kohlis held the chiefship, the Bharmis engaged in agriculture and Mehnis took to plunder. A number of menial groups (barbers, cobblers and weavers) were closely associated with the Siyals. Chuchak, who belonged to the clan of Kohlis, settled in village Kotli Baqir Shah. His domain stretched from Jabuana to Machhival. Ignoring his sons, he nominated his nephew Mal Khan as his successor. The new chief founded the town of Jhang, which was exposed to the floods of the Chenab. A thick grove of trees (*anbuwah-i drakhtan*), known as *jhang* in the local dialect, imparted its name to the place. Every year, the peasants assembled at the administrative centres of Chiniot and Shorkot to pay their land tax. A representative of the governor, arriving from Lahore at the head of a large army, collected the dues and returned to the capital. Mal Khan became an intermediary between the peasants and state. Owing to his loyal service, he was summoned to Lahore. He was recognized as the chief (*zamindar*) of Jhang and conferred the title of Khan. With this mandate, he consolidated his control over the Siyals and overcame the opposition of their rivals called Nols.[10]

Under the descendants of Mal Khan, the Siyal domain continued to expand. The death of a chief was an important event. In normal circumstances, one of his sons succeeded him. In exceptional cases, the chiefship passed on to a brother, nephew or uncle. A close relative was free to walk out of the original settlement and establish a new principality, which was manifested in the construction of a new fort and an open platform (*chabutra*) for administrative business. To begin with, a chief employed the retinue of kinsmen in his military campaigns. When the Siyal domain increased, it came into conflict with neighbouring clans including the Balochis and Kharals. Sometimes, internal dissensions broke out among the Siyals. In such situations, the chief reinforced his militia with the recruitment of soldiers on a daily allowance. Jalal Khan, a Siyal chief, died at the hands of his nephew Pahar Khan. Kabir Khan, a grandson of the deceased, marched to Paharpur and killed many relatives of the murderer. Another Siyal potentate Sultan Mahmud Khan wished to snatch Kamaliya from his Kharal counterpart Saadat Khan. The latter's complaint induced Prince Muizzuddin to dispatch a sizeable force against the Siyals. Since Sultan Mahmud Khan was found loyal, no punitive action was taken. Saadat Khan sent an emissary with a proposal to marry his rival's sister. In a bloody fight, the emissary and Sultan Mahmud Khan were killed. Lal Khan, a brother of the deceased, besieged Saadat Khan at Kamaliya and took away his herds. The Mehnis of Khiva killed Mahmud Khan (younger brother of Lal Khan) in an encounter on the inter-clan boundary.[11] The inhabitants of Jhang, including Damodar, must have been familiar with the early landmarks of local history.

Within the territory of a landed clan, the chief was a repository of power, wealth and influence. Many times, Damodar speaks of him as a mighty feudal lord, who was the master of land and rivers. His possessions comprised cultivated areas, extensive grasslands and large herds of cattle. His wealth – gold, silver and goods – flowed into his stores from diverse sources.[12] If trade routes passed through his domain, it added to his importance. Most often, he was seen in the village common (*sath*), where he held court in the presence of his clansmen. During endless rounds of consultation (*maslat*), he took decisions on local matters, agricultural activities and employment of servants. He supervised the drying of marshes, de-silting of water channels and filling cracks in embankments. When the crops ripened, he did not hesitate to wield the sickle alongside his clansmen and workers. In order to widen the cultivated area, he attracted migrants from distant places and offered them incentives. In case of a violent dispute with a neighbouring clan, he mobilized his clansmen with horses and weapons. He celebrated social functions on a grand scale. He made a lavish expenditure on decorations, food, alcohol, ornaments, robes, gifts and animals. He summoned numerous artisans and, assigning them different tasks, provided them raw materials like gold, pearls, cloth, sugar and flour. He gathered a colourful band of entertainers. The premium steeds, imported from Central Asia and Arabia, were decorated with tasseled strings and velvet pommels. He made sure that every person, ranging from the high ranking chiefs and valued kinsmen to the lowly placed menials and beggars, were satisfied. This display of wealth strengthened his position within his clan and legitimized his authority in his domain.[13] However, the chiefship was not a bed of roses. It was burdened with a variety of problems. Sometimes, an enemy intruded into his *zamindari*, while circumstances forced him to earn fresh enmities. If thieves looted a caravan of merchandize and investigative tracks led to his *zamndari*, Akbar could launch a punitive expedition against him. Damodar, who lived in the countryside of Jhang Siyal, saw frequent inter-clan conflicts and the growing power of the Mughal State in its formative stage.

The landed clans handled matrimonial alliances with great seriousness. It was an elaborate affair. The process was set in motion when the boy or girl was immature. The father and brothers began discussing the available options and, in particular, assessed the political gains envisaged in the long run. Chuchak and his sons deliberated on the match for Hir. If she were married in the land of the Afghans, the Siyal sway would extend beyond the Indus. If she were given in marriage to Akbar, the Siyals would acquire the right of collecting the land tax. They did not consider the ethnic background of the bridegroom. The daughter of a Jat *zamindar* could be married among the Afghans or Mughals. This was understandable because the landed clans and sovereign states were partners in the extraction of social surplus from the peasantry. Chuchak and his sons, far from being ambitious, were quite realistic. However, the matter was not confined to Chuchak and his family. The Siyals, as a clan, were involved in it. The clansmen, forming a body, met Chuchak and stressed the need to marry Hir off. Chuchak convinced them that he had not taken any step without their concurrence. He opened the letter of proposal only in their presence. The Siyals, not inclined to corner their chief, gave an enthusiastic response to the letter. They must avail the opportunity of forming a kinship with the Kheras, who would be useful to them in bad times. Chuchak conveyed the clan's decision to his wife. He also secured the clan's approval to the gifts intended for the emissaries.[14] Damodar appreciated the unenviable position of Chuchak, who was walking a tight rope. He kept his family and clan on the same page. He was submissive towards the emissaries, because they represented the Khera clan, not merely their chief Ali. The Siyal humility reflected the inferior position of the girl's side with regard to the relation with the Kheras.

Two emissaries, normally a Brahmin and Doom, played a crucial role in constructing a matrimonial bond. Their importance increased manifold if they represented landed clans. The boy's side sent them with a letter to the chief of the girl's clan. The emissaries, travelling a long distance on horseback, delivered the letter to the chief of the clan. Since the host clan was responsible for their boarding and lodging, they were treated as honoured guests. In accordance with the prevailing social norms, the Brahmin was lodged with the local

Brahmins, while the Doom was put up with the local Dooms. The sojourn of the emissaries extended to seven days. Damodar has created the impression as if nothing happened during this week. The emissaries, in view of the delicate nature of their task, were formal and cautious. On the one hand, they portrayed their patron clan in bright colours and, on the other hand, made respectful queries about the host clan. Acting in a discreet manner, they collected information about the political status of the host clan, its military strength, internal cohesion, relations with the central authority and control over the local populace. While returning, they attended a farewell meeting with the host clan. Besides a message for the patron clan, they received costly gifts comprising a set of clothes and a horse. They hoped to receive a similar set of gifts from their patrons, provided they were the first to convey the tidings. If the patrons heard the news from another quarter, the emissaries faced humiliation. Both material and non-material factors – hope for a lucrative reward and concern for their dignity – induced them to quicken their journey, which was fraught with obstacles.[15]

Thus far, Damodar has described the first part of the betrothal. He turned his gaze on Rangpur Khera to illuminate the beginning of the second part. The Khera chief Ali had spent the last seven days in perpetual anxiety. His mind was occupied with the conduct of his emissaries and response of the Siyals. The outcome of the mission would impact his credibility across the locality in general and among the Kheras in particular. True, he had sent the proposal with the approval of his clansmen. Similarly, he would receive the emissaries in the assembly of the Kheras, who had gathered for the purpose. When he heard the news of the Siyal consent, he could not control his happiness. The occasion was celebrated with the sharing of festive food, beating of drums and distribution of alms. The Kheras, exchanging congratulatory greetings, unanimously decided to leave for Jhang Siyal to complete the betrothal. Their large cavalcade comprised horses, camels and mules. The troupe of entertainers included jesters, mimics, musicians and dancers. At Chuchkana, Chuchak had decorated a spacious lounge, which matched Indra's court in grandeur. Two functions were held. In the evening, the guests were served intoxicating liquor and dainty dishes.

Next morning, the proceedings comprised entertainment, banquet and betrothal. Chuchak, holding a meeting of the Siyals, finalized gifts for members of the Khera entourage, including the prospective bridegroom. A large number of people converged at the site to watch the spectacle.[16]

Damodar brings us to the most important part of the betrothal. The two chiefs, Chuchak and Ali, stood facing each other. They made short declarations that were interspersed with a handshake. Chuchak made a statement highlighting his success over rival clans like the Chaddars and Nahars. Only his daughter had made him bend. Ali, clasping the hand of his counterpart, applauded the manner in which the Kheras were honoured. He showed grace in declaring that Chuchak was his lord and Hir was his honoured lady (*sahibiyani*). This act, involving a handshake and few words, sealed the Siyal-Khera matrimonial alliance. Nothing was written and no document was prepared. Everything was visual and verbal. None could imagine its violation. The presence of the gentry of the two clans and the general populace of Jhang Siyal conferred social sanctity on the alliance. There were two glaring absences, even if temporary. These were the women of the two clans, besides the boy and girl. The women were somewhat fortunate because they knew what was happening. The boy and girl were ignorant of the arrangement, which would determine their future for all times. In a short time, the two absences were terminated. Two identical ceremonies were held in Chuchkana and Rangpur Khera. Hir's mother Kundi, having summoned all the girls, performed the ceremony of happy omens (*shagun*). The girls put a morsel of rice dessert in Hir's mouth. Kundi gave a maund (*man*) of gold to Hir as offering. At Rangpur Khera, the ceremony took place on the return of the Kheras. Ali's unnamed wife, having invited all the lads, put a morsel of rice dessert in Sahiba's mouth and gave him a maund of gold. The joyful festivities, starting in the bungalows of Chuchak and Ali, spilled to every house.[17] If Damodar referred to them in case of Chuchkana, they must have been replicated in Rangpur Khera. The inhabitants of the two localities, having participated in the above rites or having witnessed them in different capacities, anticipated the fruition of the Siyal-Khera alliance in the form of Hir-Sahiba marriage.

The Siyal-Khera alliance, as Damodar has described, appeared to be a standard version of the relation. However, the Ranjha-Waraich alliance unfolded along different lines owing to its specific circumstances. Dhido was the son of Mojam, the Ranjha chief based in Takht Hazara. Dhido's brothers, jealous of his good looks, feared losing the chiefship to him and, therefore, decided to kill him. Mojam, anxious to secure Dhido's life, looked for a suitable match for him. In view of the wide fissure within the household, Mojam did not consult his sons or his clan. Acting in secrecy, he sent his emissaries to Yaqub Khan Waraich. Yaqub ensured that the letter was read in the presence of his clansmen. The Waraichs, considering the social credentials of the Ranjhas, virtually jumped at the proposal. Since Mojam could no longer conceal the move, drums were beaten along with the distribution of alms. The brothers, feeling outmanoeuvred, became insistent on killing Dhido. The growing tension prevented Mojam and his clansmen from visiting the Waraichs. He also decided to hold the marriage of Dhido at the earliest and, for this purpose, urged Yaqub to fix a date. Yaqub, apparently aware of Mojam's compulsions, sent a string of sixteen knots.[18]

At Takht Hazara, Mojam performed the rituals for the bridegroom and initiated preparations for the marriage. Following Mojam's sudden death, the brothers stopped the marriage and, dividing the ancestral property, separated Dhido from the joint household. The Ranjha brothers, it appeared, did not feel bound to the Ranjha-Waraich alliance. Mojam had deliberately kept them in the dark about it. Their late father had violated the time-honoured practice of consulting his family and clan on important matters. This grudge rankled in the mind of the Ranjha clan, which remained aloof when Dhido suffered injustice. The clan could not have been ignorant of the growing bad blood in Mojam's family. Since Damodar focused his attention only on Dhido, he did not delve into the consequences of Mojam's secretive actions. Similarly, Damodar did not tell us the reaction of the Waraichs to the cancellation of Dhido's marriage. They must have been cognizant of the tussle in the Ranjha household, besides the isolation of their prospective bridegroom Dhido in his family. They did not intervene in the internal matters of the Ranjhas, as the social conventions did not permit such a move. Moreover,

Dhido was still not married to their daughter and, therefore, he was not their son-in-law. Though they were disturbed at the situation, they could do nothing but wait and watch.

In Damodar's narrative, the Waraichs figured only in the beginning and middle. They were entirely absent in the intervening period. They appeared only when they learnt that Dhido had returned to Takht Hazara after the end of his domicile with the Siyals. Damodar does not tell us what the Waraichs had in their mind. However, the subsequent developments solved the puzzle. They wished to discuss the fate of the Ranjha-Waraich alliance and the intention of Dhido. Tahir, the eldest of Ranjha brothers, gauged the mood of the Waraichs. He was conscious of Dhido's failure to stick to the betrothal. He agreed to snap the bond, provided the plaintiff (*muddai*) gave his consent. In spite of initial differences, the Ranjhas and Waraichs arrived at a common understanding with regard to Dhido. This boy had disgraced his brothers through his improper deeds in Jhang Siyal and, therefore, had placed the betrothal in doubt. Dhido, maintaining his calm amidst provocation, withdrew his claim in the relationship and, thus, permitted the Waraichs to marry their daughter anywhere. It was easy for him to take this stance as, in his view, the pious domain of the saints was ideologically different from the worldly life of the landed clans.[19]

The Ranjhas and Waraichs, having weeded Dhido out of their kinship, did not feel satisfied. Waraichs, with regard to their daughter, were free. This freedom did not compensate them for their loss in the past. The Ranjhas, despite abrogating the betrothal, were guilty of harming the Waraichs in general and the girl in particular. They must retrieve their social credibility and salvage their social image. It was logical for the Ranjhas to take the initiative. In their eyes, the Ranjha-Waraich alliance never snapped. It had only remained in suspended animation. It could be revived with a few deft moves. Though Damodar did not state so, it was likely that the Ranjha brothers, cunning as they were, had a premeditated plan in their diplomatic armoury. Jeevan, the youngest of Ranjha brothers, made an effective intervention. The Ranjha-Waraich kinship had a long past. There had been many alliances between them. In fact, the two clans were intertwined like thick ropes (*une su vaan niayin*). They were bound to strengthen the bond. They must settle the marriage of Tahir's son with the Waraich girl, failing which the two clans would lose their honour. Yaqub Khan Waraich, initially apprehensive, gave his consent in the interest of the inter-clan solidarity and the future of his daughter. Dhido was easily forgotten as one who had died or had gone mad.[20]

Ranjha brothers, who were squarely responsible for cancelling Dhido's marriage, shifted the entire blame on him. In spite of this dubious understanding of the past, the Ranjhas managed to include Dhido in the marriage party. Tahir, playing the emotional card, declared that Dhido was the son of their parents and was like a father to his nephew. The Ranjha brothers, as per their convenience, excluded and included Dhido in their kinship. It was another matter that Dhido, contrary to his expectation, faced a lot of embarrassment while facing his former fiancée.[21] Damodar has succeeded in showing that the Ranjha brothers were absolute villains and Dhido continued to be an innocent victim of their machinations. During the Ranjha-Waraich meeting, Dhido refrained from exposing his brothers in the presence of Waraichs. Since he saw himself as a saint, he had risen above ordinary human passions.

Choosing Herdsmanship over Farming

Dhido, as a growing lad, had many opportunities of settling as a farmer. Every time, he refused to avail the chance owing to his disturbed mind, uncertain conditions and inexperience. In the time of Mojam, the Ranjha household was united and prosperous. Mojam and his three elder sons worked in the fields, while the right of *zamindari* brought in a steady income. The three brothers were married and blessed with children. Between them and Dhido, there was a wide chasm. While they toiled in the fields, he remained at home under the care of dotting parents. They were jealous of his beauty and, fearing that he would inherit the chiefship, conspired to kill him. They cancelled his marriage and divided the patrimonial property including income from the *zamindari* and movable goods. Dhido protested against the move because he was too young to bear the responsibility. If he were older and married, he might have accepted the separation, which would make him the head of a peasant household. His entreaties to Tahir, who had stepped into the shoes of Mojam, stood summarily rejected. The brothers asked Dhido to earn his livelihood like a Jat. He must uproot the weeds with a spade and hoe. Dhido could not handle the implements because his hands were covered with henna and he was preparing to wed the Waraich girl. With Mojam's death, he was pushed into mourning and was deprived of parental affection. Though he had not started tilling the soil, the tax collector (*muhassil*) had already started chasing him.[22] His brothers had created circumstances in which he had no choice but to leave Takht Hazara. His suffering was identical with that of the handsome Yusuf, who faced acute hostility from his brothers along with deep love from his father. Damodar, who was living in an Islamicate cultural space, must have been familiar with the Quranic tale.

Dhido, following his exile from the village, became a homeless wanderer. Instead of being a member of the Ranjha clan, he preferred to be a straw that kept drifting in the wind. If he thought that he had no possession, he was mistaken. He still had three things in the form of a staff, a flute and good looks. He discovered, to his surprise, that these assets created fresh opportunities for him at every step. During his stay in a mosque, a band of girls saw him. Unknowingly, he captivated a Jhinwar girl. She induced her mother to contact Ranjha for marriage. A party of Jats, who were travelling from Multan to the Jhelum, manipulated the situation to their advantage. Posing as Jhinwars and guardians of Ranjha, they accepted the marriage proposal in return for a hearty meal. Ranjha refused to be a party to the deceit of the Jats. Here was a providential opportunity. He could attach himself to the Jats and, through their intermediacy, marry the girl. With these two relationships, he could overcome his current state of adversity and slip into a secure life. Ranjha would have none of this. He was not a grabber but a renouncer. He would neither tell lies nor touch the unlawful (*haram*). He would not spoil the life of the girl and cheat her mother. Though he was immature and outnumbered, he disapproved the deceit of the Jats. His sympathies were with the innocent girl and her simple mother. He remained hungry and walked on weak legs, but did not succumb to any temptation.[23] At this stage, his aim was to go as far from his brothers as possible. The threat from his brothers was more real than the hazy thoughts of instant comfort. In spite of his young age and physical difficulties, Ranjha nurtured a deep sense of moral propriety. While travelling from Takht Hazara to Jhang Siyal, he rejected a series of worldly attractions and steadily climbed the ladder of spirituality. In the eyes of Damodar, Ranjha was a saint in the making.

Ranjha, owing to fatigue and hunger, stayed with an old couple. The hosts were inquisitive about the stranger, who was too tired to narrate the dispute with his brothers. He had no social antecedents. He was not connected to any caste, place or family. He did not have any source of livelihood. He fell from the sky and lay prostrate on earth. The host, convinced of Ranjha's vulnerability, offered to settle him as a farmer. He would assign him a well besides silting land (*sailabe banne*). He would give him a camel, mare, buffalo and cow. If he found a sister or niece, he would fix him in marriage. Ranjha, thanking the couple for their kindness, stated that he was going on a pilgrimage of the saints and might settle in the place on his return.[24] Since Damodar was occupied in exploring the turmoil in Ranjha's mind, he has told us little about the old man. Apparently, he had plenty of land that he had inherited from his ancestors. He might be cultivating a part of it, while another part was lying vacant. He was either childless or did not have a son. He was looking for a young man, who could be persuaded to settle there. He would provide this settler with the means of cultivation and enable him to raise a family. The settler, in due course, would look after the couple in old age. He did not express these desires, though he gave a hint about them. He and his wife treated Ranjha as their son-in-law. There was a subtle meaning in providing a white mattress on a red bedstead, besides butter and milk. The old man could not fathom the deepest layers of Ranjha's psychological state. At this moment, Ranjha had to save his life. He would not adopt what he had been discarding. Unconsciously, he was taking small steps on the path of spirituality. Damodar, more than anyone else, knew it.

By the time Ranjha reached the Chenab, he had moved away from worldliness and gravitated towards spirituality. He began to display miraculous powers through his flute. Panjpir, impressed with his music, heard his tale of woe and conferred Hir on him. Soon after, he told Luddan that fate had turned him into a wanderer, who was out to see the world. He was not related to anyone. His only possession was his flute, which enabled him to produce music. When Ranjha played the flute, Luddan nearly fainted and wild animals converged on the site. Luddan decalred that he would offer him a buffalo and two women. Without saying so, he wished to include Ranjha in his household at the ferry. Ranjha felt that Luddan had misunderstood him. He did not intend to settle on the Chenab. He had no faith in the world and its people. He did not have any worldly aspirations. He had distanced himself from the agrarian economy, involving ploughing of fields, acquiring official documents and paying taxes. For the first time, Ranjha declared that he had adopted the path of spirituality. Luddan, unwilling to offend a saint, brought Ranjha to sleep on the luxurious bed. When Hir reprimanded Luddan over this transgression, Luddan stated that the man was a perfect saint and, if offended, Hir could face a calamity. Soon after, Ranjha wrought a miracle with his flute. On listening to the melody, the wild animals gathered, the girls swooned and Hir lost her senses.[25] If Luddan had not urged Ranjha to stop, some listeners might have died. It may be recalled that Majnun, having withdrawn from the Bedouin society, lived among the wild animals.

As soon as Ranjha fell in love with Hir, his life underwent a dramatic change. He terminated his vagrancy and settled in Jhang Siyal as a herdsman of the Siyals. This was not an easy task, but he cleared the obstacles with the overt and covert support of Hir. Now, there was no need to conceal his identity. Speaking the truth, he familiarized Chuchak about his family background and circumstances in which he was forced to leave his village. Chuchak pressurized Ranjha to settle as a farmer and offered him a number of incentives. His words were remarkably similar to those of the old man, whom Ranjha had met before reaching the Chenab. The only difference was that Chuchak did not make any offer regarding Ranjha's matrimonial status.

The two lucrative offers to Ranjha might be contextualized in terms of two major categories of peasants, permanent (*khud kasht*) and migratory (*pahi kasht*). The former owned land they inherited, oxen and other means of cultivation. They tilled this land with family labour. They possessed substantial houses in the *zamindari*. Since they resided in a fixed spot, they did not abandon their habitations in the face of oppression. They could sell, transfer and bequeath their lands. They were not ejected so long as they paid the land tax. Even after long absence, they could resume their lands after clearing the arrears. They paid land tax at a concessional rate as the custom fixed. Exempted from imposts of the headmen, they enjoyed access to pastures, forests, ponds, fisheries, unoccupied lands and menial services. They were accorded a dignified place in socio-religious assemblies. In contrast to them, migratory peasants (*pahi kasht*) resided in one *zamindari* and cultivated land in another. Since *zamindari* denoted the settlement of a dominant tribe, caste or clan, a person moving out of it became an outsider. The migratory peasants were of two types. The first type possessed their own ploughs and bullocks, so that the headmen induced them to till cultivable wastes and deserted villages. The second type took up the cultivation of *khud kasht* lands of headmen or land grants of the religious elite. They did not possess ploughs, bullocks and seeds. They received farm accessories from the superior sections of the village. Apparently willing to move from place to place, they retained their holdings till they paid the land tax. If plenty of land was uncultivated, the migratory peasants extracted favourable terms from the headmen.[26] Ranjha, on two occasions, declined the position of the second type of migratory peasants (*pahi kasht*). He was not entitled to a higher status, as he had moved out of his ancestral *zamindari* and withdrawn from his clan. In case, he had continued to stay in Takht Hazara, he would have been a *khud kasht* peasant with a share in the income from the ancestral *zamindari* right.

Ranjha, as tutored by Hir, insisted on working as a herdsman. Chuchak and his Siyal kinsmen were inclined to accept the request, provided the candidate cleared a discreet test. As soon as Ranjha sipped the milk given to him, he fell into a rage and exclaimed that it came from a buffalo, which had miscarried. Besides, he was accurate in identifying its other characteristics. The Siyals were amazed at the veterinary skills of the candidate. Feeling puzzled, they failed to discern the secret underlying this outcome. They were convinced that Ranjha was a spiritual guide and true saint, who possessed the light of spiritual excellence (*azmat ki rushnai*). They were unanimous in recommending the employment of Ranjha as a herdsman and, according to convention, drums were beaten.[27] His work as a herdsman had a direct impact on the buffaloes. The buffaloes, recalcitrant for one reason or the other, yielded milk without ado. The Siyals surprised at the change, declared again that Ranjha was a saint.

On two successive occasions, Ranjha refused to settle as a migratory farmer. Even a package of lucrative offers failed to a attract him. Damodar has not given reasons for this stance, leaving much room for conjectures. The agricultural operations, right from preparation of soil to harvesting of crops, was extremely tough. Natural calamities and burdensome tax added to the difficulties. Moreover, a farmer worked in open fields, so that his actions were visible to the villagers. In contrast, love was subversive and clandestine. It could be pursued behind the smokescreen of grazing cattle. The tall grasses on the banks of the Chenab along with ancient trees, being distant from the village and fields, offered a considerable opportunity to the newly initiated lovers.[28] It was another matter that they were not hidden from the prying eyes of the jealous herdsmen. Hir, being intimately familiar with the locality, introduced Ranjha to the ecological features. She was the one to choose herdsmanship as a suitable avocation for Ranjha. She prepared him to face the impending interview. Possibly, she revealed the questions he could be asked and answers he was expected to give. Soon after, she spoke to her mother about discovering a herdsman, who was endowed with a number of abilities. Ranjha, with his grace, could ward of unfavourable events. He would not let the grass dry up. He would prevent the buffaloes from dropping their calves. He would protect the buffaloes from the mouth and foot disease. Over and above, monsoons would bring plenty of rains.[29] Since Kundi was likely to convey these details to Chuchak, Hir would succeed in creating the job for Ranjha and ensuring that he got it.

Damodar, while living among the Siyals, watched the clan chief from close quarters. One of his important functions was to employ a variety of servants on the landed estate. On the banks of the Chenab, the agrarian economy revolved around cultivation of extensive land holdings and rearing large herds of cattle. The Siyal clan comprised 84 villages and employed 84 herdsmen, though the figure was more metaphorical than real. In the expanding agrarian economy, there was always a possibility of employing a new servant. Even if the person was a total stranger, he could be taken in service and work found for him. Damodar has thrown light on the circumstances that led to the absorption of Ranjha in the agricultural-pastoral economy. If the chief's daughter sponsored the candidature of Ranjha and played her cards in an intelligent manner, Ranjha could get in with ease. Damodar has ably constructed the context wherein the lovers undertook four activities – grazing cattle, strengthening love, fighting against patriarchy of the landed clans and pursuing spirituality – that were inseparably intertwined.

Defiance, Courage and Articulation

Hir, during her childhood, gave enough indication of her potential as a rebel. She led a group of 360 girls of the Siyal domain. For each watch of the day, she had decided a schedule of activities including eating breakfast, playing games, savouring seasonal fruit and bathing in the Chenab. More importantly, she functioned as the Siyal chief in place of her father Chuchak. She rushed to the rescue of people in distress and, in the process, displayed qualities of leadership and diplomacy.[30] In a bold decision, she took charge of the boat belonging to the Sambhals and took Luddan under the Siyal protection.[31] Her action provoked the Sambhals into attacking the Siyals. Hir, remaining undeterred, transformed the girls into a fighting force. Covering their bodies in shawls, they armed themselves with double-edged swords and protective shields. In the battlefield, Hir led from the front because it did not behove a chief to take a back seat in crisis. She gave commands on offensive and defensive tactics. Her generalship led to the defeat of the Sambhals. She buried her dead companions amidst mourning and threw the Sambhal corpses into the Chenab. Throughout the Siyal-Sambhal conflict, Hir acted on her own. Rejecting the advice of Luddan, she refused to summon her brothers in the exigency. They sought an explanation on her failure to call them. Hir cooked up a false story to satisfy them. The girls had expelled some hungry shepherds, who had laid their hands on some creepers. For her, it was a minor issue. She might have called her brothers if Akbar had marched in.[32] Damodar has rightly described Hir's childhood to reveal her bravery, intelligence and independence. With this background, it was easy for Damodar to portray Hir as a passionate lover, a fiery orator and tenacious rebel. Further, Damodar was able to trace her long struggle against the patriarchal stranglehold of the landed clans.

From the very beginning, Hir was not secretive about her love. She was honest, bold and vocal. Two factors induced her to choose Ranjha as her lover. First, she was attracted to him on seeing his face. Second, she was charmed on listening to his flute. The impact of these experiences was so strong that she lost her senses. On recovering, she took the most momentous decision of her life. She revealed it to Luddan, Hassi and the band of girls. She was not the only one to be allured to Ranjha. Many other girls had started taking a romantic interest in him. Hir had to be quick and even reckless. Taking the initiative, she apologized to Luddan for being harsh to him. She expressed her gratitude to him for introducing her to Ranjha. If Luddan had not permitted Ranjha to sleep on the bedstead, he would have gone far from the ferry and, as a consequence, she would not have met him. If she did meet him, all credit must go to Luddan. Therefore, she bent backwards in dealing with Luddan and even rewarded him with two buffaloes.[33] She did not fear that Luddan would inform her parents about the rendezvous on the Chenab. After all, he was a mere servant and, therefore, depended on Siyal patronage. For Luddan, Hir was the chief for all practical purposes. It was easy for Hir to handle him. It was not so with Hassi and the girls. Hir became silent and gave a deep thought to her next step. After initial hesitation, she confided in Hassi. Indicating the growing agony in her mind, she could not express the germination of love in so many words. Since Hir looked upon Hassi as a confidant, she had high expectations from her. On the one hand, Hassi would maintain complete secrecy about what she had seen and, on the other hand, assist Hir in keeping a protective watch over Ranjha.[34]

Soon after, Hir turned to the girls. As she was the unquestioned leader of the group, she ordered them to leave the boat and sport on the swings. Hir brought Ranjha to the bedstead and had sexual intercourse with him. Overflowing with a sense of achievement, she made a startling announcement of her transformation. Henceforth, no one should call her Hir. She was no longer the daughter of her parents. Her connection with the Siyal clan had snapped. Her pride, flowing from an elite background, had crumbled. She had reduced herself to the level of her lover, a mere outcaste fit to be a herdsman. Since she had tied herself to his lappet, she hoped that he would accept a simple Jat girl.[35] These words, addressed to Ranjha, were also meant for the girls. From now onwards, none of them would look at Ranjha as a potential lover. Their path leading to him had been closed for good. Their leader had affixed her seal on him. Since they were present at the site, they were witness to the formation of a new bond. They would support the lovers through thick and thin. Once the gossip spread in the locality, they began to fear the consequences of Hir's action. Before their connivance was put to interrogation, they decided to warn Hir. It may be noted that the herdsmen, who grazed cattle on the Chenab, were the first to observe their new colleague with their master's daughter. Within two months, the news spread across the domain of the Siyals, who faced increasing ignominy.

Hir faced embarrassing questions from her friends, relatives and parents. She gave different answers to each of them. When friends cautioned her of the consequences of her involvement with Ranjha, she brazenly admitted that he was not only her husband but also her spiritual guide (*kamil murshid*). As her focus had shifted from the ferry to the moors, she was no longer interested in the boat and swings.[36] Women of rival families and Chuchak's daughters-in-law, forming a group, met Kundi and expressed concern over the disgrace of the Siyals. Hir, responding to Kundi and her daughters-in-law, denied the charge and insisted that she was a virgin. Somewhat undiplomatically, she registered her anguish at the Siyal disdain for the herdsman. Her subtle sympathy for Ranjha raised suspicions.[37] Chuchak and Kundi, sharing their agony, decided to check the reports before taking any step. Chuchak's brother Kaido, who was specifically sent to the moors, brought proof of the affair in the form of Hir's breadcrumbs for Ranjha. An outraged Hir burnt Kaido's hut and threatened to kill him.[38] Chuchak, himself entering the moors, saw the lovers in a compromising position. As expected, Hir's parents began preparations for her marriage with the Khera boy. At this moment, Damodar has recorded a conversation between Kundi and Hir. The tenor of arguments revealed the growing conflict between patriarchy of the landed clans and the love between social outcastes. This conversation was significant because Hir, abandoning her denial mode, boldly admitted her love for Ranjha and asserted the legitimacy of her relationship.[39] She articulated this stance during her forced marriage with Sahiba and her trial in the Qazi's court at Kot Qabula.

Kundi alleged that Hir was roaming across the moors with the herdsman. She had brought a bad name to the Siyal clan and her lineage. Such a daughter should have been killed at her birth. Ranjha, owing to his obscure social antecedents, was no match to the Khera boy. Only Hir had praised Ranjha, throwing dust in the eyes of others. Ranjha, in the absence of parental approval, could not be accepted as Hir's husband. Her parents had searched out the best match for her. As a clan, the Kheras were superior to the Siyals. For them, there was no dearth of brides. The formation of a matrimonial bond lay squarely in the domain of the clan. Once finalized, it was inscribed in the destiny of Hir. Since the Kheras had the mandate, they could forcibly take Hir away. The Siyals, having assumed authority over numerous homes in Jhang Siyal, had a big reputation to defend. Damodar, in his stout defense of love, spoke through Hir. Her parents, like the rest of the world, were ignorant of her relation with Ranjha. The worldly people could not appreciate the pursuit of love. Her betrothal with Ranjha had a divine sanction. Happening even before Adam and Eve, it was announced by the prominent saints. Ranjha had been inscribed in her lot through the divine will. When he captured her heart in the boat, she became his auspicious wife. They were fully merged into each other like two bodies of water. She was madly in love with Ranjha, who imbued every pore of her body. No one had the right to fix her marriage with the Khera without her knowledge. This false relation could not become true even if it were repeated a hundred times. The Siyals could not forcibly snatch her and hand her over to the Kheras. If such an eventuality took place, she would jump off the wedding mat.

Damodar has portrayed Hir as a strong young woman, who was passionately attached to Ranjha. Following the fixation of her marriage, she was put to a series of tests. She transformed every test into an opportunity to express her love for Ranjha and opposition to her marriage with Sahiba. She refused to go through the pre-wedding oil ceremony. Her brothers tried to use physical force, but she did not allow them to touch her body, because Ranjha had already touched her with his hands.[40] The Siyals decided to poison Hir and replace her with her niece (Pathana's daughter). They failed to effect this change as the poison could not kill Hir. She continued to live so that she could put up a fight. When she was rubbed with henna and perfumed paste, she declared that she had given her heart to Ranjha and, thus, ruled out Sahiba from her life. The Siyals, including three brothers and four maternal uncles, could not kill Hir at midnight, as mysterious black warriors protected her.[41] On the arrival of the Khera marriage party, Hir gave a big shock to the gathering. She not only touched Ranjha's feet and embraced him, but also declared him a perfect saint, who would rescue her from misery. She did not allow the Brahmin to tie the bridal thread (*gana*). When Ranjha was summoned to do the needful, Hir fell at his feet and reiterated her love for him. The Brahmin, realizing the seriousness of her resolve, pointed to the futility of the ritual. Kundi was forced to shut his mouth with a bribe.[42]

For the Siyals, the worst was yet to come. As the Qazi initiated the ritual of marriage (*nikah*), Hir declared that her brothers and uncles would not touch her, as the right was reserved only for Ranjha. When the Qazi asked her if she accepted Sahiba as her husband, she declared her attachment to Ranjha. In a sarcastic comment, she asked the Qazi to tie her mother Kundi with Sahiba. Since Hir never gave her consent, the marriage was legally invalid. The Siyals, in order to save their face, created the opposite impression. When Sahiba tried to consummate the marriage, Hir wrecked his teeth with a tight slap that left him bleeding. Calling him her brother, she sent him to look for her lover Ranjha.[43] The Siyals, demoralized at Hir's defiance, could not forcibly push her into the palanquin. Hir allowed the litter to leave for Rangpur Khera only when the Siyals agreed to send Ranjha along with it. On the way, she condemned the Kheras for beating Ranjha, who had been tied to her knot. She refused to take food because it was not imbued with Ranjha's fragrance.[44]

On reaching her marital home, she caused a big scandal in the presence of women. She agreed to receive the ceremonial morsel from her mother-in-law only if Ranjha sat beside her. Creating a big ruckus, she declared her resolve to play the game of 'Ring in Buttermilk' (*lassi mundari*) only with Ranjha, who was her bridegroom.[45] Through words and deeds, Hir tried to convince the Siyals and Kheras about her rejection of the marriage and commitment to love. She gave several opportunities to the two clans to revise their decision and let her be with Ranjha. Owing to the failure to do this, the stakeholders suffered in different ways. This led to inter-clan conflict, loss of life and judicial intervention. All this was avoidable.

In the eyes of Damodar, Hir was more than the beloved of Ranjha. Along with her pursuit of love and struggle against patriarchy, Damodar has traced her evolution as a saint under the tutelage of Ranjha. Hir's engagement with spirituality was not exceptional. West Asia offered varying models of female spirituality that revolved around sexual abstinence, former slavery and devotional acts.[46] In the Chishti circles of north India, a number of women had earned respect for their spiritual attainments. Baba Farid took pride in the mystical inclinations of his daughter Bibi Sharifa. If it had been permitted, Baba Farid would have granted the mandate of his spiritual succession (*khilaftnama*) and prayer carpet (*sajjadah*) to her. Bibi Zulaikha, the mother of Nizamuddin Auliya, was a pious woman and, through her miraculous power, secured her wishes from God. While supervising the education of her son amidst extreme deprivation, she inculcated in him the values of religious devotion, resignation and contentment. Fatima Sam was the most prominent female Sufi of Delhi. The Chishtis saw her as a man who had been sent in the form of a woman. She had memorized numerous verses pertaining to every circumstance of life. She held that providing food to the needy brought more divine favours than millions of prayers and fasts. Nizamuddin Auliya appreciated her commitment to the Chishti discipline and, in times of adversity, meditated at her grave. According to a writer of the sixteenth century, Bibi Sara was empowered to cause rain during a drought and Bibi Auliya performed forty-day retreats behind closed doors. He has also noted the location of the tombs of many female mystics.[47] In the case of Hir-Ranjha, their graves were seen near Hazara towards the close of the seventeenth century. As their unprecedented quest was celebrated in collective memory and soulful melodies, their graves evolved as sites of popular veneration, hitherto the exclusive preserve of Sufis.

A Long Saga of Suffering

Damodar has drawn the character of Ranjha in a mould entirely different from that of Hir. In spite of a prosperous social background, Ranjha was destined to suffer. Throughout his life, he found himself in adversity. In addition to poverty and loneliness, he underwent intense mental agony. As a child, he faced the jealousy and hostility of his three brothers. Deprived of parental affection, he was separated from the joint Ranjha household, which excluded him to fend for himself. Yet, he had his heart in the right place. He could not be the cause of difficulty for anyone, even if he suffered in the process. When he left Takht Hazara with an empty pocket, he kept on walking for many days. He was in constant fear that his brothers would catch up and kill him without mercy. During his stay in a mosque, he was placed in a difficult position due to the deceit of some Jats. Not only this, he was forced to leave the place in acute hunger. Pained at his helplessness, he wept to soothe his nerves. By the time he reached the Chenab, he begged Luddan to allow him to rest in the boat. Still, he could not provide any comfort to his delicate frame. If he had not shown his face to the girls, he would have received a severe beating.[48] Damodar had armed Ranjha with a flute, which proved its utility in moments of crisis. His melodies proved effective on at least six occasions – on the Chenab to attract Panjpir; on acceeding to the request of Luddan; on fulfilling the wish of Hir on the ferry; in the moors while collecting the buffaloes besides taming wild animals; to neutralize the anger of Chuchak on being caught red handed with Hir and to hoodwink the Siyal girls on returning as a Jogi. Ranjha's flute provided him some respite from his suffering.

In the early stages of his life, Ranjha was inseparable from his flute. Since it was his prized possession,[49] he carried it along while leaving Takht Hazara. During his childhood, he was too young to work on the fields. Yet, he learnt to play Indian *ragas* on his flute. This ability enabled him to survive adverse situations and even make substantive gains. On the Chenab, Panjpir were so impressed with his rendition of Raga Lalit that they bestowed on him several boons including Hir. Soon after, the boatman Luddan was amazed at the impact of Ranjha's melody on wild animals and, turning generous, allowed Ranjha to sleep on Hir's bedstead in the boat. Hir lost her senses on listening to the flute and, on recovering, reconciled with Luddan and fell in love with Ranjha. When Ranjha escorted buffaloes to the moors, his flute induced the buffaloes to break their ropes and rush out of their enclosures. While returning from the moors, they were attracted to the flute and gathered around Ranjha to return to the village. Chuchak noted the magnetic pull of the flute on the buffaloes and, therefore, restored Ranjha in his job. More than once, Damodar has compared the buffaloes to Gopis, who were attracted to Krishna's flute. If Ranjha managed to separate himself from the girls of Jhang Siyal, it was only because he rendered them unconscious with his music.[50] What is noteworthy, Ranjha abandoned his flute in the wake of Hir's forced marriage with Sahiba. Henceforth, Ranjha faced hostility from his brothers, the Kheras, the Waraichs and finally, a cruel punishment in the Qazi's court at Kot Qabula. However, he did not resort to his flute for any miraculous assistance.

Damodar has explored the conflict between Ranjha and eighty-four herdsmen, who looked after the cattle of the Siyals. They had strong reasons for their hostility towards Ranjha. He employed novel methods of grazing buffaloes and, as a result, earned accolades from the Siyals. He cultivated friendly relations with animals and plants, so that he came to virtually rule over the moors. Having fallen in love with Chuchak's daughter, he began receiving a preferential treatment from the chief's household. The herdsmen held that Ranjha had snatched their bread. Though their murderous attack had ended in a failure, it did not put an end to their opposition. It reached a flashpoint during the preparations for Hir's wedding. Owing to the withdrawal of Hir's protection and his rootless antecedents, his position became vulnerable. The herdsmen enumerated a series of complaints against him. Ranjha had been moving in the moors with a swaggering gait. When they called him, he did not care to respond. He had been piling fat on his body with the chief's milk and cream. Now, they would again join hands to kill him. Ranjha clarified that fate had decreed his livelihood in Jhang Siyal. He did not have a permanent interest in the place. He had not encroached into anyone's field. Nor had he taken anything from the moors. Since he was soon returning to Takht Hazara, there was no need to kill him.[51] He remained safe from the fury of herdsmen, but fell into the grip of Chuchak. The chief, having caught him red handed with Hir, thrashed him with a cane. He escaped dismissal from service as he proved his indispensability as a keeper of buffaloes.

On the day of Hir's wedding, Ranjha faced the unkindness of nature. In his eagerness to see the Khera marriage party, he suffered from a sudden giddiness and collapsed on the ground. In the process, he received a major injury on his foot that started bleeding. When he rode an ox to have a better view of the proceedings, the animal panicked and ran around in circles. Ranjha attracted the attention of the Khera marriage party due to his good looks and saintly bearing. The herdsmen, out of jealousy, upbraided Ranjha for exposing himself to public and asked him to leave the place forthwith.[52] When the Kheras left Chuchkana with Hir's palanquin, the Siyals induced Ranjha to join the cavalcade with a drum on his head. The episode became a permanent blot on Ranjha, who was often chided for disgracing his father and brothers. During a two-day journey, the Kheras attacked him with kicks and sticks, so that his body was covered with blood. His condition became so miserable that he begged the Kheras to kill him outright.[53] The Kheras restrained themselves to evade a stigma on their clan. In order to achieve their aim, they forced him to cross the swollen Chenab after the buffaloes, hoping that he would drown. Ranjha had a narrow escape. The Kheras, on reaching Rangpur Khera, were outraged at Hir's brazen confession of love for Ranjha. They conspired to kill him to retrieve their honour. He learnt of the conspiracy from a Doom girl and escaped with his life.

Following the marriage of Hir, Ranjha was again rendered homeless. The Siyals and Kheras were inclined to kill him. In order to save his life, he returned to Takht Hazara. During his absence of twelve years, he had erased the village from his mind. He thought of it only when facing hostile situations. Since time could wipe out past bitterness, the enmity of his brothers would have dissipated. However, Ranjha was shocked to find that they continued to nurture the old antagonism. He assured them that he had not come to claim his share in the patrimonial property and, as a proof of his detachment, pointed to his mendicancy of twelve years. His brothers, dissatisfied with the clarifications, accused Ranjha of disgracing Mojam by serving the Siyals as a menial. His sisters-in-law, with their questions on Hir, rubbed salt into his wounds. In these circumstances, Ranjha could not stay in the village. Damodar's description of Ranjha's adversity was restricted to some cursory remarks. Ranjha's friends, who had played with him during their childhood, came to his rescue. In the outskirts of the village, they built for him a hut, which was provided with basic necessities.[54] By turns, they might have brought food for him. During the day, they sat with him in the village common and conversed on matters of common interest. After sunset, Ranjha retreated to his hut. The duration of his stay in the village coincided with his thirty-five months long separation from Hir. His self-abnegation, quite visible in the public eye, would have dealt a severe blow to the credibility of his thick-skinned brothers.

Ranjha was not destined to live in peace. His brothers joined hands with the Waraichs to exclude him from the matrimonial alliance. Even after his formal withdrawal of any claims in the matter, his abasement reached a new high. When he accompanied the marriage party of his nephew (Tahir's son), his former fiancée subjected him to a fresh round of degradation. In the presence of a group of girls, he was forced to admit that he lacked the means to support a wife and physical strength to lead a conjugal life. His eldest brother Tahir, misunderstanding his presence among the girls, accused him of a dual posture. In order to preserve what was left of his dignity, Ranjha had to flee from the site without enjoying the festivities of the occasion.[55] His depression was partly lifted with the unexpected arrival of Ramu with Hir's message. By adopting the path of Jog and securing the help of Hir's sister-in-law Sehti, Ranjha was able to unite with Hir. However, their elopement from Rangpur Khera opened the floodgates of fresh troubles. If the lovers had not slipped into the protection of the Nahars, the Kheras would have killed them during a hazardous flight through the unknown countryside. At Kot Qabula, the Qazi dubbed Ranjha as a big bastard and mocked at his conversion to Jog. Ranjha, denied the opportunity to explain his conduct, was whipped in front of the people. He suffered the ultimate humiliation of seeing his beloved being handed over to the Kheras, who lost no time in beating her.[56] Only divine intervention ended their ordeal and paved the way for their final union.

Before proceeding further, we must take a close look at Kaido, who was quite an interesting character. Though he was the elder brother of Chuchak, he did not assume the headship of the Siyals. He did not participate in the deliberations of the clan. He had virtually abandoned its membership. He did not marry. Nor did he reside in the village. Having withdrawn from society, he lived in a hut outside Chuchkana. He had few belongings, though he might be receiving provisions from the Siyal household. In normal circumstances, he did not beg. He was not disturbed in his social isolation, which he had adopted for several decades. Chuchak had immense faith in Kaido's wisdom and resorted to him in a crisis. Such a situation arose when Hir fell in love with the herdsman. Kaido, like other Siyals, felt angry at the affair. Since he lived near the moors, he had seen the lovers together. He did not wish to spy on them because he was scared of Hir. He relented only when Chuchak became submissive towards him and invoked their common parentage. Kaido managed to collect the proof of the undue affinity between the lovers and, in the bargain, paid a very heavy price. He was beaten, his but was burnt and he was threatened with death. Though he protested against Hir's violence, he thought of shifting to Rajoa Syedan.[57] His dignity was restored at Hir's marriage. The Siyals, in view of Hir's resistance, did not know how to make her leave for Rangpur Khera without any fuss. In this predicament, Kaido came to the rescue of the Siyals. At his suggestion, Ranjha was sent along with Hir's palanquin. Everyone admitted that Kaido had solved a difficult problem, while Chuchak conceded that the troubleshooter was a true ascetic.[58] Kaido, with one stroke, achieved many aims. He was able to humiliate Ranjha, who had undermined the reputation of the Siyals. He demonstrated that his younger brother Chuchak was incapable of leading the Siyals. Kaido, despite his self-chosen segregation, had defended the honour of the Siyals and ensured the fruition of the Siyal-Khera alliance. Since Chuchak's credibility had taken a nosedive, Kaido abused him in vulgar language and got away with it. Kaido's mortification at the hands of Hir was forgotten. For him, it was a moment of glory.

The Art of Deception

Damodar knew that the pursuit of love was hazardous. The lovers were pitted against powerful forces. In general, the entire society felt scandalized at the violation of social norms by the lovers. In particular, the respective families and landed clans, remaining firmly committed to patriarchal principles, did not permit the youngsters to choose their partners. In these circumstances, Damodar empowered the lovers with the weapon of deception, which would lead them to union. Many a times, the lovers employed it to overcome patriarchal opposition. If they had not resorted to it, they would have no chance of survival and success. Hir was the first to make its effective use. She did not tell her mother about her meeting with Ranjha on the ferry. Instead, she stated that she had discovered a herdsman, who could be employed to graze their buffaloes. She did not know Ranjha's abilities in this regard. Yet, she fabricated a number of his qualities that were normally absent in a herdsman, particularly one who did not boast of any experience. Under his care, there would be plenty of rains and the grass would not dry. The buffaloes would not drop their calves and they would not be afflicted with the mouth and foot disease. Ranjha possessed these merits not because of his experience and efficiency. Rather, Hir attributed them to his grace (*barkat*). In fact, she introduced Ranjha to her mother as if he were a saint. Ranjha impressed the Siyals with his veterinary skills because

Hir, acting with ingenuity, passed on vital information to him and enabled him to pass the test.[59] Without these shrewd moves, Ranjha would not have been employed and love would have died a premature death. Not long after, Hir's parents deduced her covert role in the matter. They outmatched Hir with the same weapon. They deputed Kaido to unearth the reality. Kaido, wearing the garb of a mendicant, extracted a part of Ranjha's food (*choori*), which Hir brought for him to the moors.[60] The opponents of lovers could also adopt deception to suppress love.

In Damodar's narrative, the entry of Sehti raised the frequency of deception. Since she played a pivotal role in the Hir-Ranjha union, we need to focus on her. However, Damodar had decided to conceal crucial facts about this interesting woman. The reader could draw his inferences if some stray references were put together. In age, she was older than Hir and Ranjha. She was calm, wise and resourceful. Was she ever married? If yes, what happened to her husband and family? Where were her children if she ever became a mother? Perhaps, she left the village of her parents-in-law owing to unstated reasons. She might have been a widow, with or without any issue. If her husband was alive, she might have been turned out for failing to produce children or inability to adjust in the family. Though Damodar was silent on these matters, he has clarified that she lived on the edge of Rangpur Khera. Ali appeared to have assigned her a separate village for her independent maintenance. At the same time, she was provided with a house, which was located at some distance from the main Khera bungalow. Evidently, she also had a farmhouse, where she resided while supervising cultivation.[61] She alternated between these two houses depending on her responsibilities and needs. Hir and Ranjha treated her with respect, even addressing her as mother and queen. Her independence enabled her to acquire a lover in the person of Ramu Brahmin. The affair was a closely guarded secret. She did not meet him on her landholding, as the servants could see him. She found it safer to meet him at her house in Rangpur Khera.

The Kheras might have thought that two single women, apparently opposed to each other, formed an ideal living arrangement. They never imagined that the women would come together on a common platform. They discovered the compact between them when it was too late. To begin with, the Khera decision forced the two women to live under the same roof. Being practically strangers, they must have been formal and circumspect. With the passage of a few weeks, they realized that they were sailing in the same boat. On the one hand, they shared a common physical space and, on the other hand, endured the same affliction. They were ranged against the same patriarchal structure, which tended to distance them from their lovers. Sehti, endowed with age and sagacity, was quick to understand the commonality of their existence. She felt that Hir could assist her in pursuing her love for Ramu, provided she peeped into her heart and do her some favour. In spite of her best efforts, she could not make Hir reveal her secret. She had no choice but to employ deception (*fareb*) to reach the truth.

Sehti aimed at digging secrets out from Hir's heart and, assuming the role of a benefactor, made her a facilitator in her own pursuit of love. This marked the beginning of a new phase in Damodar's narrative wherein the main characters – Hir, Ranjha, Sehti and Ramu – consistently resorted to deception in order to break the stranglehold of the landed clans. Sehti would reveal her affair with Ramu to Hir, who would be encouraged to do the same. In fact, Sehti laid a trap and the unsuspecting Hir walked into it. She felt that Hir, in view of her pathological hatred for the Kheras, would never reveal anything to them. Sehti's love for Ramu went a long way in legitimizing Hir's love for Ranjha. Both affairs had the common consequence of undermining the socio-political position of the Kheras. Sehti remained absent for three days and, appearing on the fourth, pretended to be sick. Hir, feeling worried, asked the reason of her condition. Without waiting for a moment, Sehti replied that she was on the verge of death due to her separation from Ramu. Hir, anxious to see Ramu, secured a promise from Sehti. Hir was allowed to peep through the window when the lovers were locked in a sexual union. Following a single voyeuristic experience, Hir became Sehti's confidant and an emissary between the lovers. Since she could no longer keep Ranjha a secret, she revealed her love for him and sought Sehti's help in bringing him to Rangpur Khera.[62] It appeared that the two sisters-in-law struck a deal for mutual benefit. Neither of them would back out. Hir could not accuse Sehti of extracting her secret, because she also had Sehti's secret in her hands. It was in their interest to be faithful to each other.

Ramu, the lover of Sehti, performed the next act of deception. His task was both difficult and delicate. Conscious of this, the two sisters-in-law prepared him for the mission. Sehti advised Ramu to go all the way to Takht Hazara and, meeting Ranjha in secrecy, describe Hir's suffering to him. Hir was anxious to ensure that Ranjha trusted what Ramu told him. He was to narrate the Hir-Ranjha meeting in the boat at the ferry and their association with the landmarks of the moors of Jhang Siyal. He was to stress Hir's deep attachment to Ranjha, besides highlighting the pangs of her separation. Ramu played his role to perfection like an accomplished actor. On reaching Takht Hazara, he stayed with a Brahmin family. Concealing his real motive, he convinced his hosts that he was going to Kashmir for some work. More astutely, he extracted information about local agriculture and Mojam's sons. In particular, he learnt that Ranjha had become a mendicant. He stayed with the Siyals till Hir was unmarried and, following her marriage among the Kheras, he returned to the village. More difficult for Ramu was to meet Ranjha when nobody was around. He kept a close watch on the village common and, controlling his nerves, waited for the movement of people to stop. Speaking to Ranjha, he revealed his identity, conveyed Hir's message and reported her declining health. Ranjha asked Ramu to assure Hir of his arrival and left for Tilla Balnath.[63] Hereafter, Damodar did not say anything about Ramu. Of course, Ramu would have returned to Rangpur Khera and delivered Ranjha's message for Hir. Trustworthy and thoughtful, Ramu played a key role uniting the lovers. The Kheras could never discover the manner in which Hir contacted Ranjha. It remained a mystery. The deception worked in favour of the lovers.

Ranjha realized that it was extremely difficult to meet Hir. He had already earned the enmity of two powerful clans, the Siyals and Kheras. Now, he was required to pass through their territories without alerting them. If he assumed the garb of a Jogi and concealed his identity, he would be safe. For this purpose, he travelled north through the upper Chenhat Doab. Crossing the Jhelum, he penetrated the arid hills of the Salt Range and reached Tilla Balnath.

On his return, he walked south across the same terrain. Since his aim was clear, he overcame the obstacles of distance and fatigue. Sidh Bagai, the chief of the monastery, was reluctant to accede to Ranjha's request. The young man had lived in comfort, while the path of Jog was hazardous. Ranjha, in order to soften the mentor, made a truthful narration of his sad experiences including the exit from his home. At Jhang Siyal, he fell in love with Hir. Her marriage among the Kheras and a subsequent dispute induced him to seek Jog. Sidh Bagai, rejecting the opposition of his disciples, enrolled Ranjha as a Jogi. In view of Ranjha's real motive, the mentor placed Hir in his lappet and blessed his impending endeavour. His physical appearance underwent a sudden change. Wearing saffron robes, he smeared ash on his body and inserted large rings in his ears. Instead of going straight to Rangpur Khera, he went to Jhang Siyal so as to test the efficacy of his disguise. The girls, working in a millet field, were deceived. They were quite familiar with him, yet they could not recognize him. They thought that he was one of the mendicants, who often wandered across the countryside. Like them, he behaved in a strange manner. Rotating the beads of his rosary and pointing a finger towards the north, he did not utter a word in response to their querries. After a long suspense and guessing, Hassi recognized the famous herdsman of the Siyals and the lover of Hir. In contrast to the girls of Jhang Siyal, Sehti saw through the Jogi's guise at first sight. She also identified the key events of his life, which she had apparently learnt from Hir.[64]

Paradoxically, Hir was unable to recognize the Jogi, who was begging alms at her door. He received a handful of millets, but behaved in a peculiar way. He spilled the millets and, covering his face with a shawl, sat motionless. Speaking like an accomplished Jogi, he asked Hir to state her sickness, so that he could give her the medicine. Hir doubted the credentials of the Jogi, seeing a mismatch between his physical bearing and his saintly avocation. If he wished to cure her ailment, he should unite her with the herdsman. The Jogi, keen to prolong the conversation, asserted his genuineness as a Jogi, who had travelled from Bhutan to Narwar and Multan. For a moment, Hir suspected the Jogi to be Ranjha, but could not see through his covered face. The deadlock ended when Panjpir revealed the secret to Hir. The Jogi, failing to stretch Hir's predicament, stated his identity. The Jogi would no longer deceive Hir and Sehti, but would continue to beguile the rest of the society until the elopement uncovered the reality.

The two sisters-in-law smuggled Ranjha into Rangpur Khera through deception. With this success, they had achieved the first half of their task. From then onwards, they took up the second half. They created conditions in which Hir and Ranjha would stay as a couple and, then, elope to some unknown destination. The hazardous enterprise became achievable only with the escalation of deception. With Ramu out of the picture, three leading characters (Hir, Ranjha and Sehti) played new roles. Damodar, showing creative imagination, emplotted five interrelated episodes – a sham fight between Sehti and Hir, the furnishing of Hir's apartment, Hir's snakebite in a sesame field, a forty-day treatment of Hir from the Jogi and elopement of lovers from their cozy nest. A successful completion of one episode paved the way to the next. To begin with, the sisters-in-law had to show that they were opposed to each other and there was no understanding between them. To achieve this, they started a big fight. Sehti asserted that her father was a rich man, but unfortunately acquired a quarrelsome daughter-in-law. Hir argued that she had suffered abuse during the last thirty-five months. In accordance with a plan, the two women ensured that the wrangle spilled out to the neighbouring women and Khera household. Sehti tricked Ali with the request that Hir, having agreed to cohabit with Sahiba, could be given the goods brought in as dowry. Ali had no reason to doubt the fight and walked into the trap. Pouncing on the opportunity of retrieving the honour of the Kheras, he sent the goods ranging from blankets to buffaloes. Hir placed the goods in their respective spots and prepared for cohabitation. It was easy for the two women to push out the witless Sahiba because the stage, in reality, was being set to bring in the Jogi.[65]

Sehti formulated a plan and shared it with the lovers. Along with Hir, she went to a sesame field. Hir was pierced in her ankle with a thorn. As blood trickled out, a loud cry was raised that a cobra had bitten her. All villagers reached the site. Sehti, in command of the situation, asked Ali to summon the Jogi. Resorting to lies, she praised the Jogi as a renowned healer of snakebites. Ali, along with fellow *zamindars*, implored the Jogi to save Hir's life. Now, the Kheras had seen Ranjha during Hir's wedding and her journey to Rangpur Khera. If he was detected, the plan would collapse and conspirators exposed. Therefore, Sehti warned the villagers to approach the Jogi with great caution. He was an exalted spiritual exemplar with an ancient pedigree. Since he remained in a state of absorption, he did not show his face to anyone. He provided assistance only on his terms. The Jogi, on his part, kept turning his face away from the people's gaze and did not respond to their repeated entreaties. In a philosophical statement, he alluded to the transience of the world, vulnerability of living beings and intricacies of curative incantations. The Jogi examined Hir and, declaring that a crowned cobra had bitten her, prescribed a specific line of treatment.[66] His conditions were stipulated to allow the lovers to stay together for forty days in Sehti's house.[67] Since the villagers concurred with the conditions, there was no suspicion. The three conspirators succeeded in deceiving the entire populace of the locality, including 900 Khera clansmen, who were spread across eighty-four villages in the chiefdom of Ali.

Damodar has conceived the final act of deception in the form of a forty-day treatment of Hir. The Jogi, acting as an occultist, extracted poison from Hir's body through magical incantations. The treatment was a camouflage to the love of Hir and Ranjha, who had remained separate for nearly three years. Once again, Sehti became the master of the show. Under her benign care, the lovers ate rich food and enjoyed physical intimacy. After every eight days, the Khera household along with a sizeable group of villagers, came to inquire about the latest condition of Hir and her response to the Jogi's medical remedies. Every time, Sehti beguiled them with a new answer, which revolved around the strange behaviour of innumerable snakes. Owing to the increasing Khera pressure, Sehti and the lovers came under great strain. The lovers, fearful of detection, admitted that their honour was in Sehti's hands. Sehti claimed to have done everything within her means. She chided the lovers for wasting valuable opportunities in the moors of Jhang Siyal. They should have run away, crossing the Indus or climbing the mountains. Yet, it was not the time to repent. When two days remained for the deadline to end, the lovers made a breach in the wall and fled into the countryside. The inquisitive villagers were outraged. Sehti feigned ignorance of the whole affair. According to her fresh subterfuge, she had been lying unconscious for three days owing to the presence of snakes. Damodar has kept his readers in suspense regarding the great gamble. However, he was certain that the phase of deception terminated with the elopement.[68] Henceforth, he made the lovers explore other options to survive. First, he introduced the Nahars in his narrative and, then, brought the lovers to the Qazi's court. When the lovers did not attain any relief, they turned to the people of Kot Qabula and divine intervention, besides their own miraculous powers. Damodar's account has developed along these lines.

Ranjha was not the only lover to adopt Jog for the sake of his beloved. When Damodar was composing the story of Hir-Ranjha, the motif of Jogi had already entered the cultural landscape of the Indo-Gangetic plain. In the Awadhi Sifi romances, all princely lovers turned Jogis and embarked on the endeavour to unite with their respective sweethearts. What is surprising, the motif became important enough to find a place in the Persian chronicles. An outstanding example was recorded in the Afghan history of Shaikh Rizqullah Mushtaqi. During the reign of Bahlol Lodi (r. 1451-89), an Afghan plundered a village in the jurisdiction of Nimkhar near Qanauj. The attackers took away many villagers as prisoner including the daughter of a grocer. A keeper of buffaloes (*goban gaumesh*), who was in love with her, renounced his home. Turning a Jogi, he began searching for her in different places of north India. At Sirhind, he saw her as the wife of an Afghan. He begged for alms in the typical manner of Jogis (*awaz jogiana*). When the woman appeared with a handful of rice, the Jogi declared that he wanted to take her with him or die at the spot. The woman, out of modesty, declared that the Jogi was a scoundrel (*haram khwar*). The servants thrashed the Jogi and threw him on the street. After three days of misery, the Jogi began to work in the Afghan's stable and impressed the master with his dedication. He often entered the female quarters and spoke to the woman of his resolve. The woman declared that the man was a rogue (*daghabaz*), who would kidnap her. The Afghan retorted that this was not possible till she did not wish to run away. In due course, the man was promoted as manager of the household.

After two years, the Afghan joined an expedition to the east. In accordance with the directions of his master, the manager escorted the woman and, getting an opportunity, repeated his resolve. The Afghan, worried at the delay in his wife's arrival, suspected her abduction. He tied the manager to a tree and subjected him to blows of a whip. The woman complained that her husband had ignored her doubts about the manager. In an accident, the Afghan died of drinking sherbet that a snake had polluted. Before dying, he attacked the manager with a sword, but could not harm the suspect. The manager married the widow and the two lived happily thereafter. The lover, like Ranjha, became a Jogi in search of his beloved. In his quest, he grazed the mares of his master in the pasture. His beloved, unlike Hir, remained faithful to her Afghan husband and continued to snub her lover until the very end.[69]

Caricature of a Husband

Damodar has availed every opportunity of showing Sahiba in a poor light. When the Khera marriage party arrived in Chuchkana, Sahiba looked impressive in his ceremonial outfit. Exulting in his momentary glory, he could not anticipate the humiliation awaiting him. Following his wedding rite (*nikah*), he was brought into Hir's presence, so that the matrimony was consummated. Hir grabbed his nose and delivered a tight slap on his face. As his teeth were damaged and blood oozed out, his brain ceased to function. Hir turned her husband into a stranger, who had intruded into her privacy. Sahiba made a clumsy attempt to explain his entry. In his bewilderment, he created the impression as if Hir intended to hit Ranjha. If Hir was still angry with him, he would go out and search Ranjha for her. Though Hir was quick in expressing her remorse, she was bent on humiliating him to the maximum. Not only did she address him as brother, she also sent him to look for Ranjha.[70] This did not satisfy her insatiable desire to insult Sahiba. Hir saw the opportunity as soon as she reached Rangpur Khera along with the marriage party. In the presence of her mother-in-law and a large group of women, she declared that she would play the game of 'Ring in Buttermilk' only with Ranjha, who was her rightful husband. If Sahiba tried to assert himself, she would again smash his teeth. Nothing could be more ignominious for Sahiba.

Sehti was the sister of Sahiba, but she never supported him in his difficulties. Instead, she joined hands with Hir to disgrace him. Acting in accordance with a devious plan, she declared that Hir had agreed to cohabit with Sahiba. Her father Ali sent a number of household goods to Hir's apartment. When Sahiba arrived at the newly furnished space, he felt like a bridegroom coming to spend the first night with his bride. With henna on his hands, he nurtured strange desires in his mind. His deprivation of nearly three years was about to end. Unable to contain his excitement, he hoped that Hir would apologize for ignoring him in the past. The next moment, he fantasized becoming a father and rocking a child in his lap. His glorious illusions came to an abrupt end. As soon as Hir saw him, she leapt back as if she had seen a fearsome demon. Sehti spoke to her brother, who was more dazed than frustrated. He had made a mistake in coming there. He could come only when asked to do so. As for Hir, she never expected to see a stranger coming so close to her. His very sight was horrifying. He had polluted the place with his ominous presence. Hir stepped inside only after everything was washed clean.[71] Her reaction was not meant for Sehti, who knew her well. Hir made sure that the servants saw the development and carried the news to Sahiba, who would suffer the full blow of the latest round of abasement.

Damodar, in a rare attempt to be fair to Sahiba, presented him in a new incarnation. As the Kheras and Nahars escorted the lovers to Kot Qabula, Sahiba suddenly acquired confidence. His new-found belligerence would pull him out from a long misery. Numerous questions had been circulating in the air. Right under his nose, his wife had revived her affair with the herdsman and succeeded in eloping with him. His weakness was exposed as never before, while the reputation of his clan was in shambles. Sahiba became desperate to show his grit in front of everyone. He would answer all the questions and remove all doubts. He would take revenge from Hir for all the insults she had heaped on him. The firebrand Hir, being dragged to the Qazi's court in an unenviable state, became a soft target for a notorious nincompoop. Sahiba hurled a heap of invectives on Hir. She had employed a dirty trick to join the herdsman and run away with him like a thief. A keep of the herdsman, she openly engaged in fornication. Owing to her husband's curse, she would neither live nor die. In retaliation, Hir knocked Sahiba down with a vitriolic outburst. Declaring her submission to Ranjha, she cursed Sahiba in choicest pejoratives. Since he was wretched to the core, his face would be burnt. He was a useless person, who was kicked around in all directions. When God distributed love, he attained nothing. Forsaken by God, he did not get any response from Chuchak's daughter. Hir, ignoring the intervention of the Nahars, brought the Khera clan within the ambit of her verbal assault. In order to maximize the impact of her abuse, she declared Ranjha to be her rightful husband and perfect mentor since the earliest times. She hoped that the Kheras would be drenched in a rain of ashes.[72] Since these words were uttered in the presence of a large crowd, they did an irreparable damage to the Kheras. Sahiba must have repented for provoking Hir into doing something in which she remained unsurpassed. Damodar has built up a highly charged situation, wherein Sahiba was put to ridicule and Hir emerged on the top.

References to Akbar

Damodar has referred to Akbar nearly seventeen times. Though the Mughal emperor did not appear in person, he figured in the discussions among characters, particularly while engaging with local politics. At the beginning of our narrative, the Siyal chief Chuchak was seen as powerful enough to compete with Akbar. In the political vision of Chuchak's sons, the marriage of their sister Hir with Akbar would entrust them with the assessment of land tax and, as a consequence, the position of the Siyals would be strengthened. Here, the Siyals accepted Akbar's sovereignty, which was reflected in the local administrative apparatus. However, the landed clans felt an increasing pressure from the Mughal State. Hir, while exercising authority as the Siyal chief, felt strong enough to deal with the

Sambhals. Only if Akbar's offspring led an attack, she would bring her brothers into the battlefield. This statement implied that the Mughal polity was penetrating the tract along the Chenab. Watching the conduct of Hir as the Siyal chief, some people perceived her authority in exaggerated terms. Luddan stated that Hir, having brought the four rivers under her control, had deprived the Mughals of their power and did not fear Akbar. Luddan meant to say that the Siyal chief, in terms of military resources, was stronger than Akbar. Kundi, while dismissing reports of Hir's affair, asked the local women to feel agitated only if Akbar attacked the Siyal chiefdom. Similarly, Chuchak was worried more about Hir's alleged affair than Akbar's intrusion in his domain. Kaido regarded Hir as a greater terror than the Mughals. The Nahar chief, while granting asylum to Hir and Ranjha, declared that he would not surrender them even if Akbar marched against him.[73] Damodar measured the power of the landed chiefs with reference to Akbar. The poet could not ignore the contemporary political realities that underscored Akbar's emergence as a powerful political entity in Panjab.

Hir, during her trial at Kot Qabula, raised doubts about the Qazi's professional competence and ability to understand love. She argued that Akbar's government, being quite strong, had granted him the judgeship.[74] He would be accountable to the Mughal State for his dispensation of justice. Hir's statement aimed at deflating a power-drunk functionary, who was incompetent and dishonest. The Qazi, unnerved at the reference to Akbar,[75] tried to turn the tables on Hir. She should be ashamed of her connection with Ranjha, particularly because her father and father-in-law were associated with Akbar.[76] The people of Kot Qabula turned their ire against the local administration comprising the governor, judge and jurist. The destruction of the town was a serious matter. Akbar was likely to question the local functionaries, who would not be able to explain their conduct and, therefore, liable to punishment.[77]All three stakeholders – defendants, prosecutors and people – saw Akbar in different ways.

Even at the end of his narrative, Damodar could not afford to overlook Akbar. The lovers were finally united at a time when the kingship (*patshahi*) of Akbar was on the ascendant.[78] It was acknowledged that Akbar had established strong foundations in western Panjab. This conformed to the historical facts as recorded in the official chronicles as well as the Panjabi folklore. Akbar had won over the Gakhhar chiefs, who became the strongest supporters of the Mughal State. In central Panjab, the Bhatti chiefs refused to accept the land revenue system of the Mughals. So did the Baloch chiefs of Multan. In north-east Panjab, the hill chiefdoms frequently rose up against Akbar. Between Lahore and Multan, the Jat highwaymen looted the travellers, indicating a weak Mughal control. In the Sufi biographies (*Maqamat-i Daudi*, *Haqiqat ul-Fuqra* and *Tazkira Pir Hassu Teli*), Akbar was shown in a poor light.

Panjpir and Black Warriors

Since the times of Shaikh Ali bin Usman Hujweri (d. 1072), Islamic spirituality had been making a steady progress in Panjab. In particular, the Chishtis and Suhrawardis had struck deep roots in central Panjab. It was not surprising that Panjpir, a quintet of saints, should figure in Damodar's narrative as protectors of the protagonists. While crossing the Chenab in a boat, they were attracted to the melody of Raga Bambiha, which emerged from Ranjha's flute.[79] In a meeting with Ranjha, they listened to his tale of woes, including the injustice at the hands of his brothers and his current state of homelessness. They also listened to Raga Lalit on the flute.[80] Feeling pleased, each of the five saints conferred a unstated boon on Ranjha. More importantly, they tied Hir to his lappet. At the same time, they appeared before Hir in a dream and informed her that they had tied Ranjha to her lappet. They warned her against accepting anyone other than Ranjha. They clarified that it was God's will, which had ordained the development of this love. By conveying the tidings, they were merely serving as messengers and intermediaries. In order to seal the matter, they offered milk to Hir. Precisely at this moment, Ranjha attained spiritual enlightenment and began to see the future in the present. Ranjha, dedicating himself to Panjpir, attained his ideal (*var*) from them.[81]

The above episode occurred simultaneously at two different

sites. Only two human beings, Hir and Ranjha, were privy to it. It was their esoteric experience. Both had a personal interaction with Panjpir. They had never anticipated it. It was a divine act. It showed that the love of Hir-Ranjha did not begin due to human volition. Even before the two met in dramatic circumstances on the boat and fell in love, Panjpir conveyed the divine will to them. The context was the suffering of Ranjha, though Hir was at the top of the world, as she exercised the powers of her father, the Siyal chief. Ranjha's music had prepared the ground for the miraculous appearance of Panjpir. By this time, Ranjha had voluntarily withdrawn from his caste and, renouncing the worldly life, bore numerous privations that were akin to the austerities of the Sufis. His spiritual journey began as soon as he abandoned kinship, property and marriage. His strong spiritual inclination manifested in music, which had a significant place in the Indic and Islamic spiritual traditions.

The second appearance of Panjpir took place when Ranjha was in a crisis. Hir, married against her strong defiance, was carried away to Rangpur Khera. Ranjha, forced to accompany the Khera marriage party with a drum on his head, suffered torture at the hands of the Kheras. His condition became so pathetic that he wanted the Kheras to kill him. While crying incessantly, he remembered Panjpir and presented his complaint. He had never asked for Hir. They had themselves bestowed her on him and, thereafter, inflicted a calamity (*qehar*) on him. At the outset, they had enabled him to fall in love with Hir. He would bring the buffaloes to the moors and escort them back. Many times, he played on the flute, winning the affection of wild animals. Hir would come to meet him with a packet of food. They experienced the bliss of love, free from all worries and cares. Thereafter, Panjpir inflicted a calamity on him, burying him under the weight of physical and mental persecution. He was crying due to sorrow, despair and self-pity. In these dismal circumstances, Panjpir appeared before him and explained the cause of his ordeal. He need not cry at his difficulties, as they had deliberately heaped this agony on him. Though his pain had reached its upper limit, he ought to comprehend its rationale. Without this pain, he would not have become illumined (*raushan*).[82] They had chalked out a high target for him. Ultimately, he was bound to climb to the summit of spirituality. The obstacles, admittedly excessive in his case, could not dishearten him. After all, they had assumed the responsibility of protecting his life. He must move on. It might be recalled that Ranjha never enrolled himself in a Sufi lineage. Nor did he study the scriptures. In his life, suffering and music became a substitute for conventional Sufi practices. Of course, he sat in contemplation at midnight in the moors and, thus, unconsciously prepared himself for a formal initiation in Jog.

Though Hir too was in acute distress, she did not invoke Panjpir. Her mind was occupied in ruminating over the betrayal of Siyals, her opposition to the Kheras and the misery of Ranjha. However, Panjpir appeared before her after a long gap of thirty five months. During this period, she had her own share of problems. First, she distanced herself from Sahiba, repudiating her marriage. Second, she secured the support of Sehti and, sending Ramu as an emissary to Ranjha, conveyed the state of her mind. As a result, Ranjha went to Tilla Balnath and, entering the path of Jog, came to Rangpur Khera as a Jogi. Hir, reduced to a physical and mental wreck, had a long conversation with the Jogi. Since she did not discern his real identity, she raised many doubts about his credentials. Such a state could be fatal to her. At this critical moment, Panjpir arrived on the scene and, without being seen, pulled Hir out of a stupor. They revealed to her that the Jogi was none other than Ranjha. She must get up and meet him. But for this intervention of Panjpir, Hir would have failed to recognize Ranjha.[83] Damodar brought in Panjpir to break the stalemate, which might have continued without end. Since this was a sacred moment for the lovers, it was proper for Panjpir to appear without invocation and, thus, prepare the ground for their union. In the eyes of Damodar, the union was both physical and spiritual. The lines between sexuality and spirituality collapsed. This meeting took place under the umbrella of Panjpir, who represented the five prominent Sufis of Panjab.

Damodar, in his narrative, has introduced the mysterious black warriors when the lovers faced a violent death. The black warriors punished the groups of murderers, who conspired to kill the lovers for different reasons. Like Panjpir, the black warriors appeared on their own. Damodar has shown that the lovers were under the protective guardianship of God. In spite of their position as the light of spiritual excellence (*azmat ki rushnai*), they were involved in dire situations. Panjpir, being saints, could not provide any help in potentially violent exigencies. However, their role could not be discounted. Perhaps they were instrumental in deploying the black warriors. Alternatively, Panjpir might be assuming the guise of black warriors to do a specific task, which they could not do as saints. We are reminded of such an episode from the early thirteenth century.[84]

The black warriors saved the life of Ranjha from fellow herdsmen. While grazing buffaloes on the Chenab, his innovative methods earned praise from the Siyals. The envious herdsmen, feeling that Ranjha had snatched their livelihood, conspired to kill him at midnight. Forming a gang armed with double-edged swords, they rushed to do the evil deed. A large number of warriors, wearing black clothes and riding black horses, appeared from nowhere. As soon as they charged, the herdsmen took to flight. Some lost their lives, while others had broken limbs. The surviving herdsmen narrated their fate to Chuchak, who was convinced that Ranjha was divinely blessed and commanded miraculous powers.[85] On the eve of Hir's marriage, her brothers and maternal uncles conspired to kill Hir at midnight. However, they could not put their nefarious design into practice, as the black warriors stood guard around Hir. As they charged with swords, the conspirators fell on the ground and their jaws were locked. Hir's mother Kundi, who also wanted to get rid of her daughter, wailed at the fate of the victims and gave up her bad intention.[86] Out of fear, no one dared to probe the role of the mysterious saviours. The black warriors appeared again in the last scene of Damodar's narrative. At this moment, there was no fear of violence. The lovers, having overwhelmed the patriarchal forces, were leaving Kot Qabula for the south. Five black warriors, emerging from nowhere, blessed Hir. They revealed that she would not have become enlightened (*raushan*) without undergoing the recent suffering. Without uttering another word, they vanished into thin air.[87] As could be recalled, Panjpir had made a similar revelation to Ranjha when he endured torture at the hands of the Kheras.

Landed Clans and the Code of Chivalry

In an earlier section, we have seen a Siyal-Sambhal conflict long before the protagonists fell in love. Subsequently, the Siyals managed to prevent a confrontation with the Kheras over Hir's rejection of Sahiba, while the Ranjhas succeeded in effecting a reconciliation with the Waraichs. When the lovers eloped from Rangpur Khera, an inter-clan clash flared up. Now, the lovers were exposed to the wrath of the Kheras. The clan would catch hold of them and kill them, reminiscent of the fate of Mirza-Sahiba.[88] Elopement was an assault on the honour of the Kheras. The retinue of the clan, riding horses and wearing arms, was galvanized into action. The move conformed to Sehti's statement to the effect that her plan had put at stake the honour of 900 turbans. She meant to say that 900 Khera men, if challenged, would fight for the honour of the clan.[89] They faced no obstacle in their own domain. Once they entered the territory of the Nahars, they were treated as intruders. In the ensuing battle, both sides suffered casualties. But for the intervention of the Syeds of Rajoa, there would have been more bloodshed. As the inter-clan conflict swept the countryside, the state was entirely absent.

Damodar's account of the encounter between the lovers and the Nahar chief was significant. On the one hand, it revealed the nature of relation between the lovers and, on the other hand, uncovered the code of chivalry as the landed clans practised it. In the medieval times, a clan chief took a distressed person in his protection through a specific procedure, which evolved through tradition. Such a person was expected to reveal his identity and the circumstances of his distress. In our case, the lovers stood before the Nahars in a humble posture, putting shawls around their necks. It was not easy for them to reveal their identity. Since they had snapped their ties with the clan-based society, they were practically outcastes. They thought it prudent to speak the truth and, thus, avoid any complications. Hir stated that she was the daughter of Chuchak from Jhang Siyal. Her husband Ranjha accompanied her. Chuchak forcibly married her to the Khera. In despair, she escaped with her husband, while the Khera chief mobilized an army. Since she was surrounded in difficulties, she came into the protection of the Nahars. Ranjha, uttering similar words, declared that he was Dhido, the son of Mojam, hailing from Takht Hazara. He refrained from referring to his brothers, but blamed himself for the major mistakes of his life. Since he could not uphold the honour of his parents, he came to be known as the herdsman. He had devoted his life to Hir and, in the process, chose the path of mendicancy. As he walked away with his rightful wife, the Khera chief chased them with an army. He and his wife sought the asylum of Nahars, who were the lords of the land.[90] Ranjha, in contrast to Hir, stood out for his humility and self-depreciation.

Until then, only half of the procedure had been followed. The response of the Nahar chief, prompt in action and sparing in words, completed it. The Nahars were pleased to take the fugitives in their protection, assuming full responsibility of their safety. They did not surrender even the dogs in their custody. They were inclined towards the fugitives, who were the offspring of landed elite. They would not surrender them even if Akbar marched at the head of the Mughal army.[91] This statement, though rhetorical in tone, reflected the code of chivalry, which the landed clans tended to normalize in their functions. It added to their prestige and accorded legitimacy to their use of violence. The Nahar chief, while offering asylum, to the fugitives, evaded any reference to the Kheras, who were rushing in hot pursuit. He was equally dismissive of the Mughal emperor. It must be noted that the provision of asylum often led to inter-clan warfare. In the beginning of Damodar's narrative, we encounter its first example. When the Siyals provided asylum to the boatman Luddan, it led to an armed conflict between the Siyals and Sambhals. Damodar, in his own times, must have seen the tussle between the landed clans and the local representatives of the Mughal State (officers holding revenue assignments and Muslim theologians enjoying land grants). Damodar might have been familiar with the exploits of Dulla Bhatti, the rebellious *zamindar* of Sandal Bar (Rachna Doab) who, like his father and grandfather, died fighting against the Mughal State. Damodar, while describing the Nahar-Khera conflict, identified the following five sticking points.

1. At the outset, the Kheras confronted the Nahars, who were harvesting their crop of lentils. The Kheras asked for the

whereabouts of the Jogi and a woman. The Nahars, owing to the prevailing code of chivalry, denied any knowledge about the two persons. The Kheras, suspicious of the Nahars, issued a threat. The Nahars, incensed at the threat, became audacious. They admitted giving protection to the fugitives, without paying attention to the armed strength of the Khera contingent. In the inevitable conflict, fourteen Kheras and eight Nahars were killed.[92] With the arrival of reinforcements, the violence was likely to escalate.

2. The warring clans, while speaking to the Syeds of Rajoa, took opposite positions on the lovers. According to the Kheras, they had brought Hir as a legally wedded bride, without caring for the rumours of her affair. In pursuance of a conspiracy, she pretended to be bitten by a snake. Ranjha, disguised as a Jogi, eloped with her after breaking the wall. The Kheras were justified in chasing them so that they were brought back. The Nahars, disrupting their rightful endeavour, were not entitled to give protection to the culprits. On the other hand, the Nahars justified their action on the basis of tradition. For them, the fugitives were complete strangers and voluntarily came into their protection. At stake was the honour of their clan and, for its assertion, they had sacrificed the lives of their young men.[93] The Nahars drew a distinction between the original dispute and the resultant protection. They admitted their absence in the first part, but asserted their presence in the second, wherein they claimed to have followed social convention based on chivalry.
3. The two clans, following intervention of the Syeds of Rajoa, felt embarrassed at their conduct and became cordial towards each other. The Nahars, who had adopted a high moral ground, again showed their chivalry. Going out of their way, they provided the Kheras with food and accommodation. The bonhomie was short lived. A fresh dispute irrupted on the marital status of the fugitives. The Nahars had lodged them in an isolated house. The Kheras opposed the move because, in their eyes, Hir was their daughter-in-law and the Jogi was an old thief who had been chasing her for long. Bringing two unrelated persons together in the female quarter (*zenana*) amounted to supporting an illicit

relationship. The response of the Nahars was simple and factual. When they met the fugitives, they had their arms around each other. Since they were together, it was improper to separate them. The Nahars did not care if the two were married or not.[94]

4. Dust had not settled on the dispute when the Kheras were entangled in another problem. Here, Damodar has drawn our attention to the Nahar girls, who came out in support of the lovers. They were not only captivated by the beauty of Hir and Ranjha, they also exclaimed that they were most suited for each other. They observed that the relation had a divine sanction. Instead of stopping at the complements, the girls turned their ire against the Kheras. They alleged that the Kheras, by chasing the lovers with an armed brigade, had wrought a big calamity. The Kheras, thus cornered, were helpless. They could neither stop the verbal assault of the Nahar girls nor enter into a debate with them. Tired of the sarcastic monologues, the Kheras were unable to digest their food. Nor could they sleep at night. When they arose in the morning, they were suffering from a stomachache.[95] Nothing went in their favour. Perhaps, destiny had inscribed a terrible fate for them.
5. Just as the clans were about to depart for Kot Qabula, a fresh quarrel broke out between them. The Kheras were surprised that the Nahars were escorting the fugitives. The Kheras, thinking that the protection was over, objected to the intention of the Nahars. The Nahars argued that it was not safe to leave the fugitives in the hands of the Kheras. In view of the rising bitterness in the mind of the Kheras, it was feared that they would kill the fugitives on the way. For the Nahars, the responsibility of protection was still in operation. They were bound to guard the fugitives until they were produced before the legal authorities. Only after the delivery of the judgement, the court would grant Hir to the person who, according to the Shariat, was her lawful husband.[96] The plea of the Kheras was unceremoniously rejected and, at the same time, they were suspected of murderous intentions. They had repeatedly failed to counter the Nahars. These developments enabled Damodar to achieve his basic aim of portraying the Kheras in poor light.

The convoy reached Kot Qabula in the evening. The clans maintained peace in the jurisdiction of the legal apparatus. They spent the night in a compound of the court. For different reasons, they made a circle around the fugitives. The Nahars, having no stake in the legal proceedings, wished to protect them until they appeared before the Qazi. The Kheras made sure that the fugitives did not give them a slip, as they had done at Rangpur Khera.[97] The Nahars, having occupied a crucial space in Damodar's narrative from the elopement of the lovers to their prosecution in the court at Kot Qabula, made a sudden exit. In fact, Damodar could not have made them a party in the legal suit. The dispute was essentially between the Kheras and the lovers. The Nahar trail of chivalry paved the way for the decisive defeat of the Kheras and ultimate union of the lovers. This was how Damodar designed the plot of his narrative.

Divine Intervention Supersedes the Law

In the climax of his narrative, Damodar has combined three factors – divine intervention, spiritual power of the lovers and the public protest – resulting in the defeat of the contemporary legal apparatus. The Qazi, following a specific strategy, subjected Hir to a long interrogation. In his opening remarks, he praised Hir for her qualities. He had a lot of consideration for her distinguished social background. Her elders, Chuchak and Ali, were mighty landed chiefs who were associated with Akbar. Her marriage with Sahiba was valid because it had been conducted with the stipulated rites. In the eyes of the Shariat, her relation with Ranjha was illicit and, for this crime, her nose and ears would be slashed. Ranjha was an old thief who was guilty of breaching the wall. Hir must accept that she was the daughter-in-law of the Kheras. Hir, in her defence, was forthright and argumentative. Questioning the legal acumen of the Qazi, she rejected her marriage with Sahiba and asserted the legitimacy of her love for Ranjha. The Qazi was incapable of understanding the mysteries of love, as his knowledge was poor and integrity doubtful. The story of her love was beyond description. It was as old as the creation of universe, which had no witnesses. She was in love since she was a suckling baby. She did not care a bit about the power of the Siyals and Kheras. During the last thirty-five months, she did not receive even the minimal maintenance from the Kheras. Nor did she allow Sahiba to establish conjugal ties with her. Her love for Ranjha was known to the whole world, though there was no formal wedding ceremony. For his sake, she was willing to lose her caste and slip alive into the grave.[98]

The Qazi, while interrogating Ranjha, abused him in foul language and ridiculed his conversion to Jog. Ranjha, true to his sobriety and gentleness, expressed his disillusionment with the legal system. In his view, only a person conversant with love could comprehend the lover's way of life. The story of their love was quite complex. If the defendants tried to explain it, they were unfairly silenced. Ranjha, like Hir, believed that love was beyond the jurisdiction of the courts. The Qazi ordered Ranjha to be whipped. Hir held Ranjha to her chest and blocked the blows on his body. By doing so, she disrupted the operation of law. The defence of lovers threw the Qazi into confusion, so that he was unable to pronounce a judgement. At this moment, Awwal Fatta made a decisive intervention. Damodar did not tell us who this man was. His terse statement indicated that he was the executive head (*hakim*) of the local administration. He reprimanded the Qazi for shaming his office. Since the Qazi was conversant with the facts of the case, there was no need to summon any witness. He ordered that Hir be restored to the Kheras. This was instantly done. The clansmen subjected Hir to a severe beating, covering her with blood.[99] Undaunted, she seized the opportunity of castigating Ali who, in her view, was not a landed chief but an uncouth Jat. She held that the Kheras were too weak to punish her. Ranjha, owing to his spiritual power, had willed her punishment. She bore the physical pain with joy because it had flowed to her from Ranjha. She warned the Kheras that Ranjha, endowed with supernatural abilities, would avenge all atrocities.[100]

While the lovers were undergoing the ordeal, a fire broke out at the gates of Kot Qabula and spread to its interior. The people rushed out of their houses in panic. They tried to douse the flames with water but to no avail. They attributed the fire to the miscarriage of justice. The entire bureaucracy had failed in its duty. Raja Adli, having taken bribes, was absent from the scene. The people, in their desperation, cornered the Qazi and governor, who could not escape their responsibility. They were answerable to the people as well as Akbar. The Qazi had wrought a big calamity. Hir rightfully belonged to the Jogi. The Qazi gave her to the Kheras and, thus, buried the shoot of love in its infancy.[101] The Jogi remained detached, but his appeal to the divine forces engulfed the town in fire. Since the situation was volatile, the Qazi was constrained to bow before the popular sentiment. He was already demoralized at the hands of Hir's verbal onslaught. He faced a series of interrelated problems – to undo the verdict, to extinguish the fire, to save himself from the people's wrath, to prevent the news from reaching Akbar, to evade his possible dismissal from service and defend his personal dignity. In these disturbed conditions, the local officers might have decided to take remedial measures. The Qazi, without admitting his mistake, announced the modification of the original judgement, which was made on the basis of what became manifest (*zahir ditha*).[102] The hidden mysteries (*batin baat*), unknown to human beings, were bound to be considered. Hir would belong to the person who extinguished the fire. At the same time, an armed contingent was sent to bring the Kheras back. It was noteworthy that the Qazi had merely amended his verdict, but did not reverse it. Accordingly, Hir was withdrawn from the Kheras, but she was not handed to the Jogi. The Qazi seemed to accept the people's view that the Jogi's appeal had ignited the fire and, as a corollary, the Jogi was empowered to put it out. In other words, the Jogi was required to clear a test. If he succeeded, Hir would be his.[103]

Damodar aimed at proving that the Jogi and Hir possessed spiritual powers. Owing to the purity of their love and three years of suffering, they were elevated to the level of saints. This was manifested in the manner they extinguished the fire in three stages. First, the Jogi's miraculous ability made a passage through the fire, so that the army marched out of Kot Qabula to haul the Kheras back.[104] When it returned with the Kheras, the fire blocked its path. At its request, Hir extinguished the fire and enabled the troops to pass through. The fire still raged in the town as the protagonists had only made safe passages for the army. At the people's request, the Jogi stood up like a supplicant and, appealing to the saints, suppressed the fire. The people, out of devotion and gratitude, fell at the Jogi's feet. The Qazi and Mufti bowed before the Jogi and, implementing the amended order, restored Hir to him as his rightful wife. The inhabitants invited the lovers to settle in the town and offered to build a house for them. The lovers, recognized socially and morally as man and wife, blessed the people and left for the south. Damodar, while describing these events, has not ignored the Kheras. The clansmen were shocked at the amended verdict and, in their acute embarrassment, wished to slip away quietly. The people of Kot Qabula did not allow the Kheras to flee from the site. On insistent public demand, the Kheras were soundly beaten and unceremoniously expelled from the town.[105] Damodar derived immense pleasure while describing the humiliation of all opponents of the lovers, particularly the Kheras and law officers.

The lovers, despite their triumphant union, did not feel safe in western Panjab. The landed clans, particularly the Kheras and possibly the Siyals, would not rest until they had killed the fugitives. Before being a soft target of angry opponents, they sought a peaceful future in a self-chosen exile. History was replete with examples of great individuals, who undertook long travels for different purposes. Sometimes, they settled in new places far from their homes. Gautam Buddha was born in Kapilvastu (Nepal) but travelled across the Gangetic plain in search of knowledge. Prophet Muhammad migrated from Mecca to Madina to evade severe opposition. Ali bin Usman Hujweri and Muinuddin Chishti, both natives of Afghanistan, made new homes in Lahore and Ajmer respectively. Bahauddin Zakariya, born at Kot Aror near Multan, attained his spiritual mandate in Baghdad. Baba Farid, born at Kahtwal near Multan, studied in Delhi and, after staying for two decades in Hansi, settled in Ajodhan. Ibn Battuta, crossing Africa and Asia, arrived in India and spent a decade in this country. Syed Jalaluddin Bokhari spent seven years in different parts of central Islamic lands before returning to head the Suhrawardi hospice in Uch. According to Sikh tradition, Guru Nanak undertook long travels (*udasis*) to Mount Sumeru, Mansarovar, Kamrup, Jagannath Puri, Lanka, Mecca and Baghdad. Miyan Mir, born in Siwistan, shifted to Lahore for higher studies in his youth and spent the rest of his life in this city.

Damodar knew that the spiritual credentials of the lovers would be strengthened if they abandoned their domicile on the Chenab and embarked on a mysterious journey.

In the conclusion of his narrative, Damodar has raised some crucial points. In his view, he had described the story of Hir, not that of Ranjha who had been lying low throughout. The poet was familiar with several love tales that were recalled across the continents and centuries. The story of Hir was unique, as it had no parallel. There was a strong reason for this excellence. The lovers, having fallen in love, assumed a herculean task. Through the purity and steadfastness of their relation, they brought their love to perfect fruition (*jeyon chayi teyon nibhai*). As a result, their story did not remain confined to the environs of the Chenab. Instead, it had spread to the three spheres (*trey loi*) of the heaven, earth and underworld.[106] This claim of Damodar was quite modest.

NOTES

1. The Gulatis were included among the Aroras, who were traders par excellence of the Jatki-speaking or south-western Panjab, i.e. lower valleys of the five rivers. Higher up the river courses, they shared their position with the Khatris. More than half of Aroras of Panjab dwelt in Multan and Derajat divisions. Regarded as inferior to the Khatris and Baniyas, they were commonly dubbed as Kirar, a word synonymous with coward. They were active, enterprising, industrious and thrifty. Though often engaged in artisanal crafts, they were admirable cultivators. In the lower Chenab, their large proportion was entirely agricultural. Claiming a Khatri origin, the Aroras held that the persecution of Parshuram forced them to disperse in north and south. Their three major divisions (Uttaradhi, Dakhana and Dhara) were associated with territories. The constituent clans, enormous in numbers, followed different customs of matrimonial alliances and even clothing of women. Denzil Ibbetson, *Panjab Castes*, pp. 151-2.
2. Damodar, Stanza no. 963, p. 222.
3. Ibid., pp. 3-4.
4. This section, with unnumbered stanzas, has been given separately from the main text. Its first half has recorded some new facts. In it, Damodar has described the circumstances in which he arrived in Jhang Siyal and, impressed with the ways of the Siyals and assurance

of Chuchak, set up a shop. The substance of the second has been repeated in four stanzas immediately after the prologue (*manglachar*). Here, Damodar has praised the prosperity of the Siyal domain along with the qualities of Chuchak and his sons. He has also noted the birth of Hir when her mother was quite old, besides the assignment of the infant to nurses. This repetition has raised doubts about the authenticity of the introductory section, which might have been a later interpolation.

5. Damodar, Stanza nos. 144-5, p. 97.
6. Ibid., Stanza no. 491, p. 148.
7. Ibid., Stanza no. 871, p. 207.
8. Ibid., Stanza no. 900, p. 211.
9. Ibid., Stanza no. 962, p. 221.
10. Maulavi Nur Muhammad, *Tarikh-i Jhang Siyal*, Meerut: Matba Ahmadi, 1863, pp. 5-14.
11. Ibid., pp. 31-43.
12. The *zamindari* right provided its possessor with income, which varied in name, magnitude and source. It existed in the form of certain imposts that the *zamindars* levied on the peasants over and above the land revenue assessments. In Awadh, the claim (*satarahi*) amounted to 10 *sers* of crop per *bigha* along with a copper coin (*dam*). Apart from exclusive use of local assets (orchards, tanks, wells and trees), he charged cesses on crafts, houses, marriages, births, water and forest products, besides unpaid labour from menial castes. As remuneration for collecting taxes from the cultivators, he was entitled to an allowance (*nankar*), which varied from 5 to 10 per cent of land revenue. Irfan Habib, *The Agrarian System of Mughal India 1556-1707*, 2nd rev. edn., New Delhi: Oxford University Press, 1999, pp. 179-87.
13. In the early sixteenth century, ethnically diverse warrior lineages ruled the peasantry. The lineage chiefs dominated the subdistricts (*parganahs*) that were miniature kingdoms encompassing twenty to two hundred villages. These were the primary building blocks of political control in Indian rural society. The chiefs played a key role in organizing, financing and leading peasant cultivators in clearing the jungles and settling villages. The chief's residence, located in a town of the subdistrict, was protected by jungle, ditches and mud walls. The chief held a miniature court in rustic aristocratic style. He also maintained armouries, treasuries and lineage temples. His armed retinue comprised kinsmen, paid retainers and slaves. He cultivated private holdings using tenants and labourers. In addition to tax

exemption on these lands, he levied cesses on peasants, craftsmen and merchants. Within traditional limits, he demanded forced labour from lesser castes. John F. Richards, *The Mughal Empire*, New Delhi: Cambridge University Press, rpt., 2007, pp. 79-80.

14. Damodar, Stanza nos. 6-10, pp. 77-8.
15. Ibid., Stanza nos. 10-13, pp. 78-9.
16. Ibid., Stanza nos. 14-30, pp. 79-81.
17. Ibid., Stanza nos. 31-5, pp. 81-2.
18. Ibid., Stanza nos. 124-30, pp. 94-5.
19. Ibid., Stanza nos. 560-6, pp. 158-9.
20. Ibid., Stanza nos. 567-71, pp. 159-60.
21. Ibid., Stanza nos. 574-95, pp. 160-4.
22. Ibid., Stanza nos. 123-43, pp. 94-7.
23. Ibid., Stanza nos. 153-71, pp. 98-101.
24. Ibid., Stanza nos. 172-80, pp. 101-2.
25. Ibid., Stanza nos. 188-211, pp. 103-7.
26. Satish Chandra, 'Structure of Village Society in Northern India: The Khud Kasht and Pahi Kasht', in *Essays on Medieval Indian History*, New Delhi: Oxford University Press, 2003, pp. 168-84.
27. Damodar, Stanza nos. 235-55, pp. 110-13.
28. In the pre-Mughal times, the contemporary evidence points to large areas of wasteland, including fallow and forest. It meant that there was no shortage of pasturage for cattle. Firoz Shah Tughluq (r. 1351-88) established the city of Hissar Firoza on the land of two villages, Laras Buzurg and Laras Khurd. The former had fifty cattle pens (*kharaks*) and the latter forty. According to an Arabic work (*Masalik ul-Absar*) pertaining to the fourteenth century, the cattle were innumerable and sold at low prices. The large number of cattle might explain the fact that grain was principally transported on the backs of bullocks, not bullock carts. The manufacture and sale of clarified butter (*ghi*) was an important and profitable trade. A seller of clarified butter, based in a village of Ajodhan (Pakpattan) in Panjab, claimed that he had resources enough to buy forty or fifty slave girls. Tapan Raychaudhuri and Irfan Habib, ed., *The Cambridge Economic History of India*, vol. I: *c.1200 – c.1750*, New Delhi: Orient Longman, rpt., 1982, p. 52.
29. Damodar, Stanza nos. 230-1, p. 109.
30. Ibid., Stanza nos. 36-9, p. 82.
31. Ibid., Stanza nos. 51-62, pp. 84-5.
32. Ibid., Stanza nos. 69-105, pp. 86-92.
33. Ibid., Stanza nos. 207-14, pp. 106-7.

34. Ibid., Stanza nos. 222-6, pp. 108-9.
35. Ibid., Stanza nos. 227-9, p. 109.
36. Ibid., Stanza nos. 280-2, p. 117.
37. Ibid., Stanza nos. 299-301, pp. 119-20.
38. Ibid., Stanza nos. 314-35, pp. 123-5.
39. Ibid., Stanza nos. 352-79, pp. 127-32.
40. Ibid., Stanza nos. 392-401, pp. 134-5.
41. Ibid., Stanza nos. 408-16, pp. 136-7.
42. Ibid., Stanza nos. 431-41, pp. 139-41.
43. Ibid., Stanza nos. 442-52, pp. 141-2.
44. Ibid., Stanza nos. 497-502, pp. 149-50.
45. Ibid., Stanza nos. 519-24, pp. 152-3.
46. Jamal J. Elias, 'Female and Feminine in Islamic Mysticism', in *Critical Concepts in Islamic Studies*, vol. I, ed. Ridgeon Lloyd, London & New York, Routledge, 2008, pp. 298-302.
47. Amir Hasan Sijzi, *Fawaid ul-Fuad*, pp. 354-5, Amir Khurd, *Siyar ul-Auliya*, p. 191; Abdul Haq Muhaddis Dehalvi, *Akhbar ul-Akhyar*, Urdu tr. Subhan Mahmud and Muhammad Fazil, Delhi: Noor Publishing House, 1990, pp. 582-8.
48. Damodar, Stanza nos. 153-209, pp. 98-106.
49. The flute, an ancient wind instrument, figures in the Vedas, Buddhist paintings and Krishna's life. Made of seasoned and hollow bamboo tube, it has six holes in a straight line and a hole at the bottom end. The blowing hole, bigger than the others, is located at the upper end. Close to it is a wooden piece or cork, which diverts the blown air towards the holes and converts it into sound. The pitch of the flute is connected to its length and width. Longer the flute, lower the pitch. A thick thread around the flute prevents cracks due to fluctuating weather. A person can play it sitting or standing. It is held horizontally with the bottom hole pointing downwards. Three fingertips, each of the two hands, move over the six holes. These holes have a capacity of producing twelve notes of an octave. Pankaj Vishal, *The Handbook of Bansuri*, New Delhi: Pankaj Publications, 2008, pp. 57-72; Santosh Kumar, *Bansuri in Indian Classical Music*, New Delhi: Kanishka Publishers, 2019, pp. 141-4.
50. Damodar, Stanza nos. 182-7, pp. 102-3; 190-8, pp. 104-5; 209-16, pp. 106-7; 259-67, pp. 114-15; 345-9, pp. 126-7; 550, p. 157.
51. Ibid., Stanza nos. 402-7, pp. 135-6.
52. Ibid., Stanza nos. 422-30, pp. 138-9.
53. Ibid., Stanza nos. 504-12, pp. 150-1.

54. Ibid., Stanza nos. 551-9, pp. 157-8.
55. Ibid., Stanza nos. 586-97, pp. 163-4.
56. Ibid., Stanza nos. 931-5, p. 217.
57. Ibid., Stanza nos. 314-35, pp. 122-5.
58. Ibid., Stanza nos. 467-9, p. 145.
59. Ibid., Stanza nos. 231-55, pp. 109-13.
60. Ibid., Stanza nos. 314-23, pp. 122-3.
61. Ibid., Stanza nos., 601, p. 165; 623, p. 168; 706, p. 180.
62. Ibid., Stanza nos. 623-36, pp. 168-70.
63. Ibid., Stanza nos. 637-66, pp. 170-4.
64. Ibid., Stanza nos. 667-719, pp. 174-83.
65. Ibid., Stanza nos. 759-78, pp. 189-92.
66. India was unique in the sense that its magicians possessed the ability of reviving the dead. If a person suffered from snakebite, he was revived even after a span of six months. Such a person was flown across a river towards the east at the speed of lightning. When he reached Kamrup, the power of magic gave him new life. The Brahmins were proficient in the knowledge of magic and other occult sciences. When they recited sacred verses over the head of the dead person who had just died, he came back to life. Such a person could predict the future, provided the people were not afraid of him. This phenomenon was possible because the ghost had not eaten the pulp of his head. If his tongue was normal, he could speak. If it had decomposed, then he was not expected to utter any word. Amir Khusrau, *Nuh Sipihr*, Persian text, ed. Muhammad Wahid Mirza, London: Oxford University Press, 1949, p. 192.
67. Damodar, Stanza nos. 779-801, pp. 192-6.
68. Ibid., Stanza nos. 802-44, pp. 196-203.
69. Shaikh Rizqullah Mushtaqi, *Waqiat-i Mushtaqi*, Persian text, ed. Iqtidar Husain Siddiqui and Waqarul Hasan Siddiqi, Rampur: Rampur Raza Library, 2002, pp. 234-8.
70. Damodar, Stanza nos. 447-54, pp. 142-3.
71. Ibid., Stanza nos. 774-8, pp. 191-2.
72. Ibid., Stanza nos. 895-9, pp. 210-11.
73. Ibid., Stanza nos. 104, p. 91; 196, p. 105; 289, p. 118; 309, p. 121; 333, p. 124; 862, p. 205.
74. Ibid., Stanza no. 916, p. 214.
75. Abul Fazl, the official historian of the Mughal State and a contemporary of Damodar, provides an insight into the judicial system. The Emperor appointed a discreet and unbiased man as his judiciary delegate. This

person was not content with witnesses and oaths. He held diligent investigation of the first importance, for the inquirer was uninformed and litigants were cognizant of facts. By impartiality and knowledge of character, he distinguished the oppressed from the oppressor. Acting boldly and equitably, he took action on his conclusions. He began with a thorough interrogation and learnt circumstances of the case. Keeping in view each particular and taking questions in detail, he noted separately the evidence of each witness. Completing this task with intelligence, deliberation and discernment, he turned to other business and kept his counsel from others. Thereafter, he investigated the case afresh and searched it to his core. If capacity and vigour were not united, he was advised to appoint two persons, the Qazi to investigate and Mir Adl to carry out his finding. Abul Fazl, *Ain-i Akbari*, vol. II, pp. 42-3.

76. Damodar, Stanza no. 927, p. 216.
77. Ibid., Stanza no. 943, p. 219.
78. Ibid., Stanza no. 960, p. 221.
79. Though Damodar has assigned an important role to Panjpir, he has stopped short of naming them. First, the prevailing fluidity in their composition did not permit him to name them. Second, he has decided to show them as a single entity, who spoke with one voice. The Hir-Ranjha love grew under their benevolent umbrella. They appeared to the lovers more than once. In the middle and end of the story, they gave commands and advice to the lovers. Waris Shah has filled Damodar's gap and noted the names of Panjpir. Three of them (Baba Farid, Bahauddin Zakariya and Syed Jalaluddin Bokhari) belonged to western Panjab. The fourth, Lal Shahbaz Qalandar, hailed from Sind. These four were historical figures belonging to the thirteenth and fourteenth centuries. Their cults were established during the heyday of the Sultanate period. The fifth was the mythical deity Khwaja Khizr who, being pan-Islamic, was not identified with any geographical space, chronological frame or Sufi lineage.
80. Played at dawn, Raga Lalit has been ascribed to Marva Thata though some musicians placed it in the Bhairavi family. Pictorially it was represented as a Jogi with matted hair. Fair complexioned, he was loving and affectionate. Anointed with divine fragrances, he held a stag by its hind legs. According to a legend, Shankar (Shiv) performed a *yajna* to which all gods were invited. The moon (stag), seated on his traditional mount, tried to escape. Shankar, catching its hind legs, stopped the escaping moon. The stag, being active and

restless, symbolized human mind and desires. The holding of stag signified concentration of mind and complete self control. In another representation, Lalita was described as a pretty young woman with a shining gold complexion. While she held a *vina*, a cuckoo perched on her lotus-like hand. Seated beneath the Kalpataru tree (which fulfils all wishes) with highly adorned breasts, she was exceedingly amorous. Walter Kaufmann, *The Ragas of North India*, p. 323.

81. Damodar, Stanza nos. 182-7, pp. 102-3.
82. Ibid., Stanza nos. 512-14, pp. 151-2.
83. Ibid., Stanza no. 745, p. 187.
84. During the rule of Nasiruddin Qubacha in the early decades of the thirteenth century, an army of Mongols besieged Multan and encamped at the foot of the city's tower. Three eminent Sufis (Bahauddin Zakariya, Jalaluddin Tabrezi and Qutbuddin Bakhtiyar Kaki) were present in the city. One night, Kaki gave an arrow to Qubacha and directed him to shoot it in the direction of the Mongols. Qubacha did as directed. At daybreak, none of the invaders was seen at the site. All of them had fled away. Here, this Chishti source implied that Qubacha's forces were unable expel the invaders. A Chishti saint, employing his miraculous power through Qubacha, forced the invaders to flee and, thus, saved the inhabitants from loss of life and property. Amir Hasan Sijzi, *Fawaid ul-Fuad*, Eng. tr. Bruce B. Lawrence (entitled *Nizam Ad Din Awliya: Morals for the Heart*), New York & Mahawa: Paulist Press, 1992, p. 205.
85. Damodar, Stanza nos. 271-5, pp. 115-16.
86. Ibid., Stanza nos. 415-16, p. 137.
87. Ibid., Stanza no. 962, p. 222.
88. Mirza was the son of a Kharal *zamindar* of Danabad. He lived with his maternal uncles, the Siyals of Khiva near the Chenab. At school, Mirza fell in love with his cousin Sahiba. Her parents disapproved of the match and, instead, fixed her marriage with a boy of the Chanddar clan. Sahiba sent a message to Mirza to rescue her. On the day of Sahiba's wedding, Mirza eloped with her on his mare. The Siyals and Chanddars saw the act as an unpardonable social transgression. Gathering under Sahiba's brothers, they led a relentless chase from Khiva. Mirza, on his way to Danabad, slept under an acacia (*jand*) tree. He brushed aside Sahiba's warnings and fell prey to his overpowering arrogance. The fugitives were caught and killed. This episode ignited a massive inter-clan conflict. The Kharals routed the Siyals in a bloody battle and went on to destroy the town of Khiva.

89. The landed clans resorted to collective action during their struggles for survival, migration and settlement. A combination of caste and force enabled the victorious clan to acquire the *zamindari* right. According to statistics of *Ain-i Akbari*, every subdistrict (*pargana*) was identified with one or more castes holding the *zamindari* right. Since the possession of armed power was a necessary attribute of this right, the statistics also noted the size of cavalry, infantry and fortresses. For the entire Mughal State at the end of the sixteenth century, the *zamindari* troops comprised 384,558 cavalry, 4,277,057 infantry, 1,863 elephants, 4,260 guns and 4,500 boats. A *zamindar* usually drew his most loyal retainers from the members of his own caste who had come and settled with him. The *zamindars* employed his armed retinue in asserting his *zamindari* right in his domain and in defying the local representatives of the Mughal State. Irfan Habib, *The Agrarian System of Mughal India, 1556-1707*, pp. 196-208.
90. Damodar, Stanza nos. 858-61, p. 205.
91. Ibid., Stanza nos. 861-2, p. 205.
92. Ibid., Stanza nos. 862-3, p. 205.
93. Ibid., Stanza nos. 874-7, pp. 207-8.
94. Ibid., Stanza nos. 884-7, p. 209.
95. Ibid., Stanza nos. 888-91, pp. 209-10.
96. Ibid., Stanza nos. 892-3, p. 210.
97. Ibid., Stanza nos. 901, pp. 211-12.
98. Ibid., Stanza nos. 907-30, pp. 213-16.
99. Ibn Battuta, as Qazi (1344-45) of Maldive Islands, handled an interesting case. A slave of the late Sultan Jalaluddin was accused of illicit sex with one of the Sultan's concubines. The Grand Wazir, deputing witnesses to the woman's house, saw the fellow sleeping with her on the same bed. Both were arrested. Next morning, the Qazi learnt of the episode. The Grand Wazir expected the Qazi to make a statement on the case. The Qazi, as a principle, did not discuss the case until he had delivered a verdict on it. He would do so only in the Sultan's palace in conformity with the protocol. He went to the prescribed place and, calling the culprits, punished them with chastisement for their privacy. The woman was released, while the slave was jailed. The Grand Wazir, through some nobles, asked the Qazi to release the slave. The Qazi refused to favour the slave, who had violated his master's *harem*. The Qazi, pursuing the punishment, had the culprit beaten with bamboo rods that were more painful than the whip and had him paraded with a rope around his neck. The Qazi

resigned from his post in protest against the interference of the Grand Wazir. Ibn Battuta, *The Rehla of Ibn Battuta: India, Maldive Islands and Ceylon*, pp. 213-14.

100. Damodar, Stanza nos. 931-41, pp. 217-18.
101. Ibid., Stanza nos. 942-5, pp. 218-19.
102. In deciding cases, the Qazi received the assistance of fellow officers and, thus, the practice placed limitations on his functions. The investigators (*mutafahhis*) inquired into the facts, the clerks (*mutasarrifs*) maintained the records, the nobles (*amirs*) provided executive support, the jurists (*muftis*) gave the ruling and the Qazi pronounced the verdict. The judicial executive (*amir-i dad*), looking after the executive side of justice, saw that the decision was enforced. All Muslims, except those convicted of serious offences or perjury or partiality, were reliable witnesses. The Qazi could revise his judgement on the basis of fresh evidence or even reasoning on his part. If the *amir-i dad* felt that there had been a miscarriage of justice, he either drew the Qazi's attention to the fact or delayed the execution of the decision until a higher court reconsidered the matter. His office kept copies of documents registered with the Qazi. He forbade any covenant that transgressed the law. He controlled the functions of the police chief (*kotwal*) and public censor (*muhtasib*). Ishtiaq Husain Qureshi, *The Administration of the Sultanate of Dehli*, pp. 158-62.
103. Damodar, Stanza nos. 946-51, pp. 219-20.
104. Among the various categories of ascetics, the Jogis were famed for their supernatural abilities. They prolonged their lives through the suspension of breath. They predicted the future through a distinction between two nostrils. They transferred their souls to another body including that of animals. They drew out blood from the body and filled it again. They flew in the air, stayed in an underground pit with a narrow hole, floated across rivers and survived without food for months. They controlled the clouds to cause rain and stop it. Their expertise in alchemy enabled them to convert base metals into gold. They brought superhuman creatures, including demons and fairies, under their will. Like Hazrat Isa, they blew their breath to cure the sick, who had been suffering for years. Amir Khusrau, *Nuh Sipihr*, pp. 193-4; Ibn Battuta, *The Rehla of Ibn Battuta: India, Maldive Islands and Ceylon*, p. 164; Sujan Rai Bhandari, *Khulasat ut-Tawarikh*, p. 22.
105. Damodar, Stanza nos. 951-61, pp. 220-1.
106. Ibid., Stanza no. 963, p. 222.

CHAPTER 5

Successors of Damodar

During the post-Akbar period, the Mughal State consolidated its administrative structure. The twin institutions of military ranks (*mansabs*) and revenue assignments (*jagirs*) were streamlined. Kangra was annexed, the revolt of Raja Jagat Singh was suppressed and the hilly terrain was placed under two commandants (*faujdars*). The Qadiris and Naqshbandis shaped their mystical beliefs and practices. Guru Hargobind was forced to settle in the hills of Kahlur. Guru Gobind Singh revived the anti-Mughal resistance, paving the way for a wider rebellion under Banda Bahadur. Sikh guerrilla bands, comprising depressed castes, survived the Mughal repression. Ahmad Shah Abdali led several invasions into Panjab and occupied some areas in the north-west frontier. Local chiefs, both Muslim and Sikh, carved out autonomous principalities on the Mughal ruins. In the midst of these political upheavals, the cultural landscape thrived with literary activity. Ahmad Gujjar, Shahjahan Muqbal and Waris Shah re-narrated the story of Hir-Ranjha in narrative poetry (*qissa*). Bulle Shah, following in the footsteps of Shah Husain, assimilated the love tale in his mystical verses (*kafis*). Before taking up these poets, we would trace the movement of the story to unexpected quarters.

Towards the close of the seventeenth century, the story of Hir-Ranjha entered Persian historiography as well as the Sikh tradition. In 1695, Sujan Rai Bhandari completed a comprehensive history of India from earliest times to his own days. He has also provided an account of the provinces in the Mughal State. While tracing the route of the Chenab, his gaze turned to Hir-Ranjha. Their love had acquired great fame. Their tombs were located at a distance of four leagues from Hazara. Hir belonged to Jhang Siyal that was situated beyond Chiniot. The people of Panjab had put together this eternal story in the form of poetry. They sang these amazing couplets in heart-rending rhythms and soulful melodies (*ahl panjab keh dar muhabbat wa ashuftagi een har do naqsh ha-i badiya wa ashaar-i ajeeba basta sarur wa naghma dil fareb me-kunand*).[1] Not long after Bhandari, the Hir-Ranjha story penetrated the evolving Sikh tradition and the mountainous tract on the eastern edge of Panjab. Bhai Gurdas (1551-1636), the eminent Sikh scholar and scribe of the Sikh scripture, counted Hir-Ranjha among the legendary lovers and applauded their commitment to love (*piram paraati*).[2] Guru Gobind Singh (1666-1708), in a famous hymn, gave expression to the pain of Hir, who had been separated from Ranjha and forcibly married to a Khera youth. She was willing to live a life of spartan simplicity with Ranjha. Though the Kheras were rich, Hir preferred to consign her life among them to a furnace (*bhatth khereyan da rehna*). The Hir-Ranjha tale ensured its place in the voluminous text of the *Dasam Granth*, which was compiled in the court of the tenth Guru. The poet of the relevant section has given a major twist to the story and placed it in the wide canvas of Hindu mythology. Below is its brief recapitulation.

Once, a famine spread across the country. Except the rich, no one escaped from its fatal impact. Queen Chitar Devi lived with her son. She thought out a plan to beat starvation. She went to the houses of others to grind flour and, in return, brought leftovers of food to eat. During this adversity, she sold her son to the Jats. As the famine subsided, he grazed cattle during the day and returned home in the evening. Soon, he came to be known as Ranjha. His real identity was forgotten. Everyone recognized him as the son of a Jat and no one acknowledged him as the son of a king (Rajput). Since he was extremely handsome, every girl yearned to bond with him. Meanwhile, a beautiful nymph Maneka lived in the city of Rai Indra. Any king who saw her was struck with her charm and fell prostrate on the ground. Kapil Muni, an ascetic, saw her and dropped his semen. In a curse, he declared, 'Go to the world of humans and take birth in the family of a Siyal Jat. Assuming the name of Hir, you will eat food in the household of Turks.' She fell at the feet of Kapil Muni and prayed for a solution. Kapil Muni revealed that Lord Indra would appear in the mundane world as Ranjha. He would fall in love with her and bring her back to Amaravati. Accordingly, Hir was born in a Jat household that Chuchak headed. On growing up, she fell in love with Ranjha. When he returned after grazing cattle, she went crazy. At all moments, she kept him in her mind and recited his name. Her passion became so intense that she lost her appetite. She merged with Ranjha as a drop dissolved in water. Though they were two in body, they became one in soul. Hir, in her mad pursuit, disregarded all social norms (*lok laj*). Chuchak, fearing that Hir would die, married her among the Kheras. Ranjha accompanied her in the guise of an ascetic. During his begging, he found an opportunity and, taking Hir, departed to the domain of death. Their difficulties were eliminated and they reached heaven. Ranjha turned into Lord Indra and Hir became Maneka. All revered poets had sung songs in their praise.[3]

Ploughing the Field Afresh

Ahmad Gujjar did not tell us anything about himself. In a single line at the end of his narrative, he stated that he completed his work in Aurangzeb's twenty fourth regnal year, which coincided with 1682 AD.[4] At the outset, he noted the birth of the lovers and described the circumstances in which Ranjha left his home. His brothers, out of enmity, divided the ancestral land. His field was overgrown with weeds. When he wielded the mattock, his hands developed boils. In anger, he did not eat the food that his sister-in-law brought. His brothers asked him to work hard. It did not behove a Jat to sit idle at home. At least, he could take the cattle out for grazing. The brothers accused him of staring at women, besides being a thug and thief. Hurt at the allegations, he left his home in search of livelihood. His brothers tried to stop him in view of the difficulties ahead. He declared that his brothers, being arrogant, would earn a bad reputation. While walking through a jungle, he neutralized a lion with the melody of his flute. He spent the night in a mosque but did not interact with the Mulla. The boys, who were studying, brought food for him. Next day, Ranjha indicated his journey to the birthplace of his beloved. The boys blessed his endeavour.[5] On his way, he met the Panjpir who bestowed Hir on him. He spent the night on the bank of the Chenab. Next morning, Luddan refused to carry him in the boat without receiving the fare. He relented on hearing Ranjha's flute and allowed him to sleep on Hir's bedstead. Furious at this intrusion, Hir thrashed Luddan. She reprimanded Ranjha but, seeing his face, fell in love with him. She persuaded her father Chuchak to employ him as a herdsman.[6]

As Ahmad proceeded with the story, he fixed the spotlight on Hir. Every day, she met Ranjha in the moors on the pretext of delivering his food (*choori*). One day, Hir's uncle Kaido managed to take the food from Ranjha in alms. Hir felt that Ranjha had made a mistake and, in order to prevent further damage, caught up with Kaido and knocked him down. Kaido complained to Chuchak about Hir's violence and described her affair with Ranjha. If there was any doubt, he could send his men to check the facts. Chuchak was quick in his reaction. Without speaking to anyone, he sent his emissaries (Bhatt, Nai and Brahmin) to search a match for Hir among Chaudharis, who matched the Siyals in social ranking. The men went to the domain of the Kheras and selected Saida. Offering a rupee and sugar to the boy, they returned with the good news. As the preparation for marriage began, Hir tried her best to get the decision cancelled. At this stage, she entered into arguments with her mother and Qazi. Her mother pointed to the benign role of parents. Since they took great pains to bring her up, they were entitled to offer their advice. Hir did not listen to it and, instead, opposed the Kheras. Hir, in her response, condemned her parents and emissaries for keeping her in the dark about their move. She explained the unique nature of her love for Ranjha. She had acquired him from the divine court (*dargah*). God had fixed their marriage since the writing of the divine tablet (*lauh qalam*). Offering her life to Ranjha, she would not accept the Khera during her lifetime. The pain of Ranjha, penetrating her bones, had burnt her. Her parents, offering her to the Kheras, had compounded her sorrow. She endured a difficult situation through her attachment to Ranjha and reading the Quran.[7]

The parents roped in the Qazi to break Hir's resistance. This man was asked to pick an argument from the Shariat that would change Hir's mind. In his view, Hir's relation with Ranjha was unlawful in the absence of a marriage ceremony. Hir was attached to a servant, who grazed buffaloes in lieu of bread. She would face divine wrath for her sin. Hir, in her defence, asserted the purity of her love and questioned the credentials of the Qazi. She had made a promise to Ranjha in the presence of Khwaja Khizr. Their love was similar to that of Yusuf and Zulaikha. The Qazi lacked knowledge, experience and decency. He carried a Quran in his armpit, though he was ignorant of the alphabet. The Qazi, while leaving, admitted that Hir was deaf to his reasoning and advice of her parents.[8] Ahmad has described another confrontation between the Qazi and Hir that took place on her marriage. The Qazi claimed to see what he had heard. She was in love with the herdsman and rejected Saida, while the Kheras had arrived for the marriage. Hir complained that she was being snatched from Ranjha and forcibly handed over to the Kheras. She would prefer death to a miserable life. She accused the Qazi of casting an evil eye on the daughters of others. Ahmad noted the sad plight of Hir as the porters lifted her palanquin. But, the poet was entirely silent on Ranjha.

Ahmad was the first poet to introduce the device of written correspondence between the lovers. By doing so, they were able to revive their relation and, if possible, they could plan their future moves. When Hir reached Rangpur Khera, she wrote three letters to Ranjha and received two in reply. She related her agony in separation from Ranjha and requested him to meet her. She was nostalgic about the landmarks in their relationship. In particular, she recalled the bank of the Chenab, a tumultuous union with Ranjha in the boat, the magical impact of his flute, his herdsmanship in the woods and her visits with the sweetened breadcrumbs. Forgetting the millions of turbans of Chuchkana, she was called the beloved of the herdsman. The Shariat had forcibly tied her with the Khera. She spent the entire day in prayers, so that God enabled her to live with Ranjha. In his two letters, Ranjha laid emphasis on his suffering and sacrifices. Having abandoned his own herds in Takht Hazara, he became a herdsman of the Siyals without any gain. At midnight, he grazed the buffaloes in the midst of tigers, snakes and scorpions. In contrast, Hir changed her colour and went with the Khera. He could not figure out the way in which he could meet her.[9] What was noteworthy, Hir did not advise Ranjha to visit her in the garb of a Jogi. As we would see, it was Ranjha's own brainchild.

During the early stages of his career, Ranjha displayed the positive side of his character. These traits were repeatedly revealed since his departure from Takht Hazara and continued until his separation from Hir. During this phase, we see him dealing with a number of people such as his brothers, the Mulla and boys in the mosque, Luddan on the ferry, Hir in the boat, Chuchak in Jhang Siyal and Kaido in the moors. Ranjha, while dealing with them, was consistent in his simplicity, honesty and decency. At Tilla Balnath, his dual character was exposed in two stages. In the first stage, he tried to convince Balnath of his aptitude for Jog. He enumerated its numerous benefits, particularly its property of cleansing the human interior. He was quite scrupulous in concealing his past. He did not say a word about the unfair division of property on the part of his brothers. He was equally silent on his love for Hir, his failure to marry her and her marriage among the Kheras. On all these issues, he was firmly reticent. As soon as he was formally enrolled in Jog and acquired the outward symbols of the new path, he made a dramatic shift in his stance. He abandoned his single-minded honesty and adopted a brazen duplicity. Now, he revealed what he had concealed. He related that he grazed buffaloes during his stay in Jhang Siyal. He fell in love with Hir and experienced great happiness. When she left the place after her marriage, the resulting separation made him miserable. For the first time, he admitted that he embraced Jog only for the sake of Hir. Not only this, he issued a threat to Balnath. If the spiritual master did not exempt him from the condition of celibacy, he must reverse the process of initiation and mend his ears. Balnath must have been offended at Ranjha's questionable conduct. His disciples were vindicated because they had opposed the grant of Jog to a raw aspirant, who had not undertaken the hard labour incumbent on a novice. The disciples, in support of their argument, quoted the hallowed story of Yusuf.[10] Yet Balnath considered the special circumstances of Ranjha and, showing immense grace, blessed his object of uniting with Hir. Balnath paid a lot of attention to the kindness of Panjpir towards Ranjha. Following in their footsteps, Balnath secured Hir from God to the ardent lover. Our poet observed an affinity between two spiritual traditions, Islamic and Indic.

As we have seen, Ranjha acquired Jog from Balnath through clever postures. As a Jogi, he was not destined to enjoy the fruits of his ingenuity. He was unable to outwit a number of people he encountered before meeting Hir. A shepherd recognized the Jogi as the herdsman of the Siyals. Though he had changed his appearance, he could be detected and killed. Therefore, he must retreat to save his life. The Jogi, feeling demoralized, requested the shepherd to keep his secret. The shepherd assured the Jogi that he spoke in a lighter vein only to test his resolve. As the Jogi begged from door to door, he met different responses. He reached a house where a Jat was milking his cow. His loud cry gave a fright to the cow, which kicked the pot and spilled the milk. The Jat's wife, while offering a fistful of flour, protested against the loss. The Jogi, enraged at the remark, smashed her teeth with a punch. The commotion forced the Jogi to slip away. In his attempt to locate Hir, he roused the curiosity of women. He entered into an acrimonious debate with Hir's sister-in-law Sehti. This fiery young woman raised doubts about his training as a Jogi and his ability to cure the sick. She suspected that he was a herdsman wearing saintly apparel. The mendicant argued that he had been a Jogi for seven generations. He could cure ailments with his glance and amulets. If he felt Hir's pulse, she would regain her health. The Jogi failed to overwhelm Sehti and interact with Hir. In order to have his way, the Jogi resorted to deceit. He broke his begging bowl and spilled the millets, blaming the women for the fiasco. He began a sit-in strike (*dharna*) and threatened to burn the village. Under the pretext of piecing together the bowl and picking the grain, he tried to make an eye contact with Hir. The women, shocked at his audacity, pushed the Jogi out of the house. His bad luck chased him even to his retreat in Kalabagh.[11] A group of women scattered his sacred fire and fled away. Ahmad, describing these events, held that the pursuit of love was fraught with obstacles. In the process, he showed that craftiness could not succeed in all circumstances. Damodar and Muqbal have overlooked the Jogi's unfavourable encounters, whereas Waris has amplified the account of Ahmad.

The Jogi, owing to his bitter experiences, took shelter in Kalabagh. He reflected on his failures. He came to take away Hir but remained empty handed. He had seen her after overcoming numerous difficulties, but again separated from her. He could not fight the Kheras without some support. His state was like a peasant who could not pay the land tax to the ruler. Ruminating over his misery, he established an abode typical of the Jogis. He levelled the ground with a spade and, spreading out a blanket, lighted a fire. Wailing loudly and shedding tears, he recited the name of Hir. He realized that love was not meant for a Jat who was amenable to natural processes. It was reserved for the practitioners of austerities (*ahl riyazatan*). Resolving to undertake a forty-day retreat (*chillah*), he stood with folded hands facing Kaaba. Unfortunately, he was not destined to stay in peace. A group of girls, belonging to different castes, scattered his fire. Holding a crook (*fauhari*), he chased the girls and caught one of them. This moment marked a turning point in his fate. This girl, a niece of Hir, conveyed the Jogi's message to her aunt. She narrated the Jogi's yearning for Hir and persuaded Hir to visit the Jogi. Sehti prepared a tray of sugar, cream and five rupees, covering everything under a kerchief. The offering did not produce cordiality. The Jogi was upset because Sehti had offended him in her house. He criticized women as a class, while Sehti put up a stout defense. Ultimately, the Jogi performed a miracle by converting five rupees into five paisas. Sehti accepted the Jogi's spiritual eminence and promised to send Hir for a rendezvous.[12]

Sehti informed Hir of her experience at Kalabagh, particularly a miracle (*mojza*) of the Jogi. She was certain that the herdsman of Jhang Siyal had assumed a new garb for Hir's sake. Hir must go to meet him because time was ripe for the revival of their love. Hir went to Kalabagh and conversed with the Jogi. Revealing his state of mind, he recalled his sacrifices in the cause of love. He was a Chaudhari of Takht Hazara for seven generations. Hir's parents turned him into a herdsman and, getting their work done, violated their promises. In the moors, Hir fed him on rice dessert and listened to his flute. Having played with his emotions, she married the Khera and betrayed him. He was forced to escort the buffaloes to Rangpur Khera with a drum on his head. Women could not be trusted because even Raja

Bhoj submitted to them. Hir argued that she was imprisoned among the Kheras. She had distanced herself from Saida. Day and night, she suffered in separation from Ranjha. Together they had eaten the fruit of love. They must formulate a plan with Sehti to cross the sea of love. Ranjha must take her out of the custody of the Kheras. Her story was similar to Zulaikha, who belonged to Yusuf but forced to marry Aziz in Egypt.[13]

When Hir returned to the village, her friends congratulated her for a dramatic transformation after meeting her lover. More importantly, she begged Sehti to help her in uniting with Ranjha. Since both women had been afflicted with the pain of love, they agreed on a common plan. Sehti, speaking to her mother, said that the Jat women were outgoing and could not be kept in a cage. Hir had become pale due to her perpetual stay in the house. If Hir were exposed to the greenery of the fields, her health would change for the better. The mother felt that a household thrived with its daughter-in-law. Hir never plied the spinning wheel in their courtyard. Nor did she play games with the girls. Her depression was a cause of concern. Sehti received the approval of her mother and, informing the Khera girls at night, went to the fields in the morning. Sehti called the shots. It was claimed that Hir had been struck with a snakebite. The Jogi was chosen to treat the victim. Saida was sent to summon the Jogi who, with a clever interrogation, extracted a confession about the distance between man and wife. The Jogi beat up Saida on a flimsy excuse and, thus, got even with his rival. Sehti disapproved Saida's faulty interaction with the Jogi. At her instance, her father Ajju went to Kalabagh and persuaded the Jogi to attend to Hir. Sehti, with her crafty postures, ensured that various steps of the plan were executed to perfection.[14]

The Jogi declared that he would take up a ten-day treatment of Hir in a hut, which would be constructed out of the village. He agreed to shift the venue to a cell behind the Khera bungalows. The lovers would be able to meet in privacy and elope with ease. Hir's bed was brought to the cell, where the Jogi met her. At Sehti's request, the Jogi prayed to God and brought Murad to the site. The lovers, though united, had to elope at the earliest. The Jogi remembered Panjpir, who deputed Syed Jalaluddin Bukhari to demolish the wall.[15] When everyone slept, the lovers bolted away. Next morning, the Kheras mobilized an army and galloped in hot pursuit. The Jogi and Hir rushed to Raja Adli's town, where her parents had constructed a platform (*chauntra*). The Kheras captured the lovers. Hir was put on a horse and Ranjha, bereft of help from his relatives, was beaten up. According to Ahmad's plot, the lovers appeared before two officers with different results. Raja Adli, from the outset, came out in support of the lovers and threatened the Kheras with punishment. However, the Kheras managed to present their side of the story. The Jogi was a fraudster who, posing as a healer, ran away with Hir. Therefore, he must be put to death. Raja Adli, exercising his executive authority, transferred the dispute to the Qazi, who would adjudicate on the basis of the Shariat. Ranjha argued that Prophet Muhammad had conducted his marriage with Hir in the presence of the sun and moon. The longer statement of the Kheras recalled the alliance between two landed chiefs, Ranjha's work as a herdsman and their lavish expenditure on the Saida-Hir marriage. The Qazi's verdict handed Hir over to the Kheras. Hir saw the judgement as cruel and accused the Qazi of receiving a bribe. The Jogi alleged that the citizens earned their livelihood through unlawful means. Both cursed the town with destruction through fire. As the fire engulfed the town, there was a panic among people.[16]

Ahmad has drawn our attention to the benevolent intervention of Raja Adli. He ordered the prominent citizens to take care of the Jogi. He sent a special contingent (*ahadis*) to bring the Kheras back.[17] The Kheras, who were travelling in a boat, were stopped in the middle of the river. Having lost their case, they released their frustration in slapping Hir. She became furious on seeing her brother Pathana in the boat. Probably, the Kheras had brought him as their witness in the court. She castigated Pathana for supporting parental oppression, raising a dispute over her relation with Ranjha and bribing the Qazi. Her angry words were enough to deactivate him. Raja Adli claimed that he would suppress any highhandedness (*ziyadati*) and separate truth from falsehood. The right of the Jogi had been wrongly given to the Kheras, resulting in persecution of Hir. Since Hir was a Muslim and daughter of a Muslim, she must be fearless. He devised a novel way of settling the dispute. Far ahead of his times, he asked Hir to hold the lappet of the person whom she recognized as her right (*haq*). In full public view, Hir clasped the Jogi like snakes winding around a sandalwood tree, while the deceitful Kheras were humiliated. The Jogi blessed Raja Adli with a glorious rule and prosperous town (*ann dhan te lakhmi put bahute*).[18]

Though Ahmad concluded the story on a tragic note, he assigned an afterlife to Hir and Ranjha. The decision of Raja Adli united the lovers. Hir insisted on a legal sanction to her relation with Ranjha. Since her marriage with Saida stood annulled, she could marry Ranjha. If she went to Takht Hazara in her current state, people would treat her as an eloped woman (*udhal*). She proposed that Ranjha should escort her to her parental home. He should return to Takht Hazara and, meeting his brothers, come with a marriage party. Accordingly, Ranjha reached Takht Hazara and saluted his brothers. Since Hir had come into his hands with great difficulty, they should arrange a marriage party to bring her. Hir, calling out for her lover, completed her life on earth. The Siyals sent a letter of condolence through a messenger. They wrote that destiny had shattered their plans, while death had no remedy. They had no choice but to endure the loss. A Qazi was summoned to read the letter. Ranjha, seeing the torn end of the letter, uttered a sigh and died. The lovers, steadfast in physical love (*rah mijaz*) were elevated to perfection. God accepted Ranjha as a pious martyr (*pak shahid*) and Hir was raised to the status of fairies. Even after their deaths, they attained a new life. The pilgrims, on their way to Mecca, saw the figures of Ranjha, Hir and a brown buffalo. Ranjha showed the path to pilgrims, while Hir distributed food (*langar*) cooked in an oven.[19] This conclusion found a partial resonance in the account of Muqbal who, while admitting the elevation of lovers to the rank of spirituality, denied an afterlife to the deceased. In contrast, Waris has alleged that the Siyals poisoned Hir and Ranjha died of shock.

Dilution of Conflict

In the middle of the eighteenth century, Muqbal composed the story of Hir-Ranjha in 360 stanzas of four lines each. The poet, opening his short version, noted that Ranjha saw the glimpse of Hir in a dream. He did not tell anyone about it but longed to see her. His father died a sudden death. His seven brothers summoned the village elders (*painch*) and got the ancestral land fragmented. The brothers, remaining unnamed, always appeared in a body. Ranjha was disturbed on seeing that his share was covered with reeds. Other than this, he did not face any ill will from his brothers. Having lost his parents, he felt like a poor orphan (*gharib yatim*). Since he had not touched any work, he was buried under the weight of numerous tasks. Lonely and sad, he made his way through the wild growth and began to uproot the weeds. All parts of his body were shaken and his hands were covered with boils. In this pathetic state, he lay on the ground. Since he had left his home early, his sisters-in-law were worried about him. They had always loved him. He was young, handsome and innocent. They packed his breakfast (*chhah vela*) and began to search for him. They found him lying beside a plant. Observing his acute discomfort, they were filled with sympathy for him. They wanted to know the cause of his affliction. Ranjha was touched at their solicitude. Having reflected on his current state, he had made up his mind for the future. Though he wept while replying, he made an oblique reference to his interest in Hir.

Ranjha, speaking to his sisters-in-law, stated that he had spent his life in joyful comfort. It was impossible for him to do any hard work. His mind had lost its equanimity. He did not care about his landholding. Since worldly life was a dream, he was inclined towards mendicancy and starvation (*faqr faqa*). He had decided to renounce the world and become a recluse (*faqir*). He would be happy to attain the wealth of love (*daulat ishq*). The sisters-in-law, on hearing the reply, were disturbed and sorrowful. They offered a lot of advice to Ranjha and, in doing so, performed their duty. The sarcastic comments of rivals had already tormented them. Ranjha must not leave because of the impending labour. They promised to serve (*chakri*) him like menials and would even drive his plough. His decision had struck them like a thunderbolt. The specter of separation had ignited a fire in their interior. With numerous entreaties, they managed to please a beloved, who was annoyed with them since ancient antiquity (*mudh qadim*). Ranjha, in order to console them, ate the food. With his mind occupied with the thoughts of Hir, he returned to the village with his sisters-in-law.[20]

Back home, Ranjha continued to be restless. His mind was obsessed with Hir. In the name of love, he abandoned his material possessions and prepared to leave for Jhang. He tore his clothes and smeared his body with ash. His sisters-in-law spoke to him as if he was their beloved. Endowed with beauty, they did not care for property and wealth. Instead, they were scared of separating from him. If he went away, they would die. Since Ranjha was gentle to the core, he broke down. While weeping, he asked his sisters-in-law to excuse him for his faults. His destiny had induced him to be a wanderer. Offering him a pleasant farewell, they must pray for his union with Hir. The sisters-in-law, crying profusely, tried every method to dissuade Ranjha from his resolve. Unable to restrain the growth of love, they bade a tearful farewell to Ranjha. The attitude of his brothers was similar to that of their wives. As soon as they learnt that Ranjha was leaving for Jhang, they rushed to block his path. They wished to know the reason underlying his move. There were huge obstacles in his journey, while he was not ready to plunge into the unchartered sea. Ranjha assured his brothers that he was quite happy with them. If sorrow was inscribed in his destiny, it could not be altered. They must place him in the custody of God and return to the village. There was sadness on both sides. Ranjha was distressed at separating from his brothers. The brothers, sunk in despair, stopped eating. They hoped that God would enable them to meet their youngest sibling at the earliest.[21] In spite of the division of property and inability of Ranjha to cultivate his land, he was not bitter towards his brothers and sisters-in-law. Yet, his attraction towards Hir was far stronger than his affection for his close relatives.[22]

In Muqbal's narrative, Ranjha's stay in the mosque was pleasant. Here, a calm atmosphere prevailed. Students were studying. Some recited the Quran. A few wrote letters, while some others looked for omens (*faal*). The Mulla was extremely kind to Ranjha. Since he found that the visitor was sad, he was gentle in his questions. Ranjha, introducing himself, stated that he had been alienated from his life. He was travelling to see the world and, during his journey, had spent the night in wilderness without food. He did not refer to the situation in his family and interest in Hir. The Mulla asked a few boys to go home and bring food for the visitor. Their mothers prepared a platter of dessert with rice, sugar and clarified butter. The Mulla asked Ranjha to wash his hands and, thereafter, sat with him while he ate. Ranjha consumed the food to his heart's content and, taking his leave of the Mulla, prepared to leave for Jhang Siyal. The Mulla prevailed upon Ranjha to put up for the night and advised him to be wise (*siyana*). Next morning, when Ranjha was leaving, the Mulla prayed for his welfare. He hoped that Ranjha's faith would remain firm, enabling him to reach heaven in the distant future. As he left the mosque, he must have got rid of his fatigue, sadness and tension.[23]

In the eyes of Muqbal, Ranjha developed an intimate bond with Panjpir. On his way to Jhang Siyal, Ranjha encountered them. He bowed in salutation and, offering his waistcloth, sought their attention. Impressed with his devotion, they asked him to express any desire. Ranjha revealed that he was a disciple of Khwaja Khizr. He gave a brief account of his life including his affliction at the hands of Hir. They asked him to play on his flute and granted him a number of boons. They conferred Hir on him and, with a miracle, produced a brown buffalo. Ranjha milked it and offered the bowl to Panjpir. They consumed a part of it and, when Ranjha sipped the remainder (*ulush*), his sorrow vanished. They blessed his journey to Jhang Siyal and promised to come to his aid in adversity. They spent the night in the company of Ranjha. They provided him with food and, next morning, escorted him up to Luddan's ferry. In this manner, Ranjha was tied to Panjpir in a mystical relationship. Ranjha tried to swim across the Chenab with a raft. Luddan, captivated by Ranjha's looks, warned him of the risk. He carried Ranjha to the other bank on his boat. Ranjha was attracted to the red bedstead and became inquisitive about its owner. Luddan described Hir as a devout Muslim. A daughter of Chuchak Siyal and Malki, Hir was a beautiful virgin. During the day, she recited the Quran and kept fasts. At night, she remained awake and offered supererogatory prayers (*nafl*). Besides serving poor mendicants, she protected the naked and starving. Luddan refused to allow Ranjha to sleep on the bed because he did nothing without Hir's approval. Ranjha gave his ring to Luddan and secured the permission. Hir, arriving on the scene with 360 friends, was infuriated on seeing a stranger sleeping on her bed and beat up Luddan. She fell in love with Ranjha at first sight. Comparing their love with that of Laila-Majnu, she asked the girls to congratulate her. Here, the role of Panjpir became crucial. In response to Ranjha's invocation, they appeared in the boat and became witnesses to the marriage (*nikah*). They chewed a few grains of rice that were placed in Hir's lap. In a sermon, they advised the lovers to remember God throughout the eight watches. They must understand that the worldly life was transient. They must be firmly committed to love. Marriage was only a beginning and they were yet to cross the ocean of desire (*shauq*).[24] Muqbal, unlike Damodar and Ahmad, did not see any tiff between Ranjha and Luddan.

Muqbal has constructed Kaido's intervention in a distinctive way. This man did not act at the instance of Chuchak. Hir, to begin with, had no quarrel with him. In fact, she used his abode as a link with Ranjha. When Malki heard of Hir's affair with the herdsman, she forbade her from carrying his food to the moors. Hir, forced to look for an alternative, chose Kaido's hut. Every day, she baked a large loaf of bread (*rot khas*) and, crushing it with sugar and clarified butter, made a sweet mixture (*choorma*). Pouring it in a bowl, she brought it to Ranjha. Kaido, sick of observing Hir's daily mischief, decided to catch the lovers red handed. One day, Hir carried the bowl for Ranjha. Kaido saw his chance and hid behind a bush. Hir awakened Ranjha from sleep and embraced him. The lovers forgot the food and allowed their passion to reach a peak. As soon as Hir left the site, Kaido went up to Ranjha. Posing as a mendicant, he begged food to meet his hunger. Ranjha gave him the entire lump of sweetened breadcrumbs. Kaido prayed for Ranjha and departed. Hir returned to find that Ranjha had given the food in alms. Ranjha claimed that he had earned wellness, while she had attained prestige. This simple charity would protect them from any calamity. Hir, filled with rage, ran after Kaido. She caught up with him and grabbed the food. For her, the matter did not end. She felt that Ranjha had made a mistake. Kaido was sure to circulate rumours about them and, thus, create fresh problems. As soon as she learnt that Kaido had reported the matter to Chuchak, Hir burnt his hut along with household goods. Kaido complained to Chuchak that he had set up an abode on the Chenab, but did not live in peace. Owing to Hir's enmity, he could not survive in Jhang Siyal.[25]

Muqbal has portrayed Chuchak as assertive, tenacious and resourceful. Often losing his temper, he caught the bull by the horn and came out with tough solutions. When Kaido informed him of Hir's affair, he could not control his anger. Without losing a moment, he cornered Hir with many allegations. On the pretext of carrying food for the herdsman, she had befooled every one. Her birth had affixed a stigma on their family. She must give up her relation with Ranjha, failing which he would kill both of them. She must restrain herself because he would get her married at the earliest. Chuchak, dealing with Kaido's complaint, gave a number of assurances. His hut would be rebuilt and he would be given a new set of clothes. Twice a day, he would be provided with meals. His monetary compensation would be double the amount of his loss. He would also be reconciled with Hir. Soon after, Chuchak started preparations for Hir's marriage. He requested the Qazi to suggest a suitable match for her. The Qazi identified the son of Ajju Khera, whose family was wealthy for seven generations. A delegation comprising Brahmin, Doom and Nai went to Rangpur Khera and finalized the betrothal. Chuchak was relentless in his pursuit of marriage despite Hir's strong opposition. In consultation with the Brahmin, he decided that the marriage would be held after a fortnight. Chuchak learnt that Hir, in an argument with Malki, insisted on her relation with Ranjha along with a rejection of her marriage. Chuchak, enraged beyond limit, castigated Hir in harsh words. She had not stopped meeting the herdsman. She had disgraced the Siyals and ruined the reputation of the Kheras. He would kill her for gross misconduct. Hir alleged that he had lost his senses due to old age. Her life was inseparable from Ranjha, while her death was in the hands of God. Chuchak, unable to counter Hir, began to cry. In frustration, he turned his ire against Ranjha. This man was guilty of misleading Hir. He had betrayed his benefactors and brought a bad a name to Jhang Siyal. Chuchak dismissed him from service and ordered him to leave the place. Hir, in a clever move, demanded Ranjha's wages for twelve years. The claim could not be denied as the Shariat prescribed it. Chuchak could not face Ranjha. Malki took charge of the situation and, apologizing to Ranjha, reinstated him in his job. Chuchak, thoroughly demoralized, requested the Qazi to speak to Hir.[26]

Chuchak hoped that the Qazi, being Hir's teacher, would be able to change her stance. While weeping, he complained of Hir's attachment to the herdsman and her defiance towards her parents. Hir appeared before the Qazi and, standing with folded hands, offered seven salutations. The Qazi argued that she was bound to obey her teacher. The parents had the sole right to choose her husband. She must abandon her relation with Ranjha, which was unlawful and amounted to infidelity (*kufr*). Since Ranjha was dependent for his livelihood, he was not suitable for her. She could not prove the legality of her relation with him. She must accept her betrothal with the Khera and, thus, fall in line with the Shariat. Hir, in her reply, showed her courage and intelligence. Accusing the Qazi of bribery and sycophancy, she pushed him on the back foot. In principle, she accepted the authority of the Quran, Shariat and the Qazi. However, she also followed the path of lovers, perceiving no contradiction between religion and love. She had been in love with Ranjha since creation. She had begged Ranjha from God and, therefore, Panjpir and Khwaja Khizr performed her marriage (*nikah*) with Ranjha. She would remain true to Ranjha and would never substitute him with Saida. God would surely forgive her on the day of judgement. In the end, the Qazi became considerate towards Hir. Since she was conversant with all intricacies, it was impossible to debate with her. In view of this statement, Chuchak was made to appear false. This was a temporary victory for Hir in her struggle against patriarchy.[27]

Now, we will try to find if Ranjha suffered ill treatment at the hands of the Kheras and his close relatives, as Damodar has narrated. To answer this question, we must turn to the departure of Hir for Rangpur Khera. Her large dowry included 21 buffaloes that refused to leave despite blows of the stick. The Siyals were impelled to send Ranjha as an escort with the buffaloes. Carrying a drum on his head, he played on his flute and, as a result, the buffaloes left without any resistance. The Kheras, stopping in a jungle, enjoyed themselves with hunting, drinking and music. After sometime, they were shocked to see Ranjha in Hir's palanquin and wanted to kill him. Hir saved his life with a clever explanation. Since he represented her parental home, she had summoned him to pick the beads of a broken necklace. The Kheras were convinced and refrained from punishing Ranjha. On reaching their destination, the Kheras gave a decent farewell to Ranjha. When he returned to Takht Hazara, his brothers and sisters-in-law welcomed him with open arms. They showered him with love and kissed his forehead. They empathized with him for his recent loss and expressed happiness on his return. He was given warm water to bathe and a new set of clothes to wear. He was fed with a dessert (*choorma*). The sisters-in-law, having felt miserable in his absence, were jubilant on seeing his face. Day and night, they treated him with affection (*ikhlas*) and, in every possible way, boosted his sagging morale.[28] Muqbal, in describing these experiences of Ranjha, deviated from the narrative of Damodar, who emphasized Ranjha's severe repression at the hands of the Kheras as well his brothers. Muqbal was quite scrupulous in replacing conflicts with cordiality. He did not see Ranjha as a perpetual victim of adversity.

Turning to Rangpur Khera, we find that Hir stayed away from Saida. Though they did not quarrel, they maintained a respectable distance from each other. At the same time, Hir did not have any altercation with her parents-in-law. She was not made to live separately from the Khera household. She found it easy to secure Sehti's help in contacting Ranjha. She did not hesitate to reveal her painful separation from Ranjha. Since Sehti was also pining for Murad Baloch, she was quick to identify herself with Hir. She persuaded Hir to write a letter for Ranjha and engaged a Brahmin to carry it. The messenger went to Jhang Siyal and learnt that Ranjha was staying in Takht Hazara. He did not face embarrassing questions about the state of Hir. His meeting with Ranjha was pleasant. Ranjha, in his reply to Hir, underscored his suffering in love and his strong desire to meet her. However, the lovers did not exchange a single word on Ranjha's conversion to Jog.[29] We were told that Ranjha, without informing his brothers and sisters-in-law, left for Tilla Balnath. Initially Balnath was reluctant to enroll Ranjha in Jog. Ranjha did not face any opposition from the disciples of Balnath. Ranjha's long encounter with Balnath was playful and did not betray any rancour.

There were no differences on the condition of celibacy.[30] Ranjha, after his initiation, revealed that he acquired Jog only to unite with Hir. Balnath did not feel offended at Ranjha's apparent cunning and, instead, blessed the quest of his new disciple. The Jogi, on reaching Rangpur Khera, did not face any obstacle from the local inhabitants. Of course, Sehti alleged that the mendicant had adopted Jog only to peer at women. The Jogi, asserting his decent intentions, broke his bowl and spilled the millets. In spite of this deliberate transgression, the Jogi and Sehti argued in a sporting manner, which was devoid of bitterness.[31] Muqbal, while describing the events from the Jogi's arrival in Kalabagh to the beating of Saida, has largely followed the line of Ahmad. What was different, Muqbal gave a lot of space to the role of Hir's niece as an emissary between the lovers. However, he overlooked the visits of Sehti and Hir to Kalabagh before the snakebite.

The Jogi, having met Sehti and Hir in the Khera courtyard, established himself in Kalabagh. Here, he built a hut and set up a smouldering fire (*dhuan*). Giving up food and drink, he engaged in Jogic exercises. It was only after the snakebite and Jogi-Saida encounter that Sehti went to Kalabagh. In a short meeting with the Jogi, she invited him to meet Hir, who was lying in the Khera household after suffering a snakebite. The lovers, meeting after a long time, exchanged their feelings of love. At this moment, they made a plan for elopement. During the next seven days, the Jogi would treat Hir at his hut in Kalabagh. Sehti's mother was suspicious of the move. She directed Sehti to be present with Hir lest the Jogi should do an evil deed (*manda kam*). The lovers, along with Sehti, shifted to Kalabagh and locked themselves in the hut. The Jogi, at Sehti's request, sent a letter to Murad Baloch, who was hundreds of miles away. The Jogi employed his supernatural powers to develop an amulet, which brought Murad to the site in a short time. The four lovers fulfilled their desire and, without invoking Panjpir, fled from the place. Saida, shocked at the empty hut, informed his mother of the fraud involving Sehti and Hir. The Kheras began a massive chase across the countryside. They lost track of Sehti and Murad. Hir and Ranjha, hoping to get justice from the local chief Raja Adli, went to the town. The Kheras captured them on the way. They subjected the

Jogi to a severe beating. Someone wanted Hir to be killed, but the others vetoed the proposal.[32]

Muqbal was in a hurry to complete his story. He was silent on the fate of Sehti and Murad. He has removed the Qazi from the final scenario. Instead, he has focused his attention on Raja Adli, who was endowed with the legal authority, but did not have any sympathy for the lovers. He accused Ranjha of putting on the garb of a Jogi and raising a fresh deception. He was guilty of committing adultery with a married woman and, therefore, deserved to be destroyed from his roots. The lovers, speaking with one voice, urged that their enemies be ignored. Their love was traceable to ancient times and, at the moment, they were going to Mecca on pilgrimage (*haj*). Hir asserted that she was in love with Ranjha since he served her father as a herdsman. Her parents forcibly tied her to Saida, while Ranjha was her true husband. The Kheras argued that they brought Hir as a bride in the presence of entire humankind. The Jogi had disgraced this bad woman, who was an absolute liar. Raja Adli restored Hir to the Kheras and sent Ranjha to prison. The functionaries (*musaddi*), making a strong intervention, persuaded Raja Adli to release the Jogi. Following this, the Jogi appealed to Panjpir and, as a result, a fire broke out in the town. Raja Adli was afflicted with colic pain, which was not relieved with medicine and charity. The astrologers (*nujumi*) declared that Raja Adli could be cured if he reconciled with the Jogi and restored Hir to him. As this was done, Raja Adli became normal. The lovers were united, the fire was put out and the Kheras were expelled in disgrace. Hir asked Ranjha to come with a marriage party to marry her, so that she was not dubbed as an eloped woman. The lovers left for their respective villages. Ranjha remembered Panjpir and discarded his symbols of Jog. He reached Takht Hazara and embraced his brothers. Soon after, he received Chuchak's letter informing that Hir was no more. He uttered a sigh and died. Muqbal was certain that the love of Hir-Ranjha, being pure, attained the level of spirituality (*irfan da martaba*).[33]

Satire, Detail and Hyperbole

Waris Shah attained unprecedented fame as a versifier of the tale under reference. Born in Jandiala Sher Khan (District Shaikhupura), he was the disciple of a saint of Qasur. He undertook the versification of Hir-Ranjha tale in Hans Malkan, a village near Pakpattan. He has described the circumstances in which he accomplished the task. At this time, Panjab was undergoing political turmoil and social transformation. The Jats became chiefs and new authority arose in every part. The elite suffered decline, while the plebeians attained power. As a result, the landholders (*zamindars*) rose to prominence. The thief became a Chaudhari and the adulteress turned a pious woman. The gangs of scoundrels doubled in numbers. Waris, having expressed his anguish at the collapse of the Mughal State and empowerment of Sikh warrior bands, drew our attention to his narrative. He completed the work in 1766, which coincided with 1180 of the Hijri era and 1822 of the Bikrami calendar. He had begun the task at the instance of his beloved, though he completed it for the sake of his friends. He described the story of Hir-Ranjah in detail with the help of numerous parables (*tamsil*). It possessed the fragrance and colours of the spring. Its couplets were arranged like a chain of diamonds in a necklace. The young men of the country would be pleased to go through it. Waris hoped that God would protect the honour of his couplets. The poets would assess the merits of his art. He had displayed his horse in the market so that the buyers formed their opinion about it. Waris has confessed that his yearning for his beloved was similar to that of Hir for Ranjha. According to his claim, many poets had narrated the story in the past. However, none had narrated it in the manner he has done.[34]

Waris has picked his facts from the narrative of Ahmad Gujjar. However, he has also deviated from the earlier text on several points that need identification. A heated argument took place between Ranjha and the Mulla in the mosque. Ranjha ridiculed the Mulla for his hypocrisy and immortality, while the Mulla reprimanded Ranjha for his un-Islamic persona. The two wives of Luddan were attracted to Ranjha. They did not allow him to swim across the Chenab and, putting their arms around him, brought him to the bank. Panjpir appeared to Ranjha on the first day of his herdsmanship and, during a meeting in the moors, informed that God had conferred Hir on him. Hir's uncle Kaido figured in two episodes and, while complaining against the lovers, exposed his own perverted habits. Chuchak went to the moors and saw the lovers together. Hir and her friends enjoyed themselves with Ranjha in the waters of the Chenab. The Siyals did not accept Ranjha as a suitable match for Hir because they did not have matrimonial relations with Ranjha's clan and they would not give their daughter in marriage to a mere herdsman. Ranjha rejected Hir's proposal for elopement, but disguised as a woman to meet her during her marriage. He attributed his failure to marry Hir to the eternal tussle between the rich and poor. Since the buffaloes refused to move with the marriage party of the Kheras, Ranjha was made to escort them with a drum on his head. Hir, while going to Rangpur Khera, asked Ranjha to come in the garb of a Jogi. She refused to play the game of Lassi-Mundari with Saida and did not untie his wristband. Back in Jhang Siyal, Ranjha received a letter from his sisters-in-law asking him to return. Ranjha reminded them of inflicting injustice on him and indicated his intention of becoming a Jogi. Hir took the initiative of contacting Ranjha through a girl, who was visiting her parents in Jhang Siyal. This contact paved the way for correspondence between the lovers, wherein Hir again urged Ranjha to meet her in the guise of a Jogi. At Tilla Balnath, the rebellion of the disciples turned violent. They ransacked the hermitage, beat up Balnath and threw away their robes. Discipline was restored with the threat of expulsion. Ranjha's long interaction with Balnath and an acrimonious debate with Sehti uncovered the complexities of Jog. In the end, the Siyals agreed to marry Hir with Ranjha, but retracted from their promise to poison Hir.

Waris was a keen observer of his surroundings. He has painted a vivid picture of a village scene, which Ranjha saw on leaving the mosque and walking towards the Chenab. At dawn, a beautiful day spread light all around. The atmosphere became bright with red and pink colours. The entire world resumed its daily chores (*karobar*). As the sparrows began to chirp, the travellers got up and embarked on their journeys. The ploughmen placed yokes on their beasts, so that earth was broken to be planted with seeds. The housewives fixed churns in the pitchers of milk. They rotated the handmills and, turning corn into dough, baked loaves of bread in the oven. Soon after, they began turning out yarn from the spinning wheels. Those who had enjoyed their night on beds ran out to take a bath.[35] In these circumstances, Ranjha reached a ferry on the Chenab and found that the boat was crammed with passengers. Luddan, the swarthy and obese boatman, looked like a container of honey (*kuppa shehad da*) that the grocers loaded on the boat. Ranjha pleaded with Luddan to carry him across the Chenab. Since he had no money, he offered to help in plying the oars. He deserved sympathy because his unkind brothers had annoyed him. Luddan gave a curt reply and explained the rules he imposed on passengers. If a person paid in the form of a coin or a piece of cloth, he was virtually carried across in the lap. If someone tried to travel free of cost, he was thrown out of the boat on the ground. If someone barged into the boat forcefully, he was drowned in the middle of the river. Bards, mendicants and others inclined to free services were pushed away like dogs. Similarly, the sons of saints (*pirzadas*) were not allowed to step into the boat.[36]

Waris has drawn a sketch of the house belonging to a prosperous peasant like Ajju Khera. At the centre, one saw a courtyard enclosed with mud walls, wickets and turnpikes. Some earthen pots lay on wooden frames, while some were hung on the pegs fixed in walls. If one looked at the roof, one saw plough ropes, blinds for oxen and goad sticks. Little girls sat at the gate, while mature women had left the house for some work. In the interior, some unmarried girls were grinding corn and spinning yarn.[37] According to a famous proverb (*misal mashhoor*), a Jat woman was suited only for four activities. She carded wool, suckled the child, shouted at birds and grazed lambs.[38]

Waris, while describing the beauty of Hir, looked at every part of her body.[39] She looked like a heavenly fairy due to her pearl earrings, red bodice and nose ring. She was tall like a cypress of the heavenly garden. Her complexion was red like wine. Her tresses shone like stars around the moon. Her eyes were wild like those of a fawn. Her cheeks pulsated like the red rose. Her eyebrows were curved like the arches of Lahore. Her charming face matched the beautiful calligraphy of a book. Her lips were red like rubies, while her chin was shaped like a pear. Her nose was sharp like the Hussaini sword. Her teeth were like a string of lilies. Her neck was like that of a swan. Her arms were like the rolls of kneaded butter. Her breasts, made of white marble, upturned in pride. Her thighs were round and slender. Her navel was like a musk pod floating in a heavenly pool. Her loins were soft like velvet. The radiance of her lips slew the Khojas and Khatris of the market. She walked as if she was the Nawab's intoxicated elephant. Her movement was similar to the Qazilbash (Iranian) horsemen, who ran amuck through the bazaar. She was a fairy from the garden of Lanka or the court of Indra. The kohl of her eyes made her look like an army of Panjab that attacked Hindustan. On seeing her, the beholder performed the pilgrimage of Lailat ul-Qadr.[40]

Waris has recorded the content of correspondence between Takht Hazara and Jhang Siyal. The Ranjha brothers might have faced social disapproval at the departure of their youngest sibling. Having learnt that he was staying in Jhang Siyal, they made an earnest attempt to bring him back. In a letter to Chuchak, they accused the Siyals of employing Ranjha as a herdsman. The boy had left in anger. They had cultivated his land and stored its yield for him. Chuchak must send him back, failing which they would come in a body to take him. Chuchak, in his reply, clarified that Ranjha worked as Hir's servant and old shepherds obeyed him. The Jat youngman was worthy of praise because of his looks and energy. The Siyals would not return him as he was a valuable asset. If Ranjha wished to meet his relatives, they would not stop him. Ranjha's sisters-in-law also participated in the correspondence. They wrote three letters to Hir and received an equal number in response. They requested that Ranjha be returned to them in alms. He was too young for Hir, who must look for an older man. Since they were more beautiful than Hir, they perceived Ranjha as a beloved. In her reply, Hir allowed Ranjha to put the record straight. He accused his brothers of robbing his inheritance, while the sisters-in-law had challenged him to bring Hir as his wife. He was in the service of Hir, who had won his heart with kindness. Hir admitted employing Ranjha as a herdsman. He would not be returned as the past could not be reversed. He was in love with her, while she had taken a vow in the mosque with Quran as a witness. Describing Ranjha's routine in the moors, Hir alluded to the dishonesty of his brothers and the duplicity of their wives. Ranjha would not be sent back even if lakhs were paid in ransom.[41]

The brothers and their wives, thoroughly snubbed, did not interfere in Ranjha's life for some time. When they learnt of Hir's marriage, they made another attempt to bring Ranjha back to Takht Hazara. In a letter, they noted that Hir had betrayed him. Yet, nothing was lost for him. If he returned, they would offer a golden canopy (*kalash zareen*) at the local shrine. Ranjha, in his response, sounded optimistic about his love. There was no chance of his return. His brothers and sisters-in-law had taken away his land and also intended to take away his love. He resolved to join the creed of ear-cleft Jogis and return only with Hir. Fortunately for him, he received Hir's message, which a woman brought from Rangpur Khera. Hir underscored her suffering in separation and urged Ranjha to meet her in the garb of a Jogi. This message signalled the exchange of letters between the lovers. In a sarcastic tone, Ranjha accused Hir of enjoying a luxurious life with the Khera, whereas she had turned a Jat into a recluse (*faqir*). Hir, feeling distressed at the allegation, assured Ranjha of her love and her distance from Saida. For the third time, she asked Ranjha to come to Rangpur Khera in the guise of a Jogi. Ranjha, in his letter, expressed a sense of betrayal but, in practice, followed the repeated suggestion. Hir, both in her words and writings, laid emphasis on this momentous step. In this sense, Waris was different from Damodar, Ahmad and Muqbal. The latter three were certain that Ranjha, on his own, turned to Jog as a means of uniting with Hir.[42]

Waris has shown that the girls, living in the rural society of Panjab, did not live in seclusion. There was no restriction on their movements in the village and its environs. This was applicable to Hir's friends numbering sixty. At noon, they gathered on the banks of the Chenab, where Ranjha brought his buffaloes for a dip. They enjoyed themselves in different ways. Ranjha played on his flute, while Hir and her friends sang. Swimming around Ranjha, they performed a variety of tricks. One wrung her wet braid on his face, while another hugged him. One clung to his waist, while another touched her cheek with his. One of them teased him, while another dived on being chased. One rolled like a log, while another was carried away in the waves. In short, their movements were comparable to that of the birds such as duck, thrush, heron, woodpecker, eagle and crane. Hir, like a colourful fish, swam around Ranjha in circles and tried to trap him in the web of her flirtation.[43] Evidently, Waris has grafted the scene from Krishna's dalliance with the Gopis on the banks of the Yamuna.

A group of girls attending Hir's marriage indicated their adolescent interest in sex. Surrounding the bridegroom Saida, they demanded rings for their little fingers. They asked a number of funny questions, most of which were sexually suggestive. They asked Saida to bring his best man (*sarbala*) to face them. He must provide them with the milk of a virgin bird and that of a stallion. He must show the manner of working a well without bullocks. He must pitch a tent without poles. He must shake the bowl fixed in a tray. Could he put an elephant into a pot? Could his mother be married to a herdsman of the village? Saida answered all the questions with confidence and intelligence. Choosing to address one of the girls, he advised her to refrain from squabbling with him. She was given a ring because she was as beautiful as Bilqis, one of the 360 women in the *harem* of King Sulaiman. With the onset of monsoons, the grass had sprouted. He had shackled the legs of a cow to milk it. Its milk was as good as that of a virgin bird. He had milked a stallion and the girls could drink it without further bickering. A red and green dress augmented the female beauty, which exuded the fragrance of cloves. With eyes lined with kohl and lips reddened with the herbal twig (*dandasra*), her charm was reflected in a mirror. She walked like a duck that floated on water. He had vowed to offer a loaf to the local saint. He had searched out numerous worthless men, who could be married to the girls present. If they visited the fair of Dhronkal, they would find that he had pitched a tent without the necessary tools. It was impossible to produce a hen with the golden paw. Though he had married the herdsman's sister, he would take along all the girls and find suitable grooms for them.[44]

With the above gaze, Waris looked at the mature women, who were invited to Hir's marriage. Belonging to twelve castes and seven crafts, they were as beautiful as Padmini.[45] The fairies of heaven fainted on seeing them. Imbued with fragrance and endowed with sharp eyes, their faces shone with different complexions. They sang ribald songs and exchanged invectives. Their beauty filled the onlookers with longing. Their gossamer shawls covered their torso, while the waistcloth of Chenab hung from their midriffs. Some looked at the scene from above and others, removing their scarves, displayed their breasts and musk pod navels. Some clapped and danced, while others whirled like tops. Some began singing like the cuckoo and ended up hoarse like the crow. In sheer numbers, the crowds matched the vast concourse of pilgrims, who paid homage at the shrines of Shergarh, Pakpattan, Nigaha, Rattan and Thamman. The devout, beating drums and dancing in ecstasy, kissed the tombs and attained their desires.[46]

Waris has allowed Ranjha to condemn the Siyals for separating him from Hir. For the distraught lover, the Siyals were rotten and Hir was an apostate. When the elders discussed the matter of Hir's marriage, Chuchak hung his head in shame. The Siyals broke their promises and sold their daughters. Their beards resembled the husk of lentils. They hung a stone around the neck of a beautiful daughter. The village elders discarded the truth, while the Qazis were blinded with bribes. They chose a man as groom only to replace him with another. Thieves and thugs were made Panches and Chaudharis. The Kheras married Hir by force, while the honest Ranjha kept wailing. Though Ranjha blamed only the Siyals and Kheras, Waris has amplified the criticism to demonize the Jats as a caste. According to the poet, one could not trust the promise of a Jat. The Jats came into their senses only when they were made to roll in dust like the ass of the Gosains. They were pleased when mocked by the mimics and attacked by the Mughals. They pledged their daughters to strangers ignoring the right of their son-in-law. The Siyals were cheats, while their daughters were fraudsters. Deceiving the simple son of a chief, they converted him into a grazer of buffaloes. They went back on their promises and grafted their daughters on alien stalks. The Jats were thieves, waylayers and adulterers. Though all Jats were thugs, the Jats of the Chenab topped the list. The Dogars and Jats violated their faith and, as a result, their incomes were unlawful. Like them, their women led their sons and daughters to sin. They had great admiration for dubious characters like thieves and highway robbers. They vilified the men of prayer. Ignoring God and death, they broke betrothals. They pushed their daughters into bigamy and, thus, ruined their lives.[47]

Waris has combined wit and imagination to record a long verbal duel between the Jogi and Sehti. The Jogi, in a bitter contest with Sehti, claimed to be a distinguished representative of Jog. He matched the perfection of several things such as the bows of Lahore, the backbiting of Dipalpur, the magic of Kamrup, the cruelty of Nimrod, the image of China, the perfume of Khotan, the beauty of Yusuf and the magical verses of Waris. The Jogi, in his spiritual eminence, stood on a par with the most sublime in the physical phenomena of Panjab and other regions. His list included the turbans of Bajwara, the cotton fabric called Bafta, the country of Kashmir, the light of the moon, the heat of the oven, the beat of a distant drum, the earthquake of resurrection, the charm of fairies, the good fortune of the Kheras, the fragrance of musk, the stink of asafoetida and the sanctity of the Kaaba. The Jogi meant to say that he was the best among mendicants, while Sehti was the worst among women. A person breaking his promise was comparable to a warrior who fled from the battlefield and a veiled woman who came out of her house. God's will was as steadfast as the polestar and Kaaba. A rebellious woman and angry mendicant defied the authority. It was impossible for a landlord to pay the land tax and a foolish man to acquire wisdom. An unjust ruler was a fruitless tree. A disloyal wife was a bitch, while a man bereft of brain was an ass. A dancer was barren if she was not bashful. There could be no Jogi without austerities, life without breath, youth without courage, beloved without beauty, food without salt, moustaches without shame, beard without honour, army without salary, ministers without wisdom, Momin without prayer and government department without accounts. Four things (woman, mendicant, sword and horse) could not be loyal to anyone.[48] Waris was sensitive to religious diversity in medieval Panjab. Various religious communities and artisanal castes revered their own deities as listed below.[49]

Community	*Deity/Head*	*Community*	*Deity/Head*
Jogi	Mahadev	Mohana	Khwaja Khizr
Sannyasi	Devdatt	Mughal	Naqshband
Bairagi	Ramanand	Bharayi	Sakhi Sarwar

Udasi	Paramjot	Chuhra	Lal Beg
Brahmin	Brahma	Juari	Raja Nal
Hindu	Ram	Niyari	Shah Shams
All Rashis	Bishan-Mahesh	Julaha	Hazrat Shis
Suthra	Suthra Shah	Mirasi	Shaitan
Upasi	Shah Makhan	Ghumiar	Haji Gilgo
Jalali	Syed Jalal	Rafizi	Shah Ali
Khasi	Uwais Qarni	Nai	Sulaiman Paras
Madari	Shah Madar	Sunni	Ilm Pir
Bairagi	Vashisht	Ashiq	Ishq
Abhiyasi	Krishan	Jogi	Gorakhnath
Naushahi	Haji Naushah	Rakhshas	Shukar
Julasi	Kabir	Mast Hathi	Bhukh Pir
Qadiri	Dastgir	Vigrey Tigrey	Sota
Chishti	Farid	Jarrah	Daud
Mochi	Tihri	Teli	Hassu Teli
Suniara	Shams	Djinn	Sulaiman
Chhimba	Namdev	Momin	Rehman
Lohar	Luqman		

Waris never missed an opportunity to explore female sexuality. When Hir returned after meeting the Jogi in Kalabagh, she faced a barrage of embarrassing comments from Sehti, Raiba and Sairfa. They chided Hir for a dramatic change in her physical form and mental state. In this verbal exchange, references to the sexual act have been interwoven with a number of metaphors. Hir went to Kalabagh like a dead person but returned in good health. A restless mare became suddenly calm. An Id was celebrated in Kalabagh permitting the hungry to gorge sweets. A gallant knight rode a mare on a rough path. A general carried his guns to the fort and subjugated the peasantry. An armed horde of the Qandharis occupied Panjab. The Rajputs wielded swords in the battlefield, while the son of a Dhadi sang songs. Hanuman ransacked the kingdom of Lanka. Those who rolled in dust acquired political power. Robbers snatched loads of musk from traders, while the washermen washed the bales of velvet. A thief broke the lock and stole the musk pod. The wolves fell upon lambs and the mahouts mated the elephants. A pestle had been rotated in the casket of kohl. Removing the lid from the pail of milk, the cream was skimmed off. The barbers shaved off the beard of the Kheras. The ears and tail of the Kheras had been chopped as if they were Kabuli dogs. Saida proved to be a catamite (*gandu*). Turning to Hir, the girls found that her body had been pressed as if it had passed through a gin. Her tresses waved on her cheeks like butterflies. Her eyes sparkled, cheeks swelled and chest heaved. Below her vest, the torso was rubbed to redness. Her breasts were squeezed. Her mangoes were sucked and, leaving a trail of juices, looked as if the oilmen had extracted oil out of sesame seeds. Her navel was scratched with nails. Her limbs were displaced because heels were dug into her haunches. Her gaze had risen to the sky, refusing to look at ordinary mortals. Tired and exhausted, she was out of breath. Hir tried her best to divert the attention away from her body. Ultimately, she admitted that the rain, after a drought of twelve years, brought colour to the garden. The dismissed commander (*faujdar taghiyar*) was reinstated, while the tents and carpets were dusted. A boat, stranded on a shoal, was floating on the water level of Nuh.[50]

The lovers, in their protest against the Qazi's verdict, cursed the town with destruction through fire. In their separate appeals, they prayed that God would employ his wrath (*qehar*) to reduce the town to ashes.[51] Hir quoted a number of instances when divine retribution was inflicted in different parts of West Asia. Firaun was drowned. Zakariya was sawn in the hollow of a tree. Khalil was pushed into fire. Sulaiman was dethroned and consigned to a furnace. Yunus was swallowed by a fish. Ismail was slaughtered with a knife. Yusuf was thrown into a well. Shah Mardan was murdered by an attendant. Amir Hamza met his end at the hands of a female slave. Yazidis killed Imam Husain in a cruel manner. Imam Hasan was poisoned to death. In a similar appeal, Ranjha invoked God's anger (*karop*) for the devastation of the town. He quoted a number of examples from the Hindu religious lore. Indra, the incarnation of Vishnu, overthrew Mahekhasur. Daronacharya and Bhisham were harsh towards the Kauravas. The entrails of Harnakhsh were pulled out. Krishna dragged Kansa by his hair. Several armed divisions were consumed in the battle of Kurukshetra and, thus, the honour of Daropadi was vindicated. Rama destroyed the Lanka of Ravana. The nose of Sarupnakha was chopped off. Lachhman, Nal and Nil destroyed Kumbhakarna. Rama and Bali sliced the body of Taraka. Sabahu and Marich paid a heavy price for their deeds. In the foregoing discussion, Waris has erased the geographical distance between West Asia and South Asia.[52] At the same time, he assimilated two distinct cultural traditions, Islamic and Hindu, within a universal world view.

Waris wanted his readers to understand that all characters in his story represented distinct forces and values. Hir was the soul, while Ranjha was the body. They chose Balnath as their spiritual preceptor. They received the mandate of love from Panjpir, who symbolized the five senses. The Qazi signified the law, the boatman stood for conduct and the shepherd played the role of the agents of death. The lame Kaido, who exposed the lovers to a public trial, was a cursed devil. The flute produced the melody of awareness. In a fiery contest, Sehti was associated with death and Ranjha with life. Ranjha's sisters-in-law were responsible for expelling the humans from heaven. One should treat Jhang Siyal as a parental home and Kalabagh as a grave. The spinning bee appeared as the site of human follies. The Khera was the agent of death, who forcibly carried away the soul. The mosque, where one stayed for a day and night, was akin to a mother's womb. Raja Adli stood for pious deeds that restored Hir's faith in life. The Jogi was a perfect recluse, who bored his ears and rubbed ash on his body. However, salvation came into the share of only those who recollected the name of God.[53]

A Sufi Poet as Spokesman of Hir

Bulle Shah (1680-1758), a contemporary of Waris, was the most distinguished Sufi poet of Panjab.[54] In nearly sixteen mystical poems, he has referred to the tale of Hir-Ranjha. Without exception, he spoke on behalf of Hir, who saw Ranjha as a herdsman and Jogi. Hir knew that Ranjha had walked all the way from Takht Hazara for her sake. She found no difficulty in adopting him as her spiritual preceptor. When he did not visit her house, she was unable to identify her faults.

Since she repeated the name of Ranjha constantly, she felt that she had herself become Ranjha. Her friends must call her Dhido Ranjha, not Hir. Ranjha was in her and she was in him. She had erased her existence in a manner that only he remained. She longed only for him. Their love was older than creation (*kun fa yakun*), but it was not a secret. After searching in the jungle, pasture and desert, she did not find anyone like Ranjha. She asked her friends to congratulate her for acquiring him as a husband. Her day was blessed with his entry into her courtyard. Holding a staff in his hand and wearing a blanket on his shoulder, he appeared in the guise of a herdsman. His crown had fallen among the cattle and, thus, lost its value in the jungle and pastures.[55] In the eyes of the people, he was merely a herdsman. For Hir, he was her religion and faith (*din iman*). Leaving her parents, she had attached herself to his lappet. For his sake, she had put up with the reproaches of the people. She rejoiced on seeing him besides her bed. The world did not have to remind her of the social customs. She could not rest without seeing him. His love had driven her to madness. His separation tormented her body. She would die without him. If he came to her house, she would spend the night in joy and live happily thereafter. Very often, Ranjha went after the buffaloes and made her retreat from the moors. Sometimes, even the buffaloes returned to the village, while Ranjha remained elusive. She did not know the reason of his concealment. On these occasions, she removed her veil and cried like Zulaikha of Egypt. Her love for the herdsman was so strong that she wished to graze the buffaloes, carrying a staff in her hand and putting a blanket on her shoulder.[56]

The devout Muslims travelled to Mecca for pilgrimage. For Hir, Ranjha himself denoted Mecca. She wished to go to Takht Hazara, owing to the intensity of her love. Her Kaaba lay in the direction where Ranjha had his abode. This was true even if one examined the four holy books. People prostrated before Kaaba, but she pined for Takht Hazara and offered salutation to Ranjha. She hoped that Ranjha would overlook her faults and recognize her sincerity. She was ignorant of swimming and, if she drowned, Ranjha would be disgraced. Ranjha had fastened her with a hook and pulled the string. He gave a call from his seat and the commotion was heard in Mecca. The Kheras carried Hir in a palanquin, while Hir had no excuse or strength to resist. If the Kheras were dear to her mother, she should have put someone else in the litter leaving for Rangpur Khera.[57]

Hir, introducing the Jogi to her friends, described his outward appearance and inner qualities. He carried a staff in his hand and a blanket on his shoulders. Yet, he was neither a herdsman nor a servant. He had no interest in buffaloes. He had no liking for milk and curds. Nor did he suffer from any hunger and thirst. Betraying a strange lustre in his eyes, he was the intoxicated one (*matwala*). He carried a secret in his heart and did not open his mouth. He was separated from his beloved on the first night and, therefore, had come to search for her. For Hir, he was her true husband, while her father had been wrongly looking among the Kheras. On another occasion, Hir stated that the Jogi, like a consummate actor, had put up a great show. His identifying marks were clear. With rings in his ears and beads around his neck, he was a second Yusuf in appearance. His eyes were goblets that hunted like hawks. His eyes had shown something precious to Hir. With a mere glimpse of his face, her sorrows had vanished. If he was a Jogi, she was his Jogiani. Ever keen to serve him, she fetched water for his needs. She was conscious of wasting her previous life to no purpose. Now, he had entranced her. Their love, bearing a long past, had caused a commotion. Therefore, it could not be concealed any longer.[58]

Hir was enthusiastic about the arrival of Ranjha as a Jogi in Rangpur Khera. She declared her resolve to go with the Jogi after making a frontal mark on her forehead. None would be able to turn her back. She faced numerous reproaches for her pursuit of love. Ranjha was not a Jogi but the beloved of her heart. She had abandoned rational abilities since falling in love with him. She lost all control on gaining his sight. The Jogi trapped her heart with his hooks. He had cast a net of love with his sweet words. She recognized him well, though people called her mad. If he came to her house, all disputes would end. She would clasp him to her chest with a thousand omens. He had set up a fire at her door. Having changed his appearance, he was asking for Hir. Hir's aunts must not taunt Hir because fate had brought the Jogi to her house. With God's grace, he had come to practice Jog. No longer a herdsman, he was a divine light (*nur ilahi*). He played the unstruck melody on his flute. He had ruined Hir with his powerful magic. Millions had gone and thousands had come, but no one has discovered his secret. He had the privilege of speaking to Musa after he climbed the Koh-i Tur. Prophet Muhammad ascended to the heaven when Jibrail brought the mythical horse Buraq and the fairies sang. The Jogi narrated the mournful story of the martyrdom of Hasan and Husain. Hearing the Jogi's story, Sohni and Mahiwal drowned in deep waters. The Kheras, the ancient enemies of the lovers, carried Hir in a palanquin, while Ranjha went along with a drum on his head. The Jogi offered the cup of ecstasy to Hir who, after drinking it, became ecstatic and rubbed ash on her body. The Jogi was entangled in a legal suit with the Qazi and false accusations of Kaido. People did not know that Hir was married to the Jogi. She became a possession of the Jogi after the propitiation of Panjpir.[59]

In a long composition, Bulle Shah has captured the story of Hir-Ranjha in a nutshell. When the call for creation was given, Ranjha came from Takht Hazara. Though he was called Chuchak's herdsman, he was the lord of purity (*sahib safai*). Endowed with divine grace, he pulled the strings from the unseen world. He lived under the protection of Panjpir, who searched for him among humankind. When love established its camp, all patience disappeared. Hir asked Ranjha to accompany her to the shrine of Shaikh Bahauddin Zakariya, so that their desires were fulfilled. The lovers claimed to be free but the noose of love fell around their necks. As the marriage party of the Kheras descended, Hir was on the verge of death. The proud Khera arrived on a horse. Since Ranjha was not seen, Hir raised a hue and cry. On the day of resurrection, Hir would create a dispute and seek divine justice. Chuchak summoned the Qazi and, using force, performed the parental duty of marriage. A perfumed lotion was rubbed on Hir's shoulders and sandalwood paste was smeared on her forehead. Her bangles were of no use as Ranjha had retreated to the pasture. She could not endure the sight of Ranjha bearing a drum on his head. Ultimately, he threw the drum away and, meditating on Hir's name, reached the Tilla. His ears were bored and inserted with rings. He gained the mandate of Guru Gorakhnath. The Jogi, with his head and face shaven, came to practice Jog. He wore a saffron robe and a black string around his neck. He came to the town of the Kheras, particularly the house where he had a purpose. He blew his horn to invoke divine grace. As he faced resistance, his bowl was shattered and millets were scattered. No one was able to discern his deceit. While collecting the millets in his lap, he kept looking at Hir. As inscribed in destiny, their eyes encountered each other. Sehti detected this exchange. Since the two women were afflicted with the same pain, they added fuel to the Jogi's fire. Sehti devised a deception in which Hir was bitten by a snake. The Jogi came to recite the sacred verses. The desire of the lovers materialized.[60]

Hir-Ranjha in the Nineteenth Century

During the early decades of the nineteenth century, Ranjit Singh built a large empire between the Satluj and Hindukush mountains. He subverted a score of principalities and, reducing them to vassalage, assimilated them into an expanding domain. His sway extended to Multan, Kangra, Kashmir, Derajat and Peshawar. Assisted by an efficient army and hierarchy of local officers, he paid his nobles through revenue assignments and patronized diverse religious institutions. After his death (1839), intense conflict in the ruling class allowed the British to annex the kingdom. The colonial state introduced series of new laws, besides developing the canal colonies and communications. It won over a part of the old aristocracy and recruited a bulk of the disbanded Khalsa soldiery. As the small peasantry faced impoverishment and indebtedness, the moneylenders made substantive gains. In west Panjab, the Chishti order revived owing to the efforts of Nur Muhammad Muharvi, Sulaiman Taunsavi and Mehr Ali Shah. The middle classes, benefiting from widening literacy and printing technology, contributed to communitarian consciousness. The narrative poetry (*qissa*) constituted a prominent strand in the Panjabi literary tradition, which had been evolving since the early seventeenth century.[61]

Ahmadyar (1768-1845) has reproduced the tale of Hir-Ranjha in 1399 stanzas of four lines each.[62] In a graceful appreciation, he admitted that Waris Shah had narrated the story of Hir-Ranjha in an admirable way. He had tried to follow the lead of Waris, though he did not possess the ability of constructing the themes in verse. His affinity with Waris was visible throughout the text. The similarity was rather palpable in his account of the correspondence between the Ranjhas and Siyals, Hir's marriage with Saida and Ranjha's demonization of the Siyal Jats. It was equally manifest in Ahmadyar's description of the Jogi's unfavourable encounters in Rangpur Khera and the Jogi's acerbic debate with Sehti, besides the Jogi's knowledge of diseases and medicines. On some important points, Ahmadyar deviated from Waris and drew on the works of Damodar and Muqbal. Since such references were few, Ahmadyar refrained from any specific acknowledgement.

Ahmadyar's debt to Muqbal was evident in his accounts of the circumstances in which Ranjha left his home and the return journey of the Khera marriage party. After the death of Mauju, his seven sons treated Ranjha as if he were Yusuf. In a division of ancestral land, his share comprised nitrous soil and abundant weeds. The revenue collectors dragged him to the government office to extract the land tax. While grappling with these difficulties, he saw Hir in a dream and became obsessed with her. He revealed his dream to his brothers and their wives. They tried to turn his mind to cultivation and, advising him to forget his dream, promised to get him a bride of high status. Ranjha clarified that he had no complaint against his brothers. After the death of his parents, he had decided to renounce the world and go out in search of his beloved. When he was leaving, a number of people (his brothers, sisters-in-law, neighbours and clan) pleaded with him to stay on, but to no avail.[63] Apart from this reference to Ranjha's dream and cordiality with his brothers, Ahmadyar has picked up another episode from Muqbal. This incident happened when the Kheras, returning from hunting, saw Hir and Ranjha in the palanquin. They wanted to kill the bride and punish the herdsman. Hir raised her hands to shield Ranjha from the blows. She broke her necklace and, scattering the pearls, stated her position. Since Ranjha was a servant from her parental home, she had summoned him to collect the pearls. The Kheras restrained their aggression and decided to avenge themselves on reaching Rangpur. On the one hand, Ranjha sought the help of Panjpir and, on the other hand, offered to hold a hot ploughshare to prove his innocence. The Kheras were convinced of Ranjha's righteousness and believed that he was a saint who enjoyed divine support.[64] Ahmadyar, like Muqbal, has tried to minimize the conflict in the story.

Ahmadyar, by assigning a substantive role to Hir's brothers, added a new dimension to the Hir-Ranjha tradition. The brothers of Hir took a keen interest in Ranjha's employment as herdsman and his relation with their sister. Khan and Sultan were surprised to see Ranjha in the moors with their buffaloes. They asked him his native place, employment and remuneration. On receiving answers to these preliminary questions, they wanted to know the qualities of his flute, particularly its secrets. Ranjha revealed that he had received the flute from Panjpir and, owing their blessings, it displayed magical powers. When he played on the flute, the people living in villages and along rivers became ecstatic. Wherever it was heard, there was no oppression and calamity. Hearing its sound, the buffaloes collected within no time. It enabled him to seek the protection of God as well as the help of Panjpir. Hir's bothers were amused at the tall claims of the new herdsman. Soon after, Hir informed her mother that the yield of milk had doubled and attributed the improvement to Ranjha's grace (*barkat*). The brothers became doubtful of Hir's excessive praise of Ranjha and suspected her connivance with him. Ranjha declared that he had spent a lifetime in grazing cattle and, therefore, God had endowed him with the ability to diagnose the veterinary ailments. The brothers announced that they would employ him only if he cleared a test. At their instance, the Siyals assembled to see the spectacle. They were restless due to the fear of a negative outcome. Four bowls of milk were brought. Ranjha took a close look and identified the difference among them. The first belonged to a buffalo who had recently delivered a calf, while the second was associated with a mature buffalo (*khangar*). The third and fourth bowl came from two cows with the above traits. The brothers, jubilant at the result, confirmed Ranjha in his job and placed the buffaloes in his charge. They recognized the merit of Ranjha who enjoyed divine approval (*maqbul ilahi*).[65] Ahmadyar appears to have borrowed this episode from the versification of Damodar.

Ahmadyar has conferred an afterlife to the lovers. In a book, he read about pilgrims returning from Mecca after meeting Hir and Ranjha. One of the pilgrims was marooned on a shore. Walking for ten days towards the east, he reached a fort, which was enclosed in a heavenly garden and surrounded by a canal. He heard a voice reciting the Quran and listened to it for the whole day. In the evening, a man appeared with a herd of buffaloes. This man, wearing a purple turban (*chira gulnari*), carried a staff and flute in his hands. The visitor was fed with rice dessert. He learnt that the palace belonged to Hir and Ranjha, while the buffaloes were the same that grazed back in Panjab. The visitor spent the night and, next morning, reached his home in Panjab through a miracle. He was convinced that true lovers lived forever. At this time, a Sufi named Shah Rukn-i Alam Noori begged God for a glimpse of Hir. Sitting beside a river, he offered the obligatory prayer. He saw a girl walking in and sitting nearby. He reprimanded her for disrupting his prayer. She said that his mind was not focused on his devotion. She recounted her own experience. She was chopping mustard leaves and, seeing Ranjha, instantly slashed her finger tip. Her soul shifted to the body of Ranjha and breathed her last. Saying this, she walked away. Shah Noori uttered a sigh and fell prostrate. He realized that his love for God was not as strong as that of Hir for the Jat. Even a Sufi admitted that Hir's love was sublime and unique.[66]

Hashim Shah (1735-1843), famous for a classic on Sassi-Punnu, has earned the distinction of composing the shortest poem on the tale of Hir-Ranjha.[67] Since the work comprised thirty stanzas of four lines each, the poet admitted that he had ignored a number of anecdotes. Hashim has paid maximum attention to the role of Hir. The locality alleged that she had disgraced the Siyals by burning their turbans and beards. Her appearance before the Qazi attracted a large gathering including village elders, headmen, governor, revenue collector, theologians and Sufis. A series of allegations were levelled against Hir. The Qazi, having examined the holy book, declared that the Shariat did not permit a woman to maintain contact with any unrelated man. Hir was an unfortunate devil, who had raised an infamous dispute. Hir advanced a forceful reply, weighing all aspects of the matter. Her love for Ranjha was pure. God provided nourishment to all human beings such as warriors, saints and renouncers. The same God was a protector of the oppressed. Since ancient antiquity, destiny had been unkind to lovers. Though Yusuf was endowed with numerous virtues, destiny turned him into a slave. The lovers, in comparison to Yusuf, were ignorant orphans (*gawar yatim*). The arguments convinced the Qazi who turned his ire against Hir's parents. They were bereft of reason and sense. They had imprisoned God's lovers who were immune from legal injunctions. The Siyals did not profit from their opposition and, thus, proved that they were false. The parents appealed to Hir with folded hands. She must protect their honour and, in order to do this, she must go to the place of her parents-in-law. Hir, mindful of the dignity of her parents, went with the Kheras. Ranjha accompanied the palanquin with a drum on his head. It was impossible for him to serve the Siyals. He returned to Takht Hazara in acute sorrow. On seeing his brothers, he broke down and became unconscious. Despite his pitiable state, his love for Hir did not dissipate.[68]

Hir, in a letter to Ranjha, reprimanded him for returning to Takht Hazara and leaving her in the lurch. In his quick response, Ranjha adopted Jog. Smearing ash on his body, he kept matted hair and put on earrings. He acquired the knowledge about all aspects of his new creed. Holding a stringed instrument (*toomba*), he reached Rangpur Khera and raised the slogan of 'Alakh'. Hir recognized the voice of Ranjha and smelt the fragrance of his body. The Jogi was distressed at Hir's pitiable condition. Without saying a word, he retraced his steps. The villagers saw him as a physician, while Hir's sickness had remained undetected. Saida requested the Jogi to treat Hir. The Jogi used amulets of love and laid equal emphasis on medicines. After some time, he left the place in secrecy along with Hir. The Kheras chased the lovers and caught them in the town of Raja Adli. During the interrogation, Raja Adli asked Hir to explain her relation with Ranjha. Hir stated that Ranjha was her religion and faith (*din iman*), while Saida had not been able to touch her body. Raja Adli gave Hir to Ranjha and expelled the Kheras from the town. Hashim prayed for the longevity of Raja Adli's rule, which had administered justice all around. True love attained happiness only after enduring numerous tribulations.[69]

In 1849, Ganesh Das Vadhera completed a comprehensive work on the kingdom of Ranjit Singh, concentrating on history, geography, polity and religion. In a large section on the love tales of Panjab, he related the story of Hir-Ranjha. He followed the received knowledge up to Hir's forced marriage. From here on, his narrative adopted a different trajectory. Ranjha joined a group of Jogis and, after a period of intense austerities, he earned the privilege of wearing earrings. He went to Rangpur and visited every house in the guise of a Jogi. Hir doubted the medical expertise of the Jogi, who established his fire outside the village. Sehti plotted a stratagem to unite the lovers. The ruse of a snakebite brought in the Jogi as a healer. During the fake treatment in a secluded place, the outer wall was broken and the lovers escaped. Next day, they were caught near village Adilpur. The local administrator, who was an appointee of Sultan Adil, adjudicated the case. Hir's marriage was held unlawful because it was contracted against her will. She was free to go with Ranjha if she liked. Differences emerged between the lovers. Ranjha wanted to take Hir straight to Takht Hazara. Hir wished to return to her parents and, after a lawful wedding, would go with Ranjha. The difference was referred to the headman (*muqaddam*) of Maghiana. This man, upholding Hir's opinion, offered to take the responsibility of a guardian if Chuchak refused to hold the marriage. The same night, Hir died of snakebite and, not long after, Ranjha died of shock. Chuchak refused to see the corpse of his daughter, whose love had erased his honour. She was buried on the way to Jhang. Her grave, enclosed in four walls, did not have a roof. Ranjha was buried at Takht Hazara without a memorial. Vadhera was disappointed at the manner in which the survivors treated the lovers after their death. However, he assured us that the names of the lovers were enshrined in the hearts of the people.[70]

In 1863, Maulavi Nur Muhammad brought out a history of Jhang Siyal in Persian.[71] He believed that the story of Hir-Ranjha, which was the subject of a famous ballad, deserved a brief account. Dhido belonged to the caste (*quam*) of the Ranjhas, who were settled in Takht Hazara. Having become alienated from his brothers (*az biradaran khud ranjul shuda*), he came to Jhang Siyal. He took up service under Chuchak. He possessed a complete mastery in grazing cattle. Chuchak, recognizing his ability, gave him more importance than he did to other herdsmen. During this period, love developed between Ranjha and Chuchak's daughter Hir. Their love was regarded as spiritual, wherein the souls were united and there was no physical intimacy (*shehwat-i nafsani*). In spite of Hir's strong attachment to Ranjha, she was not married to him owing to the sense of honour and fear of her father. Hir was married to Saida, the son of Ajju Khera, a native and chief of Rangpur Khera in District Muzaffargarh. Ranjha gave up Chuchak's service and, adopting the ways of the Jogis (*tariq jogian akhtiar sakhta*), came to Rangpur. By now, his love for Hir had become famous. Saida Khera also knew that Hir had given her heart to Ranjha. Alienated from Hir, he divorced her. He ordered his men to push the lovers to the waterless tract west of Rangpur. After this, their activities and destination were not known. People lied that pilgrims had seen them in an island or in the holy cities (*harmain sharif*). These tales were not trustworthy because the relation between lovers was based on soul. It was believed that Hir possessed miraculous powers (*ahl-i karamat*). At present, Hir's tomb was located on the east of Maghiana Khas near the government bungalow. People visited the site to express their devotion and make offerings. Yet, they did not believe that Hir was buried there or her remains were shifted later on. There was no reliable tradition (*rivayat pukhta*).[72]

Richard Carnac Temple, the renowned folklorist, picked the tale of Hir-Ranjha from some Jats of Patiala State.[73] According to this version (1884), Ranjha had received his landholding from the Mughals. After the death of his father, he had differences with his seven brothers, though he cultivated affectionate relations with a sister-in-law Lali. Unable to make his field arable, he left his home and became a mendicant. On his way, he spent the night in a mosque. He had a tiff with the Mulla, while the boys brought him food. He reached a city and met Queen Luna. She invited him to be her guest and offered to marry her two daughters to him. He rejected the offer and walked through a jungle. The melody of his flute induced Lord Indra to send a buffalo. Ranjha milked the buffalo and offered the milk to Panjpir. The five saints announced that Hir had been given to him from Mecca and Medina. On the banks of the Chenab, he bribed the boatman Luddan and, thus, slept on a bed in the boat. The vessel belonged to Hir, the daughter of Chuchak Siyal. She saw a dream and, securing a Brahmin's interpretation, learnt that a lover had desecrated her bed. She rushed to the ferry and interrogated the intruder. Ranjha, in his previous incarnations, claimed to have been Indra, Krishna and Ramanand, while Hir had been their loving consort. When he appeared as Ranjha, she was born to Chuchak. In an instant marriage of the two, Prophet Muhammad formed the marriage procession and Brahma set up the marriage canopy. Panjpir performed the ceremony and Khwaja Khizr witnessed it.[74]

Hir asked Chuchak to employ Ranjha as a herdsman. Chuchak did not agree because the lad, owing to his aristocratic bearing, was unsuited for the job. Ranjha decided to return to Takht Hazara and Hir prepared to go with him. Chuchak took Ranjha in his service and, in the presence of 70 Khans and 72 nobles, betrothed him to Hir. Every night, Ranjha grazed buffaloes in the moors, where lions and serpents lived in plenty. At daybreak, Hir met him with a packet of food. Hir's brother Pathan reprimanded Ranjha for meeting Hir and, thus, cornered the lovers. Kaido received food from Ranjha in alms and declared that the affair had disgraced the Siyals. The clan reopened the question of Hir's future. She could be married to the goldsmith Mabbu, Raja Adli or Ranjha. Ultimately, the dominant view gravitated towards the Kheras. Hir, in an argument with the Qazi, refused to replace Ranjha with Saida. The Qazi admitted his inability to prevail upon Hir. At the suggestion of Kaido, Hir was betrothed to Saida. Ranjha lamented that Chuchak had promised Hir to him in an assembly. He had grazed the buffaloes for twelve years without any wages. The protest was ignored and Hir was married to Saida, who was one-eyed and bald-headed. Ranjha carried a drum along with the goods of the Kheras. Speaking to Hir, he recalled his sacrifices and criticized her betrayal. Hir reiterated her love for him and asked him to resume his job in Jhang Siyal. She swore on the Quran to meet him after twelve months. Ranjha walked back to Jhang Siyal and ultimately returned to Takht Hazara.[75]

According to the above narrative, Ranjha cheated Gorakhnath and Raja Adli oppressed Hir. At the Tilla, Gorakhnath was reluctant to initiate Ranjha in Jog because sainthood denied even minimum comfort to a novice. Ranjha stole the mentor's conch and buried it in sand besides a river. Gorakhnath demanded the conch and threatened to use his punitive powers. Ranjha played on his flute and conch. Mother goddess, Raja Adli and numerous Jogis were attracted to the site. Gorakhnath, pleased at the music, bored Ranjha's ears and inserted rings in them. He advised Ranjha to treat a young woman as sister and an old woman as mother. Ranjha rejected the advice. Gorakhnath, following the lead of Panjpir, declared that Hir had been granted to him from Mecca and Medina. Gorakhnath sent his crow to Rangpur Khera with a message for Hir. She sent messengers to five persons including Ranjha.[76]

The narrative, from the Jogi's arrival in Rangpur Khera to the elopement of lovers, proceeded along the familiar track. The dispute reached the court of Raja Adli, who listened to every stakeholder. The Kheras described Saida's marriage to Hir and the Jogi's deceitful act. Ranjha, invoking the authority of God and Prophet Muhammad, asserted his claim over Hir. Chuchak admitted that he had offered Hir to Ranjha in the presence of prominent Khans, but his relatives forced him to tie Hir with Saida. Hir accused Adli of taking a bribe from the Kheras and stated that she belonged only to Ranjha. As soon as Adli saw Hir, he was filled with lust. Declaring that Hir had been betrothed to him, he sent her to the upper story of his bungalow. When he approached her bed, she invoked Gorakhnath. The body of Adli caught fire. The sound of Ranjha's flute spread to distant places and attracted a large concourse of spiritual entities such as 70 saints of Mecca, Panjpir from Multan, mother goddess Durga and Sakhi Sarwar. An army, led by Hanuman, set fire to the city and cut down the royal garden. A minister said that Adli's life could be saved if he reversed his evil act. Adli adopted Hir as his granddaughter and, in the presence of citizens, married her to Ranjha. In view of the miraculous events, the narrators ranked Ranjha as the sixth saint after Panjpir.[77]

NOTES

1. Sujan Rai Bhandari, *Khulasat ut-Tawarikh*, pp. 77-8.
2. Bhai Gurdas, *Varan Bhai Gurdas,* vol. II, ed. Jodh Singh, Patiala and New Delhi, Vision & Venture, 1998, Var 27, Pauri 1, p. 143.
3. Anonymous, *Dasam Granth*, Charitaropakhyan, Charitar 98, Search Gurbani.Com pp. 1771-6.

4. Ahmad Gujjar, *Hir Ahmad*, ed. S.S. Padam, Barnala: Punjabi Sahit Sabha, 1960, Stanza no. 236, p. 285. (Hereafter cited as Ahmad.)
5. Ahmad, in the beginning of his narrative, has left a few gaps. First, he did not say anything about the circumstances in which Hir and Ranjha were born. He has entirely overlooked their families and clans. Second, he was silent on the manner in which Ranjha developed an interest in Hir. He did not see her in a dream. Nor did he hear about her from anyone. He could not have referred to her birthplace (Jhang Siyal) when he was ignorant of her. He left his home owing to the maltreatment of his brothers, not because of a desire to meet Hir whom he did not know. Only when he was walking towards the Chenab, he learnt about Hir for the first time. At this moment, Panjpir bestowed Hir on him and, as a consequence, his interest in Hir was instilled. The event happened before he encountered Luddan on the Chenab.
6. Ahmad, Stanza nos. 15-23, pp. 192-5.
7. Ibid., Stanza Nos. 24-36, pp. 196-200.
8. Ibid., Stanza Nos. 37-45, pp. 200-203.
9. Ibid., Stanza nos. 51-5, pp. 205-7.
10. In the account of Ahmad, Yusuf was born in prosperous circumstances. His jealous brothers threw him into a well. According to God's wish, a trader pulled him out. He was kept to be sold and, therefore, brought to the market of Misr. An old woman, picking up a few rolls of cotton yarn, entered the ranks of the buyers. Similarly, Ranjha cultivated a desire to meet Balnath, so that he could be called a Jogi. In the eyes of the disciples, Ranjha did not have the genuine aptitude for initiation into Jog. However, he was presumptuous enough to aspire for an exalted spiritual state. Ahmad, Stanza no. 72, p. 213.
11. Ahmad, Stanza nos. 85-137, pp. 218-42.
12. Ibid., Stanza nos. 138-61, pp. 242-51.
13. Zulaikha was the daughter of King Taimus. In a dream, she saw the handsome Yusuf and fell in love with him. She kept her dream a secret and declined in health. At the advice of physicians, she was fetterred in a golden chain but yearned for the unknown youth. In another dream, the youth revealed that he was the Grand Wazir of Egypt. Zulaikha was sent to Memphis as the wife of the Grand Wazir. She was shocked to find that her husband was not the youth of her dreams. Yusuf, after many misadventures, came to the royal court as a prospective slave. Zulaikha recognized Yusuf as the man of her dreams. She spent a huge sum to purchase him. In spite of her best efforts, she could

not win his love and remained distressed for long. Hir, in the eyes of Ahmad, endured a similar fate. Following a forcible marriage, she was separated from her lover and underwent great suffering.

14. Ahmad, Stanza nos. 162-98, pp. 252-67.
15. Syed Jalaluddin Bukhari (1308-80), famous as Makhdum-i Jahaniyan, was a charismatic Suhrawardi saint. Son of Ahmad Kabir and grandson of Jalaluddin Surkhposh, he took his early education in Uch. Shifting to Multan, he continued his studies under the supervision of Ruknuddin Abul Fateh. In 1341, he declined the offer of managing over fifty Sufi lodges of Sind. During the next seven years, he travelled in different parts of west Asia and, mastering Islamic sciences, received honorary robes of six Sufi orders. On returning (1348) to Uch, he developed the Suhrawardi establishment into a thriving seminary. While interacting with disciples, he privileged knowledge (*ilm*) of Islamic jurisprudence over actions (*amal*) comprising devotional practices. His spiritual discourses were compiled in six volumes. A close friend of Sultan Firoz Shah Tughluq, he spent long periods in Delhi. For details of his teachings, see Amina M. Steinfels, *Knowledge Before Action: Islamic Learning and Sufi Practice in the Life of Saiyyid Jalal al-Din Bukhari Makhdum-i Jahaniyan*, pp. 63-102.
16. Ahmad, Stanza nos. 199-231, pp. 267-82.
17. Ahadis were an intermediate category of soldiers, who were not included in the contingents of military commanders (*mansabdars*) and were too good to employ as ordinary troopers. Literally, the word denoted singular or alone (*ahad*). Treated as immediate servants of the Emperor and forming an elite corps, they were deployed on non-military errands and household duties. A separate department (*diwan*) and paymaster (*bakhshi*) dealt with them. During the early eighteenth century, they were paid a monthly salary of Rs. 40. With the decay of Emperor's authority, their name became a byword for laziness. William Irvine, *The Army of the Indian Moghuls: Its Organization and Administration*, New Delhi: Eurasia Publishing House, rpt., 1962, p. 43; Ishtiaq Husain Qureshi, *The Administration of the Mughul Empire*, Patna: Janaki Prakashan, rpt., 1979, p. 119.
18. Ahmad, Stanza nos. 225-31, pp. 279-82.
19. Ibid., Stanza nos. 232-6, pp. 282-4.
20. Muqbal, *Qissa Hir Ranjha*, ed. Joginder Singh, Patiala: Punjabi University, 2000, Stanza nos. 5-10, pp. 25-6. (Hereafter cited as Muqbal.)
21. Muqbal, Stanza nos. 11-24, pp. 26-8.

22. The poet indicated that Ranjha left his home for two reasons. First, he was unable to cultivate the land that fell in his share. He decided to adopt mendicancy that involved voluntary starvation and begging food. Second, in his heart, he intended to meet Hir. Therefore, he asked his sisters-in-law to bless his endeavour to attain Hir. The women were ignorant of his interest in Hir. They remained silent on the matter, though they tried to stop his departure. When Ranjha departed from his house, he knew that he was not a aimless wanderer. In a conscious decision, he took the road leading to Jhang Siyal where Hir lived. Quick to forget his family, he began to face pangs of separation from his beloved whom he had not met. While stepping out of his house, he tore his clothes and smeared ash on his body. The guise of mendicancy would facilitate his journey through an unknown tract and ensure his safety from robbers. This step had nothing to do with Jog, which would appear late in the narrative.
23. Muqbal, Stanza nos. 28-33, pp. 28-9.
24. Ibid., Stanza nos. 34-42, pp. 29-31.
25. Ibid., Stanza nos. 91-110, pp. 38-41.
26. Ibid., Stanza nos. 111-41, pp. 41-6.
27. Ibid., Stanza nos. 167-83, pp. 51-2.
28. Ibid., Stanza nos. 191-207, pp. 58-63.
29. Ibid., Stanza nos. 208-30, pp. 63-6.
30. The poet, contextualizing Ranjha's conversion to Jog, recalled the examples of Shaikh Sanan and Shaikh Ibrahim Adham. The former, a devout and scholarly Muslim, kept the holy place in Mecca. In old age, he went to Rome and fell in love with a Christian beauty. For her sake, he embraced Christianity, consumed wine and tended a flock of swine. He reverted to Islam at the intervention of Prophet Muhammad and help of friends. The girl repented of her actions and, converting to Islam, died of inner turmoil. Shaikh Ibrahim Adham (d. 777), born in Balkh, followed the Sufi orientation of Rabia Basri. He practised contemplation, defined levels of asceticism and suggested deeper ways of unitary knowing through experience. Outwardly a renunciant, he fasted for long periods and went without winter clothes. According to legend, he abandoned his father's kingdom for a life of poverty on the lines of Buddha. Fariduddin Attar, *Mantiq ul-Tair*, Eng. tr. (*The Conference of the Birds*) Afkham Darbandi and Dick Davis, London & New York, Penguin Books, 2011, pp. 68-86; Arthur F. Buehler, *Recognizing Sufism: Contemplation in the Islamic Tradition*, London & New York: I.B. Tauris, 2016, pp. 43-4.

31. Muqbal, Stanza nos. 232-49, pp. 66-9.
32. Ibid., Stanza nos. 297-337, pp. 75-81.
33. Ibid., Stanza nos. 338-60, pp. 81-5.
34. Waris Shah, *Hir Waris Shah*, ed. Piara Singh Padam, New Delhi: Navyug Publishers, rpt., 1998, Stanza nos. 618-23, pp. 233-5. (Hereafter cited as Waris)
35. Jit Singh Sital and Piara Singh Padam, in their texts, have deleted a part of the passage on the morning scene. For the complete reference, see Sant Singh Sekhon, *Hir Waris Shah*, New Delhi: Sahitya Academy, rpt., 2006, pp. 42-3.
36. Waris, Stanza nos. 42-4, pp. 68-9.
37. Ibid., Stanza no. 332, pp. 145-6.
38. Ibid., Stanza no. 403, p. 169.
39. Ibid., Stanza nos. 53-5, pp. 71-2.
40. Lailat ul-Qadr (night of power) pertained to 610 AD when the Quran descended in its entirety into the soul of Prophet Muhammad. It is one of the last ten nights of Ramzan and, for this reason, these ten days are regarded particularly holy. In that night, Angel Gabriel first spoke to the Prophet, the Quran was revealed and the divine mission began. According to Surah 97 of the Quran, 'It is better than a thousand months. The angels and the spirit come down during it, by the permission of the Lord, on account of every command. It is a night of peace until the rising of the dawn.' Aisha, the favourite wife of the Prophet, explained it as the soul of the Prophet. Since the Prophet is also all of creation in the form of a man, that night corresponds to his soul. It implies that the true nature of human soul is a receptacle of God's revelation. Cyril Glasse, *The Concise Encyclopaedia of Islam*, London: Stacey International, 3rd edn., 2008, p. 310.
41. Waris, Stanza nos. 162-70, pp. 98-100.
42. Ibid., Stanza nos. 241-50, pp. 119-21.
43. Ibid., Stanza no. 123, pp. 88-9.
44. Ibid., Stanza nos. 200-02, pp. 108-9.
45. According to ancient Indian erotica and legend, women were divided into four categories. These were enumerated as Padmini (lotus), Chitrini (art), Shankini (conch) and Hastini (elephant). Each name denoted distinct physical and mental qualities. A Padmini woman had a beautiful face like the full moon. Her body had exquisite shape. She was endowed with large eyes and firm breasts. Her skin was golden, silky and delicate. Bearing a melodious voice, she walked with grace and perfect bodily posture. Padmini was also the name of the wife of

Raja Rattan Sen of Chittor. According to the Awadhi account of Malik Muhammad Jaisi, she was originally a Ceylonese princess. Rattan Sen married her after undergoing a series of hurdles and austerities. Alauddin Khalji (r. 1296-1316) attacked Chittor to acquire her. In an unprecedented move, Padmini rescued her husband from the custody of the Sultan in Delhi. She was regarded as an epitome of beauty, courage and fidelity. Apparently, Waris had this Padmini in his mind.

46. Waris, Stanza nos. 196-7, p. 107.
47. Ibid., Stanza nos. 223-7, pp. 114-15.
48. Ibid., Stanza nos. 343-8, pp. 149-51.
49. Ibid., Stanza no. 346, pp. 149-50.
50. Ibid., Stanza nos. 511-34, pp. 199-206.
51. Ibid., Stanza nos. 603-6, pp. 228-30.
52. The text of Waris has enabled a modern writer to explore the lived experience of the Punjabi Muslims, with reference to their social structure and religious practices. This exercise has been undertaken in the social and cultural context of medieval Panjab. The text has been seen as a popular literary document about Panjabi Muslims, who lived Islam in their own vernacular way. Instead of understanding them solely via the standardized Islamic route, it tries to understand them through their own roots i.e. the historically evolved indigenous cultural canvas of Panjab. From the viewpoint of vernacular identity of Panjabi Muslims, the root vision of identity stands in opposition to the homogenizing project of the route approach to the identity question. Ishwar Dayal Gaur, *Society, Religion and Patriarchy: Exploring Medieval Punjab through Hir Waris*, New Delhi: Manohar, 2009, p. 20.
53. Waris, Stanza no. 624, p. 235.
54. Bulle Shah, according to some accounts, was born in Uch Gilanian near Uch. Some sources held that he was born at Pandoke near Qasur, a town 30 miles south-east of Lahore. His father, a religious scholar, was the Imam of a mosque and ran a seminary. Bulle Shah, moving to Qasur, received his formal education from Hafiz Ghulam Mustafa Qasuri. He took spiritual instructions from Shah Inayat Qadiri of Lahore. He appears to have lived in Lahore until his mentor's death (1728) and then returned to Qasur. His mystical poems (*kafis*) were simple in form and complex in themes. A Unitarian par excellence, he underscored a loving relation with God and lamented separation from Him. He advocated demolition of social boundaries, while mocking at theologians, rituals and formalism. He explained these

ideas through the tale of Hir-Ranjha. Shuja Alhaq, *A Forgotten Vision: A Study of Human Spirituality in the Light of Islamic Tradition*, vol. II, pp. 370-92.

55. Sutinder Singh Noor, *Punjabi Sufi Kaav*, New Delhi: Sahitya Akadami, 1997, Kafi no. 35, p. 212; Kafi no. 62, p. 233; Kafi no. 7, p. 194.
56. Ibid., Kafi no. 13, p. 198; Kafi no. 28, p. 208; Kafi no. 104, p. 261; Kafi no. 62, 233.
57. Ibid., Kafi no. 57, p. 228; Kafi no. 146, p. 286; Kafi no. 67, p. 236.
58. Ibid., Kafi no. 133, p. 277; Kafi no. 61, p. 232.
59. Ibid., Kafi no. 150, pp. 288-9.
60. Ibid., Kafi no. 142, pp. 282-4.
61. Farina Mir, *The Social Space of Language: Vernacular Culture in British Colonial Punjab*, Ranikhet: Permanent Black, 2010, p. 3.
62. Ahmadyar (1768-1845) was born in Jalalpur, a town lying to the northeast of Gujarat. He lived almost his entire life at this place. He adopted the medical profession in the footsteps of his ancestors, who were physicians. An erudite scholar and prolific poet, he composed nearly 50 works. These could be divided into two categories. He versified the indigenous love tales like *Hir Ranjha*, *Sohni Mahiwal*, *Sassi Punnu* and *Raj Bibi*. Turning to West Asia, he composed *Laila Majnun*, *Yusuf Zulaikha*, *Saif ul-Muluk* and *Jang Badr*. He wrote his famous *Hatimnama* in the hope of a reward from Ranjit Singh, who was mentioned with adulation. As expected, Qazi Mohkamuddin invited him to write a history of Ranjit Singh's reign in Persian. Raja Gulab Singh granted him the fief of Marala, where he shifted towards the end of his life.
63. Ahmadyar, *Hir Ahmadyar*, ed. Gobind Singh Lamba, Patiala: Amarjit Sahit Prakashan, 1982, Stanza nos. 11-39, pp. 63-7.
64. Ibid., Stanza nos. 633-57, pp. 156-9.
65. Ibid., Stanza nos. 159-65, pp. 86-7.
66. Ibid., Stanza nos. 1375-88, pp. 267-9.
67. With the formation of a strong state under Ranjit Singh, the craft of composing romantic poetry (*qissa*) acquired a new direction, with reference to composition, subject matter and truth content. Instead of indigenous love tales, the romantic poets (Ahmadyar, Hashim Shah, and Qadiryar) widened the scope to encompass Vedic-Indian and Arabic-Persian sources. According to a new convention, instead of awarding multiple background of social relations, experiences and values to foreground of love at the natural terrain, they tended to surround it with metaphysical and libidinal veils. Instead of

autochthonous lovers making love at the terrain of nature, their place was taken by royal lovers who had metaphysical proclivity for each other. Similarly, journey and melancholy were introduced as new motifs. With the dissolution of Ranjit Singh's empire, the craft of romantic poetry suffered a decline. Tejwant S. Gill, 'Kissa in the Times of Maharaja Ranjit Singh', *Maharaja Ranjit Singh and His Times*, ed. J.S. Grewal and Indu Banga, Amritsar: Guru Nanak Dev University, 1980, pp. 220-3.

68. Surinderpal Singh Mand, *Qissakar Hashim: Sassi Punnu, Sohni Mahiwal, Shirin Farhad te Hir Ranjhe de Mool Path Samet*, Amritsar: Waris Shah Foundation, 2011, Stanza nos. 16-19, pp. 260-1.
69. Ibid., Stanza noz. 23-30, pp. 262-3.
70. Ganesh Das Wadhera, *Char Bagh-i Punjab*, Eng. tr. (titled *Early Nineteenth Century Punjab*), J.S. Grewal and Indu Banga, Amritsar: Guru Nanak Dev University, 1975, pp. 148-50.
71. Belonging to the Siyal clan, the author was an old landholder of Jhang Siyal. Apart from Persian and Arabic, he possessed the knowledge of Muslim law and local customs. George William Hamilton, the commissioner of Multan Division, directed him to pen this work. The author treated the history of the district as the history of the Siyals. For his facts, he relied on an earlier book (*Siyalnama*), memories of old people and testimony of their Brahmins. He traced the migration of Siyals from eastern India and, following their conversion to Islam, noted their settlement along the Chenab. His scope embraced 18 generations of Siyals who lived for 350 years. With the help of numerous geological tables (*nasbnamas*), he described the role of Mal Khan's descendants in carving out their principalities through local warfare. The story was brought up to the conquest of the area under Ranjit Singh and the British. The book provides an account of agriculture, animal breeding, trade, food, clothing, customs, fairs and festivals. In the conclusion, the author has given a sketch of his own career.
72. Maulavi Nur Muhammad, *Tarikh-i Jhang Siyal*, Meerut: Matba Ahmadi, 1863, pp. 12-13.
73. Born in India, Richard Carnac Temple (1850-1931) studied anthropology at Cambridge (UK). After participating in the Anglo-Afghan war of 1878-9, he was given a civil appointment as Cantonment Magistrate of Ambala. He held high positions in Burma and Andaman-Nicobar Islands. He evolved a method of collecting folk tales of Panjab. He summoned bards to perform at his residence. His

clerk (*munshi*) recorded the recitation in rough and, taking corrections and explanations from the bards, copied in clear Persian hand. Temple transcribed the text in Roman characters and translated it. The clerk, who had heard the song, went over it. Temple revised it in consultation with the clerk. The process rooted in colonial power structure, ignored the context of nineteenth century Panjab, particularly the relations between the narrators (bards) and the folk tale-collector as a subject and ruler. Sadhana Naithani, 'The Colonizer-Folklorist', *Journal of Folklore Research*, vol. 34, no. 1, 1997, pp. 1-14.

74. R.C. Temple, *The Legends of the Panjab*, vol. II, Islamabad: The Institute of Folk Heritage, rpt. 1981, pp. 507-25.
75. Ibid., pp. 526-44.
76. Ibid., pp. 545-57.
77. Ibid., pp. 558-80.

CHAPTER 6

Conclusion

Damodar was not the first to narrate a love story. In West Asia and Indian subcontinent, prominent Persian poets had described popular love tales in narrative poetry (*masnavi*). In the Gangetic plain, Awadhi Sufi romances (*premakhyans*), revolving around the struggles of Hindu royal protagonists, served as allegories for the spiritual quest. In medieval Panjab, the story of Hir-Ranjah had attained a distinct place in the cultural landscape. It was not certain if Damodar was familiar with the works of Nizami Ganjawi, Amir Khusrau, Mulla Daud and Malik Muhammad Jaisi. Most probably, he had heard some of Shah Husain's mystical verses (*kafis*) that had imbibed the travails of Hir-Ranjha. Owing to his domicile in Chuchkana (Jhang Siyal) under the patronage of the Siyals, he became interested in the life of Hir, the rebellious daughter of his Siyal patrons. With his pioneering attempt in western dialect of Panjabi, he took the plot away from palaces and rulers and, in a decisive shift, brought it to the open countryside. Except for the powerful clan chiefs and local administrators, all his characters hailed from the lower social rungs. While describing the journey of Hir-Ranjha from physical love to pious sainthood, he uncovered the autonomy of Jat clans, authority of government officers and charisma of spiritual entities. His narrative was a mine of contemporary evidence on the medieval society of west Panjab. As a pioneer, he created a masterpiece that his successors could not equal. This was evident in the following characteristics of his work.

Damodar has found it necessary to describe the childhood of the protagonists. Even at this early stage, the two were exceptional. This trait enabled them to emerge as extraordinary individuals in their youth. At their birth, they were so beautiful that they were seen as the light of spiritual excellence (*azmat ki rushnai*). The two were born in similar circumstances. Their fathers, as chiefs of landed clans, held sway over substantial chunks of land. Both infants were brought up in the lap of material comfort. The similarities did not extend to their families. Hir, being the youngest of siblings, attracted considerable affection, so that she displayed qualities of independence, confidence and intelligence. As a leader of a band of 360 girls, she conducted several activities in the village. She exercised the authority of her father and, moving across the locality, left a mark of her sagacity, benevolence and compassion. In contrast, Dhido had a different childhood. He was brought up amidst contradictory forces. From his father, he received immense love and excessive protection. Parallel to this, he faced intense jealousy of his brothers, who even conspired to kill him. The betrothal of Hir took place in a joyous environment. The occasion was observed in accordance with prevailing social conventions involving the Siyals and Kheras. The betrothal of Dhido was fraught with secrecy and suspicion. Mojam was forced to keep his clan out of the picture and reduce the rituals to a minimum. Both betrothals came under strain owing to different reasons. In case of Dhido, the sudden death of Mojam enabled the Ranjha brothers to cancel his (Dhido's) marriage and divide the patrimonial property. Since Hir had fallen in love with Ranjha, she opposed her marriage with Sahiba. The Siyals and Kheras, owing to a tacit understanding, bulldozed Hir's opposition and used force to conduct the wedding.

Damodar's narrative was largely confined to ordinary folk. It was true that the lovers were born in families of prosperous landholders (*zamindars*), who held important positions in their clans. When they fell in love, they withdrew themselves from their elite antecedents. Ranjha abandoned his patrimonial property and became a wanderer with a streak of mendicancy. As soon as the two lost their virginity to each other, Hir decalred that she had no connection with her family and saw herself as a simple Jat girl. She enabled Ranjha to serve the Siyals as a herdsman and, identifying herself with his lowly position, grazed buffaloes along with him. Lest Ranjha should suffer from an inferiority complex, she adopted him as her spiritual preceptor and submitted to him like an ardent disciple. A number of menials played a significant role in the development of the story. Luddan, the boatman, was instrumental in introducing the lovers to each other. Dooms and Brahmins, deployed as emissaries of powerful chiefs, conducted elaborate negotiations between the clans and, thus, determined the course of local politics. Ramu Brahmin, the lover of Sehti was a ordinary man and carried an important message from Hir to Ranjha. Damodar, who figured many times in the story, ran a shop in Chuchkana with the approval of the Siyals. A number of poor people – goldsmiths, cooks, porters, animal keepers, musicians, singers, dancers and beggars – played specific roles during festive occasions and, in return, became recipients of remunerations, rewards and alms.

Though the menials were indispensable to the life of the community, they were not treated with respect. On several occasions, they became victims of maltreatment. Luddan presented an outstanding example. Noora Sambhal did not consider Luddan's advancing age and subjected him to humiliation. The Siyals did not do any better. They employed Luddan as a boatman, but he did not enjoy a peaceful tenure. Hir held him responsible for allowing a stranger to sleep in the boat. The girls, employing sticks, reduced him to a pulp. When he was half dead, they pushed him into the river. A Doom, who delivered the letter of Noora Sambhal to Chuchak, became the victim of collective Siyal anger. His face was blackened. He received a beating with shoes and fell prostrate on the ground. Though he was not guilty of any indiscretion, he was reduced to utter misery. Ranjha, while serving the Siyals as a herdsman, faced the ire of Chuchak. Caught with Hir in the moors, he was beaten with a cane and almost dismissed from service. When he escorted the buffaloes along with the Khera marriage party, he suffered severe torture at the hands of the Kheras. His condition became so pitiable that he begged the Kheras to kill him outright. When he appeared in the court at Kot Qabula, the Qazi abused him in foul language and ordered him to be whipped in public. No doubt, Ranjha was treated as an outcaste. He had walked out of his clan. The Siyals disowned him and the Kheras hated him. Adopting the path of Jog, he had eloped with the daughter-in-law of the Kheras. Thus, he was merely a piece of straw, which was tossed about in the whirlwind of dynamic situations. Since Damodar had his heart in the right place, he empathized with the sufferers of an unequal society. He did not hesitate to expose the powerful elements for their cruelty towards the vulnerable, weak and poor.

In Damodar's narrative, a large part of the action took place in the countryside of western Panjab. Time and again, the leading characters were found in the fertile plains, lush green crops, the majestic Chenab and vegetation in the moors. A ferry on the Chenab, located on the edge of Chuchkana, was an important site. Here, Luddan anchored the luxurious boat that originally belonged to the Sambhals. A number of swings hung from a thick grove of trees. Hir and her 360 companions spent the day in different locales of Chuchkana. In particular, they swam across the Chenab and, sporting on the swings, viewed the interior of the boat. The Siyal-Sambhal battle took place near the ferry. Ranjha, after leaving Takht Hazara, walked through the countryside spreading up to the Chenab. He spent a night in a village mosque and another in the house of a farmer. On reaching the ferry, he played his flute and, as a result, charmed Luddan, Panjpir, the girls and wild animals. The protagonists fell in love inside the boat under an open sky. The Siyals interviewed Ranjha in the village common, which lay in front of Chuchak's bungalow. Next to the ferry, the most important site was diffused among the moors. The buffaloes fed on the natural grasses, while the wild animals lived in peace. The lovers were emotionally attached to a dense shisham and bald fig, where they exchanged promises of love. During the day, the melody of Ranjha's flute echoed across the moors. Consuming food and drinking milk, the lovers slept on a platform (*jallar*), which had been built on the branches. At night, Ranjha escorted the buffaloes to the moors and, sitting on the platform, engaged in contemplation. It was true that the Hir-Ranjha love blossomed in the moors. It was equally true that the place exposed them to their opponents. Eighty-four herdsmen, jealous of Ranjha, made an abortive attempt on his life during a rainy night. Kaido gathered evidence of the intimacy between the lovers from the moors. Chuchak saw the lovers lying on the platform and directed his ire against Ranjha.

After Hir's marriage with Sahiba, the Khera marriage party travelled from Chuchkana to Rangpur Khera. As the convoy made its way through the countryside, the Kheras kept on beating Ranjha and brought him on the verge of death. At night, Ranjha escaped from the village and, swimming across the Chenab, met the Siyal girls in the moors. He saw the spots where he had been meeting Hir and, suffering from a sudden depression, left the place in a hurry. When he returned to Takht Hazara, he did not stay in the village. Instead, he spent his day in the village common among his friends and slept in a newly raised hut in the outskirts. Ramu took two days to cover the distance between Rangpur Khera and Takht Hazara. His meeting with Ranjha took place in the village common. Ranjha crossed the Jhelum and, walking through the Salt Range, climbed to Tilla Balnath. On his way to Rangpur Khera, he went to Chuchkana and again met the Siyal girls in the moors. Though Sehti's village was a pleasant site, Ranjha (Jogi) set up his fire in the outskirts. Hir suffered from snakebite in a field where sesame was growing. The lovers, after staying in Sehti's house for five weeks, escaped from Rangpur Khera. They rushed through an unknown wilderness, while the Khera retinue chased them. They stepped over a ominous weed and, unfortunately, returned to the same place again. They took shelter with the Nahars who were harvesting their crop of lentils. The Nahar-Khera conflict resulted in bloodshed and loss of life. The warring clans, escorting the lovers, travelled on horseback to Kot Qabula. Having reached the town in the evening, they spent a night in the compound of the court under an open sky. As the lovers lost their case in the court, Ranjha was whipped and Hir beaten up in full public view. As the people assembled on the streets to protest, the lovers used their miraculous power to extinguish the fire and, as a result, united with each other. The Kheras were brought back and, thrashed in public, stood expelled from the town. The lovers took leave from the crowd of citizens and left for the south.

Damodar has constructed the Hir-Ranjha love as a grand divine project. The protagonists did not fall in love through their own efforts. Love had been inscribed in their destiny. Even before they met in the boat, they became familiar with each other through supernatural means. God brought them together through Panjpir.

When Ranjha played on his flute on the Chenab, he saw Panjpir arriving on a boat. In a meeting, he narrated the facts of his life and played Raga Lalit on his flute. Pleased with Ranjha, they bestowed Hir on him. At the same time, they appeared to Hir in a dream and, conferring Ranjha on her, warned her to reject any other man. They announced that God had willed this union. In order to seal the boon, they offered milk to Hir. At this moment, Ranjha attained enlightenment and everything became visible to him. He felt that he had realized his ideal (*var*). However, Damodar has placed the lovers on different planes with respect to their relation with Panjpir. Ranjha not only saw them with his own eyes but also had a long conversation with them. In contrast, Hir did not see them while awake. Instead, she interacted with them in a dream. Further, Ranjha acquired an ability that Hir did not. He began to see all the happenings and, therefore, saw the interface between Hir and Panjpir. However, Hir was denied this privilege. Damodar expected his reader to be aware of the spiritual difference between the lovers. Once she had met Ranjha in the boat and exchanged vows of love with him, she began to look at him as her husband and spiritual guide. Correspondingly, she saw herself as his wife and disciple.

This unique relationship was manifest during Ranjha's herdsmanship in the moors. Every day, Hir carried his midday meal of sweetened breadcrumbs (*choori*). On every such occasion, she performed a specific ritual indicating her obedience and submissiveness. First, she respectfully offered her salutation to Ranjha. Second, she bent down and kissed his feet. Third, she picked up the dust of his feet and rubbed it on her face and forehead. Fourth, she stood before him with folded hands awaiting his command. Ranjha asked her to bring milk so that he was able to eat his food. She picked up a pot and went to milk a buffalo. In view of this humility, her manner appeared to be that of a typical Indian wife. She had no doubt that Ranjha was a saint possessing supernatural powers. In the aftermath of the Qazi's verdict, she declared that Ranjha had willed her punishment and that his wrath would fall on the Kheras. When Kot Qabula was engulfed in a fire, Ranjha extinguished it twice, while Hir did so only once. The protagonists had made a public display of their miraculous abilities. It may be recalled that Panjpir appeared to Ranjha while the

Kheras were beating him. In response to his complaint, they revealed that they had deliberately punished him and that this was done to make him enlightened. When the lovers finally left for the south, the five black warriors appeared to Hir and told her that she would not have become enlightened without her suffering. Evidently, the lovers did not climb the spiritual ladder at the same pace. Ranjha took the lead in climbing its rungs and, thus made quicker spiritual gains. Hir achieved the same success only after Ranjha. Damodar has maintained a clear difference between them. In the eyes of the poet, Ranjha was the mentor and Hir was his disciple. The two began their career as lovers and, towards, the end of Damodar's narrative, evolved as saints. Hir and Ranjha were not the only lovers tied in the mentor-disciple bond. A century after them, Shah Husain and Madho were seen tied in a similar dual linkage.

Ranjha, in the early stages of his life, was inseparable from his flute. During childhood, he was too young to work on the fields. Yet, he learnt to play Indian Ragas on his flute. This ability enabled him to survive adverse situations and even make substantive gains. On the Chenab, Panjpir were so impressed with his rendition of Raga Lalit that they bestowed Hir on him. Soon after, Luddan was amazed at the impact of Ranjha's melody on wild animals and, turning generous, allowed Ranjha to sleep on Hir's bed in the boat. Hir lost her senses on listening to his flute. On recovering, she reconciled with Luddan and fell in love with Ranjha. When he grazed buffaloes in the moors, Ranjha's flute produced a number of beneficial results. He managed to win the affection of wild animals. In Chuchkana, the sound of his flute induced the buffaloes to break their ropes and rush out of their enclosures. While returning from the moors, they were attracted to the lilting notes and gathered around Ranjha to return to the village. Chuchak noted the magnetic pull of the flute on the buffaloes and, therefore, restored Ranjha in his herdsmanship. More than once, Damodar has compared the buffaloes to Gopis, who were attracted to Krishna's flute. If Ranjha managed to separate himself from the Siyal girls at Chuchkana, it was only because he rendered them unconscious with his music. What was noteworthy, Ranjha abandoned his flute as soon as Hir left for Rangpur Khera. Having lost Hir to the Kheras, he never brought the flute to his lips.

Henceforth, he faced the hostility of his brothers, the Kheras and Waraichs, besides a cruel punishment at Kot Qabula. However, he did not resort to his flute for any miraculous assistance.

For Damodar, love meant a convergence of work, sex, spirituality and struggle. The lovers shared a life, which enabled them to earn their livelihood in conjunction with pursuing love and seeking spiritual goals. As soon as Hir met Ranjha for the first time in the boat, they were physically attracted to each other. Hir, taking the initiative, brought the handsome stranger to her bedstead and experienced the joy of sex. They exchanged vows of fidelity and realized that they could not live without each other. Henceforth, they began to spend a lot of time in the moors along the Chenab. Together, they grazed the buffaloes and gave them a dip in the river. Together, they ate sweetened breadcrumbs that were washed down with fresh milk. Ranjha, producing melodies from his flute, elevated Hir to higher levels of consciousness. It appears that Ranjha, treating Hir as his disciple, revealed spiritual secrets to her. They climbed to the platform (*jallar*) hanging between the branches of trees. For hours, they were locked in each other's arms, oblivious of the world around them. The bliss of conjugal life lasted only two months. Hir's forced marriage with Sahiba terminated their meetings. They remained separated for nearly thirty-six months. When they ultimately met in Rangpur Khera, Sehti realized that the lovers had been deprived of sex for long. Their outstanding need was sex and plenty of it.

Damodar recognized the indispensability of sex in human life. He has revealed this in the sexual life of Sehti. Though she was single and past her prime, she was not deprived of sex. Every night, she met her lover Ramu Brahmin in the privacy of her house and, thus, fulfilled her libido. She would not live a single day without Ramu. When she discovered the declining physical condition of Hir, she was quick to discern the cause of her malady. A fire burnt inside Hir, but she had been trying to conceal it. This desire was unique (*chat awwali*). It was an addiction (*amal*) that went deep into one's bones. A woman yearning for a man acquired a pale complexion. Sehti, in order to extract a confession from Hir, employed the device of sex. When Sehti slept with Ramu, Hir was permitted to peep inside. Hir walked into this trap. Abandoning her initial reticence, she confessed her love for Ranjha. The pain of his love was overflowing from her genitals (*lingin*). Her ailment could be cured only if she was able to unite with Ranjha. When he arrived in Rangpur Khera as a Jogi and a snake had bitten Hir, Sehti planned their rendezvous. The Jogi would treat Hir for forty days with only Sehti in attendance. The period was long enough to rouse the suspicion of the Kheras. Yet, Sehti stuck to her plan. She felt that the lovers, who had been separated for thirty-six months, had been deprived of sex. A union of ten or twenty days was not sufficient to quench their hunger for each other. A period of forty days was reasonable. During this duration, the lovers would do nothing except eating, drinking and making love. Sehti told a hundred lies to divert the attention of the Kheras. Needless to add, Damodar has borrowed the idea of forty days from the standard retreat (*chilla*) common in Sufi practice. The duration of this union was not a coincidence.

Damodar's emphasis on sex was rooted in the mystical discourse, which meandered from Baghdad to Bengal during the medieval centuries (1100-1600). A number of mystic ideologues, cutting across geographical distances and chronological frames, have advocated a merger of spirituality and sexuality. Ibn Arabi saw the perfect manifestation of divine beauty in human female form. He conceived a triad of God, man and woman, wherein the God-man relation paralleled the man-woman affinity. In the sexual union, a man found joy of complete annihilation and, therefore, erotic love was the highest spiritual experience. Baba Farid perceived the seeker as wife and God as husband. When she failed to enjoy the sexual union, her body smouldered like fire and her limbs were twisted. Owing to pangs of separation, she lost interest in her physical needs and felt driven to insanity. Jaideva, while celebrating the Radha-Krishna love, made a uninhibited use of sexual imagery. He did not confine Radha's beauty to her eyes, hair and ornaments. It was visible in the voluptuous form of her breasts, hips, navel and loins. The lovers, besides expressing their longing for each other, were found kissing lips, scratching the body with nails and receiving thrusts on the pelvis. Guru Nanak, in a composition titled 'Twelve Months' (*bara mah*), validated the bride's attraction towards her Divine Spouse. Conforming to the change of seasons, her mental state experienced a wide range of emotions.

In His absence, she felt distressed at her lonely bed. On His arrival, her bed attained splendour and her conjugal life was stabilized. Shah Husain compared the spiritual quest of the seeker to the life of a married woman. In her account of good deeds, only the nights spent with her husband were listed. A woman sleeping in the arms of her husband was truly chaste (*suhagani*), while the one sleeping alone was mightily cursed (*kulakhani*). If she lay alone on her bed, a fire ignited in her heart and her entire body was roasted. The foregoing stream of thought, which navigated across Asia from the eleventh to the sixteenth century, could not have failed to impact Damodar.

Damodar has divided his characters into two categories. Half of them supported the lovers and others opposed them. The poet has portrayed the former in a favourable light. The boatman Luddan, who lived on the ferry of the Chenab, enabled Hir and Ranjha to fall in love. The band of Siyal girls, particularly Hassi, created conditions in which Hir-Ranjha love blossomed. At Rangpur Khera, a Doom girl, acting through her mother, informed Ranjha of the evil designs of the Kheras and, thus, saved his life. When Ranjha returned to Chuchkana after losing Hir, the Siyal girls came to his rescue and offered to settle him in the place. If Ranjha was able to bide his time at Takht Hazara and endure the hostility of his brothers, it was solely because of the support from his friends who looked after his needs. Ramu, the lover of Sehti, travelled all the way to Takht Hazara and conveyed Hir's message to Ranjha. Sidh Bagai, the chief Jogi at Tilla Balnath, initiated Ranjha in Jog and blessed his endevaour to unite with Hir. Sehti operationalized a hazardous plan that resulted in the union of the lovers. The Nahars took the lovers in their protection and saved them from the wrath of the Kheras. The Nahar girls, impressed with the deep love between the lovers, weakened opposition of the Kheras. The people of Kot Qabula staged an angry protest against the local administration and, forcing it to reverse the legal verdict, brought the final union between the lovers.

Damodar did not discern any redeeming trait in the opponents of the lovers. Depicting them in dark colours, he ensured that they ended up in ignominy. The Ranjha brothers, owing to their enmity towards Dhido, harmed him in many ways and even conspired to kill him. The herdsmen, serving the Siyals, tried to kill Dhido due to their jealousy. When Dhido returned to Takht Hazara after the marriage of Hir, the Ranjha brothers revived their old enmity. They induced Ranjha to live outside the village. As if this was not enough, they joined hands with the Waraichs to isolate Dhido from the inter-clan relationship. In the same manner, Hir faced strong opposition from her family. Her mother Kundi reprimanded her for an intimacy with their herdsman. The Siyal women, acting as a body, cornered Hir for disgracing the Siyal clan. Hir's uncle Kaido, an expert in black arts, dug out the proof of Hir's involvement with Ranjha. Hir's parents tried to poison her and thought of replacing her with their granddaughter in the wedding. Hir's brothers and uncles used force against Hir during the wedding ceremonies. Her father Chuchak realized the futility of pressure against Hir, but he was too weak to intervene in her favour. The Kheras were the worst enemies of the lovers. On the one hand, they tortured Ranjha and planned to kill him. On the other hand, they paid no heed to Hir's rejection of Sahiba. They chased the lovers through a wilderness. They would have killed the lovers if Nahars had not intervened. Damodar ensured that the Kheras were ultimately punished in full public view at Kot Qabula. The poet took a lot of pleasure in describing Hir's vitriolic attack on the Kheras, particularly Ali and his son Sahiba. With undisguised glee, he narrated the ultimate humiliation of the Kheras. He did not spare the government officers because they had been unjust and cruel towards the lovers. He ensured that public anger overwhelmed the local administration, which was forced reverse its verdict and finally submitted to the spiritual excellence of the lovers. All opponents of the lovers, losing in the long run, were remembered with disdain.

Damodar's narrative was not confined to the travails of Hir and Ranjha. Equally, it recorded the socio-political conditions of west Panjab. Its canvas was restricted to a tract on the eastern bank of the Chenab, particularly Jhang Siyal which was situated between Chiniot and Shorkot. A number of Jat clans, living side by side, controlled identifiable chunks of land. The Siyal domain comprised eighty-four villages in Jhang Siyal. The chief, with the support of his clansman, virtually ruled over this area. Since the land lay in the flood plain and water table was high, the alluvial soil permitted cultivation of several crops and raising large herds of cattle. Though rainfall was scanty, the Chenab was flooded during monsoons. The clan was required to repair embankments, so that the seasonal inundations did not damage the crops and drown the cattle. It was called upon to drain excess water from the marshes. In order bring about agrarian expansion, it allowed outsiders to till the vacant lands and, in the process, provided means of cultivation and material incentives. It employed a large number of herdsmen to look after the cattle. The members of the clan formed a loose militia, which possessed horses and armaments. The armed retinue fought against the neighbouring clans to assert local dominance. If any member withdrew from the clan, he lost the protective umbrella and became an outcaste like the lovers. The clan chief presided over frequent meetings to deliberate on major and minor issues. The decisions were reached through open consultation and clear consensus. When a clan was aggrieved, it marched out to regain its honour. Inter-clan warfare was the most common feature of the socio-political life. This was visible in the Siyal-Sambhal clash and Khera-Nahar battle. The warring clans were not perturbed over the loss of life. In this regard, Sehti has made a crucial statement. While helping the lovers to unite, she claimed to have put the honour of 900 turbans at stake. It meant that the Kheras, during an exigency, could mobilize a known number of clansmen for a violent showdown.

The medieval state, in theory, allowed the landed clans to exercise autonomy in their domains. In practice, it could penetrate the countryside owing to its hegemonic claims and military superiority. The clans were aware of the increasing sweep of the state and, therefore, did not offend it in any manner. Nor did they cooperate with it. They did not treat the state as invincible and felt strong enough to defy it. In their discussions, they were not willing to surrender their political space to the state. If the clans were not able to settle a dispute through the conventional mechanisms, they resorted to the nearest town, which was the centre of local administration and the Qazi's court. In urban spaces, the citizens were aware of their strength and limitations of the state. They did not hesitate to raise their voice against the unjust decisions of government functionaries. They believed that the officers were accountable to the central authority, if not to them. From the angle of belief systems, the clans were undergoing a slow process of Islamization. The people, at large, had staunch faith in the Sufis and Jogis. They drew nourishment from both spiritual traditions that overlapped at the popular level.

During the Mughal and post-Mughal periods, a number of Panjabi poets narrated the story of Hir-Ranjha in different ways. According to Ahmad Gujjar, Ranjha employed dubious means to secure initiation into Jog and Balnath's support for uniting with Hir. For Ahmad Gujjar, Raja Adli overruled the Qazi and allowed Hir to choose her husband. The lovers, after their death, were seen helping pilgrims on way to Mecca. Shahjahan Muqbal would have us believe that Ranjha saw Hir in a dream and, therefore, left his home to meet her. The poet has gone out of his way to dilute the intensity of conflict in the story. Ranjha had affectionate relations with his brothers and sisters-in-law. He did not face any hostility from the Siyals and Kheras, while his encounter with Sehti had no trace of bitterness. The government officers, who witnessed the proceedings in the court, turned the scales in favour of the lovers. Though Waris Shah followed Ahmad Gujjar in the storyline, he added many new dimensions to the narrative. His sharp gaze resulted in vivid descriptions of the Panjabi countryside, while his wit was reflected in the Jogi-Sehti debate. In his ardent attempts to explore female sexuality, he has described the bodily parts of Hir, the dalliance of Siyal girls with Ranjha on the Chenab, sexist exchanges between these girls and Saida during his wedding and aftermath of Hir's meeting with the Jogi in Kalabagh. He was sensitive to the cultural diversity of medieval Panjab, with reference to artisanal groups and their deities. Since his outlook defied borders, his metaphors were traceable to the distant Islamic world and Indic cultural landscape. Bulle Shah, while speaking for Hir, identified the unique characteristics of Ranjha as a herdsman and Jogi. Besides giving voice to her feelings of love, he allowed her to berate her parents and the Kheras.

During the nineteenth century, Panjab experienced a strong polity under Ranjit Singh and the subsequent introduction of British colonialism. A number of writers narrated the story of Hir-Ranjha in poetry and prose. Ahmadyar, acknowledging his debt to Waris Shah, assigned a crucial role to Hir's brothers in the employment of Ranjha as a herdsman. Like Ahmad Gujjar, he noted the presence of lovers in Mecca after the end of their earthly lives. Hashim Shah, compressing the story in thirty stanzas, laid emphasis on Hir's appearance before the Qazi in a public gathering and allowed Raja Adli to deliver a verdict favouring the lovers. According to Ganesh Das Vadhera, the local administrator held Hir's marriage as unlawful as it lacked her consent. It was added that the headman of Maghiana resolved the difference between the lovers regarding their proposed wedding. Maulavi Nur Muhammad asserted that the love of Hir-Ranjha was spiritual as it was immune from carnal passion. He revealed that Saida divorced Hir and exiled the lovers to a waterless tract. Richard Carnac Temple wrote that Ranjha tricked Gorakhnath into granting Jog and Raja Adli cast a lustful eye on Hir. The folklorist attributed the final union of lovers to the support of Hindu and Muslim spiritual entities. Thus, the writers have introduced variations in the narrative in accordance with their sources and inclinations.

In several respects, the above writers were different from Damodar. They have traced the vicissitudes in the lives of the lovers. They have recognized the role of Panjpir and Balnath in supporting the lovers. They have discussed the conflict of the lovers with their immediate families. They have identified the means that the lovers adopted to overcome their obstacles. They have examined the proceedings at the Qazi's court in conjunction with the role of Raja Adli. Their narratives have concluded on a tragic note, as the lovers died soon after their final union. While asserting the intensity of attachment between the lovers, they have referred to the tales of Laila-Majnun and Yusuf-Zulaikha. However, they have understood the relation between Hir and Ranjha as a simple pursuit of physical love. In their eyes, the death of lovers was sudden, tragic and mysterious. They denied the lovers an opportunity of living a happy conjugal life. The lovers could have been divinely punished for defying the Shariat and social norms. Alternatively, the lovers could not outdo their opponents in the ongoing conflict. Some writers did not hesitate to confer an afterlife to the lovers, who appeared in the outskirts of Mecca and helped the pilgrims in different ways. What was significant, the post-Damodar poets did not place the travails of the lovers in a socio-political context. Except for the boatman

Luddan, they did not give space to menials in their retellings. Instead of diligent research into facts of the case, they relied on the collective memory and earlier works, besides their creative imagination and poetic skills.

In view of the above discussion, Damodar was unique in ways more than one. When he picked his pen to narrate the tale of Hir-Ranjha, he commanded an advantageous position. He was an inhabitant of the tract along the Chenab where the story emerged. He was close in time to the events that formed the essence of the story. He appeared to have visited the places that figured in the story and, during his travels, gathered facts from the bards of the landed clans. Being essentially an insider, he possessed intimate knowledge of the society, which nurtured an unusual love tale. In accordance with a divine plan, the protagonists fell in love and, undergoing long spells of suffering, evolved as saints with miraculous powers. The spiritual traditions of medieval Panjab, imbued with Jog and Sufism, legitimized a relation, which was unlawful in the eyes of the landed clans and Islamic orthodoxy. Damodar saw love as a complex endeavour comprising work, sex, struggle and spirituality. His narrative, in its most distinctive feature, showed that the life of lovers was intertwined with the Jat clans. With great ingenuity and skill, the poet has described the internal organization of these groups, with reference to their political autonomy and agrarian entrepreneurship. He has revealed the vulnerable state of menials and servants, who suffered oppression at the hands of their privileged patrons. Locating himself at the grassroots, Damodar has painted dense pictures of the Panjabi society in its diverse shades. In this sense, his work was a counternarrative standing in opposition to Abul Fazl's official chronicle, which has shown the Mughal State as perpetually engaged in subjugating the landed clans and their subordinates.

Bibliography

Primary Sources: Persian

Abbas Khan Sarwani, *Tarikh-i Sher Shahi*, ed. S.M. Imamuddin, Dacca: University of Dacca, 1964.

Abdul Qadir Badauni, *Muntakhab ut-Tawarikh*, vol. II, ed. Maulavi Ahmad Ali, Aligarh: Centre of Advanced Study, Department of History and Publication Division, Aligarh Muslim University, rpt., 2018; Eng. tr. W.H. Lowe and B.P. Ambashthya; vol. III, Eng. tr. Wolseley Haig and B.P. Ambashthya, Patna: Academica Asiatica, rpt., 1973.

Abdulla, *Tarikh-i Daudi*, ed. Shaikh Abdul Rashid and Iqtidar Husain Siddiqui, Aligarh: Aligarh Muslim University, 1969.

Abdur Rahman Jami, *Yusuf and Zulaikha: A Poem by Jami*, Eng. tr. Ralph T.H. Griffith, New York: Routledge, rpt., 2013.

Abul Fazl, *Ain-i Akbari*, vol. II, Eng. tr. H.S. Jarrett and Jadunath Sarkar, New Delhi: Oriental Books Reprint Corporation, 3rd edn., 1978; vol. III, Eng. tr., H. Blochmann and D.C. Phillot, Kolkata: The Asiatic Society, rpt., 2010.

______, *Akbar Nama*, vol. II and III, Eng. tr. Henry Beveridge, New Delhi: Atlantic Publishers and Distributors, rpt., 2019.

Ahmad Yadgar, *Tarikh-i Shahi*, ed. M. Hidayat Hosain, Calcutta: Royal Asiatic Society of Bengal, 1939.

Ainuddin Ain ul-Mulk Mahru, *Insha-i Mahru*, ed. Shaikh Abdul Rashid, Aligarh: Aligarh Muslim University, 1959.

Ali bin Usman Hujwiri, *Kashf ul-Mahjub*, Eng. tr. Reynold A. Nicholson, Delhi: Taj Company, rpt., 1982.

Allahdad Faizi Sirhindi, *Akbar Nama*, Eng. tr. H.M. Elliot and John

Dowson, *History of India as Told by Its Own Historians*, vol. VI, Allhabad: Kitab Mahal, rpt., 1981.

Amir Hasan Sijzi, *Fawaid ul-Fuad*, Eng. tr. (titled *Nizam Ad-Din Awliya: Morals for the Heart*), Bruce B. Lawrence, New York and Mahwah: Paulist Press, 1992.

Amir Khurd, *Siyar ul-Auliya*, Delhi: Matba Muhibb-i Hind, 1885.

Amir Khusrau, *Duwal Rani Khizr Khan*, ed. Rashid Ahmad Salim Ansari and Khaliq Ahmad Nizami, Delhi: Idarah-i Adabiyat-i Delli and Aligarh: Centre of Advanced Study in History, Department of History, Aligarh Muslim University, 1988.

Dara Shukoh, *Risala-i Haqq Numa*, Eng. tr. in *Sufi Meditation and Contemplation: Timeless Wisdom from Mughal India*, ed. Scott Kugle, New Lebanon: Omega Publications, 2012.

——, *Sakinat ul-Auliya*, ed. Tara Chand and Syed Razazada Jalali Naini, Tehran: Muassasa-i Matbuati-i Ilmi, 1963.

Fakhruddin Gorgani, *Vis and Ramin*, Eng. tr. and Introduction, Dick Davis, New York: Penguin Books, 2008.

Fakhruddin Iraqi, *Kulliyat-i Fakhruddin Iraqi*, ed. Nasreen Muhatshim, Tehran: Intsharat-i Zawwar, 1392 AH.

Fariduddin Attar, *Mantiq ul-Tair*, Eng. tr., (titled *The Conference of the Birds*), Afkham Darbandi and Dick Davis, London and New York: Penguin Books, 2011.

Ganesh Das Vadhera, *Char Bagh-i Panjab*, Eng. tr. (titled *Early Nineteenth Century Panjab*), J.S. Grewal and Indu Banga, Amritsar: Department of History, Guru Nanak Dev University, 1975.

Hamid bin Fazlullah Jamali, *Siyar ul-Arifin*, Delhi: Rizvi Press, 1893.

Hamid Qalandar, *Khair ul-Majalis*, ed. Khaliq Ahmad Nizami, Aligarh: Department of History, Aligarh Muslim University, 1966.

Ibn Battuta, *Rehla*, Eng. tr. (titled *The Rehla of Ibn Battuta: India, Maldive Islands and Ceylon*), Eng. tr. Mahdi Husain, Baroda: Oriental Institute, 1976.

Khwaja Nizamuddin Ahmad, *Tabaqat-i Akbari*, 3 vols., Eng. tr. Brajendra Nath De and Baini Prashad, Calcutta: Asiatic Society of Bengal, rpt., 1996.

Mahmud bin Muhammad Pir, *Haqiqat ul-Fuqara*, Eng. tr. (titled *Poetic Biography of Madho Lal Husayn*), Scott Kugle in *Same Sex Love: A Literary History*, ed. Ruth Vanita and Saleem Kidwai, New Delhi: Penguin Books, 2008.

Maulavi Nur Muhammad, *Tarikh-i Jhang Siyal*, Meerut: Matba Ahmadi, 1863.

Mobad Kaikhusrau Isfandiyar, *Dabistan-i Mazahab*, vol. I, ed. Rahim Razazada Malik, Tehran: Kitabkhana Tahuri, 1362 AH/1983 AD.

Muhammad Akram Barasawi, *Iqtibas ul-Anwar*, vol. II, ed. Muhammad Ehteshamuddin, Aligarh: Institute of Persian Research, Aligarh Muslim University, 2018.

Nizami Ganjawi, *Laila and Majnun*, Eng tr. Rudolph Gelpke, E. Mattin and G. Hill, New Labanon: Omega Publications, 2011.

Nur Ahmad Chishti, *Tahqiqat-i Chishti*, Lahore: Al-Faisal Nashiran wa Tajiran Kutub, rpt., 2000.

Nuruddin Jahangir, *Tuzuk-i Jahangiri*, Eng. tr. Alexander Rogers and Henry Beveridge, Delhi: Low Price Publications, rpt., 1989.

Shah Sharfuddin Bu Ali Qalandar, *Masnavi*, ed. Muhammad Muslim Ahmad Nizami, New Delhi: Kutubkhana Naziriya, 1383 AH.

Shaikh Rizqullah Mushtaqi, *Waqiat-i Mushtaqi*, ed. Iqtidar Husain Siddiqui and Waqar ul-Hasan Siddiqi, Rampur: Rampur Raza Library, 2002.

Sharfuddin Ali Yazdi, *Zafar Nama*, vol. II, ed. Muhammad Ilahdad, Calcutta: Asiatic Society of Bengal, 1888.

Shams Siraj Afif, *Tarikh-i Firoz Shahi*, ed. Maulavi Wilayat Husain, Calcutta: Asiatic Society of Bengal, 1890.

Sujan Rai Bhandari, *Khulasat ut-Tawarikh*, ed. M. Zafar Hasan, Delhi: G. and Sons, 1916.

Yahya bin Ahmad bin Abdullah Sirhindi, *Tarikh-i Mubarak Shahi*, ed. M. Hidayat Husain, Calcutta: Asiatic Society of Bengal, 1931.

Zahiruddin Muhmmad Babur, *Baburnama*, tr. and ed. (titled *The Baburnama: Memoirs of Babur, Prince and Emperor*), Wheeler M. Thackston, New York: The Modern Library, 2002.

Ziauddin Barani, *Tarikh-i Firoz Shahi*, ed. Sir Syed Ahmad, Aligarh: Aligarh Muslim University, rpt., 2005.

Primary Sources: Panjabi and Hindi

Ahmad Gujjar, *Hir Ahmad*, ed. S.S. Padam, Barnala: Panjabi Sahit Sabha, 1960.

Ahmad Salim, ed., *Tin Lok Varan*, Amritsar: Ravi Sahit Prakashan, 2015.

Ahmadyar, *Hir Ahmadyar*, ed. Gobind Singh Lamba, Patiala: Amarjit Sahit Prakashan, 1982.

Bhai Gurdas, *Varan Bhai Gurdas*, vol. II, ed. Jodh Singh, Patiala: Vision and Venture, 1998.

Jagtar Singh, ed., *Hir Damodar*, Patiala: Punjabi University, 2000.

Kala Singh Bedi, *Shah Husain Lahori: Jeevan te Rachna*, Chandigarh: SSB Publishing Company, 1978.

Kishan Singh Arif, *Qissa Dulla Bhatti te us di Bhav Jugat*, ed. Gian Chand, Ravi Sahit Prakashan, 1987.

Malik Muhammad Jaisi, *Padmavat: An Epic Poem*, Eng. tr. Purushottam Agrawal, New Delhi: Rupa Publications, 2018

Manmohan Singh, ed., *Sri Guru Granth Sahib*, Text with Eng. and Pbi. tr., Amritsar: Shiromani Gurdwara Prabandhak Committee, 2nd edn., 1982.

Mir Syed Manjhan Rajgiri, *Madhumalati*, ed. Mataprasad Gupt, Allahabad: Mittar Prakashan, 1961; Eng. tr. Aditya Behl, Simon Weightman and Shyam Manohar Pandey, New York: Oxford University Press, 2000.

Muqbal, *Qissa Hir Ranjha*, ed. Joginder Singh, Patiala: Punjabi University, 2000.

Qutban, *Mirigavati*, ed. Mataprasad Gupt, Agra: Pramanik Prakashan, 1968.

Surinderpal Singh Mand, *Qissakar Hashim: Sassi Punnu, Sohni Mahiwal, Shirin Farhad te Hir Ranjha de Mool Path Samet*, Amritsar: Waris Shah Foundation, 2011.

Sutinder Singh Noor, ed., *Panjabi Sufi Kaav*, New Delhi: Sahitya Akadami, 1997.

Waris Shah, *Hir Waris Shah*, ed. Piara Singh Padam, New Delhi: Navyug Publishers, rpt., 1998.

Secondary Sources: Books

Alhaq, Shuja, *A Forgotten Vision: A Study of Human Spirituality in the Light of the Islamic Tradition*, 2 vols., New Delhi: Vikas Publishing House, 1997.

Ashraf, Kanwar Muhammad, *Life and Conditions of the People of Hindustan*, New Delhi: Munshiram Manoharlal, 2nd edn., 1970.

Baldick, Julian, *Mystical Islam: An Introduction to Sufism*, London & New York: Tauris Parke Paperbacks, 2000.

Behl, Aditya, *Love's Subtle Magic: An Indian Islamic Literary Tradition, 1379-1545*, New York: Oxford University Press, 2012.

Bloch, Marc, *Feudal Society*, vol. I: *The Growth of Ties of Dependence*, Eng. tr. L.A. Manyon, New Delhi: Aakar Books, rpt., 2019.

Bouillier, Veronique, *Monastic Wanderers: Nath Yogis in Modern South Asia*, New Delhi: Manohar, 2017.

Briggs, George Weston, *Gorakhnath and Kanphata Yogis*, Delhi: Motilal Banarsidass, rpt., 1980.

Buehler, Arthur F., *Recognizing Sufism: Contemplation in the Islamic Tradition*, London & New York: I.B. Tauris, 2016.

Dalal, Roshen, *Hinduism: An Alphabetical Guide*, New Delhi: Penguin Books, 2010.

Droge, A.J., *The Quran: A New Annotated Translation*, New Delhi: Oxford University Press, 2013.

Esposito, John L., ed., *The Oxford Dictionary of Islam*, New York: Oxford University Press, 2003.

Gaur, Ishwar Dayal, *Society, Religion and Patriarchy: Exploring Medieval Punjab through Hir Waris*, New Delhi: Manohar, 2009.

Glasse, Cyril, ed., *The Concise Encyclopaedia of Islam*, London: Stacey International, 3rd edn., 2008.

Gold, Ann Grodzins, *A Carnival of Parting: The Tales of King Bharthari and King Gopi Chand as Sung and Told by Madhu Natisar Nath of Ghatiyali*, New Delhi: Munshiram Manoharlal, 1993.

Grzimek, H.C. Bernhard, ed., *Grzimek's Animal Life Encyclopaedia,* vol. VI *(Reptiles)*, New York: Van Nostrand Reinhold Company, 1975.

Habib, Irfan, *The Agrarian System of Mughal India 1556-1707*, 2nd rev. edn., New Delhi: Oxford University Press, 1999.

Habib, Mohammad and Khaliq Ahmad Nizami, ed., *A Comprehensive History of India*, vol. V: *The Delhi Sultanat 1206-1526*, New Delhi: People's Publishing House, rpt., 1987.

Habib, Mohammad, *Politics and Society during the Early Medieval Period: Collected Works of Professor Mohmmad Habib*, vol. I, ed. K.A. Nizami, New Delhi: People's Publishing House and Aligarh: Centre of Advanced Study, Department of History, Aligarh Muslim University, 1974.

Hastings, James, ed., *The Encyclopaedia of Religion and Ethics*, vol. I, Edinburgh: T and T Clark, 1967.

Hines, Naseem A., *Maulana Daud's Candayan: A Critical Study*, New Delhi: Manohar, 2009.

Houtsma, M.T. et al., ed., *The Encyclopaedia of Islam*, vol. III, Leiden: E.J. Brill and London: Luzac & Co., 1946

Huda, Qamarul, *Striving for Divine Union: Spiritual Exercises for Suhrawardi Sufis*, London & New York, Routledge Curzon, 2003.

Ibbetson, Denzil, *Panjab Castes*, Patiala: Languages Department, Punjab, rpt., 1970.

Imperial Gazetteer of India, *Provincial Series: Punjab*, 2 vols., Calcutta: Superintendent of Government Printing, 1908.

Irvine, William, *The Army of the Indian Moghuls: Its Organization and Administration*, New Delhi: Eurasia Publishing House, rpt., 1962.

Khan, Dominique Sila Khan, *Conversion and Shifting Identities: Ramdev Pir and Ismailis in Rajasthan*, New Delhi: Manohar, rpt., 2003.

Khan, Nawab Iftikhar Ali, *A History of the Ruling Family of Sheikh Sadruddin Sadr-i Jahan of Malerkotla (1449 AD to 1948 AD)*, ed. R.K. Ghai, Patiala: Punjabi University, 2000.

Mallinson, James and Mark Singleton, *Roots of Yoga*, U.K.: Penguin Classics, 2017.

Mir, Farina, *The Social Space of Language: Vernacular Culture in British Colonial Punjab*, Ranikhet: Permanent Black, 2010.

Mirza, Mohammad Wahid, *The Life and Works of Amir Khusrau*, Delhi: Idarah-i Adabiyat-i Delli, rpt., 1974.

Monserrate, Father, *Commentary of Father Monserrate*, ed. S.N. Banerjee and J.S. Hoyland, Jalandhar: Asian Publishers, rpt., 1993.

Naqvi, Hamida Khatoon, *Agricultural, Industrial and Urban Dynamism under the Sultans of Delhi 1206-1555*, New Delhi: Munshiram Manoharlal, 1986.

Nasr, Seyyed Hossein et al., ed., *The Study Quran: A New Translation and Commentary*, New York: Harper One, 2015.

Nasr, Seyyed Hossein, ed., *Islamic Spirituality: Manifestations*, New York: The Crossword Publishing Company, 2012.

Nizami, Khaliq Ahmad, *Religion and Politics in India during the Thirteenth Century*, New Delhi: Oxford University Press, 2002.

Qureshi, Ishtiaq Husain, *The Administration of the Mughul Empire*, Patna: Janaki Prakashan, rpt., 1979.

______, *The Administration of the Sultanate of Dehli*, New Delhi: Oriental Books Reprint Corporation, 1st rev. edn., 1971.

Roy, Kumkum, *The Emergence of Monarchy in North India: Eighth-Fourth Centuries BC (As Reflected in the Brahmanical Tradition)*, New Delhi: Oxford University Press, 1994.

Raychaudhuri, Tapan and Irfan Habib, *The Cambridge Economic History of India, vol. I: c.1200-c.1750*, New Delhi: Orient Longman, rpt., 2004.

Richards, John F., *The Mughal Empire*, New Delhi: Cambridge University Press, rpt., 2007.

Rizvi, Saiyid Athar Abbas, *A History of Sufism in India*, vol. I, New Delhi: Munshiram Manoharlal, 1975.

Rose, H.A., *A Glossary of the Castes and Tribes of the Punjab and North West Frontier Province*, 3 vols., Patiala: Languages Department, Punjab, rpt., 1970.

Roy, Asim, *The Islamic Syncretistic Tradition in Bengal*, New Jersey: Princeton University Press, 1983.

Siddiqui, Iqtidar Husain, *History of Sher Shah Sur*, Aligarh: P.C. Dwadash Shreni & Co., 1971.

———, *Some Aspects of Afghan Despotism in India*, Aligarh: Three Men Publications, 1969.

Singh, Nikky Guninder Kaur, *The Feminine Principle in the Sikh Vision of the Transcendent*, New York: Cambridge University Press, 1993.

Singh, Surinder, *The Making of Medieval Panjab; Politics, Society and Culture, c.1000-c.1500*, New Delhi: Manohar, 2020.

Steinfels, Amina M., *Knowledge before Action: Islamic Learning and Sufi Practice in the Life of Sayyid Jalal al-Din Bukhari Makhdum-i Jahaniyan*, Columbia: University of South Carolina, 2012.

Stutley, Margaret and James, *A Dictionary of Hinduism: The Mythology, Folklore and Development (1500 BC-AD 1500)*, Bombay: Allied Publishers, 1977.

Syed, Najm Hosain, *Sedhan, Saran te Hor Lekh*, ed. Purdaman Singh Bedi, Ludhiana: Jaswant Printers, 2005.

Tayob, Abdulkader, *Islam: A Short Introduction*, Oxford: Oneworld Publications, 2006.

Temple, R.C., *The Legends of the Panjab*, vol. II, Islamabad: The Institute of Folk Heritage, rpt., 1981.

Walker, Benjamin, *Hindu World: A Encyclopedic Survey*, vol. I, New Delhi: Indus (Harper Collins), 1995.

Secondary Sources: Articles

Alam, Muzaffar and Sanjay Subrahmanyam, 'Love, Passion and Reason in Faizi's Nal Daman', in *Love in South Asia: A Cultural History*, ed. Francesca Orsini, New Delhi: Cambridge University Press, 2007.

Bednar, Michael Boris, 'The Content and Form in Amir Khusraw's Duval Rani va Khizr Khan', *Journal of the Royal Asiatic Society*, 3rd series, vol. 24, no. 1, January 2014.

Behl, Aditya, 'Emotion and Meaning in Mrigavati: Strategies of Spiritual Signification in Hindavi Sufi Romances', in *After Timur Left: Culture and Circulation in Fifteenth Century North India*, ed. Francesca Orsini and Samira Sheikh, New Delhi: Oxford University Press, 2014.

Behl, Aditya, 'The Magic Doe: Desire and Narrative in a Hindavi Sufi Romance circa 1503', in *India's Islamic Traditions 711-1750*, ed. Richard M. Eaton, New Delhi: Oxford University Press, 2003.

Chandra, Satish, 'Mughal Relations with the Rajput States of Rajasthan: The Foundations', in *Mughal Religious Policies: The Rajputs and the Deccan*, New Delhi: Vikas Publishing House, 1993.

_____, 'Structure of Village Society in Northern India: The Khud Kasht and Pahi Kasht', in *Essays on Medieval Indian History*, New Delhi: Oxford University Press, 2003.

Desai, Z.A., 'Life and Works of Faizi', *Indo-Iranica*, vol. XVI, no. 3, 1964.

Digby, Simon, 'Abd al-Quddus Gangohi (1456-1537): The Personality and Attitudes of An Indian Sufi', *Medieval India: A Miscellany*, vol. III, Bombay: Asia Publishing House, 1975.

Eaton, Richard M., 'The Political and Religious Authority of the Shrine of Baba Farid', in *Essays on Islam and Indian History*, New Delhi: Oxford University Press, 2000.

Elias, Jamal J., 'Female and Feminine in Islamic Mysticism', in *Critical Concepts in Islamic Studies*, vol. I, ed. Ridgeon Lloyd, London & New York, 2008.

Ernst, Carl W., 'Islamization of Yoga in the Amritkunda Translations', *Journal of the Royal Asiatic Society*, Third Series, vol. 13, no. 2, July 2003.

Husain, Yusuf, 'Haud ul-Hayat: The Arabic Version of Amritkund', in *On Becoming An Indian Muslim: French Essays on Aspects of Syncretism*, ed. M. Waseem, New Delhi: Oxford University Press, 2003.

Naithani, Sadhana, 'The Colonizer-Folklorist', *Journal of Folklore Research*, vol. 34, no. 1, 1997.

Nizami, Khaliq Ahmad, 'Some Aspects of Khanqah Life in Medieval India', in *Studies in Medieval Indian History and Culture*, Allahabad: Kitab Mahal, 1966.

Singh, Surinder, 'Rulers, Zamindars and Sufis: Probing a Triangular Model of State Formation', in *Situating Medieval India: Polity, Society and Culture*, New Delhi: Manohar, 2023.

_____, 'Mughal Centralization and Local Resistance in Northwestern India: An Exploration in the Ballad of Dulla Bhatti', in *Popular Literature and Pre-modern Societies in South Asia*, ed. Surinder Singh and Ishwar Dayal Gaur, New Delhi: Pearson Longman, 2008.

_____, 'Revolt of Dulla Bhatti against the Mughal State: A Study of Oral Tradition and Modern Cultural Forms', in *Situating Medieval India: Polity, Society and Culture*, New Delhi: Manohar, 2023.

Wink, Andre, 'On the Road to Failure: The Afghans in Mughal India', in *Islamicate Traditions in South Asia: Themes from Culture and History*, ed. Agnieszka Kuczkiewics Fras, New Delhi: Manohar, 2013.

Index